W9-CLI-037

Social Theory and Archaeology

Social Theory and Archaeology

MICHAEL SHANKS AND
CHRISTOPHER TILLEY

Polity Press

CC 72
.4
.S52
1987x

Copyright ©Michael Shanks and Christopher Tilley, 1987

First published 1987 by Polity Press in association with Basil Blackwell.

Editorial Office:
Polity Press, Dales Brewery, Gwydir Street,
Cambridge CB1 2LJ, UK

Basil Blackwell Ltd
108 Cowley Road, Oxford OX4 1JF, UK

All rights reserved. Except for the quotation of short passages for the purposes of criticism and review, no part of this publication may be reproduced, stored in a retrieval system, or transmitted, in any form or by any means, electronic, mechanical, photocopying, recording or otherwise, without the prior permission of the publisher.

Except in the United States of America, this book is sold subject to the condition that it shall not, by way of trade or otherwise, be lent, resold, hired out, or otherwise circulated without the publisher's prior consent in any form of binding or cover other than that in which it is published and without a similar condition including this condition being imposed on the subsequent purchaser.

British Library Cataloguing in Publication Data

Shanks, Michael
   Social theory and archaeology.
   1. Archaeology—Social aspects
   I. Title   II. Tilley, Christopher
   930.1′01   CC107

   ISBN 0-7456-0183-9
   ISBN 0-7456-0184-7 Pbk

Typeset in 10 on 11½pt Times
by DMB (Typesetting) Abingdon, Oxon.
Printed in Great Britain by
Billing & Sons Ltd, Worcester.

Contents

Preface

Archaeologists for the first time in the history of the discipline are beginning to be faced with a wide variety of different theoretical perspectives on the past. The majority of these have only emerged during the last seven years and are currently having a major impact in breaking down the theoretical hegemony of positivism and functionalism which formed the twin pillars of 'new' archaeology. Despite the growing plethora of theories, archaeology still remains today a deeply empiricist and antitheoretical discipline. Yet it is quite clear that after 150 years of empiricism in one form or another we still have little more than a rudimentary understanding of the archaeological past. No amount of excavation, survey, ethnoarchaeological work or so-called 'middle-range' empiricism will cure the perceived fundamental isolation of past from present. This gap can only be dealt with adequately if we develop conceptual tools and theoretical structures with which to reinscribe the past into the present, to realize their interaction. This book is intended as an advanced introduction to some current debates which may help to achieve that goal.

The impetus to the development of fresh theoretical perspectives in archaeology has come almost entirely from outside the discipline and has brought archaeology into increasingly closer contact with wider debates in social theory. In the format of a single book we have neither attempted, nor do we claim, any degree of comprehensive coverage. Instead we have chosen to discuss a limited number of key areas for the reconstruction of archaeological theory. In the first chapter we discuss what theory in archaeology should be about, criticize the reduction of theory to methodology, and consider the dominant forms of textual production in contemporary archaeology. Chapters 2 and 3 consider the competing theoretical discourses of recent social archaeology, and the relationship of the individual to society. Chapters 4, 5 and 6 focus on key areas that have been quintessentially archaeological concerns: the relationship of material culture to the social and the study of change over long time spans. Here the relative lack of theorization in the discipline has been quite striking – we might expect a discipline whose primary data base is material culture to have a developed theory of its meaning and significance. Similarly, archaeologists, although dealing with long time spans, have little questioned the concept of time, and reductionist, essentialist and ethnocentric notions of social evolution have long been dominant. If we achieve little more in this book we hope at least to initiate further conceptualization and debate in these vital areas. Chapter 7 situates archaeology as a cultural practice firmly in the present and argues that it needs to become fully self-reflexive, aware of itself as political practice. We do not think it either possible or desirable to attempt to achieve a fresh unification of archaeological theory within one all-encompassing framework. The only essential unity we propose is that all archaeology ought to be cultural critique, a practice both produced in the present and contributing to the present. Archaeological discourse is a *form* of power while at the same time being the *study* of power. The final chapter sets out in a formal way a number of theses which we regard as essential to the development of a fresh problematic for the discipline.

The book is partly based on two joint undergraduate and graduate seminar courses given in the Department of Archaeology, University of Cambridge, during the spring and autumn of 1986. We would like to thank those people who kindly agreed to chair the seminars: Robin Boast, Grant Chambers, Ian Hodder, Matthew Johnson, Sandar van de Leeuw, Olivier de Montmillon, Ajay Pratrap, Colin Renfrew; and all those who participated in them and contributed to the debate. Parts of chapters 6 and 7 were also presented and discussed at the University of Tromsø. Michael Shanks would like to thank his history class of 1986-7 for their support. Grant Chambers, Tony Giddens, Ian Hodder and Mike Rowlands all kindly provided detailed comments on the text and suggested valuable improvements.

1

Theory and Method in Archaeology

THEORETICAL ARCHAEOLOGY: A PRELIMINARY AND CONVENTIONAL OUTLINE

Theory has been an important issue in archaeology since the 1960s and has taken the form of a contentious field of polemical manoeuvring within the discipline and between archaeology and other social sciences. In his essay, 'Archaeology: the loss of innocence' (1973), David Clarke, a seminal figure in British theoretical archaeology, specified different aspects of theory. He distinguished a theory of concepts from a theory of information and a theory of reasoning, terming these respectively archaeological metaphysics, epistemology and archaeological logic and explanation. For Clarke these three aspects are overlain and permeated by a series of other levels of archaeological theory; these are steps in archaeological interpretation. Predepositional and depositional theory considers the relationships between activities, social patterning, and environmental factors and the traces deposited in the archaeological record. Postdepositional theory considers what happens to the deposited traces: processes such as destruction, erosion and disturbance. Retrieval theory is predominantly a theory of the sampling of the surviving deposited traces in excavation and fieldwork. Analytical theory is concerned with retrieved information and its processing; interpretative theory considers how the traces relate to their ancient social and environmental sources which are not now open to direct observation and experience.

The literature on most of these aspects of theoretical archaeology is quite sizeable. Most of the concepts of traditional archaeology, such as 'culture' and 'diffusion', have been challenged, found wanting and replaced (e.g. Shennan, 1978; Renfrew, 1978). New archaeology in America favoured an explicitly systemic conceptualization of the archaeological past focusing on culture systems adapting to environmental factors (e.g. Binford, 1965; Flannery, 1968). In Britain the new conceptual framework of the 1970s mirrored more functionalist anthropology with organically conceived social systems functioning within environmental milieux (see chapter 2). Since the late 1970s attention has been channelled to the boundaries of such systems. The idea of interaction between social units has developed into theories of peer polity interaction (Renfrew and Cherry (eds), 1986) and world systems theory (Gledhill and Rowlands, 1982). Varieties of neo-evolutionary theory have been the most influential frameworks utilized to account for mechanisms of social change, from simple unilineal and stadial positions to more complex multilinear or epigenetic theories (see chapter 6).

In regard to the information that archaeology might reveal about the past, the new archaeology initiated a new optimism that archaeology was not confined to description of materials and technologies with the social and ideological increasingly removed from the reach of archaeological speculation: new archaeology was constituted as a new theory of archaeological information whereby it was to become anthropology (Binford, 1962).

The theory of archaeological logic and explanatory structure has been dominated by the consideration of hypothesis-based deductive reasoning processes (involving subsuming particular occurrences under generalizations) with an equivalence of prediction and explanation (Fritz and Plog, 1970; Watson, LeBlanc and Redman, 1971). The most influential aspect of such theory has been procedures of rigorous and explicit testing of clearly formulated hypotheses, known as problem-oriented research (Hill, 1972; Plog, 1974).

In retrieval theory sampling procedures have been applied to excavation and fieldwork (Cherry, Gamble and Shennan (eds), 1978; Mueller (ed.), 1975). Binford's middle-range theory aspires to a statistical correlation of material culture patterning and social behaviour (Binford, 1977; 1981). Schiffer's behavioural archaeology (1976) aims at an analogous general theory, a science of material culture patterning. Ethnoarchaeological and modern material culture studies have investigated the relation of social patterning to material culture and its deposition (e.g. Hodder, 1982; Gould (ed.), 1978; Gould, 1980; Gould and Schiffer (eds), 1981; Binford, 1978).

New ways of processing data, in particular computer based, have been developed in line with the developing range of new concepts, aiming at extracting more subtle and precisely documented patterning in archaeological data (Doran and Hodson, 1975; Orton, 1980; Richards and Ryan, 1985).

Two particular fields of interpretative theory can be briefly mentioned here: theories of artefact exchange and prehistoric exchange networks; and theories of the relation of mortuary practices to the society which practised them. In the former, different artefact distributions are interpreted in terms of changing patterns of exchange between individuals and/or groups (Earle and Ericson, 1977; Ericson and Earle, 1982); the latter considers the traces of mortuary practices and the ritual deposition of artefacts in terms of symbolic dimensions of social relations (see Chapman, Kinnes and Randsborg (eds), 1981; and chapter 2 below).

Clarke reckoned that the introspective fervour in archaeology of the late 1960s and 1970s amounted to 'a precipitate, unplanned and unfinished exploration of new disciplinary fieldspace . . . profound practical, theoretical and philosophical problems to which the new archaeologies have responded with diverse new methods, new observations, new paradigms and new theory' (1973, p. 17). Adapting Kuhn's notion Clarke identified four new paradigms (1972, p. 5) (characterized as being systems of assumptions, conventions, fields of concepts which specify data, significant problems and exemplary solutions for a 'community' of archaeologists): the morphological, anthropological, ecological and geographical. So, according to Clarke, some archaeologists focus on artefact systems, their specification and quantitative derivation. Anthropological archaeologists consider the relation of data to social patterning. Ecological archaeologists aim to delineate palaeoenvironments and the place of human communities within them. And archaeology's geographical paradigm is dominated by locational and spatial analysis of settlement and artefact distributions.

These 'paradigms' have developed in criticism of, and in addition to, archaeology's traditional paradigm – an artefact-based, particularizing and qualitative archaeology aiming at a culture history expressed in literary narrative clichés. The theoretical developments have also been inextricably coupled with technical advances forming the basis for, or arising in response to, new theoretical orientations: lithic and ceramic analyses (including trace element analysis); analysis of botanical, faunal, skeletal and environmental material. All of these have refined and augmented archaeological data quite considerably.

Clarke conceived a unity or a logic behind this proliferation of new archaeologies, approaches, theories, paradigms. It all amounted to the transformation from a self-conscious to a critically self-conscious discipline. (See table 1.1.)

Clarke's *Analytical Archaeology* (1968) was meant to provide a general theory:

> Archaeology, is, after all, one discipline and that unity largely resides in the latent theory of archaeology – that disconnected bundle of inadequate subtheories which we must seek to formulate and structure within an articulated and comprehensive system; a common theoretical hat-rack for all our parochical hats.
>
> (1973, p. 18)

Clarke's was essentially a positivist vision of a unified archaeology, scientific progress precipitating the emergence of a scientific archaeology from its pre-scientific anterior. This fundamentalist vision of a scientific archaeology has been predominant in the United States. There the emergence of the theoretically introspective new archaeology has been interpreted as a Kuhnian paradigm shift; a major disciplinary change; the inauguration of a new period of normal science; a new scientific hegemony (Martin, 1971; Sterud, 1973, 1978; Zubrow, 1972).

In Britain the positivism of the new archaeology has not achieved anything like the acceptance it has had in the United States. Traditional archaeology has successfully met the challenge. Its empiricism has incorporated the methodology of explicit problem posing and rigorous testing and came to appreciate the possibility of archaeology acquiring a far wider range and a higher refinement of data, while its scepticism has eschewed ideas of scientific objec-

TABLE 1.1 *Clarke's summary of the traditionalist and the new archaeology*

	Traditionalist	*New*
Philosophy	Historical	Experimental
Approach	Qualitative Particularizing	Quantitative Generalizing
Mode of expression	Literary Narrative	Symbolic Jargon
Attitude	Isolationist Authoritarian	Condisciplinary Anarchic

Source: Clark 1972, p. 54. Reprinted by permission of Methuen & Co.

tivity and theoretical elaboration. So theory is still most frequently conceived as abstract and secondary to data acquisition, different fashions explaining the same data, while traditional archaeology's explanations are based on common sense and natural language. There has been work within an explicit systemic framework, most notably by Colin Renfrew (1972), but social archaeology in Britain has emerged predominantly as a soft functionalism, the offspring of a colonialist anthropology.

This hegemony of hard scientific fundamentalism, sceptical empiricism and soft functionalism has received serious theoretical challenges since the late 1970s. Some archaeologists have drawn on structural Marxist anthropology and emhasized a conception of the social which differs from functionalist models in stressing internal contradiction rather than states of social equilibrium (see Spriggs (ed.), 1984). Structuralist and contextual archaeologists have emphasized the meaning and symbolic dimensions of social practices, stressing the culturally specific and variable meanings of material culture rather than simply concentrating on its patterning supposedly 'explained' within a framework of reductionist cross-cultural generalization (e.g. Hodder (ed.), 1982; Hodder, 1986). Other archaeologists have begun to examine archaeological work and explanations in the context of contemporary capitalism, critically assessing the ideology of archaeology (Shanks and Tilley, 1987; Miller and Tilley (eds), 1984). However, these challenges are only beginning to be widely acknowledged.

Fragmentation, specialization, divergent approaches, 'paradigms', theories of the social: different archaeologies. Rather than enter this labyrinth and perhaps identify the most likely archaeological exit, we intend instead to take a different line. We aim to ask the meaning of the fragmentation, the significance of the theoretical hegemony; to ask what theory itself might be; to assess the questions 'theoretical' archaeology has been posing; to ask what questions should be posed. So, in this chapter we wish to begin with some *metatheoretical* questions, questions about theory itself.

ARCHAEOLOGICAL THEORY: METHOD

The developments that have taken place in archaeology since the 1960s amount to a process of rationalization of the discipline, a reaction to fact collection, the literary narrative, and unexamined common-sense categories and concepts of traditional archaeology.

But this rationalization has, for the most part, taken the form of *methodological* inquiry, a search for methods or approaches to the data, which will give a better, more complete, more objective view or account of the past. A valid method is conceived as being as objective as possible (some would equate this with being scientific), eliminating subjective bias. Approaches may vary as to what aspects of the archaeological record they concentrate on, what different patterns in the data they isolate and claim to explain, but all must be objective, reasonable, realistic, based on the primacy of the object of investigation. Concomitantly, the primary questions of theory have been:

1 How to extract the maximum information from what is left of the past.
2 Which concepts are the most efficient at achieving the aim of establishing an objective past.
3 How to bring the archaeologist into the closest possible accordance with the object of investigation; that is, with the artefact and its depositional context.

Discussions of social theory in archaeology have, until recently, been very much undertaken in the context of these questions: reference has been made to other social sciences for concepts which might be applied to archaeological data in order to gain access to a fuller and more reliable account of the past. The aim has been to establish which social (or indeed other) concepts might be most efficiently applied to archaeological data. For example, palaeo-economy (Higgs (ed.), 1972, 1975) draws on biological and etho-logical theories of evolution, conceiving these as more applicable to archaeological data than social theory. Marxist archaeologists con-ceive their conceptualization of the social context of artefacts as more accurate than systems theory and social typologies of bands, tribes etc. (e.g. Friedman and Rowlands, 1978; Bender, 1978).

Images of the archaeologist

Within this conceptualization of theory we can sketch two dominant underlying images of the archaeologist: the archaeologist as detective and the archaeologist as therapist.

The archaeologist as detective
The simile of archaeologist as detective is one not infrequently employed in introductory texts and prefaces (e.g. de Paor, 1967;

Clark, 1969) and is undoubtedly part of the popular mythology of archaeology. The archaeologist pieces together clues in order to reconstruct the past; the archaeologist is a Sherlock Holmes. The major theme underlying Conan Doyle's Sherlock Holmes stories is the expulsion of magic and mystery. Holmes, through the rigorous application of his method, makes everything explicit, accountable, subject to scientific analysis. Holmes, an obvious genius and man of science, always manages somehow to stumble upon the deduction which unravels the subtle connections between the clues. The stories usually end with Holmes recounting with devastating simplicity how the code of the clues was broken, how he eventually arrived at his final and all-encapsulating deduction. What was initially enigma, mystery, fascination, impossibility, becomes dispelled by a simple explanation. The application of pure method renders all the mysteries and the enigmas accountable in the burning light of reason. Once the deductions are revealed the solution to the mystery always appears absurdly simple, open to the commonest common sense. Holmes' logic is applicable to all areas of human experience: his ability to predict or 'read' even Dr Watson's somewhat illogical trains of thought are repeatedly displayed. Conan Doyle's books are a celebration of the power of empiricist or positivist science – cold, calculating reason dispelling illusion, eliminating subjectivity. They are also, of course, works of literary fiction.

The parallels with archaeology are readily apparent. The past, initially mysterious and seemingly impossible to adequately grasp or comprehend from mere fragments, can be reached, probed, ultimately known, through the operation of scientific method. Archaeologists are detectives travelling in the rattling carriages of scientific logic, boarding the *Flying Scotsman*, steaming back to discover the past to shatter the illusion, to tell everyone else, all the non-archaeologists, how it really was: what happened and why, what and who created the past leading to our present. But we all know that it is really not that simple. If it was, we would already have reached the past. We could stop writing archaeology books and write science fiction instead – dream of the future. One great problem with the future is that it has an annoying tendency to always create new pasts. What has gone wrong with our logical train of positivist science, of rationalized inquiry? Rather than moving back into the past is it, in fact, shunting back and forth in a siding? Do the rails, that we are sometimes told represent the logic of a truly scientific methodology, represent a viable and coherent route back to the past?

The archaeologist as therapist
Doing archaeology, the process of acquiring knowledge of the archaeological object, has now become, with the advent of the new archaeology, a therapeutic process. Various methods represent various remedies, cures for pathological thinking, for contradiction within the process of acquiring knowledge. Most theory in archaeology today acts as a pharmacopoeia. The goal is to avoid subjectivity, the pathology. Archaeological method instills health, a healthy regard to the objective artefact. Each new approach, systems theory to middle-range theory, is an implicit or explicit remedy for the failings of the others.

It is relevant and significant to consider the roots of pharmacopoeia in the Greek *pharmakon* meaning drug, cure, remedy and poison. *Pharmakon* is related to *pharmakeus* and *pharmakos* which mean, respectively, sorcerer or magician and one sacrificed or executed as atonement or purification for others, a scapegoat (cf. Derrida, 1981). Archaeological method consists of shamanistic cures, exorcisms resulting in the expulsion of a scapegoat, itself also poison, pollution, and remedy. Method aims at an expulsion of the subjective whose absence supposedly guarantees epistemological security. Yet method's curative powers simultaneously poison the study of the past, riddling our practice with dualisms – subject becomes split from object, fact from value, past from present. Method is to provide psychological security that we have eliminated ourselves in the present in order to return to the past. By immersing us in the object world, method tries to alleviate us from the burden of choice: choice of *alternative* meanings, *alternative* pasts. Ultimately method wants to place the archaeologist in the image of god, or alternatively as mindless automaton: god because the archaeologist is supposedly able to determine how the past was for once and all; automaton because all that is required is an application of method – the archaeologist becomes spiritual medium on earth, magical representative of the absent creator of the past.

Method and objectivity

Methods are operations on the artefact, the object, the basis for providing explanations. Ultimately everything becomes reduced to the object. The data, the material traces, stand supreme. Ideas, theories, hypotheses (call them what you will), are all refracted from that great solid bedrock of archaeological data we all know exists. Kick a megalith and it hurts! However, typologists know their megaliths in just the same sense as witch hunters know their witches: both are social creations. Archaeology today amounts to excavating and processing artefacts according to positivist rational method. It does not matter which facts are subjected to archaeology because what matters is the quality the objects supposedly possess – objectivity. This is what the archaeologist is after: objectivity conceived as abstract, in itself. The quality of the object is considered not in concrete terms but abstractly or quantitatively. Objectivity is abstract, uniform, neutral, because it exists separately from the archaeologist, the observing subject. Objective 'facts' count and archaeological knowledge is thought to be entirely dependent on them. They are, after all, hard physical reality. So archaeological method (rational and objective) produces its object in advance. Artefacts have meaning primarily as objectivity and this is claimed to be the basis or origin of good archaeology.

On most accounts archaeology becomes the perception and experience of objectivity, the artefacts of the past. Such objectivity is regarded as sacred, disembodied, essential, as constituting an essence. The archaeological object is present to our senses, real, with immediate proximity. Furthermore, the object as object is regarded as being theory and value-free, in-itself, identical to itself, transcendent. Objects become, in such a conception, *archai* (originals), outward manifestations of implicit historical essence. History is supposedly to be found in the archaeological object. The artefact is a *punctum*, a punctual presence, piercing time; it is the mark of history, the historical moment. Possess in consciousness this absolute spiritual plenitude, this property, the past immediately present with us, and you have history. This is a deference, a deferment of meaning to the object. Write up this experience and interpretation and theory can supposedly follow.

Theory, data, practice

Few archaeologists believe in induction any more. Some, following a reading of Popper (1959), have suggested that an earlier advocacy of verification procedures must now give way to falsification (see Renfrew, Rowlands and Segraves (eds), 1982, section I). Most realize that facts are selected and that research must be problem orientated; facts only answer the questions the archaeologist asks of them. Paradigms have been discussed at length (Meltzer, 1979; Binford and Sabloff, 1982) and there is a growing realization that data are theory-laden. However, this has made very little difference to archaeology. There is still a wide consensus in the belief in 'objective reality' or the archaeological record.

Consider Fowler's *Approaches to Archaeology* (1977), a relatively sophisticated introduction to 1970s British sceptical empiricism. In a chapter entitled 'Theoretical archaeology' he claims that 'all archaeology is theoretical' (p. 131). He argues that theory is involved from the beginning of the archaeological process, emphasizing 'models', defined as conscious and unconscious mental frameworks *applied* to the data: 'archaeological evidence does not mean anything' (p. 132), because it is dependent on the models applied by the archaeologist. The corollary is that 'there is no ultimate, finite truth revealed by archaeological evidence . . . all interpretation of it is relative' (p. 138). What remains in Fowler's text is an assertion of the primacy of the data, archaeological information to which theory and models are merely 'applied': 'whatever the theory, in the last resort quality of interpretation depends on the quality of the evidence' (p. 152). Fowler goes further in relating quality of the evidence to the 'quality of the archaeologist' (p. 152). Data are, after all, retrieved in the practice of excavation and theory can, perhaps, be quietly forgotten.

This position regards concrete practical method as operating on the archaeological record. In such a framework methods, approaches, are the means of doing archaeology, and archaeological theory has all too often come to refer to this 'real world' of archaeological practice. A hierarchy is implied:

Excavation ⎫
Data processing ⎪
Synthesis   ⎬ Technique; method
Interpretation ⎪
Theory   ⎭

Such a common-sense conception of 'theory' is of a system of ideas, concepts or statements, abstract rather than empirical, held to constitute an explanation or account of archaeological phenomena and essentially separate from those phenomena. Traditional archaeology has frequently taken an attitude that theory detracts from the real business of archaeology. Its quietude on matters of theory results not so much from a rejection of philosophical underpinnings but rather from a largely silent consensus around empiricist norms. A general characteristic of empiricism, whether the 'straight empiricism' of fact collection and subsequent description and interpretation, or in the positivist shape of hypothetico-deductive testing procedures advocated in the new archaeology, is that theoretical reflection is always systematically discouraged in favour of the primacy of facts or methodologies geared to producing such facts. However, this suspicion of theory is ultimately itself a philosophical statement of priorities emerging in the guise of a supposedly common-sense embargo on useless speculation regarded as being a diversion from day-to-day practical work (see e.g. Flannery, 1982). This is a non-sense. Any argument that theory is irrelevant to archaeology is itself theoretical, as is another 'common-sense' proposition that the world consists of a series of observable facts whose regularities and interrelationships can only be known through observation – that the external visible aspects of artefacts exhaust their meaning.

In the new archaeology theory is similarly regarded as abstract and parasitic on method. It can sometimes be useful, but any theory which relates to the real practice of archaeology in any other way than by strengthening and perfecting the possibilities for technique and method is considered dogmatic, irrelevant or mere fantasy (Schiffer, 1981). Theory can have only one relevance to practice: perfecting method. Does it work? The question asked of us all will be: 'but what does this look like in practice?' Theory must be 'applied' to archaeological 'reality'. But this very notion of 'application' presupposes the gap between theory and practice as always already a problem. Ultimately the relation can only be conceived as arbitrary, contingent or incidental. Social theory, for example, is relevant to archaeology: it provides new models and categories which may be applied to the archaeological object world. We find patterning of structures of power and hierarchy in the neolithic where before there were tribal chiefdoms, where there were cultures and before that druids. After all, we know that we are not simply digging up objects: they must be related to their social context – eventually – or otherwise we regress into antiquarianism. However, the real practice of archaeology always tends to be separated from theory. This split is one homologous with that between mental and manual labour, decision and execution, ends and means. It is a split running throughout the capitalist division of labour. An emphasis on methodology is one on logistics, administration, management, surveillance: defining that which is 'reasonable', asserting realistic limits and goals to archaeological practice.

The effects of this relationship of theory to practice are familiar: isolated empirical, 'expert' studies; intensive empirical special-ization accompanying efforts to divest concepts of empirical content; mathematical operations; use of catastrophe theory (Renfrew, 1978a); emphasis on the formulation of laws of culture process or high-level generalization. All aim to provide an intuition of the essence of prehistory – its objectivity, its essential meaning, order and logic. But the essence so arrived at is not that different from the mythical essence of prehistory implied by ley-lines and megalith builders arriving from outer space. A rabid empiricism accompanies idealism and fantasy because empiricism is little more than an idealism of the object. Furthermore, all choice between competing archaeologies, alternative pasts, is suspended in a proliferation of archaeologies, a pluralism allowing comparison only on the terms of a conception of method which decides means of application, of execution, but not ends: there can be no comment on the social, political and philosophical meaning of particular archaeologies, particular pasts.

Idealism, fantasy, text

As a way forward into further specifying and investigating these effects of a coupling of empiricism and idealism found in contemporary archaeology, it is interesting to consider a fantasy by Jorge Luis Borges. In 'Tlön, Uqbar, Orbis Tertius' (1981) he recounts his (fictional) discovery of an encyclopaedia which catalogues the planet Tlön, a reality of complete idealism.

> Centuries and centuries of idealism have not failed to influence reality. In the most ancient regions of Tlön, the duplication of lost objects is not infrequent. Two persons look for a pencil; the first finds it and says nothing; the second finds a second pencil, no less real, but closer to his expectations. These secondary objects are called *hrönir* and are, though awkward in form, somewhat longer. Until recently, the *hrönir* were the accidental products of distraction and forgetfulness. It seems unbelievable that their methodological production dates back scarcely a hundred years, but this is what the Eleventh Volume tells us. The first efforts were unsuccessful. However, the *modus operandi* merits description. The director of one of the state prisons told his inmates that there were certain tombs in an ancient river bed and promised freedom to whoever might make an important discovery. During the months preceding the excavation the inmates were shown photographs of what they were to find. This first effort proved that expectation and anxiety can be inhibitory; a week's work with pick and shovel did not manage to unearth anything in the way of a *hrön* except a rusty wheel of a period posterior to the experiment. But this was kept secret and the process was repeated later in four schools. In three of them the failure was almost complete; in the fourth (whose director died accidentally during the first excavations) the students unearthed – or produced – a gold

mask, an archaic sword, two or three clay urns and the mouldy and mutilated torso of a king whose chest bore an inscription which it has not yet been possible to decipher . . . The methodical fabrication of *hrönir* (says the Eleventh Volume) has performed prodigious services for archaeologists. It has made possible the interrogation and even the modification of the past, which is now no less plastic and docile than the future.

(Borges, 1981, pp. 37–8)

Peeling back the layers of text in this fantasy, we might say the following about archaeology. Traditional and new archaeology represent a desire for the past in itself and for itself; a desire for an objective past, for primary originary objectivity, the essence of the past, the essential meaning, an ideal presence of the past. The past is to be perceived by the autonomous archaeologist whose subjectivity is to be marginalized in a simple immediate experience and expression of the past.

This is an idealist fiction. The past cannot be exactly reproduced. Exact reproduction is repetition, tautology, silence. The archaeological past is not re-created as it was or in whatever approximation. It is, of course, excavated away. As such, the archaeological past must be *written*. We argue that it is vital to realize the specific form and nature of this act of writing, this form of the material production of the past. Objects are recovered in excavation. They may be lodged and displayed in museums and made to stand for the past of which they are a part (metonymy). They also need to be enshrined in books (the exhortation to publish excavations is common). The archaeological object and its context are both described and represented in the informational report (metaphor). Museum and text represent metonymy and metaphor. These are not neutral vehicles for an ideal presence of the past; equally, they are not simply rhetorical detours to a picture of the past. We have argued elsewhere (Shanks and Tilley, 1987, pp. 22–3) that fieldwork and excavation are not neutral instruments for recovering the past. Their supposed passive observation and conceptual detachment with regard to the past, equated with objectivity, is rooted in a particular vision of time, a spatial time (see chapter 5) which is treated as an independent variable separating past (conceived as a problem) from a voyeuristic present. This temporality has no way of coping with the personal, active and productive (or destructive) experience of fieldwork and excavation since 'what is historic in thought – the practice of archaeology, our experience of digging – is equated with irrelevance' (Shanks and Tilley, 1987, p. 23). We have also focused (ibid., ch. 4) on the museum's aesthetic, its way of representing the past, and have argued the way the past is presented is profoundly part of what is represented. Forms of display, such as free-standing sculpture and 'realistic' period settings, make statements about the relation of artefacts to their social context and the manner in which space, time and history are themselves conceived. So, we have located the temporality of museum cases – where date, (an abstract dimensional co-ordinate) is represented as the time of an artefact – in the spatial and quantified time of capitalism where the factory clock organizes routine and discipline of an alienated workforce. The period room, essentially a visual inventory, represents history as information and indicates that a meaningful understanding of history may be gained through a window on the past where the social meaning of artefacts is to be seen in their 'naturalistic' spatial juxtaposition. We have questioned these and other meanings of the museum's aesthetic. Analogous arguments can be presented concerning archaeological writing, archaeological texts.

The archaeological text is a medium for the inscription of representations of artefacts and their meanings. The artefact and its context, the subject matter of archaeology, must necessarily be given metaphorical expression, be signified in a text. This textual production means archaeology is fundamentally expressive, a signifying practice which confers meaning on the past. Language and writing are not neutral, objective instruments. Rather than representing the world, they are a means of coping with it. In this way a purely objective representation of the past is a textual impossibility. Now archaeologists conceive writing ideally as a neutral and technical resource rather than a transformative medium, a medium arising from the relationship of the archaeologist to the artefact and its context, and from the relation of an archaeologist to an audience. Writing and language may intrude on the representation of the past, but they should not: this is the conventional position in archaeological discourse which remains largely silent on such issues. But instead we stress that language is a social phenomenon and as a corollary archaeological writing, as part of archaeological work more generally, has to be seen and theorized as social production. We need to consider archaeology as discourse – a structured system of rules, conventions and meanings for the production of knowledges, texts.

Despite the concern with theory that developed in the new archaeology there are still comparatively few works of general theory in archaeology. Textual production in archaeology is still overwhelmingly dominated by texts which describe specific sites, types of data, regions or time periods. In the section which follows we present a series of comments on four archaeological texts: a site report, a pottery study, a general synopsis and an introduction to archaeology. Texts of these kinds still account for the vast majority of the world's output of archaeological textual production. We will focus on what these texts reveal about our arguments concerning the nature of theory in archaeology.

Archaeological texts

An excavation report: archival logistics

Wainwright's *Gussage All Saints* (1979) is a report on a total excavation of a settlement of the second half of the first millenium BC. The excavation is described as a 'problem orientated project within a rescue framework, designed to look back at Dr. Gerhardt Bersu's excavation of the site of Little Woodbury which, although a partial excavation, had for many years provided the pattern for Iron Age economy in southern Britain' (Wainwright, 1979, p. vii). The project, then, is clearly supposed to be in keeping with advanced (problem-orientated) principles of excavation. Such volumes as this, published by Her Majesty's Stationery Office have also been considered almost exemplary (e.g. Barker, 1977, p. 224).

In a standard work on archaeological publication, Grinsell, Rahtz and Williams remark that site reports for the most part remain unread (1974, p. 19). The site report is not meant to be read: this implies too much of an involvement of the reader; they are to be 'consulted'. The report is a textual archive and catalogue, a spectacular text making visible and textual the reality of the past. Measured drawings, tables, measurements, lists of numbered finds, scaled photographs and third person narrative – all represent a rhetoric of neutrality, of objectivity, from which subjective experience and impressions have been purged. Of the 205 pages only 23 discuss what was found. Setting; structural sequence; chronology; summary comments on artefacts, trade and external contacts; basic details of economy, environment and population: the discussion climbs Hawkes' (1954) empiricist ladder of inference culminating in the now clichéd expression of caution and wariness regarding the difficulty of moving from the 'facts' to 'highly speculative matters' (Bowen, in Wainwright, p. 182) such as, in this case, settlement status. This would certainly seem to be the case judging from Bowen's and Wainwright's own inferences. Taking into account debris from a bronze foundry which produced 'prestige chariot fittings', they reckon the entrance to the settlement was wide enough for a chariot and 'indicative of an assured position in the social order for a member or members of the community' (p. 193). They tentatively propose, referring to classical authors, the *Mabinogion* and song of Culwich and Olwen, that Gussage All Saints is a settlement 'quite high up a settlement hierarchy', perhaps even an Ilys – the residence of a Celtic lord. Wainwright also comments:

> the arthritic farmers of Gussage should also be reviewed within the more general theme of Celtic society in which the traits of frankness, spirited temperament, bravery, boastfulness, personal vanity, feasting and love of eulogistic verse combine to produce a type which Professor Cunliffe has bleakly castigated as combining a 'furious impetus . . . and a total lack of forward planning' . . . It is in this context, imbued with tradition and personal example, that one should view the status of the Gussage farmers.
>
> (Wainwright, 1979, p. 193)

But to criticize this essentially empty and sterile speculation is to miss the point. Such comments and 'interpretation' are consciously superfluous: 'Comment, interpretation, or synthesis are repeatable experiments which vary with whatever archaeological model happens to be fashionable at the time' (Grinsell, Rahtz and Williams, 1974, p. 20). Informational reports are, then, meant to avoid interpretation. 'The ideal report would enable a reader to reconstruct the whole site layer by layer, feature by feature, each with its constituents such as clay, gravel and charcoal flecks in due proportion' (ibid., p. 58). Barker, in *Principles of Archaeological Excavation*, recommends that the core of an excavation report be the illustrations, forming a 'planned guided tour' (1977, p. 228), a tour free from interpretation. In the spectacular text interpretation is superfluous.

Writing becomes the issue of publication, of record and description, what and how, and relative time and financial cost: an archival logistics. The issue is one of rescue and preservation of data. This has been a major issue especially since the advent of Rescue Archaeology in the early 1970s. Consequently, a report by a working party of the Ancient Monuments Board for England specifies four levels of data (see table 1.2). Levels I and II are considered appropriate to an archive or museum in the site's locality. Wainwright's *Gussage All Saints* is publication at level III. The issue at stake in publication is how much and how to publish. It is in this context that the extraordinary *redundancy of empirical detail* to be found in a site report should be considered. What really

TABLE 1.2 *Levels of data according to site descriptions and loose material (Ancient Monuments Board for England)*

Level	Site Descriptions	Loose Material
I	Site itself General Notes	Excavated finds
II	Site note books Recording forms Drawings	Finds records Photographs Negatives
III	Full illustration and description of all structural and stratigraphical relationships	Classified find lists and drawings and all specialist analyses
IV	Synthesized description and data	Selected finds and reports relevant to synthesis

Source: P. Barker (1977), p. 230.

is to be made of the 52 drawn sections (detailing layering and type of infill) of pits found within the settlement? Of the tables of measurements of bones? The authors presumably assume that such things are self-explanatory and may be of interest or use. But is this the case?

An archival logistics is, then, a logic of neutrality, literally of objectivity. The site report as archival catalogue names the object world of the archaeological site, identifying, specifying, classifying each and everything. The mark of the informational report is the category. Categories reduce the heterogeneity of the object world. The conventional sequence of categories in Wainwright is:

1 Structures: enclosures; pits; settlement phases.
2 Artefact finds: pottery; stone; metal; other.
3 Organic finds: animal; human; plant.

The sequence includes 'everything' found at Gussage All Saints. The sequence of categories effects closure. But what is the origin of the categories and their social meaning? Conventionally, categories are points of method, part of reducing the data to manageable units, securing a place for everything. They are part of the law of neutral archaeological reason; categories are meant to be neutral. But why should this 'neutral' categorization be used rather than another?

And is such categorization really neutral? It in no ways cures the fundamental isolation of each self-present object in the report, the assumed basic units of empirical science. The objects remain detached from a historically located materiality, from the question of their meaning other than that of objectivity (a meaning which belongs to the historical present): the objects are simply manipulated by neutral reason. So the past is, in effect, presented with identity papers and locked up. There is a place for everything and, apparently, everything is in its place. The tendency, ideal or *telos* is a total administration of the past. No ambiguity is to be allowed, no heterogeneity. Such deviance is to be banished to the margins or eliminated.

Categories gather together, but each category is not classifiable according to itself. Categories gather but *prevent* closure. They are both inside and outside the object world. Archaeology cannot be absorbed into its object. Categories imply a signifying practice, a material practice in the present. The theorization of categories *requires* their relation to archaeology as a material and political practice in the present.

A work of synthesis

The two volumes of Gibson's *Beaker Domestic Sites* (1982) are aimed at filling a gap: drawing together and examining a neglected category of data – non-ritual pottery and sites from the second millenium BC in Britain. Gibson's study is a display of archaeological reality: objects, *archai* – original sources, an originary archaeological reality, objects through which access may be gained to the past. While presenting a history of the study of beaker domestic pottery, examining typologies, chronology, traditional problems of diffusion and influence of beaker style on other ceramic design, and considering the possibility of a category 'Beaker domestic assemblage', the bulk of Gibson's book is a catalogue of 167 pages, plus 210 pages of half scale drawings of some 5,000 pot fragments of which all but 24 are 2.5 cm^2 or smaller.

Such work encapsulates empiricism's subjective idealism: that the archaeological object is identified with the conventional and contemporary experience of it. Here we have a fetishism of the object, a blindness towards the genesis of an object, its material and conceptual production in past and present. As such, the text, the drawings, utterly fail reality. The archaeologist becomes museum scribe, copying and copying the past: ritualistic scrutiny, display and repetition. And there is also the same redundancy of detail as we noted in the site report – the detail of 5,000 diminutive pot sherds and . . . sites to be studied in the future?

The aim of such works is primarily synthesis, to draw together a body of data conceived as related according to archaeological categorization, to classify and reclassify. But the issue of categorization is again seriously abbreviated. Gibson's problem is that of beaker domestic pottery. We might ask the meaning of a study, a catalogue with commentary, devoted to such a category. He talks of the problem of distinguishing 'ritual from domestic' and defines domestic pottery as 'all finds not directly associated with a burial' and presents a diagram labelled as a 'Model for beaker context possibilities' (figure 1.1). All the categories he adopts – fabric, fine, coarse, burial, ritual, domestic – are categories of common sense, assumed as meaningful and self-evident. They remain unexamined, their definition regarded as essentially transparent. That there are variations in the meanings attached to different linguistic expressions of the same phenomena and differences in the meanings attached to the same words or phrases, according to who interprets them and according to their context of appearance, according that is to their inscription in textual and social practices, is forgotten. Nor are the categories of material culture, the social, ceramic production, critically theorized. The consequence is statements such as the following, taken from the conclusion to 92 pages of discussion: 'Domestic sites act as a type of cauldron for interaction between contemporary pottery styles. This interaction is, however, natural, and to be expected where individual potters are at work and producing goods which they regard as aesthetically pleasing' (Gibson, 1982, p. 92). Nowhere has Gibson considered the concept of interaction (of pottery styles?), style, the 'natural', the individual, work, goods, or the aesthetic. All are taken from common sense, all remain untheorized.

Gibson's study is certainly not exceptional in the archaeological literature, not even in the single-minded devotion to empiricism, to the aura of the archaeological find, required to produce measured drawings of 5,000 sherds 2.5 cm^2. Whatever the supposed value of such studies, gathering and making accessible arrays of data, they only serve to reveal the effects of the lack of critical theoretical reflection on conventional archaeological practice.

A work of synopsis
Smooth, 'readable', well-illustrated, comprehensive and relatively progressive, *Prehistoric Europe* by Champion et al. (1984) is an

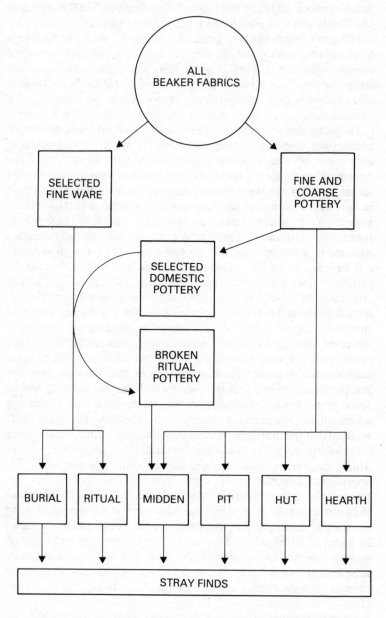

FIGURE 1.1   Gibson's 'Model for beaker context possibilities'
Source: A Gibson (1982).

excellent textbook covering all of Europe from earliest times to the Roman Empire. It is a synoptic text, a general summarizing view from a detached viewpoint. Abridging and crystallizing, this is a withdrawal from practical engagements with the archaeological object into interpretation. It represents reason's claim to legislate a truth as synoptic, rational and conceptual, with heterogeneity marginalized in a strategy of comparison, compilation and coherence.

In this book, a sophisticated example of British processual archaeology about which we will have much to say later, prehistory is brought to coherence as a kaleidoscopic interaction of the same 'essential' categories of economy, environment, population and the social: this is conceived as socio-economic process. So each chapter is an application of this conceptual scheme to stretches of prehistory, comparing different regions, compiling patterns, trends, discontinuities. The overall result is the establishment of a pattern of 'development'.

The text attempts to produce a 'balanced' account using different archaeological approaches, from palaeoeconomy to structural Marxism, different investments in the archaeological data bearing returns in the form of synoptic width. But we argue that the width, the academic neutrality, the attempted balance of different views within an all-embracing atemporal, aspatial 'socio-economic' process is ultimately incoherent. 'Materialist' explanations of material culture-patterning according to a logic of the ecosystem do not simply stress different aspects of the same socio-economic process to those theorized in structural Marxist archaeologies which give primacy to the structuring of social relations of production; they do not simply represent different interpretations of the same data (see, for example, pp. 149–51). This narrative line, subsuming fundamentally incompatible approaches, reveals such processual archaeology as an old historicism glossed with new jargon and methods. We argue instead that it is essential to question the political status and meaning of categories and theory. This applies equally to the book's theme of European prehistory. As Rowlands has argued: 'a prehistory of Europe cannot be assumed (except ideologically) . . . it does not exist except as the presentist projection into prehistory of current interest in establishing a unified sense of a "European" past' (1984, p. 154). Indeed much evidence could be extracted from this work that 'Europe' is a coherent archaeological concept only in the terms of university courses in prehistory. The explicit intention behind the book – the authors would probably agree – is to fill a particular gap in archaeological discourse and provide an elementary student text. Yet a text which does not appear to be critically aware of its own insertion within an established socio-economic political structure and smoothes over the social and political implications of choosing alternative frameworks for the interpretation of the 'European' or any other past, can hardly be expected to provide a stimulus for critical thought.

An introductory text

Attractively packaged and cleanly written, Greene's *Archaeology: an Introduction* (1983) is designed for an undergraduate course introducing archaeology. As with all introductions to archaeology, we find an overwhelming emphasis on method and technique – excavation, fieldwork and techniques of artefact analysis – involving the recovery and scrutiny of basic evidence (114 out of 175 pages). The unfortunate effect of such texts is to identify the discipline of archaeology with its technical instrumentation. Some primers may supplement this with a précis of archaeological achievements – discoveries – or, as in Greene's book, a history of archaeology, presented as the histories of the archaeological achievements of imaginative individuals (30 out of 175 pages).

In the final chapter, entitled 'Making sense of the past', Greene gives his account and assessment of recent developments: 'the hottest area of debate in contemporary archaeology is between traditional and new archaeology, and the applicability of various theoretical approaches and their resultant frameworks' (pp. 154–5). Different theories for Greene produce different frameworks which may be applied to the data. He comments that this is the excitement of contemporary archaeology, the fervent debate. But archaeology's fundamental unity is apparently not challenged. In the first place, theory is identified as essentially heuristic, as providing different ways of looking at the same data. So Greene comments:

> the new archaeology has greatly improved the quality of information in some areas of archaeology, and has produced a better framework for seeking explanations for that very reason. It is in many ways similar to the demands made by Edward de Bono in the general field of problem solving by lateral thinking.
>
> (p. 162)

Second, Greene follows Daniel in seeing a coherence in the history of archaeology as a discipline – not much has really changed since the eighteenth century! The history of archaeology apparently shows that 'the terminology and preoccupations do of course change, but the objectives and attitudes to the evidence . . . have a familiar ring' (p. 174). Daniel makes almost identical assertions: 'archaeologists have always been talking about evolutionary change and cultural process' (1981, p. 191). The underlying argument is, of course, that all that really matters are the data 'sources', nothing else really changes in its fundamentals. Greene, 'liberal' and detached, is sceptical of any final answers, any certainty. There are no wholly right or wrong answers, no final truths. The only certainty we are left with is the objectivity of the past, its 'facticity'. Hence the emphasis in such introductions to archaeology on methods and techniques, and the corollary that archaeology is detached from its historical reality as academic disciplinary practice. Its history becomes, as mentioned, a succession of individual imaginative consciousnesses.

Contemporary archaeological discourse

At the moment archaeological discourse is seriously abbreviated. It doesn't matter what you say as long as you say it in the right way; as long as you conform to the rules of empiricist/positivist discourse, rational method; as long as what you say is reasonable, not fantasy or extreme, is open to 'testing' against the data, is not overtly political, is not subjective. And if you transgress these laws of discourse, the epistemology and ontology police are waiting.

A repressive pluralism holds sway; we can only decide between different archaeologies according to prescribed laws of method and discourse. Different archaeologies are conceived as simply different approaches to the same past. Consequently, decision becomes paralysed. Contemporary archaeology has no way of coping with the perceived crisis of information, the large amount of archaeological information now being amassed, and what we identify as a redundancy of detail, other than by management and archival strategies.

Archaeological discourse is practised and dominated by experts, detached academic specialists for the most part ignoring or blind to the social conditions of their practice, conceiving these and their personal subjective experiences of archaeology as theoretically irrelevant. A subjective idealism privileges essential objectivity, the transcendental origin of knowledge, identifying the object and archaeological experiences of it. This is the only manner in which subjective experience is theoretically acceptable.

A teleology specifies the transcendental goal of archaeology as the past in itself and for itself. This goal is beyond question and decision, overriding and regulating the process and method of attaining the goal. The past is the aim; the task is to follow method, keep to the laws of discourse. Generally, contemporary archaeology can be characterized as being pervaded by a set of categorical oppositions.

Practice	Theory
Object	Subject
Past	Present
Presence	Absence
Substance	Re-presentation
Reality	Rhetoric, text
SECURITY	SUSPICION

Underlying and giving meaning to these oppositions are the two other terms: security and suspicion. 'Practice' through to 'reality' imply a nexus of security and, accordingly, these are considered primary in contrast to the questionability and suspicion underlying their opposites. Practice or doing archaeology via the application of method is given primacy over ideas and conceptualization. Hard facts are deemed to expel and annihilate soft ideas. The interpreting subject always becomes something to be regretted – all archaeologists ought to be suspicious of themselves and others, and the past shouldn't become infected with the present. Consequently, the past becomes conceived as a set of presences (artefacts and their associations) contrasted with the present, absented and distanced from the past. The past is felt to reside in an objective substance of its own – the reality, the presence, of the hand axe. However, the past clearly does not possess objective substance when described or re-presented in a text. The admittance of the relevance of theory, subjectivity, the present, writing, makes us feel suspicious, insecure, on weak ground. Essentially, it becomes problematic that people who write archaeology have different aspirations, live in the present and write texts.

The solution of the *aporiai* of these oppositions appears an impossible one. If we could go back in a time capsule would we not produce better archaeology? Ultimately on this line of reasoning, all archaeology must be suspicious, dangerous. But this is, as we have said, idealist fantasy.

ARCHAEOLOGY AS THEORETICAL PRACTICE

It is time to subvert these oppositions. Each opposed term in fact defines the other. No single term can be considered to stand on its own, self-referring. Each term is defined by what it excludes, what it denies. Consequently, subverting these oppositions requires their mediation. This is not simply to say, for example, that theory and data are equal and paired, each affecting the other, each as important as the other in archaeological practice (Renfrew, 1982). It is to contend that all the terms are aspects of the same material process, the same material practice. It is to accept our experience as archaeologists of producing the past now. Accordingly, theory is not something mental as opposed to practical, not an abstraction (distraction), which can be applied to objective data if so wished. Consider theory's metaphorical roots in the Greek:

Theaomai: to gaze at, spectate (with a sense of wonder).
Theoreo: spectate, review, inspect, contemplate, consider, to consult an oracle.
Theoros: a spectator at the theatre or the games.
Theorema: object of contemplation, subject of investigation.
Theatron: place for seeing, for assembly.
Theoria: mission to an oracle, contemplation, consideration.

Theory is not separate from practice. Theory is reflection, critique, performance, a theatre for action, an act and object of contemplation: these are aspects of the same material process, the theoretical practice of archaeology. So knowing the past means producing it in the present. Past and present are mediated in the practice of archaeology, in excavation and the writing of archaeological texts.

The archaeological text represents the necessary inscription of the artefact. Inscription is signifying practice which cannot be absorbed into the archaeological object. The object and its context (the subject of archaeology) must *necessarily* be given metaphorical expression, be signified in the text. As we have argued, simple, unmediated, immediate experience and expression of the past is an idealist fiction. No text is a transparent medium expressing an essential meaning of the past. Writing occurs in the present, it is a material means of production. As a social practice it is a threading together of the social, historical, linguistic and personal. There is no escape from this nexus. Archaeology is, then, immediately theoretical, social, political and autobiographical. Subjectivity, in the sense of autobiography, relating practice to the living of which it is an aspect, is not a deviation from real archaeology; it is the gesture which defuses the power of the *public* law of archaeological reason or discourse. To express it another way: to contend that we can only know the mediated object requires the mediation of the object world and the archaeologist's subjectivity. The subjective becomes the form of the objective because both are aspects of the same material process.

To return to categorization: a materialist emphasis on theory as practice requires a redefinition of the object world, a reconceptualizing centred on mediation. Instead of self-contained objects possessing identity, there are fields of relations. Identity presupposes difference from something else. There are no conclusive categories which can incorporate the differential and relational complexity of material reality and production. No concept or category is ever adequate to that which it signifies; the world cannot be compartmentalized according to categories of consciousness. There are, then, flaws in every concept and these make it necessary to refer to other concepts. Each category, apparently self-referring and inside itself, is in reality defined by what it excludes, by its chronic relation of difference to other categories. The result is a texture of webs of meaning. Meaning is never fully present, never fully disclosed, never final or conclusive; it is always deferred, in some ways absent, subject to redefinition and negotiation.

Categories are never adequate to the past. Interpretation does not produce stability nor effect closure. In the same way there are no universal truths to be found in the past. We, as archaeologists, are not gradually piecing together a better and better or more complete account of the past. Truths apply to the historical conjuncture and are wrapped up in the historical, social and personal mediation of subject and object, theory and practice, past and present. Interpretation, rather than effecting closure, opens up or discloses, creating *discontinuity*, difference.

The past, then, is gone; it can't be recaptured in itself, relived as object. It only exists now in its connection with the present, in the present's practice of interpretation. So it is not the objects of the past and their preservation which matter so much as the relations revealed and created between them in the historical act of interpretation. Instead of a past whose meaning is transparent to enlightened reason, or lost in mystery, we emphasize the act of interpretation. Indeed, according to our contention of the mediation of past and present, subjectivity and objectivity, theory and data, the past like an oracle *requires* interpretation.

Interpretation cannot be reduced to a methodology. We decry method as a way back to an absent past and refuse a rigorous method-ology. Method must instead be understood to arise out of a practical confrontation with the object. It is the affective as opposed to the effective. To argue that the past is chronically subject to interpretation and reinterpretation does not imply that all pasts are equally valid. Nor can it be accommodated in a shrug of the shoulders or a scepticism which would doubt the ultimate validity of any archaeology. It means the past forms an expansive space for intellectual struggle in the present and that we must accept the necessity for self-reflection and critique, situating archaeology in the present. Critique involves evaluation and makes taking sides a necessity, accepting responsibility for a decision as to why and how to write the past, and for whom. This responsibility belongs to us however much we might try to privilege the objectivity of the artefact or the neutrality of academic discourse.

What is the substance of this theoretical practice? What should be the focus of archaeology? There are the following unavoidable and crucial questions.

1 How is social reality created and structured?
2 What is the place of material culture, archaeology's object, within social reality?
3 How is social reality related to time; how and why does social reality change?
4 What is the meaning and form of gaining knowledge of past social reality?

There is no question of whether or not a consideration of social theory is needed in archaeology. The question to be asked is what kind of theory it should be – a strategic question. The questions posed above can receive no simple answers prior to being worked out in practice. So we are not proposing to replace a bad theory with a better theory, of archaeology, society, or whatever. To propose another theory to be applied, a theory reckoned to be better in some way, is to reproduce the split between theory and practice and to add to the proliferation of archaeological 'approaches' to the past. We are not going to argue that any particular method or approach or concept is automatically and wholly to be rejected. To do so abstractly would be to commit the error of theoreticism. What we shall do in the following chapters is to consider each of the above questions and examine and emphasize theory as a practice which cannot be separated from the object of archaeology, itself indelibly social, and the present socio-political context of this practice, this mediation of past and present.

2

Social Archaeology

Archaeologists have long realized the necessity of going beyond antiquarianism, the collection and study of artefacts for their own sake, and have attempted various forms of historical narrative and social reconstruction, setting artefacts in their context. This has predominantly involved relating material culture to units which subsume the individual – cultures, societies, culture systems: social totalities. This is because archaeology's data have been thought to require a conceptual occlusion of the agents who were originally responsible for producing the past. Before considering this striking absence of the individual social actor in archaeological theory we will examine the project of a social archaeology as it has developed in Britain by examining a series of texts.

SOCIAL ARCHAEOLOGY: A TEXTUAL CRITIQUE

The social narrative of traditional archaeology

A synopsis of prehistory from the first farmers to the Roman empire, Piggott's *Ancient Europe* (1965) is a chronological narrative of archaeological material, selected as outstanding or exemplary. For Piggott the narrative is one of a contrast to Western civilization: aggression and violence, barbarism and brutality, the less endearing attributes of humanity (p. 14ff). And the narrative is the traditional one of change explained by invasions, folk movements, cultural diffusion and warfare.

Piggott's account of the societies acting out this narrative is entirely descriptive, rooted in common-sense categories of the social. He proclaims (p. 7) that prehistorians 'move in a world of anonymous societies, defined by their distinctive traditions in the style and manufacture of everyday objects'. So the book outlines the ways of life: early farmers' house design (invariably peasant), economy, and when evidence is available, clothing and hairstyles. Examples are given of craft skills and workmanship, and artistic achievement is suitably appreciated:

> In Celtic art, 'man is a stranger' . . . attractive and repellent; it is far from primitiveness and simplicity . . . is refined in thought and technique; elaborate and clever: full of paradoxes, restless, puzzlingly ambiguous.
>
> (p. 243)

Temples, henges, cursus monuments, ritual accoutrements – all attest to the limitations of archaeological inference: 'we have no information on the beliefs which prompted the construction of these sacred places, nor of the rites performed within them' (p. 116). Such material expressions of religious or ritual phenomena are shrouded in mystery; they can only be described Occasionally, however, from evidence such as 'the presumed cult-figures of obese women' in Malta (p. 115), a guess may be made of the existence of some divinity.

In the terms of Piggott's empiricism the structure of society cannot be directly perceived, although inference from a diversity in the quality and richness of artefacts and burials may lead to a conception of a ranked society. Social hierarchy is consistently and simply seen in terms of princes or chieftains: this is the extent of Piggott's analyses of social ranking. For example, the rich round barrow burials in Wessex, England are described in terms of princely panoply: ' "they are assuredly the single sepulchres of kings and great personages . . ." wrote William Stukeley in the eighteenth century of the barrows on Salisbury plain, and he was right' (p. 129).

A repeated stress on the limitations of archaeological evidence is accompanied by its literary elaboration and enlivenment. Here is Piggott on the Celtic chieftain:

> The panoply and equipment of the battle-drunk, screaming tribal chieftain in his chariot hung with the decapitated heads of his foes, the air raucous with the sound of the baritus and the carnyx . . .
>
> (p. 243)

The values, aspirations and theoretical outlook of such works (for Hawkes (1968) the distillation of history from disparate facts, 'writing of quality and humanity' (p. 256)) are still held today by many archaeologists. Burgess's work, *The Age of Stonehenge* (1980), aspires to such an example. The first 130 pages of this 330 page book are an artefact-centred chronicle of British prehistory (3200 – 1200 BC) interspersed with rudimentary social sketching, again rooted in common-sense categories. So Burgess comments that far-reaching social, ideological and spiritual upheavals are indicated by important changes in material culture, in burial practices, and in the fate of the great public centres of the third millennium (p. 79). Artefact change means social change. And, somewhat earlier, 'the bewildering variety of burial customs which emerged in the Meldon Bridge period in part reflects the very complex structure of society at that time' (p. 61). After the chronicle, Burgess presents a description of society in this 'Age of Stonehenge': what the people were like, what they wore, what sort of settlements they lived in, the agriculture, crafts and industries they practised, their means of transport and communication, their burial ritual and ceremony are all featured. For Burgess, such description represents society as available to the archaeologist. Simple statements about social stratification (chiefdoms, paramount chiefs and superchiefs) are elaborated by reference to later literary sources (particularly Irish sagas). This, along with discussion of Celtic origins, amounts to the full extent of Burgess's social analysis.

In this index card (already a floppy disc?) archaeology, the particularity of the past is preserved in descriptive detail: description of hair styles, inventories of cinerary urns, discussions of post hole patterning. The sort of speculation as to the meaning of such variety is, perhaps, encapsulated in Burgess's comments on the reason for increasing deposition of bronzes in rivers, lakes and springs at the end of his period: 'with the increased precipitation and waterlogging after 1500 BC a development of water-cults makes good sense' (p. 351). People were fed up with the rain!

Systems theory

Renfrew's *Emergence of Civilisation* (1972) was the first major application of systems theory in British archaeology. Following Clarke's general programmatic statement of a systems-based archaeology (1968), Renfrew set out to explicitly theorize the workings of Aegean society in the third millennium BC and trace an explanation for the emergence of the 'civilized' palace economies of Crete and mainland Greece.

Society is conceived as a system, 'an intercommunicating network of attributes or entities forming a complex whole' (Clarke, 1968, p. 42). These entities are subsystems which amount to regularized patterns of social behaviours (figure 2.1). The interconnections are mechanisms of negative feedback maintaining balance or equilibrium. Each subsystem, and the system itself, are kept within assigned limits or maintained in a stable state by homoeostatic mechanisms which counteract any disturbance. So, for example, poor fishing means less fish to eat; negative feedback results in more fishing or use of food other than fish. Relations of positive feedback involve the amplification of an initial deviation, extending and increasing processes already present. Renfrew defines a particular variant of positive feedback as the 'multiplier

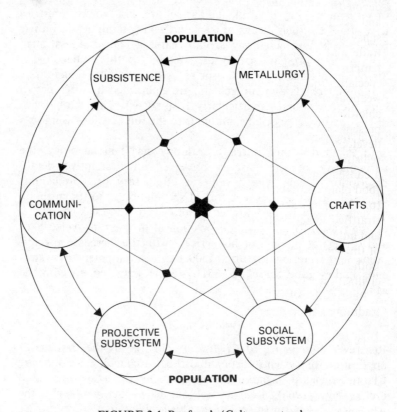

FIGURE 2.1 Renfrew's 'Culture system'
Notes: All the subsystems are linked with each other and the external system environment with relations of positive or negative feedback.
Source: From C. Renfrew (1972). Reprinted by permission of Methuen & Co.

effect', where a deviation in one subsystem has the effect of bringing about innovation in another:

> Changes or innovations occurring in one field of human activity (in one subsystem of a culture) sometimes act so as to favour changes in other fields (in other subsystems). The multiplier effect is said to operate when these induced changes in one or more subsystems themselves act so as to enhance the original changes in the first subsystem.
>
> (p. 37)

The multiplier effect is Renfrew's explanation of the emergence of Aegean civilization. In what he claims as a 'necessary preliminary' (p. 17) Renfrew produces 160 pages of traditional archaeological discourse specifying and describing details of cultural sequences. This is followed by a description of 'culture process' – a chapter is devoted to the parameters of his system (environment, population and settlement pattern), and individual chapters to the various subsystems (subsistence, metallurgy, crafts, social, the symbolic, trade and communication). For each he summarizes the general patterns and trends: for example, the development of craft specialization and metal working enabling new tools and new weapons and new forms of wealth; transformation of tribe into chiefdom, into principality or state. In the final chapter Renfrew presents two multiplier effects: 'the decisive factor for the development of Aegean civilization was the development of a redistributive system for subsistence commodities. This emerged as a consequence of the intensive exploitation of a new spectrum of food plants, notably tree crops, yielding a new diversity in produce' (p. 480). The second: 'the decisive factor . . . is the emergence of a stratified society, where high status correlates with material wealth and military prowess. These features arose largely as a consequence of the development of metallurgy and of maritime trade' (p. 483). Both are taken as models offering explanation for the emergence of civilization.

Renfrew's systems framework offered many advantages over traditional archaeologies:

1 it required explicit theorization of the social.
2 It directed attention to social process as lying behind material culture patterning.
3 In focusing on social process it involved considering explanation and causality rather than simple documentation of variety in space and time.
4 It involved a stress on complex causality: 'no single factor, however striking its growth, can of itself produce changes in the structure of culture' (p. 39).

5   It necessitated a consideration of subsystem interaction within a cultural whole, rather than permitting concentration on any single cultural phenomenon, such as subsistence or ceramic design.

However, in common with other uses of systems theory in archaeology, culture is conceived as man's extrasomatic means of adaptation (p. 13). The social logic of Renfrew's systems theory is that of function. Each subsystem is 'explained' in terms of its function in maintaining the existence of the whole cultural system, while the system itself is conceived as a mediatory entity, biologically adapting a population to its natural environment. Civilization, Renfrew's ultimate theme, thus becomes a socio-cultural form of adaptation to nature: 'civilisation is the complex artificial environment of man; it is the insulation created by man, an artefact which mediates between himself and the world of nature. Since man's environment is multi-dimensional so too is civilisation' (p. 13). This logic of adaptation and functionalist explanation has long been questioned in the social sciences, and criticism within archaeology is also well established (e.g. Hodder, 1982; Tilley, 1981a, 1981b). Theorizing a cultural entity as adaptive or functional simply affirms its existence and provides little comprehension of its specific form of articulation. To say that institutions and regularized customs of society are artefacts and can be regarded to fulfil functions broadly analogous to those of material artefacts which mediate between people and the natural environment, as Renfrew does, is to say nothing about why the institutions and customs take the specific form they do.

To conceive culture as adaptive means that societies are regarded as primarily conservative – maintaining equilibrium within their environment through homoeostatic negative feedback devices. Change becomes a problem:

> This conservative nature of culture cannot too strongly be stressed. In terms of our model it is the natural tendency of culture to persist unchanged . . . it is change, any change, which demands explanation.
>
> (p. 487)

Stability, apparently, just happens – it does not require explanation. For Renfrew the multiplier effect is 'needed to overcome this innate conservative homoeostasis of culture' (p. 487). The problem of change is solved by reference to a mechanistic relation between subsystems, and the notion of 'relation' becomes reified. The mechanism is conceptualized as existing separately from the entities it unites: subsystems can be defined independently of their relations with other subsystems. This begs the question of the ontology of both subsystem and relation: what is negative feedback? what exactly is a subsystem? do subsystems and systems exist? how are they to be defined? Patterns of interactions, activities and artefacts would seem to be Renfrew's answer (pp. 19–23). Renfrew accepts that these regularized patterns are arbitrary categories imposed in analysis (p. 20). This throws the burden of their specification on to theory but Renfrew gives no justification for specifying subsystems as 'subsistence', 'technological', 'social', 'symbolic' and 'communicative', other than convenience. Why are they convenient, and for what purpose? Renfrew does not confront the meaning or significance of such categories. He accepts that boundaries are difficult to define: 'Criteria of different degrees of uniformity will lead to the definition of larger or smaller units' (p. 21). But what is to specify the application of different criteria? Intuition? Usefulness? Obviousness? Again, this is not theorized. In Renfrew's book the categories of system and subsystem are descriptive, referring to empirical patterning. The entire procedure of systems analysis is heuristic, its usefulness being its stress on complexity and interaction. Renfrew has realized this (p. 495) and his later work with catastrophe theory (1978, 1979) may be seen as an attempted solution, a solution involving the quantification of culture and the specification of a mathematized social process.

The interactions of negative and positive feedback are, as we have said, reified mechanisms between arbitrary analytical categories, mechanisms derived from cybernetic theory. They are *not* a social logic but based on analogies with machines, analogies which take no account of human agency and praxis (cf. below).

In that subsystems and interactions are defined independently, the synchronic is separated from the diachronic, static analysis from the explanation of change. This relates to society being conceived as naturally conservative, denying change, being naturally timeless, and change being problematic, that which is to be explained (see chapter 5 below).

Renfrew's systems analysis proceeds by successive reduction of empirical detail to categories, a process of simplification. So culture sequence is transformed into systemic categories, subsystems, whose general patterning and trends are isolated. These general trends are then encapsulated in a dual model of emergence of complex society – 'civilization'. The result is an extraordinary redundancy of detail (the redundancy already noted in chapter 1). The relation between the culture sequence of part I and the processual analyses in part II of Renfrew's book seems to be that the first is chronicle – neutral exposition – while part II is theory *applied* to this data as an explanation. Archaeological remains from over a thousand years of Aegean prehistory are reduced to some 24 pages of multiplier effect (pp. 480–504). Now, of course, simplification and generalization are essential to any analytical or theoretical practice but it is as essential to pose the question of the meaning, significance and character of this generalization. We argue that Renfrew's study is an application, an imposition of pre-defined categories of system and subsystem on to the 'data'. It lacks self-reflexiveness. The categories of system, subsystem, feedback, exist in no 'real' or 'theoretical' relation to the object of study. The only relation is that of application (p. 18); it is purely methodological – theory is held to exist separately from data. This is the corollary to the arbitrary definition of subsystem and the non-social cybernetic logic of the mechanisms of interaction. The concomitant of this is that any complexity claimed for the explanation is entirely a function (sic) of the model of system (the applied theory) and does not necessarily apply to the data which are meant to be explained. This imposition throws into focus the politics of Renfrew's theory – the stress on the conservative nature of society, and the adopted model of *homo oeconomicus* (see esp. pp. 497ff).

Renfrew's *Emergence of Civilisation* prefigures many of the major aspects and developments in the social archaeology of the 1970s and early 1980s:

1 Procedures of applying social theories to archaeological data.
2 Processual explanation based on an identification of patterned behaviours from archaeological remains and specification of their complex interaction.
3 Theoretical use of social typologies: evolutionary sequences of bands, tribes, chiefdoms, etc.
4 A related focus on the identification of social ranking.
5 An emphasis, often economistic, on the general importance of social control of material resources.
6 A focus on the analysis of mortuary remains from a structural-functionalist and role-model perspective.
7 The development of models of trade and exchange.
8 Use of the notion of prestige goods economies.
9 Use of cross-cultural generalizations.

In the following sections we analyse some of these developments in archaeological theorizations of the social.

Social typologies

The social typology, band, tribe, chiefdom and state (Sahlins, 1968; Service, 1962) has had tremendous influence on social archaeology. While forming the basis of various forms of evolutionary thinking in archaeology it has also, more generally, provided a vocabulary for social archaeology. The static and descriptive nature of the categories has meant that change from one category to another is problematical and has led to the claim that identification of a particular 'type' of society somehow constitutes an explanation. This is clear from Renfrew's 'recognition' of chiefdoms in neolithic Wessex, southern England (1973). He first specifies 20 features of chiefdoms (following Sahlins and Service), including ranking, the distribution of surplus by chiefs, 'clearly defined territorial boundaries', 'frequent ceremonies and rituals serving wide social purposes' (p. 543). There is no discussion of social process, of the working of a chiefdom social system. Renfrew proceeds to identify territorial divisions on the basis of ceremonial monuments – causewayed camps – in the earlier neolithic. He thinks these were emerging chiefdoms coalescing in the later neolithic into one greater chiefdom with constituent tribes. The archaeological evidence is considered to fit into this social categorization: mobilization of humanpower; craft specialization; religious specialization. For example, the Stonehenge area with major ceremonial monuments is considered evidence of the existence of a paramount chief. This checklist archaeology, and the social typologies on which it is based, although much criticized (e.g. Tainter, 1978) for its reductive subsumption of variability, nevertheless remains in use (e.g. Collis, 1984; and see chapter 6 below).

Ranking, resource and exchange

The volume *Ranking, Resource and Exchange* (Renfrew and Shennan (eds), 1982) in many respects represents the culmination of the programme of functionalist social archaeology in Britain, covering almost all of the elements of what is now a virtual theoretical hegemony standing opposed to traditional archaeology. The fifteen essays exemplify three routes for exploring ranking: settlement ranking and political structures involving ideas of co-ordinating political centres and core–periphery relations; the mobilization and organization of surplus labour especially in ceremonial monument construction; ranking and status of individual social personae identified particularly in the analysis of mortuary remains.

The predominant focus is on resources and their control and management. Sherratt considers agricultural wealth in the Carpathian basin from the sixth millennium BC, proposing regional exchange networks linking nodal lowland areas and highland hinterlands involving domestic cattle. He argues this is a primary feature in emerging social hierarchy. Shennan and S. Champion consider the role of rare exchanged items, amber and coral respectively, in the earlier Bronze and Iron Ages of central and western Europe. Both propose prestige goods ranking systems, hierarchical societies where social position depended on consumption of prestige goods. Haselgrove has an elaborated prestige goods system in the late pre-Roman Iron Age centralized polities of south-east England, elaborated in its incorporation at the periphery of an expansive Roman empire, the core polity and source of prestige goods. Thus one process in social hierarchization is identified as relating to trade, exchange and societal interaction. Another process relates to the intensification and specialization of production of agriculture and crafts and subsequent management and control. Chapman considers control of critical resources – land, water, copper and interregional traded items – as a determinant factor in the development of social ranking in Iberia, 4000–1000 BC. The Rhine Main basin, 1500–500 BC, is considered by T. Champion who derives the pattern of settlement relocation, subsistence innovation, enhanced social ranking, technological development and ritual activities ('Urnfield' phenomenan) from an imbalance between subsistence resources and population.

This social logic of giving priority to relations between population, subsistence and environment is frequent in such 'processual' studies. So Halstead and O'Shea present a self-styled 'adaptive model' for the emergence of redistributive economies and apply it to the 'palaces' of Bronze Age Crete. Accumulation of tokens of value which may be exchanged for foodstuffs in times of shortage is termed social storage – an adaptive response to periodic failure in food supply. The tokens used in social storage – craft items, durable and convertible – 'would have permitted the sustained accumulation and manipulation of wealth and power and so have facilitated the emergence of institutionalised social inequality' (p. 98) – the Cretan palace civilization. Gamble relates settlement nucleation and political developments in the Bronze Age Aegean (Melos) to agricultural intensification and control.

There is no doubt that this volume of studies represents a considerable advance over traditional archaeology in its concentration on the patterning of social process. But this is conceived in purely descriptive terms (cf. Whallon, 1982). The relations between a limited number of cross-cultural variables are described in their various combinations (figure 2.2). These variables amount to resources and the mechanisms of their control as is indicated by the reduction of social ranking to the effects of two processes: those of exchange and societal interaction, and intensification of production.

The functionalist logic of such processes is very apparent in many of the studies. So, for example, T. Champion talks of the strain on subsistence resources in late second-millennium BC Germany:

> The particular strategy adopted to meet this strain was to minimise risk and provide a buffer against subsistence failure. This required increased levels of managerial control internally and of exchange relations externally, and had an inbuilt predisposition towards growth.
>
> (p. 65)

So the different parts of the system – production, ranking, exchange, ritual – interact coherently in a whole adapted to its particular environment. The task of archaeological explanation has become that of describing the workings of such systems which are held to account for patterning in the archaeological record. Analysis of ranking is reduced to tracing the development of complexity.

This emphasis on descriptive process is in accordance with the structure of the whole book – the attempt to develop a coherent narrative of the emergence of hierarchical structure: appearance of salient ranking; discussion of the resource base of early states and post-collapse resurgence, the first millennium BC and post-Roman dark ages. This background narrative to the individual studies is foregrounded in the editorial introductions to each section. The relations of this project to neo-evolutionary theory are also clear in the functionalist frame of reference adopted and the use of cross-cultural comparison associated with the identification of particular instances of general processes claimed to have universal relevance (Halstead and O'Shea, p. 98; Renfrew, p. 91). Hence it is possible to reduce several thousand years of prehistory essentially to the particular manifestations of the two processes outlined above.

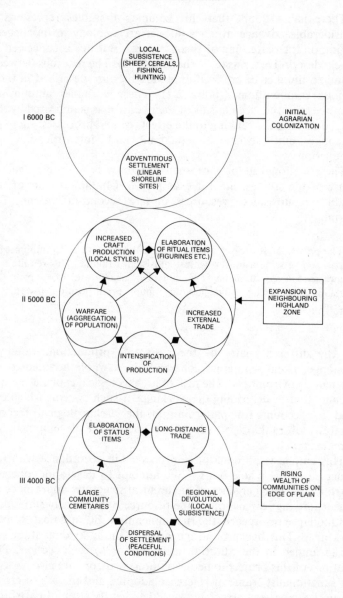

FIGURE 2.2 Sherratt's social model for the Great Hungarian Plain
6000–3500BC

Notes: Rectangles represent external factors.

Source: From Renfrew and Shennan (eds), (1982). Reprinted by permission of
Cambridge University Press.

The separation of process and its manifestation in the archaeological record relates to the separation of theory and data, the general and the particular, a separation which is frequently duplicated in the structure of the essays themselves: general points followed by empirical illustration. However, a more serious criticism must be the lack of theorization of archaeology's primary data – material culture. Identified patterning in material culture is conceived as an immediate expression of social process; it is not (see chapter 4).

Peer Polity Interaction

The effects of the simple descriptive basis of much processual archaeology are very evident in the recent volume, *Peer Polity Interaction and Socio-Political Change* (Renfrew and Cherry (eds), 1986). The concept of peer polity interaction refers to a series of empirical observations which have been noted to occur together in several instances. They are: (1) polities occur in regional clusters; (2) organizational changes occur not singly within these clusters but in more than one polity at about the same time; (3) changes in, for example, conceptual systems for the communication of information in artefacts associated with high status and in ritual activities occur together and seem to be attributable to no single locus of innovation (Renfrew, pp. 7–8). It is proposed that the changes are the result of interaction between autonomous polities within a single geographical region. These interactions include competition; warfare and competitive emulation; symbolic entrainment (adoption of a more developed symbolic system upon contact with a less developed one); transmission of information; and exchange of goods. The book consists of a series of illustrations of these generalizations and processes in Aegean city-states, Minoan palaces, complex chiefdoms in the European Iron age, Classic Mayan centres, the Midwestern Hopewell, USA.

The concept of peer polity interaction usefully emphasizes societal interaction and complex processes of transformation rather than synchronic analyses of the workings of a single polity. Attention is also drawn to interactions which might be termed symbolic or stylistic. However, as with the systems approach, there is the very real problem of defining the units of interest – here peer polities. Such a concept is clearly much easier to apply to early civilizations with literary evidence available (Cherry and Renfrew, pp. 150–1; Champion and Champion, p. 63). Elsewhere there is the usual reliance on social typologies. Again the descriptive nature of the concept is evident, leaving untheorized so much of the social logic of the phenomenon, in particular the role of material culture. Renfrew and Cherry clearly think that peer polity interaction allows consideration of the symbolic and the stylistic as well as the economic and technological in a processual rather than an 'idealist' context (p. viii). But the recurring assumption is that symbolic entrainment, symbolic interaction, would be manifested as stylistic similarity or homogeneity. We have already commented that the relation of material culture to the social is not such a simple matter. We might agree with Sabloff: 'we must be able to tie the interactions of the hypothesized peers to specific features of the archaeological record' (p. 116).

Analysis of mortuary practices

The pioneering work of Saxe (1970) and Binford (1972a) opened up the analysis of mortuary practices as a primary means of investigating past social systems. They developed the general argument that mortuary practices need to be analysed in the context of variations in types of society and social complexity. In his paper Binford argued that:

> We would expect that other things being equal, the heterogeneity in mortuary practice which is characteristic of a single sociocultural unit would vary directly with the complexity of the status hierarchy, as well as with the complexity of the overall organization of the society with regard to membership units and other forms of sodalities.
>
>   (1972a, pp. 221–2)

And

> It is proposed that there are two general components of the social situation to be evaluated . . . First is what we may call, with Goodenough (1965, p. 7) the *social persona* of the deceased. This is a composite of the social identities maintained in life and recognized as appropriate for consideration at death. Second is the composition and size of the social unit recognizing status responsibilities to the deceased. We would expect direct correlations between the relative rank of the social position held by the deceased and the number of persons having duty-status relationships vis-a-vis the deceased.
>
>   (Ibid., pp. 225–6)

According to Binford, the main features which archaeologists may be able to detect with regard to prehistoric social organization from an analysis of mortuary practices are: (1) the type of organization present, whether or not it was essentially egalitarian or stratified, whether or not the presence of distinct and/or competing corporate groups is indicated; (2) the complexity of past social systems or, in other words, how much structural differentiation there appears to be. The main dimensions of social persona or roles which might be recognized are age, sex, social affiliation and position as well as, in certain cases, the conditions and locations of death.

The volume, *The Archaeology of Death* (Chapman, Kinnes and Randsborg (eds), 1981), fleshes out this position and succinctly summarizes the theoretical position developed in the archaeological literature at the outset of the 1980s. As Chapman, Randsborg and Brown comment, effort has predominantly gone into analysing the variety within the mortuary practices of a particular social unit in attempting to identify social ranking. Attention has thus focused on the range of artefacts deposited with the dead, assuming that certain artefacts will symbolize social status (e.g. S. E. Shennan, 1975). Effort expenditure on the treatment of the deceased has also been proposed as a key variable: greater expenditure correlating with higher rank (e.g. Tainter, 1975, 1977, 1978). Other analyses have considered the demographic structure of skeletal populations searching for physical indications of social difference (e.g. Buikstra, 1981). Analyses of mortuary practices have relied heavily on the utilization of a range of statistical techniques, many computer based, ranging from simple tests of statistical significance to multivariate techniques such as cluster analysis and principal components analysis.

The general strategy in such studies is the identification of pattern and its correlation with social complexity. Questions asked of the data include: do certain artefacts regularly occur with others in individual graves, or with sex or a particular age set of the burial population; are certain burials orientated in a particular direction as opposed to others; to what extent is the arrangement of burials in a cemetery random or regularly patterned; how does the spatial organization of burials differ within and between cemeteries; what are the demographic parameters of deceased populations and what symbolic dimensions (e.g. use of burial monuments as territorial markers) might be inferred. Attention has also centred on the arrangement of artefacts in graves and attempts to calculate measures of effort expenditure. Such work has drawn heavily on cross-cultural ethnographic 'tests' or surveys, with attempts being made to set up more or less directly deterministic links, or 'behavioural correlates' between people, resources, and mortuary practices. These surveys are of dubious value and can hardly be considered to vindicate the overall approach. A correlation is a very different thing from an explanation, and there is no reason to suppose that ethnographically documented cases of mortuary practices provide a representative sample of forms of prehistoric social organization.

There has been increasing awareness of the complexity that might be encountered and a call has been made for investigation of processes of the formation of the archaeological record, processes which may complicate the expression of social organization in mortuary practices (O'Shea, 1981, 1984). In his study of 5 Plains Indian cemetries O'Shea reaffirms the direct expression of social organization in burial practices but focuses on the additional relationship between the practices and their archaeological observation. It has also been noted that status need not be directly reflected in burial but may be suppressed as a form of ideology (Chapman and Randsborg, 1981, p. 14). However, rather than directing attention to the need to theorize such aspects of material culture they have been conceived primarily as just adding further complexity, distortion to be counteracted in the derivation of social pattern from the patterning of mortuary practices: 'what matters here is that the archaeologist evaluates the degree to which the mortuary data do reflect the social structure by means of complementary data (e.g. settlements and settlement patterns, metal hoards etc.)' (Chapman and Randsborg, 1981, p. 14).

The entire theoretical perspective on which this work is based draws heavily on structural-functionalist and role theory, as developed in anthropology and sociology (Firth, 1971; Dahrendorf, 1968; Merton, 1957; Nadel, 1957; Radcliffe-Brown, 1952). However, the theoretical basis of this work remains scantily discussed. In the *Archaeology of Death* volume discussion of the theoretical basis underlying the archaeological approaches and analyses is virtually absent, apart from a few passing references to the work of Goodenough. Within the perspective offered in this book the notion of social structure implicitly employed is more or less equivalent to pattern. Significantly, the concept does not even appear in the index. Social structure (referred to in processual archaeology predominantly in terms of ranking) is considered to reside in the network of patterns of interactions between individual agents, arising either from an analysis of empirically given realities in social life, or abstractions based on these, such as the notion of social persona or role. Such a conception is directly analogous to that of anatomical pattern in biology, where the skeleton and organs may be held to provide a physical support for the body. Radcliffe-Brown considered social structures in terms of three basic problems: What kinds of structures are there and how best may we categorize them? How do they function and maintain themselves? How are the structures of different form constituted? For him, the basic unit of structure was the 'elementary family' from which other structural relations or kin ties could be deduced (1952, pp. 178–80). In role theory a number of different roles forming an actor's social persona are held to be enacted in different situations, with the roles changing according to whether they have been ascribed or achieved, and in terms of temporal enactment and context. Various roles may be acted out by any one person (e.g. a bank manager may also be a father and a Conservative Party official).

In any role system there may be various degrees of role summation, coherence, dependence or independence, within society or with regard to other roles. Such a theory provides an implausible and deterministic model of the relationships between individuals and groups. As Giddens notes, 'the actors only perform according to scripts which have already been written out for them' (1976, p. 16). A person's role is regarded as given rather than negotiated and renegotiated in practice. Actors merely slot into a number of prescribed roles and act in conformity with them. But it is people and not roles that actually constitute society. A serious debilitating effect of this conception of social structure adopted in processual archaeology is that it lacks any explanatory significance. Conceptions of role, social persona, or social structure only have significance as redescriptions of the archaeological evidence, they are not explanatory. Function, rather than structure, plays the explanatory role as human society can exist only in its activity; but as we have argued, the specification of function is yet another form of redescription of social practices and similarly remains non-explanatory. The possibility that underlying principles of social conduct exist in social forms, not directly discernible in terms of perceived social relationships or roles, does not exist within the framework of processual archaeology (cf. the consideration of social structure below and in chapter 3). This lack may go some way to affording an understanding of its predominantly descriptive emphasis and lack of explanatory content.

Marxist archaeologies

From an explicitly Marxist outlook, Rowlands in his later work (1982, 1984a) has outlined an alternative programme for a social archaeology. With Gledhill (Gledhill and Rowlands, 1982, pp. 162–4) he has proposed a conception of the social totality which differs markedly from the mechanical interactions of a systemic perspective, or the largely untheorized concepts of 'society' used in traditional archaeological narrative. Avoiding the formalism of Althusser's conception of the social formation with its determinate levels of economic base and superstructure and ultimate economic determinism and functionalism (see chapter 6), Rowlands has emphasized the necessity of theorizing total social systems with no implied hierarchy of determination:

> theorising about long term socio-economic change in prehistory involves us in the construction of models of total social systems in which ideological, political and economic processes are linked to each other in a dialectical interplay rather than as determinate levels in a social formation.
>
> (Gledhill and Rowlands, 1982, p. 145)

But rather than an indeterminate interplay of relations Rowlands gives weight to the political:

> History, in a concrete sense, emerges as the resolution of continuous antagonisms existing between social subjects. What defines the social whole, therefore, is the form of political articulation that constitutes the totality of social relations . . . it has no particular locus (in the state, for example) . . . It follows that politics is not definable in any institutional form but refers more generally to power struggle and to the idioms, symbols, and other means used to define relative status and position.
>
> (Rowlands, 1982, p. 167)

We shall take up these points in more detail below (pp. 57–60; 72–8). Rowlands has also raised the issue of the boundaries of units of analysis. First, in advocating world systems analysis, inter-societal exchange and interdependency, involving especially the development of core and periphery areas (e.g. Frankenstein and Rowlands, 1978). So,

> The distinction between 'internal' and 'external' relationships is therefore only a viable one in a limited sense. At given moments of time, existing societies can be linked together in new ways, and the results of this linking are not predictable without understanding how this change in external conditions of reproduction bears on internal structures.
>
> (Gledhill and Rowlands, 1982, p. 148)

Secondly, Rowlands points to the analytical process of classification and categorization. So the notion of society 'forms a category only because archaeologists classify it as such, as part of the taxonomic space within which they operate and as part of the definition of their own discipline' (Rowlands, 1982, p. 164). Ultimately notions of society relate to the emergence of nation-states in Western Europe in recent times (ibid.) He also emphasizes the importance of analysis of contradiction within social forms or totalities – the internal generation of processes of transformation. This is associated with a call for a genuine theory of history 'centred on social dynamics and transformation processes' (Gledhill and Rowlands, 1982, p. 145), a denial of the opposition between the synchronic and the diachronic found in systems theory and functionalist archaeology more generally.

Rowlands stresses the materiality of the political and the ideological and, therefore, that both are written into the archaeological record. The dialectical conception of social relations and social totalities advanced (as opposed to mechanical articulation) means, for example, that the economic and socio-political cannot be separated. It also means that the conception of totality is inseparable from its place in analysis. In Rowlands' words:

> Analysis proceeds from the abstraction of the whole to that of its parts and back to the whole again and from the abstract to the concrete at each of these levels. Such a view is always partial in the sense that some things are always left out, and the whole may or may not correspond to what may be isolated empirically as a concrete 'society'. The totality is therefore a conceptual entity that has reality only in the sense that it forms a mental appropriation of a real world that exists separate from thought process. In this sense, population, society, or a mode of subsistence could all be totalities and abstractions at the same moment, the validity of their application depending on how they relate to each other in the analysis of concrete situations.
>
> (Rowlands, 1982, p. 163)

This forms part of Rowlands' rejection of the categorical opposition between materialism and idealism, facts and values, the objective and the subjective, and the concept of reality (Rowlands, 1984a), replacing these with a recognition of the active intellectual production of the past, with a critical awareness of the insertion of archaeological categorization and theorization within a Western political and intellectual context. This is, of course, in accordance with his conception of the political.

It will be clear from the discussions which follow in this book, and elsewhere (Tilley, 1982; Shanks and Tilley, 1982; Miller and Tilley, 1984a, 1984b; Tilley, 1984, 1985; Shanks and Tilley, 1987), that we fully endorse Rowlands' programmatic statements concerning a true 'social archaeology'. However, we must reserve criticism for the specific form of the development of models of general processes of social transformation (Friedman and Rowlands, 1978) (see chapter 6).

Those archaeologists drawing inspiration in particular from recent Marxist anthropology (see Spriggs (ed.), 1984, for a bibliography) have made significant advances over competing social archaeologies. They have produced more sophisticated conceptualization of social totalities, extending consideration of the political and ideological issues of legitimation from a narrower focus on subsistence adaptation and interactions between technologies, environment and population found in processual functionalist archaeology (see above). However, most of Rowlands' aims for a Marxist social archaeology have unfortunately not yet been achieved.

Consider, for example, Parker Pearson's work on the early Iron Age of Denmark (1984a, 1984b). He makes a series of reasonable abstract statements about the implications of a Marxist archaeology:

1 Marxist theory has practical (political) implications.
2 Central to social analysis are conceptions of contradiction and conflict.
3 The role of ideology of articulating action and belief is another key concept requiring theorization and analysis (1984, pp. 60–3).
4 This last point implies that artefacts cannot simply be categorized according to economic, social or ideological criteria: a hoe may be as ideological as a law code.
5 Institutions may embody the social, economic and ideological; the economy conversely may be considered religious or ideological practice. (1984b, p. 71)

However, this theorizing appears quite separate from its application to the Iron Age of Denmark. In fact, what is 'applied' to the data is Friedman's model of social change among the Kachin of Burma (Friedman, 1975, based on Leach, 1954). Parker Pearson correlates and compares patterning in conventional classes of data in prehistoric Denmark (burial, votive and settlement evidence), tracing the supposed expressions of Friedman's transformational cycles leading to the emergence of states. He claims that his study has attempted to outline one way of transforming material remains into social insights (1984a, p. 69). This involves a consideration of legitimation – conspicuous consumption, manipulation of ancestors and consciousness of social identity in ritual practices. So Parker Pearson produces some interesting comments on the possible relations between the living, the dead, ancestors, gods, tradition and spiritual sanctioning (1984a, p. 64). But the relation of material culture to practice is predominantly, for him, one of exemplification or expression. The particularity and detail of votive deposits, grave goods, bronze forms, pot designs, are simply absorbed into the general model.

Parker Pearson fits together a coherent social logic of transformation, one of competitive aristocracies, inflationary spirals, appropriation of surplus production and its legitimation (1984, p. 89). The only significant difference between this and the processual archaeologies outlined above is its emphasis on relations of production, their structuring effects on the social totality, and their ideological legitimation. However, this consideration of ideology needs to be taken much further (see chapter 3 below).

The reduction of vital insights and principles of Marxist theory to the status of just another approach to be applied to archaeological data is even more clear in Kristiansen's work on prehistoric Denmark (1984). Marxist theory is to supply an evolutionary and systemic explanatory superstructure able to cope with all forms of archaeological data (1984, pp. 74–5). For Kristiansen, in effect, Marxism simply provides different boxes and connecting arrows (figure 2.3). The real strength of approaches derived from structural Marxist anthropology lies in the attempt to overcome a functionalist separation and reification of religion, politics, economics etc. as separate interacting subsystems. However, in practice, in the process of writing an account of the past, this seems to have made very little difference, hence the frequently adopted economistic models and 'applications'. Kristiansen places great emphasis on the distinction between cultural form and material function. Basically this amounts to saying that it is necessary to consider the material function of cultural manifestations: so Kristiansen regards megalithic monuments as an extension of the organization of production; this is their material function (pp. 80–1). Religion may have an economic role (p. 76). This highlights ideological legitimation: cultural form may have a legitimating (ideological) material function. This, of course, gives

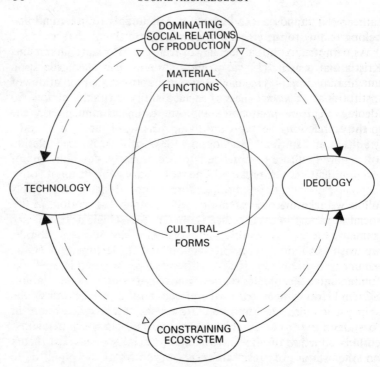

FIGURE 2.3 Kristiansen's 'Basic theoretical concepts' for the analysis of
the social formation

Notes: The solid lines represent selective pressure; the broken lines represent
adaptive response.

Source: From K. Kristiansen (1984). Reprinted by permission of Cambridge
University Press.

primacy to the social relations of production – that which needs
legitimation. For Kristiansen ideology thus becomes a 'subjective'
representation of the 'objective' – that which pertains to the social
relations of production (settlement, subsistence, technology) (p. 78).

A functionalist logic and economism are quite evident here.
Kristiansen proceeds to apply his general social model to the data,
assuming the well-worn distinction between territorial megalithic
chiefdoms and segmentary tribes of the Battle-Axe culture (social
typologies again) (p. 77). It turns out that these represent an
'agricultural' as opposed to a 'pastoral' tribal economy (p. 85).
This, apparently, is the essence of 1,200 years of Danish prehistory.
The different categories of data are mobilized around this
distinction, described as 'very different cultural manifestations of

rather similar material functions of production' (p. 77); that is both belong to the category of tribal economy.

As with the processual social archaeologies, Parker Pearson and Kristiansen present us with a complex and often ingenious and imaginative interplay of social process involving more or fewer institutional categories such as economy, ritual, technology, ideology. This interplay is held to account for patterning identified in the archaeological record.

SOCIAL ARCHAEOLOGY: A SUMMARY

While we acknowledge that the developments in conceptions of the social advances in archaeology since the early 1960s represent an immense theoretical improvement *vis à vis* traditional archaeology, we wish to follow Hodder (1982a, 1982b, 1985, 1986) in his summary critique of social archaeology. Hodder draws the fundamental distinction between social system and structure. System refers to the patterning and organization of social relationships; structure refers to the rules and concepts which give meaning to system. He argues that social archaeologies have been almost entirely concerned with the workings of social systems. This focus on system has several aspects and implications:

1 The concept of system emphasizes relations of power (dependence and authority and hierarchy, the movement and control of resources), exchange and trade, the character and control of subsistence, and in Marxist-influenced work strategies of ideological legitimation.

2 This conception of the social has been mobilized in archaeology as research strategies of the recognition and description of pattern. This has involved classification and ordering of artefacts according to their attributes, definition of types and styles, and correlation with other features of system; analysis of artefact distributions for possible correlations with social groups, activities, exchange networks; site locational analysis, searching for site hierarchies; analysis of the patterning of mortuary remains for correlation with original social context; societal categorization – the description of the past in terms of bands, tribes etc., its degrees of complexity; the description of subsistence strategies. These research aims have provided justification for the utilization of a wide range of statistical and mathematical techniques (e.g. Hodder and Orton, 1976; Doran and Hodson, 1975).

3   In its descriptive emphasis the focus is on what people do (although Marxist archaeologists may also focus on the structuring effects of social relations of production). The recognition of system (not necessarily implying the explicit adoption of a systems theory framework) is the recognition of regularized patterns of behaviours. There is little or no theorizing of social *action*, the intentional and meaningful practice of knowledgeable social actors.

4   The focus on *behaviour* rather than social *action* reduces material culture to an epiphenomenon of the social relations within which it is inserted – a product of social behaviour; a material resource to be controlled, exchanged; a sign of social interaction or difference; or a technology mediating population and environment. Hence the relative lack of theorization of material culture.

5   The descriptive emphasis involving behaviours rather than social action and reduction of material culture to epiphenomenon allows the fragmentation of theory. Economy may be theorized separately from ritual because it refers to different sets of behaviours (compare the outline of archaeological theory at the beginning of chapter 1).

6   The reduction of material culture to epiphenomenon also allows the development of levels of theory. Binford's 'middle-range theory' (1977, 1983, chs 17, 23–5, 28), as opposed to high-level social theory, depends on it being possible to predict artefact deposition without reference to social process.

7   The aim of processual archaeology is the specification of relations between variables such as subsistence, environment, technology, social ranking. These variables are the regularized patterns of behaviours just mentioned. Hence such social archaeologies can often be reduced to synoptic diagrams of social process: boxes and arrows, flow diagrams such as those illustrated above. A function of the emphasis on description, this reifies the variables and relations. There is little questioning of the meaning of the variables which remain essentially arbitrary: why subsistence, technology, ideology, rather than another categorization? There is a lack of theorization of the location of these variables in the *practice* of archaeological analysis. Usually their choice depends simply on the acceptance that the variables are analytical.

8   These variables are defined prior to analysis and, as just mentioned, are reified categories. This permits and encourages cross-cultural comparison and generalization. But historical particularity then becomes a problem: why any particular subsistence strategy?

9   The emphasis on description of system as relations between variables of patterned behaviours results in a radical occlusion of the individual. The individual social actor is reduced to a support (theoretically absent) for the patterns of behaviours or becomes aggregated into just another variable – population.

10   A specification of the relations between variables, the working of the system, and its correlation with, or identification in, archaeological data is held to constitute an explanation. This is often implicitly or explicitly functionalist: a variable is held to be explained if it functions in the working of a whole. But this singularly fails to explain anything about the particularity of any variable. Again: *why* this subsistence strategy, this form of burial rather than another? Function is not an explanatory concept when applied to the social; it remains descriptive. Function also tends to be separated out from style which then becomes a problem: why this pot design rather than another? (See chapter 4.)

11   The other problems of functionalism are also present; concepts such as homoeostatis or adaptation mean that change becomes a problem originating necessarily in dysfunction or alteration of parameters external to the system, in the society–environment relation. This separates statics and dynamics: specification of the workings of a system is separated from processes of change.

12   Processual social archaeologies have treated the theorization of social totality as an issue of definition or specification. The problem of social units and their boundaries and interaction has been recognized with the development of concepts of world system and peer polity interaction. However, there has been little theorization of the structuring of the totality: what structures the whole; what is the meaning of the particular relations between the constituent variables and the wider question of the meaning of categories such as band, chiefdom; and theorization of societal boundaries.

13   Social change tends to be conceived purely descriptively as the empirical rearrangement of the variables of patterned behaviours. In that these variables are reified and defined prior to analysis, neo-evolutionary cross-cultural frameworks of cultural change are facilitated. These are extensively criticized in chapter 6. We simply comment here that the particularity of the historical event and context becomes a problem, occluded in the description of social process.

Hodder has stressed the necessity of considering social structure – the context of meanings of any social act; the generative rules which form structured sets. A question such as why one subsistence strategy existed in a particular social totality rather than another, equally 'adaptive', can only be answered by considering the meaningful context of the subsistence strategy, the rules which generate any particular social action – this is the question of structure (cf. the notion of structure adopted in processual archaeology in the analysis of mortuary practices discussed above). It is necessary to consider the meaning context and structure of, for example, a particular system of ranking or a particular subsistence strategy, not least because 'behind the social system is a structure of meaning which determines the relationship between material culture and society' (Hodder, 1982b, p. 153). As archaeologists we are concerned with how social system extends into material culture; this requires a theorization of material culture which must take structure into account. We take up the concept of structure in more detail in chapter 3 and consider it in relation to material culture in chapter 4.

SOCIAL ARCHAEOLOGY AND A LOGIC OF NECESSITY

In extending our critique of social archaeology we now take up some ideas developed by Laclau and Mouffe (1985) and consider two assumptions which lie behind most social archaeology:

1 That the social constitutes an intelligible totality, conceptually explicable and definable (in whatever senses).
2 That the history of society has a rational substratum (this is, of course, the rationale for evolutionary archaeology of whatever sort).

We argue that both of these assumptions involve a *logic of necessity*. Key elements of 'society' or the social totality are defined in the abstract and related by some form of social logic: descriptive, cybernetic, economistic, functionalist etc. These elements become the metasubject of History. The concrete, the particular is subsumed beneath the abstract categories; the mass of data is brought to order, classified, reduced to its essentials.

There are two basic arguments in this process:

1 An argument from appearance: surface appearances, differences can be *reduced* to identity.

2   An argument from contingency: if surface data or differences cannot be easily incorporated into a category, they do not matter, or at the very least are irrelevant, contingent to the social model being used.

A logic of necessity defines the necessary categories, the necessary character and relations of elements of the social. It specifies which things are necessary for society to be society. A logic of necessity involves a research strategy of *recognition* – recognizing pattern in the data which relates to elements or categories or concepts defined and related in the assumed social model. Pattern becomes an emanation of the pre-defined and eternal *essential*: what necessarily constitutes the social totality. History and the social totality are conceived as having essences, essential features, which operate as their principle of unity. They have something in common: the essential, the necessary. History itself is ordered according to processes of selection (of that which supposedly pertains to its essential meaning), incorporation into general abstract and necessary categories, and exclusion of that which is deemed irrelevant. History is brought to order. Everything is to be accounted for, whether in terms of incorporation or exclusion, conceived as representing the necessary or the contingent. So the *telos* of a logic of necessity is totality: everything in its place. Selection, incorporation and exclusion thus become a legal system behind the order; they represent reason's pretension to legislate and control history, bringing order to an anarchy of dispersed particularity and difference.

Consider Bradley's book, *The Social Foundations of Prehistoric Britain* (1984). This is a thematic synopsis. It brings the mass of data to order through the literal application of models drawn from anthropology and anthropologically informed archaeology. Each chapter takes a theme as a means of explaining a particular stretch of chronology. Hence in chapter 2, entitled 'Constructions of the dead', scenarios are sketched for the period 3500–2500 BC involving the possible relation of farming communities to economic resources and ancestors and focusing on the construction of communal tombs. Test implications are drawn (how to recognize each scenario or model); then the patterning in the data is assessed against the model. It is, again, a search for empirical patterning directly representing social process. But there is a remainder to Bradley's effort: variety. He comments: 'within the general framework suggested here [chapter 7: a general synthesis], there are numerous variants . . . I doubt whether this book has come to terms with the sheer complexity of the evidence' (p. 166). The range of explanatory models appearing in the book are very limited: prestige goods economies (some with core/periphery distinction); ritual in agricultural society; conspicuous consumption. Bradley ends up with three cycles of prestige goods economies explaining 4,500 years of prehistory in Britain.

But what happens to all the detail? It is all subsumed? Does it simply support the models? Will there always be this remainder? This contingency? The irrelevancy of so much detail? One answer offered to this problem is that of pluralism. It is accepted that different archaeological approaches emphasize or select different aspects of the data base. So subsistence studies supplement social evolutionary work supplemented by palaeoenvironmental studies (e.g. Rowley-Conwy, 1986, p. 28). Such pluralism is considered healthy, fostering debate, adding to the richness of archaeology as a discipline (Renfrew, 1982, 1983) and covering a wide variety of aspects of the archaeological past.

However, the different approaches may well imply different totalities conceived as explanatory context for archaeological data: for example, the ecosystem for palaeoeconomy as opposed to social formation for Marxist archaeologists. How are these different totalities to be reconciled? One answer has been the search for a metasystem, a totality, theoretical or substantive, which can incorporate all approaches. Clarke's project of an analytical archaeology (1968; cf. 1973) can be viewed as such a totalizing systematics. More recently, Kristiansen (1984, p. 74) has claimed that Marxism (or, at least, his version of it) provides an integrative framework which supposedly incorporates all archaeological aspirations (for him a systemic and evolutionary outlook). On the other hand, we have already argued that any approach may be deemed to be acceptable so long as it conforms to the canons of what is presupposed to be rational method (see chapter 1). Hence different approaches are simply irreconcilable; their sole unity is simply that they have been used by those individuals who label themselves archaeologists.

None of these answers challenge a logic of necessity. The result is as we described in chapter 1: archaeology labouring under an extraordinary redundancy of detail, so much apparently irrelevant particularity, theoretically fragmented, a labyrinth of borrowed approaches and levels of theory.

We have described a logic of necessity as involving a set of categorical oppositions:

Totality	Fragment
Necessity	Contingency
Essence	Appearance
General	Particular
Abstract	Concrete
Identity	Difference
Incorporation	Dispersal
Legality	Anarchy

The left hand column is given priority over the right. Ultimately this relates to the general conception of the archaeological record (mentioned at the beginning of this chapter) which involves an occlusion of the individual; social actors are conceived as essentially lost in comparison to the social unit or whole of which they were a part. The social whole is thus split, theoretically and substantively, from the individual. As in chapter 1, we shall use the strategy of mediation as a way forward. First, we shall outline a logic of contingency, and then in the next chapter present a theory of the individual and social practice.

A LOGIC OF CONTINGENCY

We argue that 'Society', in the sense of the social totality of a logic of necessity, doesn't exist. There can be no general and abstract categories nor systems of logic which coherently represent social totalities or history. Nothing exists in itself, self-identical, a full presence to itself in a relationship of total interiority. Such existence is by definition transcendental; so involving a metaphysical assumption, an appeal to foundational legislative authority, *substantia*, the Cartesian *cogito*, a legal system (such as rational method), a logic of essences. There is no ultimate literality, literal existence, objective substance, 'society', from which artefacts, social relations etc. can be derived; there are no identities fixed for all time. It is therefore not possible to specify society as the object of archaeology (Rowlands had made this point in advocating 'world systems', stressing the problem of the edges of 'society'; cf. also Giddens, 1981, pp. 23, 82–3, on societal space-time edges). Instead, we wish to stress internal relations (relations which have no existence separate from the entities they relate, being part of those entities). On the question of identity – the identity of anything does not consist of a list of attributes (to what would they belong?), but must be referred to a relational order. As we argued in chapter 1, identity presupposes a relation of difference to something else. Identity is differential, depending on systems of difference, relational sequences. Identity is always incomplete, never final because of the potential infinity of relations of difference. There is always a surplus of meaning because the presence or trace of some things in others (their internal relations) prevents total fixation, prevents meaning being pinned precisely down. And that identity is regularity in a relational system presupposes a practice of establishing order. Identities are established in practice. All this means that every identity – social, conceptual or material – is negotiated in practice. This act of negotiation is a political practice.

To adopt such a position is to assert that the social is open. Social *order* is an achievement of practice, it is a domestication of difference, a political project of creating order, fixing identity, cutting down the surplus of meaning. 'Society' is not a datum, an abstract given, but a construction. Hence 'necessity', as we have used the term, doesn't refer to underlying principles or essences (that which is necessary for 'society' to be 'society'), but refers to a practice of fixing contingency. This is also to accept *over-determination* (Althusser's use of the term) of entities – the 'economic' may be overdetermined by the 'religious' because the economic has no essential identity, no automatic necessity, its meaning is established in social practice.

At this point it is instructive to consider another 'remainder' in Bradley's book (1984): the series of epigraphs heading the chapters. What is their purpose? Entertainment? They appear unnecessary, contingent; some seem to be held to convey eternal truths about the human lot, but none are discussed or taken up in detail. The epigraphs punctuate the text, punctuate history. As literary devices, they are a presence of textuality. They draw attention to the book as text; but textuality, discourse, is an absent theoretical presence in Bradley's synopsis. Bradley's discourse is one of plenitude – compilation, the filling out of a theme, a position. The text fills a gap. Its presence presents the past; it conveys the past more or less transparently; language is conceived as a neutral vehicle to present the past. That discourse itself is an event is eclipsed (existing only in the gaps, at the margins – in Bradley's epigraphs). But, as we have stressed, we write archaeology now. Discourse is not identical with the past; concepts are not identical with the past. It is essential to realize this. There is no necessity about doing archaeology or writing archaeological texts; archaeological discourse is a contemporary event, not abstract plenitude. Knowledge is not a recognition of the eternal (as implied in a logic of necessity) but is fundamentally part of contemporary social practice, rooted therefore in political relations of power.

We can now draw some points together:

1   We argue against social archaeologies which are reductionist or essentialist, reducing the particular to an abstract social logic, to a priori categories, defining and searching for essential features of society and history.

2   This means there can be no hierarchy of determination: for example, that the economic, or more general relations between population and environment, determine the general form and trajectory of society as opposed to other institutional forms such as the 'political' or the 'religious'.

3   Concomitantly, there are no universal series of social units, such as band, tribe, lineage, mode of production, available for use in archaeological analysis. Such over-generalised concepts need to be abandoned.

4   We wish to stress not a better definition of 'society' as a layer cake or flow diagram, but rather the construction and constitution of social order in social practice. The social is an overdetermined relational whole, an open field of relations, an indeterminate articulation. Social order is constituted in the practice of individual social actors which relates to historical context, not an abstract universal pattern. This is to stress the primacy of the political: practical negotiation, strategy and power in the structuring of social reality.

5   A corollary of the fourth point is the need to stress the practical constitution of the past in the discipline of archaeology. Archaeology is a discursive event; its practice is a mediation of archaeological subject and object, present and past. Neither can be reduced to the other. The archaeological object cannot be precisely and conceptually captured. Past and present can only be held together in their difference, in their non-identity in the event of interpretation. Rather than a totalizing systematics of precise self-contained concepts, this requires a different and critical set of concepts themselves rooted in the event of interpretation. For example, 'totality' is not to be regarded as an affirmative, but as a critical category – the idea of critique finds its roots in the Greek *krinein*: to separate, distinguish, judge, condemn, contend, struggle. This is to affirm the importance of polemic; only polemically, we might also say politically and rhetorically, does reason present itself as a total reality. Hence a total system is a political project of fixing

everything in place, a legal system of control. In this sense we need to convict totality of non-identity with itself, to deny a totalizing systematics, the final solution to all archaeological ills. But at the same time material culture can only be understood through teasing out its relations with other entities, setting it within a relational whole, tracing its dispersal, its meaning within social practice.

6   We need also to appreciate the *materiality* of the archaeological object. The artefact is a material fragment, a riddle neither directly revealing nor concealing 'the past', 'society' or whatever category. Artefacts do not represent the past, they are not a property of the past. Artefacts signify. Signification requires reading, interpretation, not an application of 'method' which produces its object in advance. Consequently, there are no progressive stages through which analysis must pass, for example moving from the more general to the particular, or incorporating data in wider and wider scales of categories. We conceive interpretation as an act renouncing finality, as a denial of universal history, the idea of coherent unity and completed development. Interpretation is associated with a strategic knowledge (Shanks and Tilley, 1987, ch. 5), not abstracted from its social conditions of production, but polemically responding to specific conditions, attending to historical and political circumstances, a knowledge rooted in contemporary structures of power.

In the chapter that follows we present a set of concepts which we intend as a contribution to this programme of a critical social archaeology, beginning with the concept of the individual or the subject.

3

The Individual and the Social

ARCHAEOLOGY AND THE INDIVIDUAL

If, as Wheeler claimed (1954, p. 13), archaeologists are digging up people, how is this the case? Where is the individual in the archaeological past? Are archaeological data collective, going beyond the individual personality? If so, in what sense? Individuals have appeared in the archaeological literature as powerful but anonymous agencies, for example a 'paramount chief' might be inferred from the construction of Stonehenge, Silbury Hill or the Bush Barrow in the second millenium BC of Wessex. The work of an individual artisan may, perhaps, be recognized from examples of their work (Hill and Gunn (eds), 1977), but here individuality is reduced to idiosyncracy and creativity. Literary sources may, of course, rescue an individual from anonymity. However, archaeology has been predominantly concerned with units larger than the individual. We now want to assess this absence of the individual in considering the mediation of the individual and society.

Other cultures and other subjects

In the conclusion to his Huxley Memorial lecture of 1938 Mauss wrote:

> From a mere masquerade to a mask, from a role to a person, to a name, to an individual, from the last to a being with a metaphysical and ethical value, from a moral consciousness to a sacred being, from the latter to a fundamental form of thought and action . . . who knows even if this 'category', which all of us believe to be well founded, will always be recognised as such.
>
> (Mauss, 1979, p. 90)

The 'category' that Mauss was referring to is the concept of the human subject, here conceived as a muted and variable entity radically open to different forms of constitution, both temporally and in different societies. Such a notion conflicts with our common-sense, twentieth-century Western ideas about what it means to be a human subject and the manner in which people live, think and relate to others.

There has probably never been a society which did not recognize the individual subject by such means as naming or being able to differentiate between and perceive physical bodies, but we should not conclude from this too readily that a transhistorical or transcultural form of subjectivity has ever existed, or exists now. Persons are not in any sense to be regarded as given and unproblematic entities. Conceptions of the subject differ between cultures and have altered historically in tandem with the practices, institutions and forms of reference constituting subjectivity; the obvious concomitants of this are differences in bodily gesture, practices of discourse, and patterns of conduct and interaction. Mauss (ibid.) usefully challenges any notion of a person as being reducible to a set of natural (biological) processes or as arising as a transcendental spin-off of a unitary 'human experience' of the world or society; or equally, as being a datum related to some supposed universal consciousness of individuality. Particular ways of specifying the individual or individuality may arise in all societies, but this does not necessarily entail a specification of subjects as being in any sense unique entities imbued with a distinctive consciousness, will or intentionality. Although naming of individuals is a commonplace in societies, i.e. the specification of a subject within systems of persons, this naming does not necessarily imply the constitution of persons as distinctive individual beings. In other words names and statuses while specifying persons do not necessarily individuate an autonomous ego as a separate agent with a personalized consciousness and independently constituted mode of individuality. In regard to Zuni: 'on the one hand the clan is conceived as constituted by a *certain number of persons*, activities, roles; and, on the other, the purpose of all these roles is really to symbolize, each in its own portion, the pre-figured totality of the clan' (Mauss, 1979, 65). In ancient China the individuality of a person was his or her *ming* and this removed from individuals all the connotations of perceptible, individual being:

> the name, the *ming*, is a collective noun, it is something that has come from elsewhere: the corresponding ancestor had borne it and it

will be inherited by a descendant of the bearer. And when the matter
was considered philosophically, when in certain metaphysical
systems the attempt was made to express the matter, it was said that
the individual is a compound of *shen* and *kwei* (two more collective
nouns).

(Ibid., p. 76–7)

This suggests that actual concepts of personage may vary
markedly from one group to the next and that the modern Western
conception of a person as a bounded, unified and integrated being,
a subject of distinctive cognition and dynamic centre of awareness,
emotion, action and judgement is a rather peculiar idea. The ethnocentric bias of such a notion is very clearly brought out in Geertz's
analysis of individuality in Javanese, Balinese and Moroccan
societies. The Javanese concept of a person is arranged in terms of
two sets of essentially religious symbolic contrasts: inside/outside;
refined/vulgar – both of which subsume individuals. The former
contrast differentiates between relations of human experience and
spirituality and is contrasted with the observed realm of bodily
behaviour, but both are considered to be an identical component of
all individuals; the latter distinguishes between different sets of
conduct. Individual persons become the momentary locus through
which the two sets of oppositions prevail and confront each other
– a passing expression of the permanency of these oppositions in
human existence (Geertz, 1979, pp. 230–1). In Balinese society all
aspects of personalized individuation are completely stylized, so
that individuals become, in effect, dramatis personae in a symbolic
play of affective emotions and actions. Physical subjects become,
according to Geertz, 'incidents in a happenstance history' (p. 232).
In Morocco personal being has a chameleon-like quality, differing
according to the context for action, and individuals become
effectively kaleidoscopes in the mosaic of social organization.

Construction of the self: the imaginary and the symbolic.

Lacan, in his rereading of Freud, has explored the problematic
relation between the subject and the social. This relation, he
proposes, can be conceptualized in terms of two modes or realms in
which the subject apprehends reality: the symbolic and the
imaginary. As these are interdependent, the subject is always
located at the intersection of the criss-crossing axes of the real, the
symbolic and the imaginary. The symbolic order is that which
confers meaning and relates the subject to a place in the social
order of other subjects. The imaginary is the order in which the

subject develops a self-centred consciousness. The real is always an absent presence – that to which the symbolic and imaginary relate. Such a conception leads to the decentering of individual consciousness which is no longer regarded as the origin of meaning, knowledge and action.

Lacan proposes that the child, at birth, is a *hommelette*, a little person and also 'like a broken egg spreading in all directions' (Coward and Ellis, 1977, p. 101). The child, at this stage, has no sense of its own identity and no possibility of conceiving of itself as a unity distanced from that which is other or exterior to it. In the 'mirror phase' (Lacan, 1977, pp. 1–7), the child learns to recognize itself through the mirror as a being distinct from the outside world, yet this identity is also imaginary because it is an imaged or a specular knowledge. The child's imaginary identity with its image in the mirror (the 'other') is the manner in which the infant forms an image of itself as a distinctive objective entity. The imaginary relation of the ego to the body characterized by the mirror phase is constituted via a specular counterpart and so the relationship between subject and ego is essentially narcissistic. The image is more constituent than constituted for the infant. This specular form situates the agency of the ego prior to any social determination in an imaginary or fictional direction – imaginary and fictional because it suggests some degree of permanency to the I, rather than the I as always something being constructed. In the mirror phase the subject is represented as an image or something other, a stand-in reflection of the self and yet, paradoxically, this image constitutes part of the subject's self-knowledge and self-awareness.

It is only with the child's entry into language that it becomes a 'full' subject entering into a determinate field of signification, of which the paramount example is language use. Speech entails the differentiation of *I* from *you* and creates a division between the subject of the *enunciation* and the subject of the *énoncé*, between the I that speaks and the I that is represented in discourse and that ultimately disperses the unity of the subject. The subject is situated in discourse by the 'I' and yet this I is always a substitute for the subject that speaks. The child that speaks always has to identify with the I yet this I is formed in terms of a matrix of symbolically defined relations and subject positions. As the subject is always linguistically and discursively constructed he or she is always a displaced or decentred subject, displaced and constituted across the whole gamut of discursive symbolic and material practices making up the social field. Hence there can be no unmediated discourse, no pure constitution of the self. The self is always created in relation to the other and the subject loses control over meaning and signification in the parallel objectivity of discourse (Lacan, 1977, p. 70). Rather than being a given, the subject is an entity linked to and dependent on various strata of consciousness so that 'a signifier is that which represents a subject not for another subject, but for another signifier' (Lacan, 1973, pp. 180–1). Signifiers do not link individuals to other individuals, or even to the world, but to other signifiers. The subject therefore becomes an effect of the realm of signifiers within any particular socially constructed symbolic field and the subject's 'reality' is situated within this order. The subject should be considered as a *subject in process*, in a constant state of definement, individuation and construction: a network rather than a point in the social field. The reality of the subject, produced by discourse, is a transindividual reality. This entails that the experience of the subject has to be located at the level of the symbolic. The capacity to symbolize allows people to situate themselves in reality and yet subjects are never in a position to establish any control over the symbolic because people do not produce their own meaning: structures of signification are always given to them. Signification is a function of language and material practices which are both part of the being of the subject and yet at the same time distanced. Language is always received ready-made for subjects to use. At the same time it is through language use that the individual gains an identity and a capacity to transform the conditions of his or her existence. The subject cannot find his or her truth in a cogito because identity is dispersed in a field of signifiers in which the individual locates himself or herself and yet is dependent on a dimension which is always something more. The realm of the imaginary constructs and organizes a world centred on the subject while the subject's existential reality is radically decentred. The thought of humanity

> always faces the exhausting task of going back from the thought to the thinker; everything it says about man, is said by man, and this man is man only through that which isn't he, through the life of him and the culture around him . . . he is always other, the other of others, and the other of his self: subject when he is object, object when he is subject.
>
> (Dufrenne, 1967, p. 73, cited in Racevskis, 1983, p. 144)

History and the subject

It is, perhaps, most fully in the dialogue promoted by psychoanalysis that the paradoxical nature of the Western myth of the autonomous ego is most clearly revealed:

Does the subject not become engaged in an ever-growing dispossession of that being of his, concerning which – by dint of sincere portraits which leave its idea no less incoherent, of rectifications that do not succeed in freeing its essence, of stays and defences that do not prevent his statue from tottering, of narcissistic embraces that become like a puff of air in animating it – he ends up by recognizing that this being has never been anything more than his construct in the imaginary and that this construct disappoints all his certainties? For in this labour which he undertakes to reconstruct *for another*, he rediscovers the fundamental alienation that made him construct it like another, and which has always destined it to be taken from him *by another*.

(Lacan, 1977, p. 42)

Lacan notes that the 'ce suis-je' of the time of Villon (mid-fifteenth century) has become completely reversed in the 'c'est moi' of the contemporary subject (ibid., p. 70). The subject and subjectivity in mathematics, politics, religion or advertising animates contemporary society and yet the symbolic character of these cultural interventions has at the same time never been more manifest. Yet this symbolic culture appears to us as having the character of an objective plenitude, the 'objectivity' of the mathematical symbol, the 'objectivity' of law and political discourse, of religious statements and the advertising image.

Foucault, in stating that 'man is an invention of recent date' and that were the structure of contemporary discourse transcended he would be 'erased like a face drawn in sand at the edge of the sea' (Foucault, 1974, p. 387), is making more than a rhetorical point. Foucault's archaeologies of Western culture, of knowledge, the clinic, incarceration and sexuality, have all signalled poignantly the radically different conception of the subject in Western capitalism as compared to that existing in pre-capitalist social formations. His focus on the decades around 1800 in *The Order of Things* is especially significant in so far as this was the period in which the 'sciences of man' – those sciences which privileged humanity as a centre and *telos* of their domain – were originally constructed, soon to take on their recognizable modern positivity. This was the appearance of Western humanity as a subject *in* and *of* discourse. Sometime at the end of the eighteenth century humanity appeared. Previously discourse had provided a fairly transparent medium of representation with linguistic forms and relations corresponding to specific elements in the world in which God had arranged a great chain of being and drawn language into correspondence with it. Humans were merely one kind of creation among many, each with its allotted space, the essences, natures and definitions of which could be read off from a table of beings. There was no need for a finite being, MAN, to make representation possible or posit the existence of the nature of being in the world: 'In Classical thought, the personage for whom the representation exists, and who represents himself therein as an image or reflection, he who ties together all the interlacing threads of the "representation in the form of a picture or table" – he is never to be found in that table himself' (ibid., p. 308). Instead of humanity as a being amongst other beings, he or she becomes a subject amongst objects and both the subject and object of self-understanding, knowledge and the organizer of a spectacle for self-appearance: 'the threshold of our modernity is situated not by the attempt to apply objective methods to the study of man, but rather by the constitution of an empirico-transcendental doublet which was called man' (ibid., p. 319).

Under this doublet 'man' appears as (1) a fact among other facts to be studied empirically yet at the same time providing a transcendental grounding for this knowledge; (2) surrounded by that which cannot be comprehended (the unknown) and yet as a potentially lucid cogito and source of all intelligibility (the cogito of Descartes); (3) a product of history, the origins of which could not be reached, and also the source or foundation for that history.

Formation and constitution of the subject

The subject of Western society is a subject very much bound up with and arising from the field of capitalist social relations and lending support to the principles underlying capitalist production (entrepreneurial freedom, competition etc.) Forms of property, law and contract, notions of individual mortality and the proprietal subject enjoying certain 'rights' all arise from the reality of individual private possession linked with commodity exchange (Hirst, 1980). The proprietal subject who owns and acquires commodities also has certain possessive rights. Notions of greed, selfishness, laziness etc. only make sense in terms of, are ideational prerequisites for, and concomitants of capitalism which produces and reinforces subjects of a specific type – subjects who must be held accountable for their doings in the capitalist market place and who are supposedly free to radically alter the conditions of their own social existence.

This is not to claim that the mode of production simply determines the nature of subjectivity but that subjectivity is inextricably bound up with it. As we have argued, any social totality must be viewed as an ensemble of partially integrated symbolic systems including language, economic relations, cultural production, religion, politics, which are mutually determining without there being any primacy of determination at any one level. Different forms of social life coexist in the form of an overall and overdetermined set of correspondences made possible by the symbolic nature of human thought and interaction. It is in terms of this network of correspondences, which do not exclude the possibility of gaps or fissures, that the subject finds explanation and justification for a particular mode of being and action. The subject becomes a transindividual relation made possible by the symbolic order both permitting the existence of subjects and the symbolic experience of those subjects. So-called 'humanist' attempts to explain society and history by taking as their starting point a human essence, the free subject of needs, work, moral and political action, find their reflection in the 'free' subject that is also the subject of the Law, playing a key role in the reproduction of capitalist social relations. As Barthes notes, the judicial notion of a consistent and unitary subject derives its power only in the form of being a particular representation:

> this pyschology has . . . the pretext of giving as a basis for action a pre-existing inner person, it postulates 'the soul': it judges men as a 'conscience' . . . in the name of which you can very well today have your head cut off [and] comes straight from our traditional literature, that which one calls in bourgeois style literature of the Human Document.
>
> (Barthes, 1973, p. 45)

Social relations cannot be reduced to the fiction of a domain of interacting and free agents.

The very idea of a subject that can both speak and be spoken about entails a paradox inherent in the use of the term in ordinary language. The subject of discourse can be that which denotes as well as that which is denoted. The subject understood as an embodiment of thought is a subject that creates or sustains sense. The subject can also be something that is brought under domination or repressive control: that which has the *capacity to subject*. So, the subject can be a support or medium for discourse and at the same time be controlled or dominated by discourse or material practices: an active agent and an agent acted upon. This brings us to subjectivity, subjugation, agency and power.

Subjectivity and power

The appearance of humanity in a field of discourse, as documented by Foucault, can be regarded as issuing in a new mode of social existence in which people become subjectified and reified as objects of knowledge – 'bodies' in a field of forces constituted by power-knowledge strategies instituting an integration of the subject in terms of the overall social field.

New methods of classification, hierarchization, codification, surveillance and a disciplinary technology focusing upon the body developed in the nineteenth century, producing fresh types of coercion and subjectification. The prison (Foucault, 1977) remains one example, among many, of the technology of discipline, surveillance and punishment – one of the most visible and clearly articulated sites of practices widespread in society. In Foucault's terms Western societies are disciplinary societies. In the present context this is important because discipline creates a new type of subject, a fresh form of subjectivity, and a novel manner of subjugation.

1   Discipline operates on the body. The subject is approached as an object to be analysed and separated into finely controlled constituent parts: arms, legs, head etc. The aim of these operations is to produce a docile and easily manipulated body. For example different parts of the body may be minutely trained, as in army drill, with a standardization of operations being the ideal.

2   Discipline results in the control of time and space. Discipline requires precise control of time and the regular repetition of practices in time, for example the school timetable. Space and the organization of individuals in space is produced in specific ways; hospitals, prisons, schools, factories and military establishments all establish and operate in terms of ordered grid patterns allowing individuals to be divided, organized and supervised. The act of looking over and being looked at is a central means by which individuals become controlled in disciplinary space and time.

3   Discipline results in a proliferation of discourses enmeshing the subject and individualizing him or her. By means of the compilation of detailed records and dossiers on individuals every subject becomes a subject that can be known, subjected to a normalizing judgement and discourses of power. Deviancy from the standards of the disciplinary apparatus can be measured, defined and controlled.

Discipline in contemporary Western societies is a manifestation of power. The development of Western discursive practices, especially in institutional and official bureaucratic forms, has favoured the development of discourses and practices that actualize domination and repression throughout the social field: the family, the school, the museum, the hospital, the factory. Thus a new potential for violence and subjugation is actualized in the very systematism of power strategies. What constitutes the subject and forms of subjugation is the operation of power, both as a positive and as a negative force in society, by producing knowledges and actualizing them in specific forms. We might then say no power without subjects and subjugation and no subjects or subjugation without power.

What we are stressing is the centrality of power in social life. Power is a force and process to be found in all social totalities and, historically, different modalities of the operation of power produce different subjects, forms of subjectivity and types of subjugation. One concomitant of this is that the subject in capitalist social formations will have a fundamentally different type of subjectivity and be subject to different forms of subjugation than in other societies. Specific forms of practices which produce subjects in contemporary western society might be delineated:

1 Modes of inquiry which produce 'truths' giving themselves the status of sciences and objectivizing the subject in various ways: for example the positivist social sciences.
2 The development of practices in which the subject becomes divided from within or without so objectivizing him or her: for example divisions between the criminal and the upright citizen, the sane and the insane, the healthy and the sick, the sober and the alcoholic or drug user.
3 Discourses in which people turn themselves into subjects: for example as subjects of sexuality or capital accumulation and commodity exchange.
4 Creation of subjects in terms of ethnic or social or religious divisions.
5 Creation of subjects in terms of those who possess knowledge and those who do not.
6 Creation of subjects as effects of the division of labour and economic exploitation separating individuals from what they produce.
7 Forms of property, law and contract create subjects with specific 'rights' and 'claims'.

8 Creation of subjects in language, communication through material or linguistic forms, i.e. the realm of the symbolic.
9 Ideological practices create subjects, practices which are interbedded and intertwined in points 1–8 above.

An examination of the category 'person ', 'subject' or 'agent' reveals it to be by no means universal, nor a homogeneous unity. Following Lacan we might also argue that individual consciousness is not the simple origin of meaning, knowledge and action. Instead the human subject is situated in a social and symbolic field. The conception of an autonomous ego, is, after Foucault and Lacan, historically specific; a feature of the emergence of the human sciences, the agent must be situated within historical practice. This draws attention again to archaeology as discourse, a practice constituting objects of knowledge. Foucault's work also shows the centrality of power in the constitution of subjectivity, and in social practices more generally. Social practice involves subjectivity and subjugation, *power to* and *power over*, agency and control. So power is both creative and oppressive and social actors are knowledgeable, not passive.

In the last chapter we questioned the category of the social, interrogating its coherence and definition and pointing to its location within archaeological practice. We argued instead for an open conception of social order stressing its constitution in social practices, which immediately involve relations of negotiation, strategy and power. In this chapter we have extended this position in arguing that the individual social subject is dispersed and decentred, situated in a nexus of power, historical and political practice and the symbolic. We now focus on the mediation of the social and the individual in considering social practice and structure.

SOCIAL PRACTICE AND STRUCTURE

In social practice the individual agent is always already positioned in relation to structure: relational sets of meanings, concepts, signs which provide principles for conduct in a meaningful life-world. Any social acts draws upon these already existing structured sign systems or conceptual schemes for the ordering of experience; but every manifestation of structure in an action is a concretization of structure through its effects on social practice and on the object world. This realization of structure contains the possibility of the reordering or transformation of structures because meanings and principles for conduct are re-evaluated in practice, in the negotiation between and manipulation of social agents, in the historical and conjunctural circumstances of practice, and through the contingent effects of unintended consequences of practice.

Action, in other words, is in dialectical relation to structure and social context. It begins in structure, is mediated by structure, and ends in structure, but its realization in the world may result in the rearticulation or transformation of structure. This is the concept of structuration: structure is both a medium and an outcome of social practice (Giddens, 1979, 1984). So individuals pursue projects which make sense in terms of structure. Negotiation and strategy are central to this social practice which is a chronic relation of forces between social agents with differing aims and interests. This is what we mean in emphasizing social practice as fundamentally political, in emphasizing the centrality of relations of power.

POWER

Power, in archaeology, has been conceived primarily in terms of ranking and control. As a possession, some sections of society have more power than others; they have more status. In this way power is conceived to flow from the top to the bottom of society. Ranking comes to refer to the unequal distribution of power. Power seemingly requires theorization in terms of some sort of essence which may be possessed. The concept is reified. Archaeologists have concentrated very much on the role played by power and ranking in the reproduction of society, on describing patterns of hierarchy and control of resources (see chapter 2).

We take a different line. Any analysis of power concerns us with the social roots of power, attempts to achieve and maintain power, and counter attempts to subvert power strategies and sap the social bases of power on the part of those subjected to its exercise. Power should not be understood in terms of an all-important essence in society residing at a specific place, something which may be possessed, 'taken up' and exercised. Instead, power is a feature of society which is irreducible to individuals or groups or specific areas of the social field such as the economic or the political. In other words, power has no necessary and unitary form of existence. Rather than being conceived as *a* feature of the social we regard it as being coextensive with the social field as a whole. Relations of power are thus interwoven and networked with respect to the specific conditions of existence and effects of social practices. Power resides throughout the entire gamut of social practices and in the structural ordering of society. Power is that aspect of human practices which *brings about effects*, or permits the achievement or attempted achievement of outcomes. These may or may not be transformative in intent. Power may usually be connected with the sectional interests of individuals or groups involving exploitation, domination and subjection, and resistance to these practices, but this is its usual effect rather than part of its definition. Power is also a positive and not just a repressive feature of the social.

Power resides in all social intercourse because in any social encounter actors inevitably employ, to a greater or lesser extent, different sets of resources, material or non-material. Power relates to and works in terms of these material (technologies, raw materials, control over coercive and non-coercive media) and non-material resources (knowledge, information, position within the overall field of social relations, competences and skills), which individuals, groups and collectivities draw upon routinely in their day-to-day conduct. Power is dialectically related to these resources. It both draws upon and reproduces them. This is why power is not something exercised by individuals, something which can be possessed, but the effects of its operation usually result in a structured asymmetry of resources benefiting certain individuals or groups as opposed to others. Power is, therefore, to be linked with interests, but not as a reflection of interests but rather a feature which works through interests in a variety of forms and without a predetermined outcome. Consequently power, and struggles operating in terms of power, form a fundamental feature of societal reproduction and transformation (see chapter 6).

THE SYMBOLIC

We have already discussed how the subject is situated in a symbolic field: the symbolic, signs and signification, is an essential dimension of social practice. It, too, mediates practice.

Actions are not just constrained and limited by external conditions such as the friction of physical space but also by the conceptual categories by means of which the social is constituted. Cognition, however, does not simply posit limits but also creates a field of possibilities for action. The social world as cognized by social actors has both referential value and existential meaning. Any conception of history as meaningful must recognize that signs are always already situated in structures but whose meaning may be reconstituted in action. Signs relate to other signs in structure as a collective symbolic scheme providing meaning for action. In structure signs have an abstract sense, signifying within a collective scheme of signification in terms of their relations with other signs (see chapter 4, pp. 136–43). Although signs relate to other signs in structure in an abstract fashion, their relationship to action entails a different significance. It is one of potential rearticulation and the constitution of fresh meanings. In action signs become positioned in a contingent relationship with regard to individual purposive activity and collective social strategies. In the contextual matrices of situated social activities signs become set in a contingent relationship to objects. They may take on a particular rather than a purely abstract referentiality and become subject to combination and recombination with objects and other signs from which fresh form and meaning may arise. In other words, signs, codes, symbols and categories may always take on new meanings because their meanings have their realization in relation to specific political projects and strategies.

So in social practice signs are brought into a referential relationship to the objects of actions. Action grafts particular contextual meanings to the conceptual values of signs. Secondly, they become subject to contingent relationships affecting their semantic values because signs are not just experienced by actors as something standing outside themselves but are always dialectically related to their political *interests*. As Sahlins point out:

> the sign represents a differential interest to various subjects according to its place in their specific life schemes. 'Interest' and 'sense' (or 'meaning') are two sides of the same thing, the sign, as related respectively to persons and to other signs . . . Reference is a dialectic between the conceptual polysemy of the sign and its indexical connection to a specific context. Notoriously, signs have multiple meanings as conceptual values, but in human practice they find determinative representations, amounting to some selection or inflection of the conceptual sense. And because the 'objective' world to which they are applied has its own refractory characteristics and dynamics, the signs, and by derivation the people who live by them, may then be categorically revalued.
>
> (1981, pp. 69–70)

Put more simply, what this suggests is that signs or conceptual categories are always dialectically related to situated social action and the interests and values of actors. Meaning is precarious; its reproduction may result in its reconstitution, because action results in the re-evaluation of the meaning of the sign in practice, in a fundamentally political and historical context of power, interest and strategy.

IDEOLOGY AND SUBJECTIVITY

As a concomitant of the considerations advanced above, we argue that no social practices exist without signification and without being situated within an overall symbolic field. Signifying practices have specific determinations and effects in the field of social relations, creating, reproducing or transforming this field. They are a necessary element in any form of social practice.

Ideology is a form of signifying practice which acts to constitute subjects in a specific way in specific circumstances in order to reproduce rather than transform the social totality. Consequently, ideology can only have an existence and an effectivity through subjects. As a form of power it subjugates subjects. Following Althusser (1971) we can regard ideology as an imaginary relationship between people and their conditions of existence. It is not an illusion or a 'false consciousness' of that reality. Rather than regard ideology as a set of illusions we can think of it as forming a set of representations (discourses, images, myths, practices) concerning the real relations in which people live. This notion of ideology as representation in and for subjects emphasizes its familiarity and naturalizing qualities. Ideological practices are always likely to be practices that are recurrent, practices presented in a new way, practices that are already 'obvious' from previous discourses and practices. Ideology may be particularly effective in the constitution of forms of subjectivity and in effecting subjugation because it tends to represent not the real, or even a distorted reflection of the real, but that which is supposedly natural, obvious or beyond question. What ideology systematically suppresses is the nature of its own construction in signifying practices. As emphasized by Althusser (1971, p. 155), ideology is both a real and an imaginary relation to the world: real in that it is the way that people *live* their subjectivity within the field of social relations that governs their existence; imaginary in that it systematically prevents full self-reflection of the conditions of existence in which subjects find themselves. Within the ideologies of capitalism it is perfectly 'obvious' that we are all autonomous individuals, possessing a distinctive will and consciousness, an enclosed, personal subjectivity, and 'free' to participate in the capitalist market and to direct the development of our own destinies. As individual speakers it is also 'obvious' that we are both the owners and origins of our utterances.

In considering Lacan's work in psychoanalysis we have already been concerned to demonstrate the construction of the subject in language and the symbolic order. Since the symbolic order must be considered to be, in part, an ideological order all subjects are constructed in and constrained by ideology. The network of subject positions which make action possible are produced in the symbolic realm of human signifying practices and ideology tends to displace the contradictions which exist between different forms of signifying practices. As ideologies are not merely reflected in the psyche but lived they are always inscribed in the materiality of social practices and objectified in material manifestations. Subjects must necessarily live their relations to their conditions of existence and hence they must live through ideological practices. Ideology operates by positioning the individual as a subject in relation to a certain meaning. So, ideology both produces individuals with a subjectivity and also subjugates them within the social totality with its always already existing sets of contradictory principles for action, motivation and meaning. As Coward and Ellis note, 'ideological practice is necessary to societies of whatever kind because the individual is not the centre of the social whole: the social process has no centre, no motivating force' (1977, p. 74). If ideology is necessary to any society in the process of subjectification and subjugation then we must distinguish between two senses of ideology: ideology as a necessary and positive force; and ideology as legitimating systems of repression and social domination. The former creates subjects; the latter, as a dimension of power, subjugates subjects in the interests of certain hegemonic individuals, interest groups or classes (we take this up further in chapter 6).

The concept of ideology has already been taken up in archaeology. Some have used the concept as part of a social reconstruction of the past: ideology refers to that part of society which masks social inequality or contradiction in society and so prevents radical social change (e.g. Shennan, 1982; Kristiansen, 1984). Others have applied the concept to archaeology itself and have shown how archaeological reconstruction, for example in museums, may hide social inequality or contradiction in the present. The concept of ideology is here central to the project of a critical archaeology (see chapter 7) which aims to investigate the production of the past in the present (e.g. Leone, 1981, 1984; Meltzer, 1981).

Hodder has produced an effective critique of such use of the concept (1986, pp. 61–70). He argues that people are not fooled by ideologies; they do not simply succumb to 'false consciousness'. And that if ideology masks 'real' reality, how is *objective* social reality to be defined? How are we to decide between different definitions of social reality (masked by ideology)? Hodder also criticizes the cross-cultural nature of the concept: that it pays insufficient regard to the specific historical context; and it pays little attention to the production of particular ideologies, where they come from.

While we also criticize the identification of ideology with false consciousness (Shanks and Tilley, 1982, p. 130) and the simple functionalist use of the concept as masking contradiction, we hope to show how ideology may be situated within particular social practices (see above and chapter 4) and is involved in social change (chapter 6), while the concept remains central to a critical awareness of archaeology as a disciplinary practice (Shanks and Tilley, 1987; chapter 7 below).

We have presented a case for a fresh notion of subjectivity – a position which goes beyond dogmatic humanism or anti-humanism. Any position which displaces or decentres the subject is regarded by some (e.g. Thompson, 1978) as fundamentally dehumanizing, a Stalinist intervention. What such a position tends to overlook is the constitution of different types of subjects in different societies and the historically peculiar conception of the subject in our own society and its relation to capitalism. The free, autonomous subject going around conferring meaning and significance at will is also an ideological component of capitalist social relations. We should not, of course, seek to abolish the subject or humanity. To the contrary, we should restore that humanity by founding a critical position for conceptualizing a new type of subject: the subject as a *trace* within the social field; as constructed in language, by relations of power and signifying practices; a subject ideologically constituted but also aware of the possibility of being subjugated by that ideology. To regard human subjects as being constructed is to recognize their sociality, their insertion within a symbolic field. Any subject is therefore transindividual, a locus for action rather than a point from which that action arises. The subject is always present, always doing, creating, knowledgeable of many aspects of his or her social existence. But this presence, action and knowledgeability also entails an absence

– the absence of the other – of the domain of the symbolic, a primary area of which is material culture. We must therefore aim to divert attention from the essentially *isolated* subject of the capitalist market-place to focus on a social subject that is created in the otherness of human existence. We are refusing that symbolic violence which ignores who we are, that would make us a mere component of the system, and we refuse the inquisition of those 'scientific' practices which would place us in a field of objectifying determination that goes beyond the social. This brings us to a position where we may tackle material culture, the primary object of archaeology, as a signifying practice.

4

Material Culture

We wish to address two basic questions in this chapter. First, how do we interpret material culture; what meaning, if any, does it possess? Secondly, how does material culture patterning relate to the social? As a way of approaching these questions we wish to briefly examine some of the answers provided by both traditional and 'new' archaeology.

TYPES, CULTURE AND COGNITION

In traditional archaeology the question of the relationship between material culture and society was addressed in a fairly limited fashion and was very closely bound up with considerations of artefact classification and the establishment of typological sequences. The attempt to establish a spatio-temporal systematics for the pigeon-holing of artefacts formed the backbone of research in Anglo-American archaeology until the relatively recent rise of the new archaeology.

Given that artefacts exhibited demonstrable variation across both time and space, one of the primary aims of traditional archaeology was to bring order to this variability by stipulating redundancies in the form of classificatory schemes often explicitly modelled on the basis of biological analogies in which artefacts were to be sorted and 'identified' in a manner equivalent to plants, animals, or mushrooms and toadstools. For example, the 1930 Pecos Conference concerned with the formulation of procedures for classifying American south-western ceramics adopted the following scheme: 'Kingdom: artefacts; Phylum: ceramics; Class: pottery; Order: basic combination of paste and temper; Ware: basic surface colour after firing; Genus: surface treatment; Type or

Subtype . . .' (Hargrave, 1932, p. 8, cited in Hill and Evans, 1972, p. 237). Clark notes that 'the fact that industrial and art forms are subject to evolutionary processes is a great aid when it comes to arranging them in sequence . . . [The problem is] to determine the direction in which the development has proceeded, to determine in other words whether one is dealing with progressive evolution or with a series of degeneration' (Clark, 1972, pp. 134–6, cf. Kreiger, 1944, p. 273). One task of the archaeologist was to determine *types*, usually descriptively labelled according to the locality where first identified (e.g. Flagstaff red pottery; Folsom point; Peterborough Ware), or presumed function, or a mixture of the two (e.g. La Tène fibulae). Artefacts could then, ideally, be assigned to these type groupings on the basis of perceived similarities and differences. Different groups of artefacts, associated together in hoards, burials, settlements, votive deposits etc., could be grouped together in more inclusive entities, 'cultures'. But what did the 'types' and the 'cultures' mean in social terms?

Meaning and artefact types

Traditional archaeology provided three main answers to this question. The first largely evaded the question of social meaning altogether. Types were developed as purely classificatory devices to bring order to the immense range of archaeological materials discovered and to facilitate comparison of specimens and expedite field recording and cataloguing (Kreiger, 1944, p. 275).

The second answer was that the types defined by the archaeologist were expressions of the 'mental templates' of their makers:

> It may be said that, ideally, an archaeological type should represent a unit of cultural practice equivalent to the 'culture trait' of ethnography. Each type should approximate as closely as possible that combination of mechanical and aesthetic executions which formed a definite structural pattern in the minds of a number of workers, who attained this pattern with varying degrees of success and interpretation.
>
> (Kreiger, 1944, pp. 272, 278)

Rouse makes a similar point when he writes: 'Types are stylistic patterns, to which the artisan tries to make his completed artefacts conform' (1939, p. 15). Compare Gifford:

> When entire cultural configurations are taken into account certain regularities are discernible that are due to the interaction of

individuals and small social groups within a society, and these are observed as types. Types in this sense are material manifestations of the regularities of human behaviour . . . The basic attributes involved in any type come together in the combination of a mental image plus the motor habits of the prehistoric artisans of a culture in such a way that when executed in clay, they fulfilled the requirements of the ceramic and stylistic values of that culture.

(1960, pp. 341–2)

And Chang:

The 'right' categories are those that reflect or approximate the natives' own thinking about how their physical world is to be classified, consciously or unconsciously, explicitly or implicitly, within which framework they accordingly act.

(1967, p. 78)

The third answer, very closely related to the second, was that types and cultures primarily had meaning as historical indicators of temporal and spatial relationships between human groups:

We find certain types of remains – pots, implements, burial rites, house forms – constantly recurring together. Such a complex of regularly associated traits we shall term a 'cultural group' or a 'culture'. We assume that such a complex is the material expression of what today would be called a people.

(Childe, 1929, pp. v–vi).

The ideas of artefacts as 'types' reflecting basic ideas, mental images, preferences or culturally prescribed ways to do things, and of regularly occurring patterns of different material items as representing peoples or ethnic groups, formed the interpretative basis for assigning meaning to material culture and the archaeological record. It is represented perhaps most succinctly in the 'type-variety' concept developed in the US, initially for classifying ceramics (figure 4.1).

European and American prehistory was, in essentials, written as the history of cultural continuity and change of types and cultures. A number of assumptions underpinned such an approach. Learning formed the basic means for cultural transmission between generations in any particular cultural group, while diffusion of ideas between discrete non-breeding populations accounted for cultural similarities and differences. This cultural transmission of ideas took place in inverse proportion to the degree of physical or social distance between them. Concomitantly spatial discontinuities

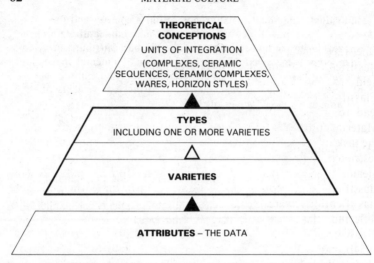

FIGURE 4.1 The Type-variety method of ceramic classification, after Gifford

Source: From J. Gifford (1960).

in culture resulted from either natural boundaries to interaction or social value systems inhibiting the acceptance or adoption of new ideas. Internal cultural change was deemed to be essentially slow and incremental resulting either from an inbuilt dynamic or 'drift' away from previously accepted norms governing artefact production, vagaries of fashion, or technological innovation. Alternatively, obvious discontinuities in the archaeological record were explained as resulting from the development of exchange networks with other groups; migration or invasion of populations; or diffusion of radically new and powerful ideas, for example religious cults. Binford termed such an interpretative framework the 'aquatic view' of culture:

> Culture is viewed as a vast flowing stream with minor variations in ideational norms concerning appropriate ways of making pots, getting married, treating one's mother-in-law, building houses, temples . . . and even dying. These ideational variations are periodically 'crystallized' at different points in time and space, resulting in distinctive and sometimes striking cultural climaxes which allow us to break up the continuum of culture into cultural phases.

(Binford 1972, pp. 197–8)

Artefact classification

One idea underlying the development and refinement of the classificatory schemes was that the act of classification was usually held to be a neutral device and independent of theory. Classification followed data collection and once carried out could lead to inferences being made from the materials thus sorted. Material culture had a meaning or significance inherent in itself and the task of the archaeologist was to extract this meaning which was restricted, i.e. each artefact retained within itself one or a few meanings. Much debate centred on how artefacts might be *best* classified (e.g. Rouse, 1960; Sears, 1960) and whether these classifications were 'real' or 'ideal', i.e. whether they actually reflected the ideas of prehistoric artisans which were then discovered, or were imposed by the archaeologist (Ford, 1954a, 1954b; Spaulding, 1953, 1954). Because many of the typologies obviously worked, at least as limited temporal indicators, they were assumed to be in essentials correct and the 'types' and 'cultures' became canonized in the literature as *the* types and *the* cultures: 'pottery types are not primarily descriptive devices but are refined tools for the elucidation of space-time problems' (Sears, 1960, p. 326).

As we have mentioned above, the meaning of archaeological data was its supposed direct relationship to cognitive structures collectively held by peoples or ethnic groups; but despite this interest traditional archaeology never really developed such concerns because to identify types, cultures and spatio-temporal relationships between them became ends in themselves. This was coupled with a pessimism in which it was claimed that little could be known beyond the realms of technology and the economy (Hawkes, 1954; Piggott, 1959, pp. 9–12).

The cognitive and social reality of artefact taxonomies and cultures have been much disputed during the last 25 years. As regards artefact classification, it has begun to be recognized that classification is not independent of theory (Dunnell, 1971; Hill and Evans, 1972) and that there is no such thing as a 'best' classification. All classifications are partial and select from observed features of the data set. Attempts to create some kind of 'natural' classification, good for all purposes, and dealing with all possible variation within the data set studied is simply unattainable. Any form of classification involves the definition of significant criteria (significant to the classifier) to be used in the process of forming classes. This may involve the arrangement of these criteria in some order of importance which depends on theory or what we know or want to know. The link between classificatory systems and theoretical knowledge of the data universe to be studied is insoluble. Classifications are dependent on and derived from theory; they are not in some sense independent formal schemes which may be considered to be more or less convenient or useful. An infinite number of different classificatory systems may be developed for the same data set and there is no automatic obligation for the archaeologist to model, or attempt to model, his or her taxonomic systems on the basis of those utilized by prehistoric artisans.

Cognition and the past

Archaeological taxonomies and descriptions of the past may tell us a great deal about the manner in which the archaeologist thinks about past socio-cultural systems, but is there any reason to think that they tell us anything about the manner in which prehistoric social actors thought about their culture? Is this irrelevant anyway? One answer is provided by Eggert (1977) who makes four points:

1   A native people's way of thinking about and explaining their world should represent a starting rather than an end point for inquiry and this inquiry has to be undertaken from another (scientific) frame of reference.
2   Material forms not explictly devised for communicative purposes, unlike language, are too ambiguous to reflect in an unequivocal manner the ideas embodied in them.
3   Cognitive systems are abstractions of the anthropologist. They are idealized and tend to subsume or ignore the considerable degree of individual variability in action sequences and thought.
4   People's conceptions of what they do and how they should act may differ markedly from their actual practices.

Eggert concludes that any attempt on the part of the archaeologist to study or infer or attempt to model taxonomic systems in terms of prehistoric cognitive systems is fundamentally misguided.

Some ethnoarchaeological studies, on the other hand, have attempted to demonstrate that cognitive systems are embodied in material culture and cannot be ignored by the archaeologist if he or she wishes to arrive at an adequate understanding of that being investigated (e.g. Arnold, 1971; Friedrich, 1970; Hardin, 1979, 1983; and see the discussion below pp. 148–58). Arnold suggests that

Since artifacts are the result of what people actually do and not what they say they do, it seems more reasonable to attempt to reconstruct non-verbal behaviour from ancient artifacts rather than from anything else. But, if it can be demonstrated from an analysis of verbal behaviour, non-verbal behaviour, and from the material aspects of culture that a cognitive system common to a particular group is really conditioning all of these factors, then, it seems reasonable to suggest that cognitive systems should warrant some attention as a significant factor in the production of artifacts.

(Arnold, 1971, p. 22)

Arnold's study attempts to demonstrate a clear relationship between the cognitive ethnomineralogical system used by potters in Ticul, Yucatan, and verbal, non-verbal and material aspects of processes involved in selecting and using raw materials for making pottery. He finds a correlation between certain emic ethnomineralogical categories of raw materials used to make pottery (clays, temper etc.) and actual (etic) composition as determined by X-ray diffraction studies. However, studies such as those by Arnold and Hardin seem to fall rather short of mapping a cognitive *system* in terms of material culture patterning – a point we wish to elaborate by returning to consider Eggert's strictures.

Even if an archaeologist were able to reproduce an exact replica of a prehistoric taxonomic system how much would this tell us? It appears to be insufficient to regard such an attempt at a reconstruction of the 'templates' of prehistoric artisans as providing an *explanation* of material culture patterning. An archaeologist duplicating a prehistoric taxonomic system would be arriving at a *description* of that system, but such a description of the manner of ordering and thinking about artefacts is itself in need of explanation or further description in relation to social strategies and practices. Material culture should be regarded as not merely a *reflection* of cognitive systems and social practices but actively involved in the formation and structuring of those practices. So, we are never likely to be dealing with a simple correspondence relationship between idea and/or action and material culture form but a situation in which material culture actively mediates ideas and practices. The fact that material culture differs from language in its communicative form and effect does not require that we evaluate the communicative intent of material culture negatively, in terms of its difference from language, and conclude that material culture as a communicative form is too ambiguous to repay study. Cognitive systems are, of course, attributed by the anthropologist or the archaeologist to ethnic groups and material culture patterning.

Such systems are constructs; but this in no way implies that they do not exist or that the actions of individuals might be contradictory or variable. In fact, as we argue in chapter 6, societies are inherently contradictory entities. The idea of society as being constituted in terms of a normative (and cognitive) set of beliefs held and subscribed to by all social actors cannot be sustained. The problem with the studies by Arnold, Hardin and others is that while they do usefully point out the significance of cognitive bases for social action and their manifestation in material culture, in common with the work of traditional archaeologists the assumption is made that all social actors in a society share an undifferentiated and normative set of beliefs. There is little consideration of the negotiation and renegotiation of meaning frames within the context of social strategies which may very well be oppositional and contradictory. An emphasis on contradiction and conflict of interest goes some way to explain why social practices, as often as not, conflict with idealized models of these practices.

STYLE AND FUNCTION

In much of the literature post-dating the mid-1960s the notion of material culture as more or less directly relating to cognition or peoples was challenged or abandoned by many. A realization developed that archaeological cultures could simply not be correlated in any direct or immediate manner with ethnicity and there were in fact multiple factors affecting the nature of distributions of material culture items perceived in the archaeological record (e.g. Hodder (ed.), 1978). The types used to define cultures were as often as not atypical features of the archaeological record in any particular region (e.g. Clarke, 1968, pp. 29–31). What traditional archaeologists took as representing ethnicity might instead refer to functional variability in the types of activities carried out on different sites. This point provided the essence of the debate between Binford (1973) and Bordes (1973) regarding the meaning of assemblage variability in Mousterian sites in south-western France: Bordes arguing that the differences reflected ethnic identity, and Binford claiming they related to functional variability between different activity sets. Clarke (1968) argued that cultures were to be polythetically rather than monothetically defined and that such cultures were distinct analytical entities in themselves with no necessary relationship with ethnicity. Renfrew (1978) questioned the existence of homogeneous assemblages, suggesting that cultures were little more than arbitrary taxonomic categories imposed on a continuum of change.

In short, the interpretative basis of the meaning of material culture provided by traditional archaeology was undermined. Instead, material culture was granted a fresh significance which became grafted in terms of the opposition between two dichotomous terms: style and function. Much of the debate which has taken place during the last 15 years about the relationship between material culture and the social hinges on the definition and use of these terms and whether primacy can (or should) be granted to one or the other in an understanding of the past.

Material culture: system and adaptation

Two major developments in thinking occurred. Firstly, culture became redefined as a system composed of distinct subsystems. It became fashionable to talk about the interaction between sub-systems rather than people, the latter being effectively screened out of the analysis (see chapter 2). Secondly, Binford (1962), following White (1959), redefined culture as an extrasomatic means of adaptation. Consequently the primary meaning of material culture was its role as an interface between people, the environment, and interactions of individuals regarded as components of social systems. Culture was no longer to be regarded as something shared by people but as participated in differentially:

> A basic characteristic of cultural systems is the integration of individuals and social units performing different tasks, frequently at different locations . . . Within any one cultural system, the degree to which the participants share the same ideational basis should vary with the degree of cultural complexity of the system as a whole.
>
> (Binford, 1972, p. 199)

As Binford regarded material culture as an extrasomatic means of adaptation it was entirely consistent that he should regard it in wholly functional terms. It either had a direct utilitarian function or a social function. In an early paper Binford (1962) defined three distinct classes of artefacts: technomic, sociotechnic and ideotechnic, functioning respectively in coping with the environment, social and ideological relations. Residually cross-cutting these three functionally defined artefact classes was style: 'formal qualities that are not directly explicable in terms of the nature of the raw materials, technology of production, or variability in the structure of the technological and social subsystems of the total cultural system' (1972, p. 25). Style functioned in terms of promoting group solidarity, awareness and identity. Later recognizing that it was impossible to sustain any meaningful distinction between functional classes of artefacts operating in different social subsystems, Binford (1965) redefined artefacts as possessing primary (utilitarian) and secondary (stylistic) functions cross-cutting morphological and decorative variation (in the case of ceramics). Primary functional variation referred to utilitarian use (e.g. the difference between a drinking vessel and a plate). Secondary functional variation referred to the social context of the production and use of material culture: 'this variation may arise from a traditional way of doing things within a family or a larger social unit, or it may serve as a conscious expression of between-group solidarity' Binford, 1972, p. 200).

The examination of what Binford termed primary and secondary functional variability in the archaeological record has played a major role in the recent development of archaeology. In prehistoric and ethnoarchaeological studies much attention has focused on technologies of artefact production (e.g. Semenov, 1964; Van de Leeuw, 1976; Kramer, 1985, pp. 78–83; Howard and Morris (eds), 1981; Steponaitis, 1983). A second area that has been investigated is the determination of the utilization of particular artefacts (e.g. Hayden (ed.), 1979; Wilmsen, 1968; Braun, 1983; Hally, 1986). In such studies attention has focused on the suitability of particular artefact types for different purposes which are supposedly strictly delimited by the physical properties of the artefacts themselves. Characterization studies of sources of raw materials have been used to suggest the existence of exchange networks or social interaction spheres (e.g. Earle and Ericson (eds), 1977; Ericson and Earle (eds), 1982; Sabloff and Lamberg-Karlovsky (eds), 1975), and attention has been paid to the rate of breakage of artefacts, discard and reuse patterns (e.g. DeBoer and Lathrap, 1979; David, 1972; Kramer, 1985, pp. 89–92; Schiffer, 1976; Binford, 1979). Other studies have investigated sites in terms of the relationship between artefact patterning and different activities such as tool manufacturing, food processing and group size (e.g. Binford, 1978, 1981; Schapiro, 1984; Kent, 1984; Hietala, 1984). Such work has certainly alerted archaeologists to the complexities of the formation processes of the archaeological record but the symbolic and social meaning of artefact production and usage has been neglected. Meaning tends to be only investigated insofar as it can be reduced to an effect of various technologies or utilitarian considerations.

Ceramic sociology

Some innovative research in the 1960s and 1970s on ceramics was based on the assumption that degrees of stylistic similarity in material culture patterning might reflect social interaction. In cases where it could be assumed on the basis of ethnographic evidence, as in the American South-West, that residence was uxorial and women made the pottery intended for household use and traditions of pottery manufacture and decoration were passed down from mother to daughter, the spatial concentration of micro traditions in design style would be expected to indicate distinct clan or residence groupings within a settlement (for synchronic studies see e.g. Longacre, 1970; Hill, 1970; and for a diachronic perspective Deetz, 1965; Whallon, 1968).

On a broader regional scale, degrees of social interaction resulting in the borrowing of designs or design fields would be reflected in the degree of stylistic similarity between sites (Engelbrecht, 1978; S. Plog, 1976; Washburn, 1983). Such studies have been subjected to much critical assessment (Allen and Richardson, 1971; Hodder, 1982; Stanislawski and Stanislawski, 1978; Longacre, 1981; S. Plog, 1978), focusing on the feasibility (or necessity) of reconstructing kinship patterns from archaeological data given that concepts such as matrilocal kinship are often second or third order anthropological abstractions themselves. Ceramics may also often be produced by groups rather than individuals and learning networks may differ considerably from a simple transmission from mother to daughter within a social unit essentially conceived as isolated. Nor is there any necessary correlation between interaction and stylistic similarity because style may be actively used to mark out boundaries of different social groups where there is intense interaction between them. The theory assumes that style is a passive reflection of group or social identity and the cross-cultural generalizing perspective, in terms of which this research has often been framed, denies the specificity of cultural context, that in some situations style may relate to learning networks while in others it clearly does not. We need to know why this is the case. In one sense the idea that decorative style reflects the composition of social groups in space and time bears a very close resemblance to traditional archaeology, but at a fine-grained level.

Choice, function and information

Many archaeologists, however, have always realized that given consideration of technological and utilitarian parameters there still exists a latitude for choice in the manner in which artefacts may be produced and the meanings which they may carry. But how much choice and what are these social meanings?

Choice is predominantly regarded as strictly delimited by environment and function:

> If our interest resides in ancient artefacts and our aims in the most powerful interpretation of these artefacts, then we must realise that archaeological artefact systems express the individually modified imprints of environmental constraint on particularly valued cultural matrices.
>
> (Clarke, 1968, p. 83)

According to Braun,

> Where pottery making is a domestic craft, we can then assume a selective process. Pottery techniques that produce vessels that are inefficient as tools, require relatively high labour or material costs, or require relatively frequent placement, will tend to be avoided in favour of techniques that produce more efficient results, at lower costs . . . The mechanical uses of ceramic vessels directly constrain the kinds of decoration they receive and hence the kinds of social information they carry.
>
> (1983, pp. 112–13)

And Arnold:

> Viewed from the perspective of cybernetics, weather and climate can provide either deviation counteracting feedback or deviation amplifying feedback for pottery production depending on the character of the climate . . . In areas where a wet, cold and foggy climate persists for the entire year, the negative feedback is totally effective in preventing the development of pottery making, even if the craft is introduced by innovation or diffusion.
>
> (1985, pp. 76, 83)

Such statements are so widespread in the literature that they require no further documentation. While rigid environmental and functional constraint on the choice of the form and nature of material culture is usually emphasized, meaning is sometimes addressed in a purely abstract manner as 'information' and in terms of information flow structures (e.g. Johnson, 1978; Van de Leeuw, 1981).

Clarke (1968) defined material culture as a separate subsystem of society providing information, the messages being 'accumulated survival information plus miscellaneous and random noise peculiar to each system and its past trajectory' (1968, p. 85) and this general approach to meaning as survival information has been frequently advocated in debates about the significance of style and function in material culture. Dunnell regards style as denoting 'those *forms that do not have detectable selective values. Function* is manifest as those *forms that directly affect the Darwinian fitness of the populations in which they occur*' (1978, p. 199 emphasis in original). A priority of function is asserted in purely adaptive terms with the significance of style marginalized in terms of stochastic processes – trivial socio-cultural variation. On the other hand, style may be regarded as important but only insofar as it can be explained away as just another form of adaptation to the natural and social environment (e.g. Conkey, 1978; Fritz, 1978; Jochim, 1983).

Wobst regards style as a strategy of information exchange with both functional and adaptive significance. Artefacts convey messages and Wobst conceives the content of such messages as being more or less isomorphic with spoken language. Consequently he suggests that because it is relatively costly to produce messages in the stylistic mode of artefacts as opposed to conveying information through language, only a relatively narrow range of information will be expressed in the form of simple invariant and recurrent messages – messages of emotional state, social identification, group affiliation, rank, authorship and ownership, behavioural norms, religious and political belief (Wobst, 1977, p. 323). Stylistic messaging will usually be 'targeted' at individuals beyond the immediate household or residence group but loses its usefulness in relation to socially distant populations because they will either be unable to encounter or decode the messages. This leads Wobst to claim that

> the majority of functions of stylistic behaviour should relate to processes of social integration and social differentiation. Stylistic messages of identification, ownership, and authorship link efficiently those members of a community who are not in constant verbal contact and who have little opportunity to observe each others' behaviour patterns . . . it makes social intercourse more predictable.
>
> (Ibid., p. 327)

So style transmits information about social group membership and internal differentiation, functioning to keep a society running smoothly by reducing stress or conflict, and may be used to maintain social boundaries. This general perspective has been frequently adopted in the subsequent literature (e.g. Weissner, 1983; Pollock, 1983; Graves, 1982; S. Plog, 1980, pp. 126–39; Braun and S. Plog,

1982). All such a perspective purports to explain is the existence or non-existence of style; it is incapable of telling us anything at all with regard to its specific form and nature, such as why pots might have one set of designs rather than another.

Style and meaning

Whether explicitly stated or implicitly assumed, in most studies style is regarded as something left over in material culture after utilitarian function has been taken into account. It is generally regarded as having social significance which may or may not be regarded as important and possible or impossible to study with any degree of 'rigour'.

Underlying much of this discussion are two assumptions: (1) style can be separated out from utilitarian aspects of artefacts; (2) it 'functions' in social rather than utilitarian areas of life. In a series of papers Sackett (1973, 1977, 1982, 1985) has been specifically concerned to stress the inseparability of style and function, challenging the idea that stylistic aspects of artefacts merely constitute a residue, something left over when function has been taken into account. He argues that style does not constitute a distinct domain but is to be encountered in all formal variability in individual artefacts and that style and function share equal responsibility for the finished product, a view which we wish to fully endorse. It is impossible, for example, to separate out the style and the function in either vessel shape or projectile point morphology. There is no way in which we can meaningfully measure and determine what proportion of a vessel's shape performs some utilitarian end, the remainder being assigned to the domain of style. To take a chair – what proportion of this is functional as opposed to stylistic? No answer can be given; the style inheres in the function and vice versa. Furthermore, ascribing any specific or strictly delimited function to an object is in many, if not all cases, an extremely dubious exercise. A chair may be to sit on, it nominally fulfils this function, but chairs can also be used for standing on, or for knocking people over the head with, as pendulums, rulers, or almost anything else. This is not to deny the banal point that objects have uses and may normally be used in just one way, but it is to suggest that such a position represents, at best, a starting point rather than an end point for archaeological analysis.

The second point is far more crucial, and we will consider it in relation to Sackett's work. What is at issue here is the *social mean-*

ing of style. Sackett argues that 'any artifact has an *active* voice which connotes function . . . [and] a *passive* voice which connotes style' (1977, p. 370; our emphasis). The implication here is that function is something dynamic and active depending on the use of artefacts and the roles they play as technology or in social terms, while style merely reflects aspects of the social world, playing no significant role in either creating or transforming it. Sackett distinguishes between two domains of artefacts: those which may be taken to be utilitarian in function; and those which are primarily non-utilitarian, for example a crown or a head-dress. Both may be cross-cut by adjunct form, for example pottery decoration. Stone tools, by contrast, have no obvious adjunct form. Sackett's non-utilitarian class of artefacts clearly embraces both Binford's sociotechnic and ideotechnic classes, while adjunct form is that which is normally taken to be stylistic in the archaeological literature. Sackett's further and most important argument is worth quoting at some length:

> Although the form of any given object may be entirely appropriate to its function . . . there exists nevertheless a great range of alternative forms that would be more or less equally appropriate. In other words, there usually is a variety of functionally equivalent means of achieving a given end, whether these concern the design of a weapon with which to kill reindeer, the execution of pot decoration that symbolically identifies a specific residence group, or the manufacture of a chisel-ended burin. The seemingly equally valid and feasible options we may regard as functional equivalents with respect to a given end constitute a spectrum of what I choose to term *isochrestic* form . . . The artisans in any given society tend to 'choose' but one, or at most but a very few, of the isochrestic options that at least in theory are potentially available to them from this spectrum . . . Given the large number of options that are at least potentially available, chance alone dictates that any single one is unlikely to be chosen by two societies which are not ethnically related in some fashion; and chance would appear to exclude altogether the possibility that the same combination of several such choices in different spectra of isochrestic form could be made by two unrelated societies . . . Since material culture is largely the product of learned behaviours that are socially transmitted, there exists a strong and direct correlation between the specific choices a society makes and its specific position in the stream of culture history.
>
> (Sackett, 1982, pp. 72–3)

In this formulation style, viewed as isochrestic variation, has no social meaning whatsoever other than being a habitualized expression of ethnicity and, apparently, neither suggests nor requires any further explanation (Sackett, 1985, p. 157). Sackett's position, while being sensitive to the detection of style in all artefacts, at the same time explicitly avoids any consideration of its meaning and significance because in his view style just happens as a product of habit and socialization processes; hence the claim which he makes that style is function writ small.

To summarize: while in traditional archaeology the meaning of material culture was its supposedly direct reflection of ethnicity and (unspecified) ideas, the new archaeology reduced its meaning to function – as an adaptive interface between people and the environment (as technology) or as a means of cementing together social groups or symbolizing group identity (as style). In the case of Sackett's work this is a purely passive process, while for Wobst and others it has a more active dimension as a form of social signalling. In all accounts, function has either been privileged in relation to style or style has been explained away as existing because of an inherent social function. However, specifying a social function for stylistic aspects of material culture patterning tells us virtually nothing about its specificity, for example all the multitudes of different chair forms, past or present, their shapes, decorative features, arrangements in different rooms or types of rooms. The general conclusion that may be drawn is that the term function is virtually redundant.

When we are dealing with material culture we are analysing a world of stylistic form and conceptual choice, creating things in one way rather than another. The corollary is that the archaeological record is a record of form according to specific cognitive orientations toward the world. The first stage in trying to understand material culture is to accept it as a stylistic cultural production. The second stage is to make full use of the range of variability in the material culture patterning apparent to us and not to subsume this variability under high-level generalizations. Exploiting the variability in material culture patterning is of vital importance: it gives us clues on which to hinge our statements and ensures we realize the full potential of the archaeological record.

Place a brick somewhere in London. Imagine that London represents the totality of the social relations and practices existing in a prehistoric society. The brick represents the archaeological evidence from which we have to extrapolate to come to an understanding of that past social totality. Obviously the variability in the brick is of vital importance if we are going to understand anything at all. However, for many archaeologists, it appears as if even our solitary brick in the centre of London is too variable and complicated, so much so that high-level generalizations must be employed to further reduce the brick to a few fragments via the operation of certain methodological hammers. One of the most powerful of these hammers – the hammer of function – has already been discussed above, and is often combined with another even more powerful tool, the sledge hammer of cross-cultural generalization (e.g. Arnold, 1985; and see the discussion above), which finally manages to reduce our brick to fine particles of dust. London appears to be lost.

HISTORY, STRUCTURE AND MATERIAL CULTURE

Most of contemporary archaeological discourse concerns itself with the delimitation and analysis of constraints, usually of an asocial nature, impinging upon societies – environment, ecology, population pressure, economic resource availability – presupposing that human potentialities are strictly bounded and limited. However, in most of the substantive analyses, such a position is simply assumed rather than demonstrated, and there is little, if any, evidence to support it. Rather than thinking in terms of asocial constraints, perhaps we should think in terms of human potentialities and possibilities for action. In any given determinate social field societies to a greater or lesser extent constrain themselves, rather than being constrained by external forces or purely utilitarian considerations. Such a move parallels a shift from viewing material culture as primarily functional to regarding it as constituting a symbolic, active communicative field. How then do we conceive of material culture and its relation to the social?

Perception, history and material culture

Very broadly, a history of perception or the manner in which people regard the world provides one link between the content of thought and the structuring of society (Lowe, 1982). Merleau-Ponty, in *The Phenomenology of Perception* (1962), emphasizes three main features of perception together creating a perceptive field: the subject as perceiver; the action of perceiving; and the content of that perceived. The perceiving subject from an embodied spatial location always approaches and conceives of the world as a lived, dynamic, open, horizontal field. The act of perceiving unifies the subject with that perceived and the content of the perceived resulting from the act of perception affects the subject's actions and relationship with the world. Perception is bounded by three fundamental factors: (1) common media framing and facilitating the act of perception; (2) the senses themselves – hearing, touching, smelling, tasting, seeing – structuring the subject as embodied receiver; (3) epistemic or cognitive presuppositions ordering the content of that perceived. Together these constitute a field of perception within which knowledge of the world becomes possible. From such a perspective we can view material culture as being involved actively in a process of perception and as media framing and facilitating the act of perception and gaining knowledge of the world. The question we next have to ask is: how important is material culture as framing and communicative media in society; and, historically, has it had a differential importance?

All communicative media from the patterns on a pot to television and video not only transmit information but also form, package and filter it. If the medium doesn't actually constitute the message it certainly alters it. Historically, media for communication have changed dramatically, from oral cultures in which there was no written language, script or text, to cultures where writing was the preserve of an elite minority, to the introduction of print and an increase in literacy, to the mass media electronic communicative forms of today. These changes have been additive rather than substitutive. Ong (1967) and Lowe (1982) have claimed that such changes from oral to chirographic to typographic to electronic cultures are correlated with a changing hierarchy of the senses. In oral cultures speech has to fulfil the role of both preserving knowledge and framing communication, for only in the act of speaking can knowledge be preserved. Speech, memory and a primacy of hearing as perception go together: oral communication is primarily aural communication. A priority of hearing over seeing is implied. It is only with the advent of a typographic culture that sight assumes priority.

This perspective, while privileging language, overlooks the role of material culture as a perceptive medium and as a framework for communicating knowledge and information. In an oral culture it would seem to be quite plausible to regard material culture as a communicative medium of considerable importance for transmitting, storing and preserving social knowledge and as a symbolic medium for orientating people in their natural and social environment because of the relative permanence of material culture *vis à vis* speech acts. So material culture can be regarded in oral societies as a form of writing and discourse inscribed in a material medium in just the same way as words in chirographic and typographic cultures are inscribed on a page. It is then possible to go on to suggest that as a communicative discourse material culture becomes successively transformed in importance with the advent and spread of communicative media directly related to spoken language – writing, printing and the mass media of today, which do not transcribe speech but actually transmit it.

With the development of mass industrial production as opposed to craft production the role of material culture as an active symbolic transformative intervention in the social world is certainly altered. In a world capitalist economy we may be wearing jeans at the same time as a Lebanese gunman. The material form – in this case jeans – remains the same but its meaning will alter according to the context. Jeans will be consumed in different ways, appropriated and incorporated into various symbolic structures according to historical tradition and social context. In a prehistoric situation not only will the meanings differ but so will the particularity of the material form. Consequently it is possible to argue that there is likely to be a closer relationship between material form and meaning content than exists today.

Material culture, the individual and society

In considering the nature of material culture as communication, as a form of writing and silent discourse, we need some perspective on the relationship between the individual subject and society. In other words, we need to consider to what extent material culture production is simply a product of individuals and to be related to their intentions, individual psychology and personal make-up, or to what extent it can be considered a social production. How important is the individual as individual in cultural production? Is material culture to be regarded as a largely autonomous expression of individual personality, or as indelibly structured in relation to social processes which themselves encompass, define, create and articulate the individual? We have already provided answers to these questions in the previous chapter. It does not seem to be at all theoretically acceptable to pursue a view of the human subject as endowed with specific capacities and attributes, as the source of social relations, font of meaning, knowledge and action. We should insist, therefore, on the logical priority of the social and the structuring of social relations in accounting for all social practices including material culture production. Material culture is in no sense to be regarded as a product of unmediated individual intentionality but as a production of the intersubjective social construction of reality. Individuals are structured in terms of the social and, concomitantly, material culture is socially rather than individually structured.

The intention here is not to uphold a radically anti-humanist position in the manner of Althusser and Balibar (1970) but, as we argued in chapter 3, to regard individuality as created and constructed in a social and symbolic field over which the subject has no immediate or direct degree of control or possibility for radical intervention. This is to decentre the subject and to regard material culture as a social production created in terms of a socially mediated symbolic field. We are placing emphasis on the constructedness of human meaning and that meaning is not a private experience but a product of shared systems of signification. Language and material culture pre-date the individual. The agent does not so much construct language or material culture but is, rather, constructed through them. Meaning is by no means a natural extension of personality but a product of linguistic and material culture systems. Reality is not reflected by language or material culture as much as actively produced by it. The meaning an individual is able to articulate in relation to the world is dependent on the construction of that world through language and material culture.

Material culture and structure

We now want to explore the relationship between material culture and structure. The central proposition that follows from a position in which the subject is decentred *vis à vis* material culture production is that the archaeological record must be regarded not in terms of just a random collection of artefacts or attributes of individual artefacts but as a structured record, structured in relation to the social construction of reality and in relation to social strategies of interest and power and ideology as a form of power. The position we are taking is that material culture as communication is a structured sign system. The point has already been made that material culture can be considered as a form of writing and in the absence of writing as we know it today as a textual production it can be considered to play a much more powerful role as a signifier in the comparatively less complex oral cultures archaeologists typically investigate. If we take up this notion of material culture as a form of writing does this imply that it can be considered in just the same manner as language – as a form of non-verbal discourse with grammars, codes and specific units of signification? In other words does material culture act as a structured series of signs which signify something in social reality, or does material culture form a kind of discourse signifying itself rather than something external to it? If material culture signifies the social or aspects of social reality in what manner is this effected? Is material culture a supplement to language acting in a similar way with an equivalent pattern of meaning structure? These questions take us into the realm of structuralism, semiotics, post-structuralism and deconstruction.

Saussure, the father of contemporary structuralism, in his *Course in General Linguistics* (1978), regarded the study of linguistics as one day forming part of a general science of signs. This would seem to suggest that language forms one sign system among many and that there might be a relative autonomy among different semiotic systems. Barthes, in his *Elements of Semiology* (1967), strongly criticized such a view regarding all sign systems as part of language. For him there could be no non-linguistic semiotic system. Rather than adhering either to Saussure or Barthes' position it would seem best to regard material culture as forming a system of discourse which has a relative degree of autonomy from a language, a second order type of writing which shares some essential features with linguistic systems while at the same time not being directly assimilable to, or reducible to, language. So, in what manner does material culture as a signifying system have a relative autonomy from language and what features does it share with language? The answer to this question depends, of course, on how we regard language as a signifying system.

Saussure in his *Course* viewed language as a system of signs which must be studied synchronically rather than diachronically. Each sign is made up of a signifier (sound-image or graphic equivalent) and a signified (a concept or meaning). According to Saussure the relationship between the signifier and that signified was entirely arbitrary, a matter of cultural or historical convention. Each sign in a system only had meaning by virtue of its difference from other signs. For example, badger has meaning because it is not rat, dog or pig; but its relationship with the four legged, black and white striped creature is entirely arbitrary, a matter of convention. In Saussure's conception of a linguistic system emphasis is placed therefore on relational difference. Meaning does not inhere in a sign in itself but by virtue of its difference from other signs. Saussure was not particularly interested in actual speech (*parole*) but with objective structures making speech

possible (*langue*), i.e. the rules underlying and structuring any particular real speech act in the world. The nature of *langue* as a
system of rules lies underneath and governs the relative superficiality
of day-to-day speech. If language is an exchange of messages
constituted in their difference, governed by an underlying system of
grammatical rules and is taken as a paradigm for social and cultural
analysis, then the move made by Lévi-Strauss (1968) to view
kinship as a structured exchange of mates within the confines of an
abstract system of underlying unconscious rules, the economy an
exchange of goods and services, politics an exchange of power and
so on, is quite easy to understand. But what of material culture? If
language is an exchange of messages, then material culture might
be thought to act as a kind of second level back-up, mirroring in
some sense this message exchange and reinforcing it by virtue of its
very materiality and relative permanence.

There are two major problems with this structuralist perspective.
First it systematically diverts attention from history, the manner in
which people have altered and do alter their objectifications of the
social. A structuralist perspective concentrates on the synchronic
investigation of order, the codes underlying the order, and the
significance of the experience of the order.

In archaeology formal analysis of pattern in material culture is
now well established. The aim has been to investigate pattern, to
establish the logic behind the patterning and establish rules for
constructing the patterns. Washburn (1978, 1983) has used
symmetry (repetition, rotation, reflection of a design element) as a
logic lying beneath pottery decoration. Hodder (1982, pp. 174–81)
has claimed a generative grammar for the decoration of calabashes
among the Sudanese Nuba, a system of rules operating on an
originary cross motif, which can generate a wide variety of actually
occurring calabash designs. His analysis included computer
simulation – 'testing' the rules he isolates as generating the designs
to see whether they fitted observed patterns. Fritz (1978) has identified symmetrical relationships in the organization of the directional orientation of settlement space in the Chaco Canyon in the
American south-west. Fletcher's (1977) work on the formal
arrangement of settlement space can be mentioned here – an
analysis aimed at identifying a syntax of space.

In addition to attempts to identify rules of symmetry and design
combination and space syntax, analysis of pattern or structure
in archaeology has employed the use of binary oppositions
such as bounded/unbounded, horizontal/vertical, left/right,
hierarchical/sequential. Hodder (1982d) has described a transfor-

mation of the structure of designs on Dutch neolithic pottery according to a horizontal/vertical distinction: from bounded designs hierarchically organized, to later horizontally zoned sequential designs. As in orthodox structuralism the meaning of such patterning remains a problem. Hodder links the changes in pottery design in the Dutch neolithic to a change from strongly bounded to incorporative social groups; so designs are held to directly mirror social entities. Another way of assigning meaning is to invoke oppositions or distinctions such as male/female (as in Leroi-Gourhan's early work (1965) on upper paleolithic cave painting), culture/nature, domestic/wild, living/dead, settlement/burial, and these may be held to be cognitive universals as implied by Hodder (1982, p. 215f).

Secondly, a structuralist position privileges language and this may hinder the recognition of the importance of non-verbal signifying systems. Granting priority to the verbal, and suggesting that non-verbal forms of communication merely directly mirror (inadequately) linguistic structures and forms of signification is, as Rossi-Landi points out, rather like

> asserting the priority of digestion upon breathing, or of rivers upon seas, or worse, of downhill roads upon uphill roads. Since language and all other sign systems of a community are in reciprocal relations in reality, we don't understand in what possible way one can attribute to any one of these sign systems a *real* priority.
>
> (Rossi-Landi, 1975, pp. 20–1)

Material culture as a coded sign system constitutes its own 'material language', tied to production and consumption. It does not simply reflect the significative structures of language in another form. Like language it is itself a practice, a symbolic practice with its own determinate meaning product which needs to be situated and understood in relation to the overall structuration of the social.

If for Saussure the relationship between the signifier and that signified is entirely arbitrary within the context of an overall system of difference, then for Derrida (1976, 1978), the later work of Barthes (1977) and for Foucault (1981) this difference can be extended infinitely. If meaning is a matter of difference and not identity, taken to its logical conclusion language cannot be held to constitute a stable closed system. Meanings of signs are always elusive, for if a sign is constituted by what it is not, by difference from other signs, there can be no final relationship between one signifier and something that is signified, as the signified is always already the signifier of another signified. Meaning is then the result of a never-ending play of signifiers rather than something that can be firmly related to a particular referent. The meaning of one sign depends on that of another; signifieds keep on changing into signifiers and vice versa. Signs confer value as much by virtue of what they are not as what they are. The concomitant of this position is that meaning in language is floating rather than fixed – dispersed along whole chains of signifiers as each becomes in effect a residue of others, a trace of language. For signs to have any capacity for meaning they must be repeatable or reproducible: something that occurs only once cannot count as a sign. The reproduction of signs constitutes part of their identity and difference but the very fact of their reproduction entails a lack of any unitary meaning or self-identity because they can always be reproduced in different contexts, changing their meaning. Signifieds always become altered by the chains of signified– signifiers in which they become embroiled through usage.

Material culture, language and practice

We want to suggest that material culture can be considered to be an articulated and structured silent material discourse forming a channel of reified expression and being linked and bound up with social practices and social strategies involving power, interests and ideology. As a communicative signifying medium material culture is quite literally a reification when compared with the relatively free-flowing rhythms of actions of individuals in the world and the spontaneity of spoken language. If we take up Saussure's notion of the diacritical sign – i.e. the sign whose value is independent of denoted objects and rests upon its insertion in a system of signs, and Derrida's deconstruction of the notion of the sign as possessing a plenitude of meaning by virtue of its relation to other signs – we arrive at what might be termed the *metacritical* sign: the sign whose meaning remains radically dispersed through an essentially open chain of signifieds–signifiers. If we conceive of material culture as embodying a series of metacritical signs then we must regard the meaning of the archaeological record as being always already irreducible to the elements which go to make up and compose that record, characterized as a system of points or units. What we will be involved with will be a search for the structures, and the principles composing those structures, underlying the visible tangibility of the material culture patterning. Our analysis must try to uncover what lies beneath the observable presences, to take account of the absences, the co-presences and co-absences, the similarities and the differences which constitute the patterning of material culture in a particular spatial and temporal context. The principles governing the form, nature and content of material culture patterning are to be found at both the level of micro-relations (e.g. a set of designs on a pot) and macro-relations (e.g. relationships between settlement and burial), but they are irreducibly linked, each forming a part of the other; hence any analysis which restricts itself to just considering one feature of the archaeological record such as an isolated study of pot design is bound to be inadequate.

Material culture can be considered to be constituted in terms of a spiralling matrix of associative (paradigmatic) and syntagmatic relations involving parallelism, opposition, linearity, equivalence and inversion between its elements. Each individual act of material culture production is at the same time a contextualized social act involving the relocation of signs along axes which define the relationships between signs and other signs. The meaning of these signs is constituted in their lateral or spatial and horizontal or temporal relations. The signs reach out beyond themselves and toward others and become amplified in specific contexts or subdued in others. Material culture does not so much signify a relationship between people and nature, since the environment is itself socially constituted, but relationships between groups, relationships of power. The form of social relations provides a grid into which the signifying force of material culture becomes inserted to extend, define, redefine, bolster up or transform that grid. The social relations are themselves articulated into a field of meaning partially articulated through thought and language and capable of reinforcement through the objectified and reified meanings inscribed in material culture. The material logic of the relationships involved in the contextual patterning of material culture may run parallel to, subvert or invert the social logic or practices involved at the sites of the production, use, exchange or destruction of artefacts. Material culture as constituted by chains of signifiers–signifieds should not be treated in a simplistic fashion as necessarily representing anything in particular, such as red ochre or use of red as symbolizing blood or pots of shape X as signifying male and pots of shape Y as signifying female, *on its own*. The signifying force of material culture depends on the structure of its interrelations, and the signification of any particular artefact or item can be seen as being intersected by the meanings of other items. So, particular objects form nodes in a grid of other objects. This follows from a view of material culture as being constituted in an open field rather than as a closed system of signs. The material culture record is a set of conjunctions, repetitions and differences, and meaning shifts across from context to context, level to level, association to association. Despite that, material culture forms part of the encoding and decoding strategies involved in the active social construction of reality helping to constitute a common cultural field and tradition along with action and speech. It would be naive to suppose that material culture expresses exactly that which might be expressed in language but in a different form. The importance of material culture as a signifying force is precisely its difference from language while at the same time being involved in a communication of meanings. Material culture forms part of the social construction of reality in which the precise status of meaning becomes conceptually and physically shifted from one register to another: from action to speech to the material. Meaning can be communicated in all these areas but the medium alters the nature and effectivity of the message. The depth of social meaning in the world derives partly from the use of multiple channels for its transmission. Material culture constitutes an external field to the intersubjectivity of social relations and is dialectically related to them, its signifying relations affecting the constitution and transformation of the social.

Material culture may be regarded as revealing its structure and the principles which underlie it through its repetition. This is why, as has long been recognized, consistent patterning in the archaeological record is so important for understanding its nature. Material culture as a communicative discourse solidifies, encodes and reifies the social relations in which it is embedded and from which it is derived. Social action is the product of discourse and from this discourse both action and material culture arise. Material culture plays less the role of signifying social relations than acting in terms of established and fixed relations.

We can argue, therefore, that artefacts constitute a code of signs that exchange among themselves. The production, utilization and consumption of material culture on the part of the individual agent can be regarded as an act of *bricolage*. Material culture is used to organize the existence of agents and invest this existence with meaning and significance. The *bricoleur*, or handyman (Lévi-Strauss, 1966, 1969), who uses odd scraps of wood, a bent saw or whatever, to do a reasonable patching up job, cannot by the nature of his or her situation create something entirely new, but is trapped by the 'constitutive sets' from which the elements came. The bricoleur is never fully in control or master of the situation with which he or she is confronted. Similarly, the agent produces and uses material culture, but is never aware of the entire system of material significations. The agent lives through the world metonymically. That which is being utilized, produced and consumed is never the individual artefact or object (although it may appear as such), but rather the entire symbolic structured system of objects or artefacts of which it forms a part; the use and production of artefacts is simultaneously the use and reproduction of the system of which they form a part.

The primary significance of material culture is not pragmatic, its utilitarian or technological use-value, but its significative exchange value. In our argument, we agree with Baudrillard (1981) in suggesting that a theory of material culture simply cannot be established in terms of biological needs and their satisfaction, but must be based on a theory of signification and regarded as a symbolic production, part of the social constitution of reality:

> the empirical 'object,' given in its contingency of form, colour, material, function and discourse . . . . is a myth. How often it has been wished away! But the object is *nothing*. It is nothing but the different types of relations and significations that converge, contradict themselves, and twist around it, as such – the hidden logic that not only arranges this bundle of relations, but directs the manifest discourse that overlays and occludes it.
>
> (Baudrillard, 1981, p. 63)

We need to analyse artefacts in terms that go entirely beyond them, in relation to meaning structures and the social strategies to which they are related, to determine what specific place in the social is occupied by material culture as part of an overall pattern of significations.

STUDYING MATERIAL CULTURE

Material culture and social practices

A growing number of recent archaeological studies are beginning to work towards the position we have been proposing. Braithwaite's (1982) ethnoarchaeological study among the Azande (southern Sudan) brings out the active use of material culture in processes of definition and maintenance of social categories and boundaries. Male/female differentiation and asymmetrical power relations related to this differentiation form a fundamental feature of the Azande social world. Power relations between the sexes are played out in terms of the sexual division of labour and its articulation with the timing and spacing of productive activities. While men are in a position of social domination, and greater prestige is associated with their activities and labour product, this domination is nevertheless dependent on their relationship with and competition for women who possess a more muted but nevertheless important strength and influence. The male–female relationship is one of considerable tension and ambiguity. Clay pots are made by the men and used and owned almost exclusively by women in the domestic sphere of labour. The male/female opposition involving the negotiation and renegotiation of social position is related to the use of decorated and undecorated pottery. Pots only used by a single sex are not decorated while the decorated pots are those used in the transfer of foods or drink from one sex to another, e.g. a woman serving a man food from a cooking vessel. So, pottery decoration is associated with and serves to mark out situations in which there is transfer of food across fundamental social boundaries; it serves to mark out areas of concern and importance in Azande society.

In the Wessex area of south England a new type of pottery, finely decorated beakers, appears in the late neolithic at a time when the social landscape is dominated by the use of large-scale ceremonial monuments in what appears to have been a dispersed and acephalous society with legitimation of authority being ritually based in the activities taking place at the henge monuments. Although the building of these monuments must have required considerable labour input and co-ordination, contemporary burials show little evidence of hierarchy or status differentiation (Shennan, 1986, p. 145). Thorpe and Richards (1984) and Shennan (1986) note that the new material culture form – the finely decorated beakers – occur in graves on the peripheries of the assumed areas of ritual influence of the henge monuments and moreover in graves in which we have the first evidence of status differentiation. They suggest that these beakers were actively adopted and used by those excluded from the traditional power structures associated with the use of the henges and mark the beginning of the development of an alternative and competing structure of authority and power. This is a markedly different kind of explanation for the adoption of beakers than those previously proposed in the literature where their introduction was discussed in terms of the appearance of new peoples in the framework of traditional archaeology, or as a prestige good in the new archaeology. Thorpe and Richards and Shennan display sensitivity as to the particular context in which beakers occur in Wessex and argue for their active use in competing power strategies; however, neither explanation is able to cope with the specificity of the local context in which finely decorated beakers first occur in large areas of Europe: these frameworks were unable to explain why beakers appear in some areas in a particular context (in graves or settlements or ritual structures) and not in others.

These studies are also unable to explain within the framework adopted the specificity of pot decoration. For example all that Braithwaite's explanation does is to tell us why decoration might occur – but what of its form? Similarly, why use beakers in Wessex rather than decorated ox bones?

Hodder's ethnoarchaeological studies, reported in *Symbols in Action* (1982), usefully emphasize two important features of material culture. First, and again, that material culture plays an active symbolic role in social relations. Interacting groups manipulate and negotiate, consciously and unconsciously, material symbols according to their strategies and intentions. For example, particular types of body decoration worn by young men and women in the Baringo area of Kenya are a means by which the authority of older men is contradicted. In the Lozi kingdom material culture is used by status groups to legitimate authority. In both these cases it is clear that material culture does not simply reflect social relations but actively mediates intentions, strategies, attitudes and ideologies.

Secondly, material culture is meaningfully constituted; it is produced in relation to symbolic schemes, structured according to the system of meanings of particular social groups. These structured meanings mediate social practices and material culture. Hodder argues that all aspects of Nuba material culture, from burial to settlement to decoration to refuse disposal are related to the same symbolic scheme. Among the Nuba there are well-developed local groups, while roles and networks of individual relationships are only weakly defined. Following Douglas (1970), Hodder associates these features with an emphasis on the purity of the group, the distinction insider/outsider, and on classification and categorization:

All these aspects of ritual and world view are present in Nuba society, and particularly in Mesakin society . . . from the emphasis on spatial group seclusion to the pollution taboos, to the concern with body, home and granary boundaries, to the ritual surrounding the boundary between life and death and the breaking of items associated with a dead man, to the regular placing of items in particular places in the huts, to detailed classification and categorisation of form and design, to the logically consistent set of generational rules in the art.

(Hodder, 1982, p. 183)

As indicated here, however, Hodder emphasizes a single unitary logic within a social system which may nevertheless contain tensions:

Each material item has significance in terms of its place in the whole. This is not to say that the patterns in the different types of data are always direct mirror images of each other. Rather the identifiable patterns are transformations, often contrasting, disrupting, or commenting on basic dichotomies and tensions within the social system and within the distribution of power.

(Ibid, p. 212)

The concomitant of such a position is that any unitary logic must be argued to be historically specific and not a universal principle of analysis.

We have suggested (Shanks and Tilley, 1982) a series of principles generating the patterning of human remains from communal tombs (long barrows and chambered passage graves) in neolithic Wessex and Skåne, Sweden, based on the distinctions individual/group, bounded/unbounded, male/female, right/left, culture/nature and basic body symmetries such as body/limbs, upper/lower in respect of disarticulated/articulated remains. Such distinctions were argued to be part of what Bourdieu has termed habitus (1977), aspects of lineage-based social systems, involving social strategies arising from opposed structuring principles of social control by individual lineage heads or elders in contradiction with collective production, and direct, unmediated reciprocity and exchange relations between kin groups. In such a social context we argued that communal burial asserts the collective rather than the individual. The regrouping of disarticulated remains, which we identified, incorporates in the expression of symmetry between body parts a denial of asymmetrical relationships in relations of production. In this manner we focused on the possible ideological dimension of the form and nature of material culture, how it may act to naturalize and misrepresent other social practices.

Tilley (1984) has extended the analysis to cover all aspects of material culture patterning in the middle neolithic of southern Sweden, identifying structural homologies running through the directional orientation of tombs in the landscape, to burial practices, ceramic designs and uses of settlement and mortuary space. These homologies are related to social strategies of group competition in the context of status display and ritual elaboration. Incorporating the distinctions ancestors/living, spiritual/social, material culture is analysed as an ideological comment on other social practices. Related transformations in diverse aspects of material culture patterning are traced through to the emergence of the Battle Axe/Corded Ware tradition. It is proposed that the manipulation of material culture in the sphere of ritual activities was part of an ideological order which eventually failed to misrepresent structural contradictions and justify asymmetries in social relations, leading to a legitimation crisis and wholesale social change: the emergence of the more egalitarian Battle Axe tradition.

Miller (1985a) has similarly used concepts of ideology and a legitimation crisis in the context of the Indus or Harappan civilization. He articulates the material remains around a culture/nature distinction and in relation to an emphasis on order, standardization and purity. He invokes Foucault's notion of power as relating not merely to coercive social processes manifested by particular individuals, institutions or groups but as an overarching and pervasive principle which generates as well as constrains social forms. Arguing against notions of priest-kings and redistributive temple beaucracies, he suggests that power resides in a multiplicity of organizational forms, this very dispersal of power ensuring the reproduction of the social order.

Miller's (1985) analysis of Indian Dangwara pottery is a sophisticated elucidation of some of the principles we have been emphasizing in this chapter. He represents a formal symbolic framework summarizing the variability of pottery in Dangwara society established by relating the pot forms, colours and uses to cultural categories and codes such as food, gender and caste (figure 4.2). Having noted different classifications of the pottery categories (e.g. according to colour, semantic label and function) and related the pottery code to other codes or category systems, Miller stresses that this formal order is his objectified postulation which is to be superseded:

> rather there is a set of individual and transient realisations in particular contexts and strategies, which treats these alignments as generalised potentials rather than rules of meaning . . . the formal is constantly qualified as category (to the different actual pots of the same form), code (to the variety of classifications) and grid (to the variety of 'evocations') into the informal and realised, which produces an array of different and sometimes inconsistent patterns.
>
> (p. 175)

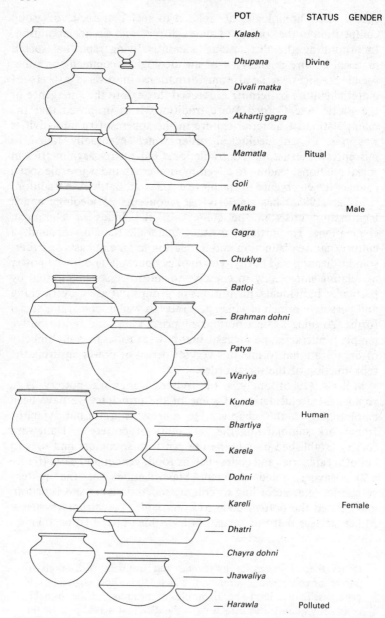

FIGURE 4.2 The associations between pottery and major social variables in Dangwara society, India, according to Miller

Source: From D. Miller (1985). Reprinted by permission of Cambridge University Press.

COLOUR	CASTE	CONNOTATION	CONTENT	EXCHANGE	HEAT	RIGHTS
	Brahman					
Red painted				*Jajman* system		
						Contractual
		Auspicious				
			Water		Cold	
				Embedded exchange		Proprietorial
	High castes					
Red and buff						
	Middle castes		Milk			
			Wheat	Market system		
		Inauspicious				
						Non-contractual
	Low castes					
Black			Sorghum			Non-proprietorial
			Pulse	Monetary economy		
	Untouchables				Hot	

The variability apparent in the interpretation of the meaning(s) of the same pot depends on the particular context in which the interpretation takes place. Miller adopts the term 'pragmatics' to refer to this relationship of conceptualization and context. Two important concepts of pragmatics are 'cue' and 'frame'. Cues and frames divide off various contexts in which interpretation may occur. Pots themselves may act as framing devices (see above), providing cues as to the significance and meaning of events taking place, controlling spheres of evocation. The notion of pragmatics introduces substantial multivalency with regard to pottery, and through pots acting as frames, into other categories.

Context implies not only other category sets but also human practice: the production and use of pots. Miller also considers the relation of pot categories to social strategies – in particular 'emulation', a process in which attempts are made to raise status through utilizing particular pot forms associated with dominant groups; and 'naturalization', in which the socially contingent appears natural. He rightly emphasizes this as an important feature of material culture. Its frequency, apparent triviality and practicality or simple functionality lend themselves to naturalization. Arbitrary cultural distinctions may be superimposed on apparently natural (functional) associations, without becoming a discursive focus of attention.

We may note several conclusions from Miller's work:

1 The notion of a formal set of discrete categories as forming the basis of classification systems is to be extended. Categories include non-incidental variability. Such variability involves the heterogeneity of social context and practice and does not involve a denial of structure (p. 202). The material artefact is polysemous.

2 Material variability is not a simple symbolic reflection of a prior social classification. Categories of social relationship such as caste or class are like the material dimension – 'constructs which capture and in turn constitute elements of culture, but within an array of alternative, sometimes complementary and sometimes conflicting representations. There is no privileged real "society" that is being represented: there is nothing else behind these mirrors. The term "representation" refers to a circle of form and understanding, and culture is exhausted by the same constructs through which it is understood' (pp. 202–3).

3 This means that different social dimensions are not reducible, one to the other (such as stylistic form to adaptive function).

4 Consequently archaeologists are not in a weak position with regard to social analysis in the sense of having no direct access to the understanding of social actors which may be linguistically articulated. We have analogously argued above that archaeological analysis is not a recovery of a lost life-world through empathetic reconstruction of the consciousness of an ancient potter: 'a society studied through its material rather than its linguistic manifestation is in no sense less immediate or less real' (p. 198).

5 This requires a theorization of material culture not readily available in contemporary sociologies. This will not be a specifically archaeological theory but theory directed at material culture and its particular properties: as an important aspect of Bourdieu's doxa, a representation of the given order of the world that constitutes an environment for living (Bourdieu, 1977, pp. 164–71); as an effective frame for social action; as ideologically informed due to its perceived simple functionality, concreteness and triviality which facilitate naturalization and misrepresentation.

Our work (Shanks and Tilley, 1987) with the design of contemporary beer cans in Britain and Sweden also exemplifies some of the features of material culture analysis we have been proposing. Involving detailed analysis of the material culture of alcoholic drink, both packaging and advertising, we located the design of beer cans within a social context of brewing, commercial marketing, consumerism, consumption and the relation of drinking to images of health and the body. Eschewing cross-cultural generalization with its resultant problems of lack of explanation of specific features of material culture, we compared the two capitalist nation-states Britain and Sweden, analysing the historical development of brewing, drinking, the welfare state and technologies of disciplinary power. We argued there was a contradiction embodied in the material culture of drink in Britain and Sweden, between alcohol as commercial product and alcohol as drug. The differences between British and Swedish can design can be understood as different ideological mediations of the contradiction between promoted consumption and disciplinary control of drink. So design can hardly be conceived as reflecting a separate social reality but is a structured mediation inscribed in commercial, institutional and individual social practices and strategies.

Material culture and the archaeological record

We have argued for a view of material culture as a constructed network of significations, linking this position with some recent
studies. Considered in terms of the archaeological record material
culture obviously has boundaries and thresholds in terms of its
content and internal structure. It is not reducible to, nor deducible
from, a universal code because material culture is intimately linked
with social praxis and it is through praxis that it comes into being as
an objectification and in an objectified form. Material culture is
structured in relation to a specific social totality and is historically
and spatially constituted.

Individual material culture items are concrete and particular.
They are, after all, empirical objects. At the same time material
culture items in the archaeological record are meaningfully
constituted and linked in structural relationships underlying their
physical presence, forming a network of cross-references. The
individual item forms part of the totality and the totality in part
serves to constitute the nature of the individual artefact, its value
and significance. The interrelatedness of the meaning of material
culture in the archaeological record refers to the intersubjectivity of
human actions. Material culture production, in any particular
context, is not an isolated act but is always already established as a
juncture: a relation to the material culture which already exists in a
cultural tradition both spatially and temporally. Any fresh or novel
material culture production is always a response to an established
tradition. The space and time of material culture patterning is
charged through with the space and time of the social relations to
which it refers and relates. This is not quantitative space and time
but lived human space and time (see chapter 6). Meaning is
distributed across space and time through repetition and
difference, contextualized parallels, associations, inversions and so
on. While the meaning of material culture is relatively fixed as
compared with the nuances of speech, i.e. it is likely to possess
fewer syntactic links, and differences between right and wrong are
likely to be more clear cut than in speech, the meaning of material
culture can by no means be regarded as stable. It can possess
different meanings at different times and in different locations. A
large tomb such as a megalith is unlikely to possess exactly the same
meaning 1,000 years after it was first constructed and this point
leads us on to a consideration of how we, as archaeologists, go
about interpreting material culture.

Translating material culture

The past is not an eternally open site in which the archaeologist rambles around conferring meaning and significance at will. Regarding material culture as meaningfully constituted forming a signifying field inevitably involves the archaeologist in a complex process of interpretation, decoding or translation. The single most important feature of material culture is that while it is irreducibly polysemous with an indeterminate range of meanings we can't just ascribe any old meaning to it. Material culture patterning is not a reality to be questioned in the way in which a hypothethico-deductive analysis might suggest but a reality that has to be constructed in the process of translative, interpretative analysis. Gaining a representation of the significance of material culture forms a process in which the significance is achieved by making visible or drawing out certain features of the data rather than others.

In translating from the past to the present we are not trying to convey exactly the form and meaning of artefacts in terms of their significance for prehistoric social actors. They had their point of view; we have ours. Is one any better than the other? Are our categories their categories? Much archaeological discussion, particularly that concerned with erecting typologies, has concerned itself, as we discussed earlier in this chapter, with this distinction. Our present analysis of the archaeological record provides one perspective on that record, and as all material objects have to be interpreted, whether they exist in the present or the past, we cannot restrict ourselves to some arcane attempt at a recovery of original meaning for there is no such thing as original meaning given the intersubjective context of the production and use of material culture. In this the position of the archaeologist is no different from an anthropologist faced with an essentially alien culture. So we are not trying to convey form and meaning from an original, somehow untainted past context into a present-day context as accurately as possible. Such a perspective would find it hard to define the nature of its own accuracy and, therefore, could shed no light on what actually is important in the process of translating the past. In the act of translating the past we change it just as we change a text in translation from one language into another. No translation or conceptually mediated intervention would be possible if it strove for an absolute degree of identity with the original (see Benjamin, 1970). Translation is always active, it changes the past while being constrained by that being translated, the foreignness, the otherness. Translation is a mode of recovering the meaning in the past, an active remembering on the part of the archaeologist. The past does not somehow form a slate which we can wipe clean since materiality is inscribed or written into it. No interpretation can ever be complete or whole or exhaust the meaning of the past because of the polysemous nature of the structured series of metacritical signs that compose it. Content and form in the past form a whole, like a banana in its skin. Our interpretations can either envelop the past like a gigantic octopus with ample tentacles to suck it in or, alternatively, can try to come to terms with the otherness through a theory–data dialectic in which we allow the data to challenge our presuppositions while at the same time not privileging that data as in standard empiricist approaches. This is in part a realization that all archaeology is essentially derivative, derived from that which it studies.

The artefact constitutes both a point of departure and a point of return. The point of return is a translation of the archaeological record into a fresh constellation. Truth does not reside in a recovery or reproduction of some supposed original meaning but in the process of the transformation of the past. The difference between a translation of the past and the empirically perceived past indicates the similarities and not vice versa. Because material culture relates to and was produced in a past social context we should not think of it as being mute and enclosed in an isolation which can only be broken by an infusion of our present consciousness. The past still speaks in its traces, in the signifying residues of the texture of the social world in which it was once located. It is up to us to articulate that past in our own speech; to come to terms with it as a vast network of signifying residues, to trace the connections down the signifying axes and place them back in our present.

CONCLUSION

In this chapter we have argued that to try and explain material culture in functionalist terms or subsume it under cross-cultural generalizations is entirely unsatisfactory. Instead we should be thinking in terms of human potentialities linked with social constraints rather than the asocial and the environmental. Material culture forms a set of resources, a symbolic order in practice, something drawn on in political relations, activated and manipulated in ideological systems. In other words, material culture is actively involved in the social world. We have suggested that material culture should be regarded as a social production rather than an individual creation. Conceived as a form of communication it constitutes a form of 'writing' and is located along structured axes of signification. We are not attempting to argue that material culture, in a manner analagous to language, directly represents things, features or concepts in the social world, but that it is ordered in relation to the social. The structure of this ordering is of vital significance. Material culture is polysemous, located along open systems of signified–signifiers or metacritical signs. This means that we can never exhaust or pin down its meaning once and for all. Material culture in the archaeological record consists of a set of conjunctions and repetitions with meaning shifting between different levels and contexts. Interpreting material culture might be regarded as a kind of translation which is essentially transformative and does not aim at a recovery of original meaning. Given the intersubjective context of the production and use of material culture there is no original meaning to be recovered as the meaning depends on the structured and positioned social situation of the individual.

5

Time and Archaeology

In about 2400 BC people began to live in a small community of stone houses at Skara Brae in the Orkneys. They kept cows and sheep, ate shellfish, made furniture out of stone, and made basically the same sort of pots for perhaps 500 years. It would seem that little changed over that stretch of time. How are we to understand those centuries of life when compared with time in comtemporary capitalism and consumerist change? The issue is one of the meaning of material culture and the character of social structures which we have considered in earlier chapters. It is also an issue of the meaning of time itself.

Most of the human past is the province of archaeology: vast stretches of time. Yet there is virtually no discussion of time in archaeology. It is assumed as an unproblematic dimension. We aim to direct attention to this lacuna, to challenge conventional assumptions about time. Is time a dimension? What is the meaning of chronology? How is time related to social change? Is time the dimension of the historical disciplines? Is there a specifically archaeological time – long term as opposed to short term? How are past and present related in terms of time? We intend to argue that these questions are vital to a critical reflection on contemporary archaeology.

THE TIME OF CHRONOLOGY

Chronology: spatial time

Any inquiry into the past which does not reckon with the dimension of time is obviously nonsense; the past *is* the past by virtue of the place it occupies in the time-scale.

(Piggott, 1959, p. 63)

The archaeological text legislates on chronology. Relative and absolute; stratification and radiocarbon: time in archaeology is presented as sequence and date. Time is identified as a dimension. Each object or feature has a temporal attribute, objective and quantifiable. This is its date, a universal index or scale according to which everything may be related and compared. Time as dimension is thus conceived spatially as location and distance. As a diachronic dimension (abstract in that it is a neutral attribute separate from that to which it refers), time provides a framework or context within which the traces of the past may be situated and ordered.

Time in the space of excavation

Chronology is applied to the traces of the past to bring order and sense. It is a technology for the reduction of difference and the production of meaning.

It is the excavation which establishes difference. The excavation produces variety and variability in space – the three dimensional volume of the site containing artefacts, features and layers. The archaeological imperatives are to reduce this difference to similarity, order, and to establish meaning. Reduction of difference involves the identification of spatial pattern and temporal sequence. The concept of stratigraphy translates variation in space into variation in time, establishes relationships in time. Technologies for identifying spatial pattern include taxonomics (locating artefact, feature and site in a hierarchy of ordering taxa) and spatial analysis.

Chronology and change

It is not now often accepted that any pattern produced is meaningful in itself. There is the problem of the origin, meaning and development of the ordered, classified archaeological universe. The traditional answer to this problem is a narrative of 'cultures', involving concepts of innovation, diffusion of ideas, population shift and, more generally, notions of evolutionary progress – from savagery to civilization.

The new archaeology of the 1960s and since conceives of the explanation of an identified pattern and sequence in terms of culture process, the workings of culture systems, social systems and cultural evolution. The problem of *social* change has been foregrounded. Agents of change have been variously proposed: prime movers such as population pressure and adaptation to environment; the technomics of economic rationality; the mechanisms of mathematical logic (see the discussions in chapters 2 and 6).

Time is assumed to be a theoretically unproblematic dimension like space. With time and space separable from that to which they refer, change becomes a problem. Change becomes variability associated with time as abstract sequence. Change becomes a catalogue of difference with an abstracted essence, the universal motor of history, generating variability. Time conceived as chronometric space is conceptually separate from social production and reproduction. It is present only as a context, with change as a problem.

Time is separate from space; both are separate dimensions. This separation is associated with a distinction between synchrony and diachrony, social statics and dynamics, with dynamics or change apparently belonging to time. Such a separation is related to functionalist conceptions of the social, organic units open to synchronic analysis; it is related to static conceptions of social entities ordered in evolutionary sequence: band, tribe, chiefdom, early-state module . . .

BAILEY IN THE *APORIAI* OF TEMPORAL LANDSCAPE

The most sophisticated and illuminating discussion of time in archaeology has been produced by Bailey (1981, 1983) and it merits some considerable attention. Arguing for a duality within time, between time as objective process and time as socially and so subjectively represented, he identifies a series of distinctions (not necessarily coincident or parallel):

occurrence	representation
objective	subjective
duration	event
long term	short term
durable	ephemeral
collective	individual
present explained in terms of the *past*	past explained in terms of the *present*
nature	history

Time as process is a function of objective occurrences. This may be distinguished from time as existing in its representation as a product of concepts which are to be related to their social context. The single event, visible in the short term, is distinguished by Bailey from long-term process possessing a duration, *ex hypothesi*, longer than the event. Long-term process is presented by Bailey as going beyond the individual and consequently having a collective aggregate character (not necessarily 'social').

These features of two aspects of time (Bailey assumes that chronology is objective time, its representation is secondary and subjective) are associated with a distinction between academic disciplines. Environmentalist disciplines and the natural sciences aim to explain the present in terms of the past. The present is a dependent category within neutral and objective temporal scales and involves long-term biological and ecological pressures which eclipse the individual. Their frameworks employ cross-cultural and generalizing regularities. For Bailey the social sciences and history extrapolate from necessarily short-term behaviour in the present to explain the past. They assume time to be internal to the social, as part of the social, and regard the social as an independent variable.

To be distinct and non-derivative a discipline must formulate its own concepts and theories, conceptual schemes derived from its own data base. Arguing that archaeological data refer to aggregate behaviours, he proposes that archaeology's temporal index is not the single momentary event but long-term process. Archaeology's temporal scale is *not* that of the other social sciences whose concern is with the short term. To be a distinct and autonomous discipline archaeology must view the past in terms of processes probably not visible in the present. Bailey claims that criticisms of concepts such as adaptation apply only to the scale of the social sciences. In archaeology's scale of long-term continuity the concept of adaptation is meaningful. Archaeology, then, is to be grouped with the natural sciences having an environmentalist perspective.

Scale and the discipline of archaeology

For Bailey archaeology should be concerned with a different order than that of the social sciences, for its scale is different. He suggests that archaeological data refer to aggregates of behaviour, averages which go beyond the individual event, short-term social process, which are the focus of the conceptual schemes of the social scientist. Social process is defined as short term by Bailey, or rather he has it applying to a scale different to that of aggregate behaviour. This definition is simply asserted; he only states that the social sciences must show that social process can be long term. But the ancient city-state displays a continuity of social process that can be historically documented for over a thousand years (de Ste. Croix, 1981; Anderson, 1974). What constitutes long term as opposed to short term? Bailey makes the point that environmental phenomena can be as sudden as social phenomena: flood, drought, earthquake. Clearly the answer cannot be a simple quantitative reference to chronology: short term referring to year by year; long term referring to century by century.

Bailey relates temporal scale to process: different scales refer to different processes. The processes pertain to a hierarchy of natural entities from subatomic particles to organism to society to environment to cosmos. Scales apply to this hierarchy of entities and moreover are incommensurate. The social sciences have their scale and processes; archaeology shall have its own independent scale and processes. The disciplines are incomparable. They exist side by side (although within the same abstract temporal context – chronology). The individual subject of the social sciences has no relation to long term structure.

But this surely implies a contradiction between his assumption of time being chronology and time being specific to process, a contradiction between empty abstracted time and a saturated time inseparable from the process of an entity, a substantial time. How can scales be, in Bailey's own terms, incommensurate within a chronometric time? Furthermore, the process of archaeology he outlines is the logic of economic and ecological relations, adaptive logic within empty chronometric time; the logic and the time are separate. Is there not, in fact, a confusion of logical sequence and temporality? What is the temporality of scale? What is the temporality of all these separate processes? Bailey needs to explain how scale and process or logic has anything to do with temporality. We might say with John Berger that 'reality should never be confused with scale, it is only scale that has degrees' (1984, p. 53).

A great deal is made of the claim that archaeology must be an independent discipline with its own conceptual framework and body of theory. Bailey's arguments about scale are meant to support archaeology being defined as a specific discipline and are meant to resolve or rather neutralize the increasingly emergent splits within it. These rifts have been especially obvious to him at Cambridge, origin of both palaeoeconomy (Bailey's subdiscipline) and the symbolic-structuralist-post-structuralist approach associated with Ian Hodder and others. To Bailey both are acceptable; they simply ask different questions, apply to different processes, different scales. It is pointless arguing one against the other but environmentalist palaeoeconomy is more archaeological. Post-structuralist archaeologies are for Bailey essentially derived from the present. They are nonetheless interesting.

But isn't this simply a way of justifying essentially arbitrary divisions between academic disciplines with the individual separate from an independent realm of long-term 'structural' logic, with incommensurate scales existing within the same spatial time? We argue that all social disciplines, including archaeology, are historical; long and short term, all deal with social practice. Bailey is proposing a disabling theoretical fragmentation for the sake of justifying archaeology as a separate discipline.

A subject of history

The distinctiveness of Bailey's archaeology lies in its aggregate data. Again the objective is given primacy. But what constitutes aggregate behaviour? He makes the point that the whole is more than the sum of the parts. But what are the parts and what is the sum? To what, in his natural hierarchy of entities, does archaeology refer? What is the subject of 'archaeological' process? It is presumably not 'society' but a natural, as opposed to a social, entity. Is it 'Man' ('Woman') and 'Nature'? Whatever Bailey's answer (he does not provide one in the two papers concerned with time), he must report to a metaphysics, an idealism. Bailey's proposed archaeology is idealist in that it assumes an essential principle or subject of archaeological history. History is assumed as a coherent order, the workings not of social process (incoherent in the long term) – but of what? A *ratio naturae* with its adaptive logic? The logic of hyperscale?

Bailey opposes history to nature, taking the natural as the ontological first principle – *prima ratio* – the eternal against which 'Man' is measured. History is defined as a separate and incommensurate order. In this sense his archaeology is no history at all.

Bailey's archaeology is a universal history applying to 'humanity' from the moment such an entity can be defined. His scales and separate subjects assume an independent regularity, single themes for different scales. The archaeologist is to become initiate in the as yet mysterious laws of this reason, searching for the key to diversity, the pattern, the regularity. Time is divided into subject and law, metaphysical entities *natura* and *ratio*. In Bailey's non-historical history human experience and suffering are dismissed as belonging to another scale, subjective, contingent; absorbed, rationalized into adaptive logic; subjected to the Law:

natural reason, *ratio*, a goddess wreaking vengeance on those who mark not the will of *natura*.

Past and present

Archaeology is to find its essential reality, its subject and its scale. The archaeologist is observer of this reality; Bailey's idealism is contemplative. Archaeology is locked into its time, the present, observing a distant or rather incommensurate archaeological past. But this temporal distance is postulated a priori. It is a function of associating tense with date: conceiving the 'past' as of a different date and so distant from the 'present'. Where is the present in Bailey's spatial time? It becomes a durationless and invisible instant in the overwhelming flow.

Bailey's scheme of independent scales is logically connected with the paradoxes of the division of time as dimension. The possibility of the infinite subdivision of a chronometric time ends in the durationless instant. This becomes the essence of temporality, just as abstract space ends and begins in the dimensionless point.

The material event is the province of the archaeological past, a past which cannot, in Bailey's idealism, be thought as a present. He presents no conceptual apparatus for dealing with the past as a present – it is over and lost because of the nature of archaeological data, and for Bailey the data are determinate. To treat the past as a present, he says must result in archaeology being a derivative discipline. The data are far better now for producing generalizations about social process. But this is to privilege generalization and again assumes a homogeneous past, a unified and rational past.

Nor is there an adequate consideration of the past in the present, the presence of the past, the time of the archaeologist, the historiographic issue of the production of the past. He considers that different archaeologies merely ask different questions of the same data. The relation between present archaeologist and past artefact is assumed to be unproblematic – simple reflection in thought? The titles of both of his papers on time in archaeology ('Concepts, time-scales and explanations in economic prehistory' and 'Concepts of time in Quaternary prehistory') refer to *concepts* of time, but what is the relation of concept to 'reality'? This is not considered.

Bailey's dual conception of time amounts to a radical separation of past and present and a valuation of the former; the past is where we are to find ontological and disciplinary security. The present and subjective time, that is time as experienced and lived, time as implicated in social relations, is marginalized. Human consciousness is treated as an event like any other. Objective occurrence is distinguished from representation in symbolic structures. He thus adheres to a split between material event and mental appropriation. Bailey does mention that time is related to social structure, but this relation is again lost in the archaeological past. He also accepts that ideas of time may have had an influence on behaviour in the past and refers to time scheduling and budgeting in subsistence practices: a logistical time of calculation.

CHRONOLOGY AND ITS ORIGINS

But what is the meaning of such temporality – the time of measurement and calculation? Is such a conception of time itself atemporal? We argue that temporality itself is historical, that any definition of history is itself historical, and deny any chronology which claims universality.

Spatial neutral time, the time of archaeological taxonomics, Bailey's fragmented temporality, are capitalism's chronometry.

> History since the French Revolution has changed its role. Once it was the guardian of the past: now it has become the midwife of the future. It no longer speaks of the changeless but, rather, of the laws of change which spare nothing . . . Social life which once offered an example of relative permanence is now the guarantor of impermanence.
>
> (Berger, 1984, p. 12)

Change is transformation, metamorphosis of the object. It belongs to the object. But chronology is an index, a law applying to all events, a single all-powerful force. Change under the law of chronology becomes an aspect of time itself. Time as chronology, abstract and inhuman, the law or principle which applies to everything, becomes in Bailey's archaeology death triumphant over all, adaptation, *fatum naturae*. No longer a condition of social existence and life, time becomes sentence and punishment. The archaeologist becomes the executor of the law and people become the objects of history.

Contemporary chronology flows. The past is lost in the distance in the unceasing flow, exotic, mysterious and a problem. The past is no longer organically related to the present. The present represents ephemerality; the present is itself lost in the flow. This corresponds to the impermanence of consumerism, but also refers to the possibility of social change in the non-Western world, the promise of social revolution. Contemporary historical existence, historicity, is both violence and possibility: violence to life, actual and symbolic, and the possibility of revolution and change (Berger, 1984).

Capitalism's chronometry is the calculus for organizing and programming labour. It is a commodified time allowing the calculation and comparison of incommensurate labours. It is an ideology of production. Chronometric time is money. Chronometry is the time of the factory clock. The private and the public are separated as work-time and leisure-time. Lived time is marginalized; times other than chronometry destroyed, condemned as subjective, irrational, superstition.

This is not to long for an age before capitalism's colonization of time. Contemporary historicity is the emergence of a sense of possibility, a possibility enabling a prospect of social justice, that the present may be changed, that it is not under the guardianship of a mythical past. Not nostalgia, but what is needed is a mediation of Bailey's oppositions.

This is to undo the identification of reason with reality, the identification of chronology with the reality of time. In this way nature and history come to mediate each other: what appears as natural is historical production, and the identification of history with what happened – objective occurrence – is dissolved in terms of the concrete existence of the past. So the past is not assimilated into the time of the archaeologist but realized as discontinuous with the present, realized as being more than its representation by the archaeologist.

TIME AND PRAXIS

We can agree with Bailey that time is to be grasped in relation to particular processes. Time is thus substantial, not a dimension, not a context. Context is to be subverted. Context is not exterior; there is no stable 'event' and its 'context'. Temporal interval does not consist of emptiness. Time exists in the relation between presence and absence, both physical and temporal. Intervals are a part of presences, defining, marking edges, structuring difference. There is a chronic reciprocity between past, present and future. So the archaeological past exists as a future project in the present, in the social practice of archaeology. No time then exists in itself as abstract date or whatever. Time is not an abstract existent, contentless form. As we have argued, this would require a metaphysics of time. Substantial time is to replace the momentary present with the event of *presencing*. Presencing is a historic present, 'mutual reaching out and opening up of future, past and present' (Heidegger, 1972, p. 14), holding them together in their difference, a relational nexus. Time is the event of praxis. So instead of length of time we should refer to the density of relations of practice.

Time is a condition of social practice. As we have stressed earlier (chapter 3), in social practice social actors draw on structures which enable action and in the action reproduce those structures. So every social act implicates different temporalities: the occasion or event of the action; the life history of the social actor; and the institutional time of structure. This is the *social* logic of 'scale'.

In arguing against a 'Hegelian' total and abstract time, Althusser proposes multiple temporalities within a social formation – times specific to the separate instances: economic, political, legal and ideological (Althusser and Balibar, 1970, chapter 4). There is thus no single unifying time, no single 'now'. The only unity to different temporalities is their location within a structured social formation. While not agreeing with Althusser's characterization of 'social formation' we agree that time is unavoidably implicated in social logic. So chronology does not explain, nor does it provide a context. It is part of that which is to be understood.

Time may not involve chronology, as we shall illustrate in a moment. Synchronic does not necessarily mean at the same date; at the same date does not mean that two events were necessarily synchronous. Dates act as taxa, uniting 'events' according to an abstract calculus. We argue instead that any synchrony and diachrony must arise out of the social structures of which they are a part. Bailey was lost in the abstract landscape of a quantitative and spatial time. We can conceive a substantial time as an eventful landscape of continuity and discontinuity: structured difference.

A history of times

Our point is that different temporal orientations shape history itself.

'The moment is a moment' (Bourdieu reporting an Algerian peasant)
(1963, p. 59)

Time for the Algerian peasant is not measured but marked. There are not spatial points of division, segments of regular succession, but self-enclosed, discontinuous units. Points of reference are supplied by experience of the agricultural cycle: a ritual calendar. The peasant temporality of tradition is not coincident with chronology.

Marked time	Measured time
Submission to the passage of time	Managed time
Self-enclosed recurrent moments	Repetitive segments of regular succession
The *forthcoming*: exalted by tradition	*Future* void, open
Imitation of past; conformity with ancestral model	Design of a projected future
Concrete horizon of the present; single context of meaning	Mutually exclusive possibility
Reading signs to which tradition provides the key	'Rational' calculation
Deferred consumption (hoarding)	Abstract absent accumulation
Gift	Credit
Social imperative	'Rational' choice
SUBSTANTIAL TIME	ABSTRACT TIME

The measured time of abstract chronology, to be managed, calculated, saved and expended, is distinct from the peasants' immersion in a substantial time, a mythology in action, a submission to the passage of time, with no one dreaming of 'saving time', 'spending time'. The future in an abstract quantitative chronometry is a void of mutually exclusive possibilities, a time to come to be forecast; the forthcoming of substantial temporality is a single context of meaning, the concrete horizon of the present exalted by tradition, to be an imitation of the past, conforming to the ancestral model. To presume to calculate the future is hubris. So rational calculation of the future, opening up possibility, opposes a prophetic readings of signs for which tradition furnishes the key, a reduction of possibility. Provision for the forthcoming involves hoarding, concrete deferred consumption, opposed to abstract absent accumulation. The gift, with debt a social and moral issue, is distinct from credit. Social imperative opposes rational 'economic' choice.

Reason (1979) locates what he calls the textual time of the peasant and capitalism's abstract time in the organization of production and relates this distinction to different forms of classification. Socialized production by the peasant family is orientated towards use-values of anticipated products that are qualitatively distinct and strictly not commensurable. Accounting practices and orientation to abstractly commensurable exchange-values are inapplicable. Peasant work-time is substantial, rooted in concrete labour: 'work time is a physiognomy of subsistence' (Reason, 1979, p. 229). Conversely, capitalist labour presupposes an abstract temporal frame: time is money. Reason opposes abstract repetitive temporality to a textual time, a temporality that constitutes and is 'constituted in, the narrative account as the prime formula for reflecting [upon] the curses and causes of events, and provides the essential means of explicating the sense of the accomplished facts of life . . . With textual time, we deal not with a dimension but with a way of grasping one's living' (ibid., pp. 230–1). He relates textual time to a world composed by exemplification – 'the production of signs which "possess" that to which they refer' (p. 237) – categorization as opposed to a system of classification.

Classification implies a separation of sign and sense, an arbitrary signifier with a stable structure of rules and articulatory criteria of identity which transcend the particular occasion. Reason here refers to Saussure's observation that in linguistics 'as in political economy we are confronted with the notion of *value*: both sciences are concerned with a *system for equating things of different orders* – labour and wages in one and signified and signifier in the other' (Reason, 1979, p. 241, citing Saussure, 1974, p. 79; Saussure's italics). In both, time is an indexical quality. These orders of temporality are clearly implicated in social practice. It should also be noted that they are not mutually exclusive: we can understand the time of the peasant, just as the peasant can understand chronology. The important point is the *structural relation of time to social practice*, the social and historical production of time.

Lévi Strauss has written that

The characteristic feature of the savage mind is its timelessness; its object is to grasp the world as both a synchronic and a diachronic totality and the knowledge which it draws therefrom is like that afforded of a room by mirrors fixed on opposite walls, which reflect each other (as well as objects in the intervening space) although without being strictly parallel. A multitude of images forms simultaneously, none exactly like any other, so that no single one furnishes more than a partial knowledge of the decoration and furniture but the group is characterised by invariant properties expressing a truth. The savage mind deepens its knowledge with the help of *imagines mundi*. It builds mental structures which facilitate an understanding of the world in as much as they resemble it. In this sense savage thought can be defined as analogical thought.

(Lévi-Strauss, 1966, p. 263)

He has distinguished systems of totemic classification from history. In totemic system 'history' is eliminated or integrated; in the Western present the historical process is internalized, becoming a force of change. As we have already described, Western chronology transcends discontinuity and difference, closing gaps, relating events and objects to one another. The totemic system remains faithful to the timeless model of the past, the authority of tradition, the legitimacy of absolute antiquity. The mythical past appears as separate from the present. The ancestors, creators, were different to ordinary people, their imitators; the mythical past is joined to the present because nothing has been going on since the appearance of the ancestors except events whose recurrence periodically overcomes their particularity. The historical process is not denied but admitted as form without content. There are before and after, but each reflects the other.

The traditional is the predictable, bringing past into present, shortening chronology into present memory and model of the mythical past. This predictability is not the mechanical predictability of the identification of prediction and explanation which depends on a temporality of date and sequence. It is a predictability which arises from incorporating or eclipsing historicity, breaking chains of events which have not occurred before, a predictability which is a social accomplishment.

The rhythm and nature of social change is related to social temporality. Tradition's temporality is short, a thin overlay on the authority of a timeless and mythical past. Chronology is thus compressed. We might say that tradition's temporality is of a different 'scale' to that of contemporary Western historicity.

We can make reference here to Gurvitch's (1964) typology of time. He specifies the parameters and forms of social time and relates these to types of social frames and societies. His eight forms of social time depend on different relations between past, present and future, greater and lesser duration, continuity and discontinuity, contingency and necessity, qualitative and quantitative. *Enduring time* (the time of slowed down long duration) involves the past

> projected in the present and in the future. This is the most continuous of the social times despite its retention of some proportion of the qualitative and the contingent penetrated with multiple meanings. For example, the ecological level moves in this time, particularly its demographic aspect. The past is relatively remote, yet it is dominant and projected into the present and the future: the latter thereby risks annihilation. It loses much of its concrete and qualitative coloration, and for this reason can be expressed in ordinary quantitative measures more easily than all other times. The quantitative measures, however, always remain inadequate. Kinship and locality groupings, especially the rural, are the particular groupings which tend to move in this time.
>
> (Gurvitch, 1964, p. 31)

Other types of time include cyclical time where past, present and future are mutually projected into one another with an accentuation of continuity and a weakening of contingency with the qualitative element emphasized (ibid., p. 32); and explosive time where the present as well as the past are dissolved in the creation of an immediately transcended future: discontinuity, contingency and the qualitative are stressed (p. 33). Other parameters are real lived time as opposed to the perception and awareness of time, and the control and mastery of time.

Gurvitch's social frames and societies, correlated with these different times, include social levels (ecological base, practice, symbol and value systems, collective consciousness), interpersonal and intergroup relations, structured and unstructured social groups (such as kinship groups, organizations), social classes, archaic, historical and contemporary societies. While we oppose the strong typological basis of such work it is nevertheless a useful heuristic. What needs emphasis is the social production of times – their relation to determinate structures of power and interest. So we need to consider the ideological implications of the temporality of tradition (described above) and the relationship between writing and time.

Writing transforms the temporality of tradition, extending time, producing the absent present in the graphical trace. Writing first appears as the list, as a means of storage. No longer the storage of ritual information in the memory of the initiate in tradition, writing allows the creation and control of information, of records and archives (cf. Goody, 1978). As such it is the basis of the development of surveillance and forms of social control. Inscription is duration; writing transforms temporality, but temporality itself is not neutral. As an aspect of social practice, temporality is related to social control, written into relations of power.

From historicism to the historicity of discourse

Zeno says what is in motion moves neither in the place it is nor in the one in which it is not.

Diogenes Laertius IX, 72

Aristotle summarises Zeno's third paradox: The arrow in flight is at rest.

Physics Z9 239b30

Zeno seems to have argued as follows:

1　The arrow at rest in the present moment is contained in space just its own size.
2　The arrow in flight in the present moment is contained in space just its own size.
3　In the present moment the arrow in flight is at rest.
4　The arrow in flight is always in its present, a sequence of present moments.
5　The arrow in flight is always at rest.

This is the paradox of statics and dynamics, synchrony and diachrony, of time as date, moment, sequence, and duration as length.

But there is at least one resolution: the arrow flies and is at rest when it is drawn. The paradox is resolved in the act of inscription (Barthes, 1982a, pp. 232–3).

The *telos* of objective chronologies is historicism where the artefact is explained in terms of its location within its time, within events and relations contemporary with it. Past is separated from observing present, each located on a chronometric continuum. The *telos* is eternal image. But what of the event of observation, of excavation, of analysis, of writing? Objective chronologies eclipse this *historia rerum gestarum* with the *res gestae*; discourse is eclipsed by artefact and attribute, digging by the site.

Mediating past and present

Time is established as social practice. Archaeology is established as social practice; it is a relation between past and present, the story told and its telling. The artefact then is not in itself; it emerges in the social practice of archaeology. So archaeology's object is not an eternal image. Archaeology is act of excavation, act of writing. Archaeology is a specific act of engagement with the past. So we need to move from contemplative, distanced representation, an image that goes beyond time, to the material act of production, act of excavation and inscription, acts which have their own time. The past is 'the subject of a construction whose locus is not empty time, but the particular epoch, the particular life, the particular work' (Benjamin, 1979, p. 352); each is to be broken from historical continuity in the act of engaging with the past. So understanding the past is not to look back along a continuum which has led to the present. It is not to escape the present to see the past in itself. Understanding the past is to break with the past.

This is not to put the past at risk. The past can only be determinate by virtue of the present. To be in itself the past requires the exteriority of the present interpreter, the archaeologist. Past and present must be held in tension, in relation. To conceive of the archaeologist as executor of the laws of time, of change, of natural reason is to disguise the assimilation of the time of the past to a universal homogeneity. To preserve the time of the past we must accept paradoxically the past's coexistence with the present, its relation in the present. What separates past from present is not knowledge, it is not date: it is the temporality of the past, the experience of time as it was in the past. This means that people of the past cannot be controlled as is implied in their assimilation to abstract chronology. We can only trace them in the time they live and we perceive. The past, the time is theirs. But the meaning of the past is the present's.

The tension between the past and the present involves a redescription of past events in the light of subsequent events unknown to the actors themselves; it involves the creation of temporal wholes, historical plots. It is not possible to know of the past as witnesses of the past. This is the fallacy of empathy: that the subject, the social actor of the past is the locus of history. To understand the past as archaeologist is to know the past as temporal wholes. It is vital to emphasize that these do not involve the foregone conclusions of universal history, but there are successions or developments in the past and it is the task of the archaeologist to elucidate and understand them. As Adorno has remarked, 'no universal history leads from savagery to civilisation, but there is one which leads from the slingshot to the hydrogen bomb' (Adorno, 1973, p. 320). It is the archaeologist in the present who develops the plot, the narrative.

The event of archaeology; the archaeological event

There is no *one thing*, no *some thing*, nor *such a thing whatsoever*. But it is from motion or being carried along, from change and from admixture with each other that everything comes to be which we declare to 'be', speaking incorrectly, for nothing ever is, but always becomes.

(Plato, *Theaitetos* 152d)

To say 'what is emerges' is to say that nothing exists in itself but emerges or comes to be in a field of relations with others, emerges as different to something else. It is also to say that what is emerges from its transformation. For archaeology this transformation occurs especially in the text.

The past is excavated away. It must be recorded. The artefact is described, drawn, symbolized; the event is similarly represented. The past emerges in the archaeological text. Metaphor and allegory are thus central to archaeology. Archaeological metaphor: an assertion of identity in difference; the past is represented but the difference, the tension between the past and its archaeological representation remains. The archaeological past cannot be simply represented or precisely imitated. There is no unmetamorphosed reality of the past now.

The past decays, is dismantled, and is constructed. The past is not 'discovered' or simply presented to perceptive consciousness. Artefact is not simply added to artefact, event to event, to accumulate an archaeological past. The past is dis-closed; its elements are grasped together in the archaeological judgement which constructs meaningful wholes, meaningful pasts. So the artefact is not simply the past but is inherently reflective, mediated and mediatory, uniting past and present. It is critical, that is existing in the time of *krisis* or judgement, the archaeological act which brings together past and present. Archaeology then is a mediated relation between what happened and its representation, between being historical and doing history. So our historicity is in part doing archaeology: this is simply to say that the past is temporally inseparable from the event of archaeology.

Now the archaeological event does not exist: the event has no existential reality. There is no stable 'event', singular objective occurrence, 'this happened then'. So what is an event? The idea of event was the focus of the ideographic/nomothetic distinction as applied to archaeology especially by Trigger (1978). Is archaeology a historical or a natural discipline? Is its subject the unique and particular historical event, or a logic of the (social) event in general? This distinction was often assumed to coincide with the difference between traditional and new archaeology, between humanist historical narrative and hard science providing explanation through generalization. But a universe of radically dissimilar particular events is meaningless, a literal chaos or non-sense; while a scientific archaeology subsumes the particularity of the past beneath an abstract concept of occurrence – an event is conceived as simply that which occurs. This is to oppose abstract concepts of the particular and the universal and begs the whole question of the meaning of history.

An event is an abstraction but an abstraction from a configuration of which it is a component; an event only makes sense in terms of a meaningful whole, a historical plot. So an event cannot exist in itself; it cannot be separated from its context, its relations with other events and meanings which contribute to the understanding of plot. The event is more than singular occurrence. And scale is not a reality but a construction.

So the practice of archaeology is a construction of pasts. It establishes event as event, artefact as artefact. The event emerges from archaeology; the event, time, duration is inscription.

We can draw some implications. We said above that metaphor and allegory are central to archaeology; archaeology is unavoidably historio-*graphesis*. It is a system of regimes for production of the 'past'. What is needed is a theory of archaeological inquiry: an archaeological topology (a rhetoric); an archaeological tropology (a stylistics); an archaeological poetics asking how the past is to be written, how the past can be represented without identifying it with its inscription in the present. To say the past is written, that it emerges in inscriptions, is not to give primacy to text. It is to direct attention to the tension between the traces of the past, now over, completed, and their representation in discourse. It is to direct attention to the mediation of the historical and fiction, the fictive, that which is created. How can the past be expressed as completed without making it a point in an abstract temporal continuum? It is necessary again to challenge a unified past of formal coherence, to point attention instead to the meaning of archaeological plot and ask the meaning of third-person report, of synthesizing narrative, the disguises of figure and allegory. It is to ask why archaeologies are written *now*; how and why they make sense, if they do.

The question of time in archaeology is not a neutral and academic question of method. Archaeology is not simply filling out an empty time with the debris of history. Time is not simply a neutral dimension in an academic discipline. Archaeology's appropriation of the past is a moral and political act. Choosing a past, that is constituting a past, is choosing a future; the ideology of contemporary archaeology's temporality is that it is imposing a Western valuation of measured abstract time on a multitude of pasts which cannot answer for themselves – even the dead aren't safe. The event of archaeology is disguised in a separation of past and present with present disappearing and past becoming spectacle, entertainment, illustration. We hope to have initiated a challenge to this regime of archaeological temporality, and in the following chapter consider the implication of time in social change, one of the most important areas of archaeological theory.

6

Social Evolution and Societal Change

In this chapter we wish to address the question of social change and the manner in which transformations in the archaeological record may be described, assessed and interpreted. Nowhere is the intimate connection between archaeological theory and wider social theory so evident as in considerations of social change in terms of a long temporal perspective. In a very real sense the study of long-term social change marks out an intellectual field in which archaeology and social theory do not just come together, with perhaps slightly different perspectives, but actually coalesce. Consequently, we will be concerned to analyse conceptualizations of long-term change within the broad context of the sociological literature and archaeological texts, and in historical perspective.

The question of why and how social change occurs is vital to archaeology. Indeed, for many archaeologists it provides the justification for archaeology as a worthwhile academic pursuit. What other discipline can boast such a temporal perspective on humanity? By comparison, sociologists and anthropologists (even historians) lack such temporal data. They can, at best, hope to provide fairly synchronic 'snapshot' views of social totalities in which processes governing change have to be inferred from a delimited 'slice' cut through an ongoing temporal sequence. Despite such claims, frequently made in the archaeological literature, it is worth noting that no distinctive theories of change have been produced by archaeologists, nor does it seem likely that there will be any in the future. All theories of social change utilized in the discipline are derived from the wider social sciences and then used as modelling devices for considering temporal and spatial alterations in archaeological sequences. As in all other areas of archaeological theory and practice, views of the past are thoroughly embedded in the present.

Both social theorists and archaeologists, when considering social change over long time spans have relied heavily on some notion of evolutionary development, whether working within a Marxist or non-Marxist framework. It is almost impossible to exaggerate the profound influence an evolutionary conception of society has had in considerations of the relationship between past and present. A tendency to think in evolutionary or developmental terms has been pervasive in Western thought since, at least, the Enlightenment. It forms part and parcel of the nineteenth-century origins of both archaeology and sociology as academic disciplines. Archaeological views of the past have been greatly influenced by social theory of an evolutionary type and, in turn, archaeology has been used in social theory to provide a broader temporal perspective for its consideration of the nature of change.

We discuss a number of influential evolutionary perspectives used in archaeology and social theory to conceptualize change, studies relating change to forms of economic exploitation and the environment within a systemic framework, cultural evolutionary, Marxist and structural Marxist perspectives. In particular, we intend to urge that any notion of social evolution is theoretically flawed and almost always embodies unwarranted ethnocentric evaluations. We suggest that evolutionary theories, of whatever kind, need to be abandoned in favour of a theoretical framework that can adequately cope with the indelibly social texture of change within a framework avoiding both reductionism and essentialism.

SOCIAL CHANGE AND SOCIAL SYSTEM

Systems theory

Systems theory was introduced into archaeology primarily in order to explain change. Paradoxically, as utilized, it is a conservative theory of persistence and stability (see chapter 2). Accounting for change has always been the major problem with the approach. This is a result of the emphasis put upon homoeostasis and pattern maintenance, and owes much to the old Hobbesian problem of order, or how is society possible in the struggle between competing individuals, in the battle between all against all? In classical sociology, and in the systemic perspective, this 'problem' becomes resolved by the internalization of social facts, norms or values into the consciousness of individuals in the form of needs dispositions providing motivational referents for individualized action. Society becomes treated in a reified manner in which change takes place 'behind the backs' of social actors who become irrelevant to the analysis, mere 'components' of the system (Cooke and Renfrew, 1979). The sole theoretical function of the individual is to act as an offset to the social realm, so serving to establish, in this difference, the existence of the specific realm of the social.

Systems theory provides a form of functional analysis no different from the Malinowskian functionalism which dominated anthropology until the late 1950s or the functionalist sociology of Parsons (1952) or Merton (1957), based more or less on organismic and physiological analogies. Any functional explanation of change presupposes some needs, wants or goals. In other words it is teleological in form. Something occurs as the result of reaching towards or pertaining to a desirable state. Individuals may be very well said to have needs. Indeed it is a fundamental feature of humanity to have aspirations and desires. By contrast, social systems themselves have no needs, they have no need to function, to survive, to attain a goal range or to seek out homoeostatic states. The needs of the social system cannot be independent of the actors which make it up so any notion of system function or subsystem function or the function of rituals or other institutionalized practices is entirely irrelevant and misplaced. But in a systems perspective feedback processes cannot be conceptualized except in terms of some goal unless they are just random, but to anthropomorphize such processes is invalid.

Why change should occur becomes a very real problem in a systemic perspective because the system has been defined in such a way that stability is a norm. In other words, systems theory, as utilized in archaeology, has a theoretical structure describing how a system is maintained but not how it is transformed. The theoretical structure is not isomorphic with the ontological structure it seeks to represent. Change via positive feedback mechanisms is always circumscribed and does not really penetrate the internal structure. The concepts used to analyse change are no different from those used to explain system equilibrium, and the processes operating to change a system are the same as those serving to maintain it in a stable state. They are only different forms of regulated feedback. So in order to explain change a position of exogenous causality must be resorted to. As a normative consensus is attributed to the social actors within the system (whom, we are led to suppose, all live together in a fairly harmonious fashion, with few internal conflicts, tensions, struggles for power, and contradictory sets of interests or wants), changes can only occur as a result of pressures induced from outside the system. Hill (1977, p. 76) claims that to think that internal tensions might promote systems change merely 'begs the question' as to why these arise and this must result from factors external to the system impinging upon it. Plog argues that changes *are* constantly occurring in systems but these will always be 'deviation-countering changes' (1974, p. 47). However, under 'abnormal' conditions

> there are conditions under which a change is so great that the response fails to restore the initial equilibrium. These conditions are called *environmental changes*, and the behavioural or sociocultural responses to them are called *morphogenic* or *deviation-amplifying* changes.
>
> (Ibid, p. 47)

The view is that the cumulative effect of regulatory mechanisms and deviation countering devices will offset and countermand change unless there is a particularly violent oscillation in the system's environment which causes the normal operation of the homoeostatic mechanisms to break down. Positive feedback processes are then set into operation until a new state of equilibrium is reached.

Despite the general view, repeatedly advocated (most recently by Juteson and Hampson, 1985), that a systems framework is superior to other models of change because it enables change to be explained in terms of multivariate causality, in practice the approach all too often leads to the postulation of a few 'prime movers' such as exchange (Renfrew, 1969, 1972), population increase (Cohen, 1977) or the environment (Binford, 1964; Flannery, 1968; Plog, 1974). Of these the second, population increase, is undoubtedly the most popular and it is difficult to find texts ostensibly explaining change which do not use this supposedly independent variable to explain why change – any kind of change – occurs (e.g. Bradley, 1981; Sherratt, 1981; Dolukhanov, 1986), irrespective of whether or not a systems perspective is explicitly adopted. This kind of universal recipe is, in fact, no more than an easy way out. It remains non-explanatory in precisely the same way as the 'normative' diffusionist theories to which the new archaeology so strongly objected.

Plog (1974) in his 'dynamic-equilibrium' model of change isolates four features promoting change, which he also refers to as 'growth': population, differentiation, integration and energy. The first refers to the size of the system; the second to the number of 'parts'; the third to the strength of internal system ties; and the fourth to the nature and quality of the resources utilized in the system. His analysis, in common with many others, suffers from *double determination*. Plog characterizes systems as having inbuilt emergent properties and as changing adaptively in relation to the environment. These two modes of determination of systems change are theoretically incompatible. Plog states that differentiation 'refers to evolution from multi-functional role structures to more special ones' (1974, p. 62) while also stating that 'changes in the loci of resources being utilized by an adaptation and experimentation with new resources may account for changes in differentiation' (ibid., p. 64). On the one hand, then, systems change becomes teleological, an inbuilt capacity towards change in the direction of increased differentiation; and at the same time change occurs as a result of environmental adaptation. The effectiveness of the one would appear to preclude that of the other.

Systems theory and cultural evolution

Binford asserted that White's cultural evolutionism (1959) had 'laid the theoretical basis for a logicodeductive science of culture' (Binford, 1972, p. 110) and this involved viewing culture as an extrasomatic means of adaptation. He argued that evolutionary change was change occurring within maximizing systems which included the adaptation of social systems to their environments, the more efficient use of resources and energy flux. Concomitantly, 'evolutionary processes are one form of ecological dynamics' (ibid., p. 106). The unit of evolutionary relevance is not changes in parts of social systems which, according to him, may be given a functional explanation, but changes in the integrated system as a whole. Evolution thus takes place as a result of the interaction of the total social system with its environmental field, and adequate explanations 'must make reference to forms and kinds of selective pressures operative in concrete environments' (ibid., p. 109). For Binford, if statements are to be explanatory rather than descriptive, this requires the formulation of evolutionary laws to relate relationships between the environmental field and the socio-cultural system. The search is for universal processes underlying different empirical sequences of societal change, and the reason for this change is environmental adaptation.

Flannery's linkage of systems theory with a cultural evolutionary perspective is important because he is prepared to view change as arising from within as well as from outside the system. He criticizes 'prime mover' explanations, concentrating attention on one or a few variables and proposing multivariate causality. For him, an adequate explanatory framework requires us to distinguish between: (1) the processes of evolutionary change; (2) the mechanisms by means of which these processes take place; (3) the socio-environmental stresses which serve to activate the mechanisms (Flannery, 1972, p. 409). According to Flannery, the processes and mechanisms are universal features of evolutionary development not only in human societies but in all living systems, whereas different selective stresses may be specific to any particular trajectory or evolutionary sequence. Social evolution is to be understood in terms of increasing segregation or differentiation and centralization or integration. Two possible mechanisms are discussed, promotion and linearization, corresponding to the twin processes of segregation and centralization. Promotion is the mechanism by means of which an institution or lower level office such as chiefdomship moves to a higher position in the total system with expanded and generalized functions. It results in increasing segregation of the system. Linearization or the expropriation of lower order by higher order controls leads to increasing centralization of the system. Segregation, then, is the agent of change.

For Flannery, each member of an evolutionary series (e.g. chiefdom or state) forms a set of structural conditions for further segregation to a higher level of institutions, functions, offices etc. These become, as it were, crystallized at various stages or levels of complexity of articulation by centralization processes. Segregation cannot proceed unabated for the social system would simply tear itself apart from the centrifugal tendencies of promotion mechanisms. In the long run the trend to increasing segregation cannot be stopped as more complex forms of social organization develop as a result of the failure of the simpler forms to fulfil their functions effectively. The new offices and institutions are more flexible than those they replace. So segregation is viewed as a process of development and maturation. It is beneficial and may serve to cure internal 'pathologies' subjecting the system to stress:

> In a multivariant model, we might see the state evolving through a long process of centralization and segregation, brought about by countless promotions and linearizations, in response not only to stressful socio-environmental conditions but also to stress brought on by internal pathologies.
>
> (Flannery, 1972, p. 414)

The use of the term pathology indicates quite clearly the biological analogy that Flannery wants to make and also serves to indicate that a failure of internal system function is a quite extreme condition contrary to an assumed norm of systemic compatibility or, translated into social terms, a normative consensus existing between individuals. It is adaptation to socio-environmental stresses that, for Flannery, as for Binford, provides the overall meaning and direction for evolutionary change. Without it there would be no reason for the segregation and centralization processes. Evolution permits an increasing degree of efficiency and control over the environmental field. If any particular social system is unable to adapt through segregation it is no longer able to maximize its environmental control and resultant energy yield and must be extinguished in the long run. Societies, or those that survive, attain new and higher levels of adaptive efficiency and are able to compete more successfully with their neighbours.

Sanders and Webster reiterate the point that environmental stimuli are 'basic causes of cultural evolution' (1978, p. 251). The model they use outlines various possible evolutionary trajectories from egalitarian societies to states conditioned by the permutation of environmental variables and assumes that population growth occurs, that rates of growth remain constant, and that this is a necessary precondition for evolution (ibid, p. 297). Adaptation simply accommodates people to their environment and permits the development of societal growth and higher order social structures.

SOCIO-CULTURAL EVOLUTION: CHANGE AND DEVELOPMENT

The 'new' archaeology has generally been regarded as marking a revival of explicit interest in evolutionary theory on the part of archaeologists, rather than the largely implicit adherence to vague notions of social evolution found in much of the traditional archaeological literature. The connection made by Binford and Flannery (among others) between the conception of society as a functional system and evolutionary change of such systems through time is thus understandable. However, evolutionary perspectives have *always* played an important role in the discipline, used for example to explain artefact change (see chapter 4, p. 80). A recent survey of American archaeologists carried out in the mid-1970s listed 'the rise of civilisation' and 'sociocultural evolution' as among the top research interests (Schiffer, 1978, p. 154). The literature on evolution continues to grow (e.g. Bintliff (ed.), 1984; Cohen, 1983; Dunnell, 1980; Foley (ed.), 1984; Flannery and Marcus (eds), 1983; McGuire, 1983; Segraves, 1982; Van de Leeuw (ed.), 1981; Wenke, 1981 – to mention only a few examples in the more recent literature).

Social evolution: a nineteenth-century view

The current popularity of evolutionary theory in archaeology seems to be indicative of the discipline being unable to break free from the shackles of its nineteenth-century origins. It is striking how little the level of conceptualization of the social has really altered over the last 120 years.

A general unity of conceptualization underpinned the evolutionary schemes developed during the nineteenth century by Spencer, Morgan and Tylor, among others, irrespective of the details of the various frameworks advocated (Smith, 1973, pp. 27–8). This can be summarized by the following seven points:

1　A totalizing holism. The primary object of study was the entire history of humanity. Culture with a capital C was writ large and conceived as essentially unitary.
2　Gradualism. Social change was conceived to be an incremental and cumulative process without significant discontinuities or ruptures in the historical process.
3　Universality. Change was a generic and natural process shaping humanity and social institutions.
4　Potentiality. Change was conceived as being endogenous and an inherent feature within human societies.
5　A directional trajectory. Social change was neither cyclical nor random but conceived as a unified process leading to human fulfilment.
6　A deterministic perspective. Change being both irreversible and inevitable led from the simple to the complex, from the homogeneous to the heterogeneous.
7　A causal reductionism. Change was at all times and in all places subject to the same causal laws which conferred an underlying logic to the total social process.

Most of these features occur in one form or another in varieties of twentieth century evolutionary theory.

After Spencer became an evolutionist in the early 1840s he wrote sociology as the history of societal evolution. There was no alternative to this since not to consider the social life of human beings as an all-embracing developmental totality would entail the abandonment of large areas of social life as being random and arbitrary. For Spencer, evolution was a unitary process and the theory he advocated covered all types of natural processes from the development of animal species, the maturation of the embryo and the evolution of the solar system, to the development of human society. He did not so much start from the phenomena to be explained as from an ethical and metaphysical position to be established. This was the doctrine of the universality of natural causation and its inevitable corollary, the doctrine that the universe and all things in it have reached their present forms through physically necessitated successive stages (Peel, 1971, p. 132). The source of evolutionary change was derived from an inverted account of Malthus' account of population increase: 'from the beginning population has been the proximate cause of progress . . . It forced men into the social state; made social organisation inevitable; and has developed the social sentiments . . . It is daily pressing us into closer contact and more mutually dependent relationships' (Spencer, 1852, cited in Peel, 1971, pp. 138–9). Population pressure is only a proximate cause and the ultimate source of change Spencer invokes is the inevitable differentiation of human society from homogeneity to heterogeneity: 'from the law that every active force produces more than one change, it is an inevitable corollary that through all time there has been an ever-growing complication of things' (Spencer, 1972, p. 47). Spencer did not just produce a totalizing history; his conception was, quite literally, cosmic. Everything could be reduced to a unitary process.

While the contemporary literature on evolutionary theory in archaeology is not quite so all-embracing as the framework adopted by Spencer and other nineteenth-century evolutionists, the 'explanatory' perspective remains surprisingly similar. European social evolution, from the neolithic to the Iron Age, according to Bintliff, can be explained in terms of

> the relative balance between population density, resource availability and extraction efficiency (cultigens, technical skills). It is suggested that imbalances lead to regular or cyclical 'crashes' of population and linked political superstructure; that dramatic rises in *absolute* population density produce cumulative increases in the surpluses of food, raw material and manpower capable of supporting social hierarchies and complex division of labour; that high levels of *absolute* population density produce authoritarian potential and conflict resolution needs that are met by the elaboration of leadership roles.
>
> (Bintliff, 1984, p. 29).

Bintliff endorses fully the role of population increase as the causative agent in social evolution, asserting that the archaeological record is entirely in keeping with Malthus' postulate of relentless population increase (Bintliff, 1984a, p. 174). Population density, resource availability and extraction efficiency, together with population increase, 'cause' social evolution.

Segraves (1982) similarly asserts the relation of population pressure to available natural resources as a cause of evolutionary change (1982, p. 294) and claims that 'people's "beliefs" and even their value systems as a whole will ultimately change as the mutual and reinforcing feedback between population size and technical and economic organization presses the system in a new direction' (ibid., p. 297).

Such examples indicate how little this evolutionary theorizing has moved beyond Spencer's speculations. Over and over again, the same old 'mechanisms' and 'processes' are drawn out of the hat. And if environmental adaptation, population pressure, resource extraction efficiency and the like are not stressed, then equally reductive explanatory mechanisms are drawn upon. Cohen, for example, states quite unequivocally that 'evolutionary changes in organizations of social relations are exogenic' (1983, p. 164) and that change may be explained solely in terms of boundary–cultural relations of inter-societal dependence for harnessing goods and resources.

Our aim, in the sections that follow, is not to provide a detailed descriptive review of the uses of evolutionary theory to explain societal change in the archaeological record. Instead we wish to identify and criticize some of the fundamental assumptions (found in both nineteenth- and twentieth-century uses of evolutionary theory) underlying the use of an evolutionary perspective, of whatever particular kind, in both social theory and the archaeological literature. All forms of social evolutionary theory, we contend, involve one or a number of the following four features which undermine their validity for an understanding of social change: (1) a spatialized view of time; (2) essentialism and reductionism; (3) problematic connections with biological evolution; (4) ethnocentrism. We shall consider each of these in turn.

Spatialized time

One of the primary justifications for evolutionary theories has always been the claim that they are ideally suited to the study of long-term change over long time spans. Evolutionary theories depend upon a particular conception of time: time as spatial, uniform and abstract; time as a measurable empty duration, or container utterly separate from the human activities that take place in this flow of time (see Chapter 5). Time is supposedly a continuous whole, a spatialized matrix for action. This time is repeatable, vacant, a commodified time utterly different and opposed to lived human time, the time of action and human practice. Such time allows and permits the production of a homogeneous history, a history that claims to be the history of the whole of humanity. It provides justification for the 'equal' treatment of human culture at all times and in all places: the comparative method. Such time permits general classificatory stages to be developed. It allows culture to be compressed into evolutionary sequences.

A qualitative view of substantial human time which would recognize difference is replaced by quantitative classificatory time. So, all 'tribes' are considered to be equal and hierarchically placed in relation to 'chiefdoms', 'bands' or 'states'. History is asserted to be an intelligible unity and continuum, a longitudinal totality made up of logical progression or developments in which there is a continuous concretization of particular social forms. Spatial time becomes equated with change such that in most evolutionary theories the terms time and change become more or less interchangeable. A succession of societal forms in the distance of spatial time invites ethnocentric evaluation and a constitution of the other: the savage, the primitive. Spatial time lends justification to the idea of necessity in the historical process, that things could not be otherwise, they had to happen this way. But people do make history in accordance with an awareness of history, of the humanity of history; that history is a contingent and not a necessary process.

Essentialism, reductionism and social typologies

As well as a spatialized view of time, and partly as a concomitant of it, social evolutionary theories are characterized by either essentialism or reductionism or both. These features permit and encourage its ethnocentrism. Although evolutionary theories are ostensibly about change in spatial time, by means of a reductionist line of argument they contradict this emphasis and instead assert stability – the static developmental processes or essential characteristics of social forms that are supposed to induce change.

Beneath the transformations in social and political systems evolutionary theories attempt to reveal stability, and paradoxically this is always considered to be primary when dealing with social change. Evolutionary theories seek out and attempt to elevate to the status of generalities or laws supposedly irresistible processes, iron constraints on human action and underlying tendencies that transcend history. This is an attempt to reveal the essential features moving beneath and governing individual events and the thick empirical layers of the archaeological record. Everything is to be boiled down, reduced and fitted to one single totalizing framework which presupposes some underlying continuity, whether emergent, divergent, progressive, regressive, cyclical, lineal or multilineal, in the relationship between past and present. The archaeologist becomes an investigator who pores over the past, sorting out the essential from the inessential, the necessary from the merely contingent, the wheat of process from the chaff of event. Ultimately the past becomes domesticated in its essentialist, continuous inevitability. But this inevitability is at the same time an intellectual construct, a form of power which in the attempt to produce a totalizing history reduces that history to the shadow world of essence, of economic and behavioural process.

When the term evolution is used in any discussion (unless merely used as a grandiose term for change – one of the most frequent uses, or abuses of the term) what is implied is one or a series of developmental and cumulative processes that lead somewhere. Axiomatic authority is invariably given to the reality of the term evolution. Exactly why this term is supposedly beneficial in understanding change is rarely explicitly questioned. Emphasis is instead placed on processes: is this or that process evolutionary? does such and such a trait have evolutionary potential? In this manner the validity of an evolutionary framework becomes internally safeguarded. Archaeological research becomes a strategy of recognizing what is evolutionary as distinct from what is not, what is necessary rather than what is merely contingent.

Evolutionary theories have generally relied upon typologies of social forms: band, tribe, chiefdom, state (Service, 1962) and many other variants. These have had an enormous impact upon archaeological research with various attempts being made to identify and define these stages in terms of the archaeological evidence (see chapter 2). There have been those who have questioned the validity of such typologies (Dunnell, 1980; Yoffee, 1979); but others are still claiming the general utility of a typological model and it is still very influential as a way of thinking about the past. The use of such typological frameworks creates a view of history as an overall intelligible unity and continuum. History itself becomes a continuous process of concretization of abstract, paradigmatic stadial forms. It is also always an approximation – 'we haven't got it quite right yet.' Bintliff, the major contributor to the volume *European Social Evolution* (1984), claims that 'the overall sequence [in the Bronze and Iron Age] is strongly comparable to the neo-evolutionist model of band/big–man/tribe/chiefdom/early state module' (1984, p. 30). He asserts the reality of developmental stages and claims that 'the totality of archaeological data for the European Bronze Age points to the dominance of small scale chiefdom organisation throughout Europe' (1984a, p. 158). The mass of archaeological data has been reduced to order with the 'recognition' of a chiefdom-type social organization. The concrete and the particular become subsumed in terms of an abstract category permitting the ordering and classification of the data, a reduction to its essentials. Any that don't quite fit become merely contingent to the model being used.

Such a typological framework systematically excludes *difference* and instead asserts *identity*. Identity is always the primordial term. Although each documented chiefdom or hunter-gatherer band is distinct from any other chiefdom or band, in an evolutionary framework these differences become subsumed and relegated as secondary or contingent. Hence all instances of hunter-gatherer social organization become relegated to the classificatory stage 'band'. This is a reductionist search for the 'essential'. The supposed identity of all hunter-gatherer societies permits a classificatory distinction separating them from other forms of human social organization divided into other categories, e.g. chiefdom or state. However, difference is not to be derived from the supposed identity of differential social forms – it makes these abstract categories possible in the first place. The concomitant of this is that a notion of difference, difference between forms of human social organization, deconstructs any possibility of erecting rigid social categories such as a 'band'. Bands, tribes etc, have no identity, no reality whatsoever. What is primary is not the sameness of human societies but their uniqueness. In order to be posited at all the notion of band presupposes both an abstract identity and a difference from some other abstract identity such as a chiefdom. Differences between forms of human social organization both permit the abstract identities of bands and chiefdoms to be posited and, at the same time, deconstruct the possibility of these abstractions having any analytical significance.

A typology of social stages is an attempt to create self-sufficient and exclusive categories. These are intended to order history

FIGURE 6.1 A Bronze Age chieftain
Source: Modified from C. Burgess (1980). Reprinted by permission of J. M. Dent
& Sons.

conceptually. They also order it normatively. Plural differences between societies become reduced to abstract forms, which in turn support a normative hierarchy of good and bad. Any empirical instance of an actual society undermines the efficacy of any such typology. Social typologies are not only theoretical fictions, they are also idealist fictions. Notions such as 'band' provide semblances of conceptual unity, permitting and yet simultaneously preventing and moulding thought. They promote a vision of homogeneity in the archaeological record. The complexity and variability in the archaeological data becomes ordered, fixed and shaped according to an ideal model created from the 'detached' subject position of the observer. The identity of social forms is only possible and discoverable by fitting them into a diachronic totalizing framework: an inexorable succession of stages allows the multitudes of different social forms to be divided into abstract phenomena, their necessary characteristics to count as a band etc, to be separated from contingent detail, and such a division is made according to the degree to which societies approach modernity.

Biological and social evolution

One particular aspect of the use of essentialist and reductionist frameworks in evolutionary theory is the relationship posited between social and biological evolution, which merits some more detailed discussion. Despite the fact that notions of social evolution developed before the publication of Darwin's *Origin of the Species* (1859), it is in biology that evolutionary processes have been most successfully defined through work on the concepts of natural selection and adaptation. Any use of the term evolution after the publication of Darwin's work in the social sciences in general, or in archaeology in particular, has not been able to avoid some kind of conceptual connection with biological evolutionary theory. In practice most authors writing about social evolution have made explicit links between social evolution and biological evolution. We wish to make two main points in this section: firstly, that any author adopting the term 'evolution' cannot avoid some kind of homology between biological and social processes or the term would become redundant. Secondly, any notion of biological evolution is fundamentally incompatible with an attempt to understand the social.

Biology and technology

Childe, throughout his work, asserted a position of technological determinism in relation to a requirement for populations to adapt to their natural environments and this provided not only a fundamental principle but also an ontological vindication and justification for archaeology. A perspective in which societies were viewed as being involved in an endless series of technologically governed environmental adaptations gave a 'clue' for the analysis of the archaeological record and a way of reducing its complexity to 'an easily comprehensible order' (Childe, 1947, pp. 71–2). This order was for Childe an evolutionary order in which social evolution was deemed to form a logical progression from biological evolution, while retaining many essential features in common.

> Prehistory is a continuation of natural history . . . there is an analogy between organic evolution and progress in culture. Natural history traces the emergence of new species each better adapted for survival, more fitted to obtain food and shelter, and so to multiply. Human history reveals man creating new industries and new economies that have furthered the increase of his species and thereby vindicated its enhanced fitness.
>
> (Childe, 1936, p. 15)

The bulk of *Man Makes Himself*, as with almost all Childe's works, is devoted to empirical description and discussion of culture sequences and, in this book, such sequences are characterized as being punctuated by a series of revolutionary developments which result in denser population concentrations supposedly illustrating the higher degree of adaptive fitness of technical innovations: the neolithic revolution, the urban revolution and the 'revolution in human knowledge' with the advent of literacy. Innovations (e.g. the arch, bronze, the seal, irrigation and bricks in the urban revolution) are explicitly likened by Childe to biological mutations (Childe, 1936, p. 228). In *Social Evolution*, Childe claimed that a Darwinian framework could not only be transferred from biological to social evolution, but was 'even more intelligible in the latter domain than in the former' (1951, p. 175), and that rigorous processes of selection operated on cultural innovations in the same manner as natural selection (ibid., p. 177). Cultural evolution, like biological evolution, could best be represented as 'a tree with branches all up the trunk and each branch bristling with twigs . . . differentiation – the splitting of large homogeneous cultures – is a conspicuous feature in the archaeological record' (ibid., p. 166). However, cultural evolution is to be at least in part distinguished from organic evolution because of the property of 'convergence' between different cultures brought about through diffusion of techniques and knowledge (ibid., p. 168).

Much of the recent literature on social evolution in archaeology differs remarkably little from Childe. Connections between biological and social evolution generally remain on the same level of a vague general analogy:

> Divergence from a common ancestor is one of the fundamental aspects of biological evolution, and it has undoubtedly played a major role in the evolution of a bewildering variety of human cultures with which the anthropologist is confronted. Each of those cultures also has a complex series of legacies from its evolutionary past, perhaps reinterpreted and integrated with adaptive innovations.
>
> (Flannery, 1983, p. 2)

Or, again:

> In the process of both biological and societal evolution we witness a progressive differentiation of structure and a corresponding specialization of function: 'Wherever we look we discover evolutionary processes leading to diversification and increasing complexity.'
>
> (Segraves, 1982, p. 292, citing Prigogine, Allen and Herman, 1977, pp. 5–6)

Adaptation and natural selection

In Childe's work or in books such as *The Cloud People* (Flannery and Marcus (eds), 1983) and *European Social Evolution* (Bintliff (ed), 1984) notions of biological evolution, vaguely translated into social terms, seem to play very little theoretical role whatsoever and are entirely swamped in the morass of empirical detail. In most social evolutionary theories adaptation is usually called upon to play the major explanatory role but there is no counterpart in social theory of Darwinian evolutionary theory. Societal adaptation always has to do double service as both cause and consequence of change. This can only lead to tautology when the concept of adaptation is used to explain or account for the existence of particular traits. To say that adaptive traits are present in a society or that those traits present are adaptive adds nothing to our understanding. Arguments normally amount to little more than saying that those traits present in a society are adaptive, therefore those traits are present; or those societies that survive are adaptive, therefore they survive. As Giddens notes, 'if it were the case that there were some sort of generalized motivational impulse for human beings progressively to "adapt" more effectively to their material environments, there would be a basis for sustaining evolutionary theory. But there is not any such compulsion' (Giddens, 1984, p. 236). Cohen, however, does suggest one such 'compulsion': that in small-scale societies direct producers have an interest in reducing unpleasant labour or toil and so will accept innovations that reduce toil and/or increase productivity (Cohen, 1978, pp. 302–7). Such an argument overlooks entirely the nature of 'toil' as socially constituted in the first place and that in hunter-gatherer societies at the bottom of the evolutionary ladder toil seems to be very limited. In societies characterized by forms of class exploitation there is anyway no necessary correspondence between development of the productive forces and reduction of labour time. When one reads attempts to provide accounts of why adaptation occurs the level of reductionism involved often becomes almost absurd. Socio-cultural systems, for example, may be portrayed solely in terms of feeding behaviour (just who or what is feeding is rather unclear!):

> More complex sociocultural systems tend to be more generalized in their overall feeding behaviour by virtue of their particular feeding specializations. This gives them a versatility when intersystem competition occurs. They can better exploit new energy sources, but also the complex sociocultural systems persevere because success in the long run goes to the specialist who can harness the greatest number of kilocalories.
>
> (Gall and Saxe, 1977, p. 264–5)

Dunnell (1980, p. 77) notes that although the archaeological literature is full of references to adaptation and adaptive process, it tends to be rather short on selection. Although critical of cultural evolutionary theories Dunnell wants to reinstate modern biological evolutionary theory, suggesting that 'evolution is a particular framework for explaining change as differential persistence of variability' (ibid., p. 38). This entails that biological evolutionary theory involving natural selection, mutation, drift etc. should be translated in terms of the archaeological record: for example style and function can be defined in terms of natural selection (Dunnell, 1978). Even if human beings are indeed animals and subject to processes of natural selection in an equivalent manner to badgers, hedgehogs or guinea-fowl, this by no means implies that any adequate explanation or understanding of social totalities, institutions or material culture patterning can be achieved by reference to either natural selection or adaptation. Most social and material practices have no demonstrable physical survival value for human populations whatsoever (see Shanks and Tilley, 1987).

Societies, unlike individual organisms, do not have any clear-cut physical parameters or boundaries, nor do societies have conscious problems of self-maintenance or a need to adapt. Individuals may have these characteristics but they cannot be validly anthropomorphized in terms of entire social totalities. Furthermore, evolutionary theories must apply to some unit, a society or a cultural system, and here again there is a problem. Is British society of 1987 a society or cultural system in just the same sense as a group of palaeolithic hunter-gatherers? Clearly not, and this leads one to reject any totalizing account of change framed in terms of basic processes supposedly good for all times and places. Societies construct their own social reality and the reproduction of societies entails far more than physical, biological reproduction.

Ethnocentrism

Although evolutionary theory logically need not involve ethnocentrism and in Darwin's biological theory of natural selection there is no such implication, theories of social evolution in practice have always been riddled with ethnocentric evaluations. By ethnocentrism is meant the manner in which a group identifies with its own socio-cultural individuality and creates a privileged and central image of itself in relation to others. This normally involves an explicitly or implicitly defined valorization of the achievements, social conditions etc. of a group (the in-group) with which the individual or author identifies himself or herself and a reference to other groups (the out groups) which are usually defined, conceptually constituted and evaluated by reference to the in-group adopting specific concepts, norms, measures of difference and criteria (figure 6.2). Ethnocentrism in one form or another is likely to be found in all societies and in the discourses those societies produce.

The Enlightenment and the colonial encounter

A very significant 'discovery' of the eighteenth century was the idea of progress which emerged as a consistently reiterated feature of social philosophies on a grand scale, permeating all aspects of social and political thought (Sklair, 1970, ch. 2). Scientific progress, material progress and moral progress were all conceived as being inextricably linked in an overarching conception of the

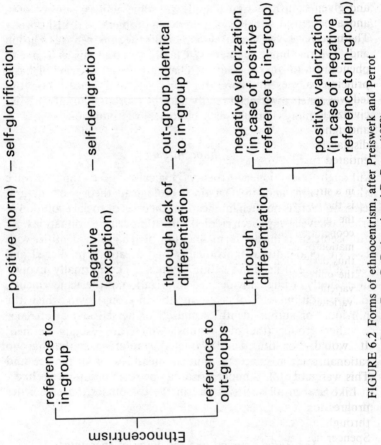

FIGURE 6.2 Forms of ethnocentrism, after Preiswerk and Perrot
Source: From R. Preiswerk and D. Perrot (1978).

growing perfection of human society which was both natural and inevitable. The social evolutionary theories of the nineteenth century gave substance and justification to the notion of progress as providing the dominant classification and explanation of social institutions and the history of humanity.

Evolutionary theories were shaped during the period of British world dominance and the consolidation of empire, a world shaped and given significance by a confident and ascending middle class and a perceived equation between scientific and social progress. The nineteenth-century evolutionary schemes of Spencer, Morgan and Tylor, among others, did not so much start from the phenomena to be explained but from an ethical and metaphysical principle to be established. For Spencer the goal to which evolution led was perfection, and in terms of human society progress led to civilization, the conditions of origin for this process being savagery and ignorance. A natural outcome of social evolution was the displacement of less developed societies by those that had differentiated further along the road to perfection:

> in a struggle for existence among societies, the survival of the fittest is the survival of those in which power of military cooperation is the greatest, and military cooperation is that primary kind of cooperation which prepares the way for other kinds. So that this formation of larger societies by the union of smaller ones in war, and thus destruction or absorption of the smaller ununited societies by the united larger ones, is an inevitable process through which the varieties of men most adapted for social life supplant the less adapted varieties.
>
> (Spencer, 1967, p. 78)

It would be difficult to find a more clearly articulated rationalization for the British imperial subjection of the colonies. This was, after all, a natural and inevitable process.

Like Spencer, Tylor and Morgan were leading exponents of the progressionist argument that all societies and institutions go through a gradual and natural process of development. While Spencer used the biological organism as a useful analogy for social analysis, Tylor and Morgan favoured the development of science as an appropriate model. Just as sciences pass through stages utilizing erroneous theories (e.g. alchemy), human societies develop through the thrusting aside of false and inadequate knowledge. Societies low on the scale of evolutionary development possess a high degree of ignorance, superstition and error. Evolution occurs because, at least in the long run, logic and rationality must prevail: 'it is a law of human progress that thought tends to work itself clear' (Tylor, 1881, p. 341). Morgan's stages of savagery, barbarism and civilization were the product of a process of historical generalization, but history could not have happened otherwise. The evidence showed that 'the principal institutions of mankind have been developed from a few primary germs of thought; and the course and manner of their development was predetermined . . . by the natural logic of the human mind and the necessary limitation of its powers' (Morgan, 1963, p. 18). Analysis was facilitated by the study of primitive 'survivals' which provided both proof and examples of the stages leading toward civilization. To Tylor in particular, cultural similarities and differences in artefacts or customs were of no significance and 'little respect need be had in such comparisons for date in history or for place on the map' (Tylor, 1871, vol. I, p. 6). Archaeology played no significant role in the development of these theories, but was occasionally harnessed to provide the necessary historical back-up, and general conceptions of evolution were adopted (e.g. Lubbock, 1865).

The evolutionary schemes of the nineteenth century provided a picture of continuous and sustained endogenous growth gratifying to the Victorian consciousness, making it possible to look down benignly on the lowly savage (in some more literary works elevated to the status of the noble savage). The social functions of anything that was superstitious or supposedly irrational could only be recognized provided they were someone else's beliefs, or a mere relic and a transitory feature of Victorian society. This provided a means of being both relativist and non-relativist at the same time, 'of admitting that many diverse modes of organising and interpreting social life might have something to say for them, and might play vital roles in the lives of human beings, while continuing to maintain the absolute validity of one such mode – the positivist' (Burrow, 1966, p. 263). The social order of laissez-faire capitalism became validated in terms of an inevitable all-embracing process. It represented the highest point humanity had reached and, if not perfect, was nearly so. If Marx (1859) was to dissent from all this, socialism was only around the corner, predicated on the growing contradictions between the social relations and forces of production.

Evolution and progress

The ethnocentrism apparent in nineteenth-century evolutionary thought hardly needs to be spelled out in detail. What is possibly not so readily apparent is the presence of ethnocentrism as an underlying theme in varieties of mid-twentieth-century and contemporary evolutionary schemes.

The stadial perspectives of Childe (1951), Fried (1967) and Service (1975) are, in essentials, only refinements of Morgan's scheme. Steward's multilineal approach (1955) with its societal typologies shares many of the assumptions of the stadial models, while the primacy given to adaptation is clearly reminiscent of Spencer. White stated in the introduction to *The Evolution of Culture* that his position did not 'differ one whit in principle from that expressed in Tylor's *Anthropology* in 1881' (White, 1959, p. xi). White dealt with the entire history of humanity as Tylor had done but this history was now primarily a history of technological progress. Human culture was a means of adaptation and developed as the efficiency of energy capture increased. This was the 'law' of cultural evolution and culture was progressive, permitting a steadily increasing control over the forces of nature. Furthermore the process of cultural evolution was *sui generis*: people were swept up in a cumulative process of exponential growth which was impossible to control. Steward's multilineal evolution was not, according to him, concerned to develop an a priori scheme but 'deals only with those limited parallels of form, function and sequence which have empirical validity' (1955, p. 19). He considered that cultural laws or regularities could only be founded on the detailed consideration of comparative sequences. However, the differences between simple and complex societies could not be conceptualized as being solely quantitative (an increase in size etc.) but, more fundamentally, were qualitative in form, involving new types of societal integration. Steward suggested that 'progress must be measured by definable values' (1955, p. 13). In his perspective progress was a necessary component of change, an 'attribute' of development. Quoting Kroeber (1948, p. 304), Steward goes so far as to list three criteria for the measurement of progress:

1 'The atrophy of magic based on psychopathology.'
2 'The decline of infantile obsession with the outstanding physiological events of human life.'
3 'The persistent tendency of technology and science to grow accumulatively.'

(Ibid., p. 14)

Such statements would have been readily embraced by any Victorian social theorist! A point very similar to the first has been made by Habermas in his attempt to develop a revised version of historical materialism in evolutionary terms (Habermas, 1979). Drawing on Piaget's theories of cognitive development in children Habermas proposes that homologies may be found between ego development and the evolution of world views. In small-scale societies thought is bound up with myth and it is only with the transition from archaic to developed civilizations that there is a break from mythological thought towards accounts of the world with 'argumentative foundations' (ibid., pp. 104–5). The modern world, for Habermas, is more enlightened than the 'primitive'. Traditional cultures form closed and non-reflective worlds compared with contemporary rationality which brings with it potentiality for change. Small-scale societies are composed of individuals who have not yet undergone the 'learning processes' that bring enlightenment. The highest forms of human rationality turn out to be those of the contemporary West.

Childe always maintained a rigid separation could be held between facts, values and interpretations, expressing this as early as the epilogue to *The Danube in Prehistory* (1929) in which he maintained that he had always attempted to consign to separate paragraphs interpretations of data as opposed to their factual description (1929, p. 418; cf. Childe, 1936, p. 2). Approaching history in a 'humble and objective manner' meant that, paradoxically, a notion of progress was both objective and scientific and non-objective and irrational. On the one hand to ask whether hydroelectric power represents progress in relation to, say, a neolithic technology could only be to Childe a meaningless question involving dubious value judgements; one could still ask, on the other hand, 'what is progress?' Childe's answer to the latter was that the historical record itself was a record of progress and that archaeology, given its long time scales, was ideally suited to document this record of progress, illustrating 'improving technical skill, accumulating knowledge, and advancing organization for securing a livelihood' (Childe, 1936, p. 34). The traditional periodization of archaeology in terms of the technological stages of stone, bronze and iron, broadly correlated with hunter-gatherer, agricultural and urban economies, provided unassailable proof of progress (ibid., p. 35), and this coloured all Childe's interpretations. Prehistoric hunter-gatherers certainly lived in no Garden of Eden:

Faced with the terrifying fact of death, their primitive emotions shocked by its ravages, the bestial-looking Mousterians had been roused to imaginative thinking. They would not believe in the complete cessation of earthly life, but dimly imagined some sort of continuance thereof in which the dead would still need material food and implements. The pathethic and futile tendency of the dead, [is] thus early attested.

(Ibid., p. 55)

Elsewhere he writes: 'getting food and shelter and indulging in sexual intercourse . . . were presumably alone available to lower palaeolithic savages' (Childe, 1944, p. 114).

In *Progress and Archaeology* (1944) and *Social Evolution* (1951) Childe admits the occurrence of certain 'dark ages' in which technical progress seems to have halted, even declined. Such periods are brushed aside as merely temporary phases (1944, p. 109) in an overall cumulative development leading up to the twentieth-century pursuit of scientific knowledge (ibid., p. 115). History itself is defined by Childe as progress and science as the mode of thought in which progress culminates. Consequently history becomes the unfolding of scientific rationality and it therefore becomes possible to make the claim that present-day reality is reason itself: i.e. it is reasonable, ordered in accordance with rationality. So the capitalist market system with its division of labour and treatment of labour as a commodity is rational(ity). It is also possible to claim that a 'scientific' history represents actual history. Reason and contemporary reality become identified; subject is collapsed into object, object into subject.

Sahlins and Service (1960), in their well-known attempt to reconcile the positions of White and Steward, coined the terms general and specific evolution. General evolution, or White's conception, was considered by them to be 'the central, inclusive, organizing outlook of anthropology, comparable in its theoretical power to evolutionism in biology' (ibid., p. 44). This entailed the 'determination and explanation of the successive transformations of culture through its several stages of overall progress' (ibid., p. 29). Evolution was, of course, a necessarily good thing and if it had not taken its course the 'civilized', industrial West would never have come into being and distinguished itself from other cultures.

Parsons, in his paper on 'evolutionary universals in society' (Parsons, 1964), was concerned to develop a generalized analytical theory and remained opposed to any view that evolutionary theory should be historical in the sense of historicism. Hence he only adopts, tacitly, a two-stage model of social growth: the 'primitive' and the 'modern'. He shuffles the evolutionary cards so as to distinguish between evolutionary *universals* and evolutionary *prerequisites*. An evolutionary universal is identified as being 'a complex of structures and associated processes the development of which so increases the long-run adaptive capacity of living systems in a given class that only systems that develop the complex can attain certain higher levels of general adaptive capacity' (ibid., pp. 340–1). Evolutionary prerequisites are universal elements in all human societies and Parsons lists four of these, their presence marking a minimum for a society to be considered truly human: technology, language, kinship and religion. He identifies six evolutionary universals:

1   Social stratification.
2   Cultural legitimation of differentiated social functions.
3   A bureaucratic organization or the institutionalism of the authority of office.
4   A money and market complex.
5   Generalized universal norms, i.e. a formal legal system.
6   A democratic association or a liberal, elected leadership.

The first two of these evolutionary universals are of primary importance for societies to 'break out' from a primitive stage of social organization. The rest have served to promote advanced industralization, our present social order. Now, as Gouldner (1970, p. 367) is quick to point out, what all this implies is that capitalist America happens, conveniently, to embody all those evolutionary universals which, according to Parsons, have ever been invented. Furthermore, the communist nations are structurally unsound, inherently unstable, an evolutionary dead end:

> I must maintain that communist totalitarian organization will probably not fully match 'democracy' in political and integrative capacity in the long run. I do indeed predict that it will prove to be unstable and will either make adjustments in the general direction of electoral democracy or . . . 'regress' into . . . less advanced and politically less effective forms of organization.
>
> (Parsons, 1964, p. 356)

In part, this is because 'those that restrict [the markets and money system] too drastically are likely to suffer from severe adaptive disadvantages in the long run' (ibid., p. 350). Had Parsons not assigned technology to the status of an evolutionary prerequisite but to an evolutionary universal, the socio-political conclusions that he draws regarding the relative merits of American and Soviet society might not have been so readily forthcoming.

Valorization: from 'simple' to 'complex'

In the 'new' archaeology the term 'progress' is rarely used. It has become conceptually shifted into the realm of adaptation and relative adaptive efficiency. Nevertheless ethnocentric valorization is hardly missing and one of the primary arenas in which this takes place is in discussions of societal complexity. A string of examples are readily to be found in almost any recent publication; here we identify just a few from Marcus's conclusions to *The Cloud People: Divergent Evolution of the Zapotec and Mixtec Civilizations* (Flannery and Marcus (eds), 1983). 'Low population density could be seen as a factor *delaying* divergent evolution [in the Archaic period]' (Marcus, 1983, p. 356; our emphasis). It is implied that evolution has reality as a process, is inevitable and that a high population density is necessarily a good thing: 'The development of urban centres in the Mixteca Alta seems to have *lagged a few centuries behind the Valley of Oaxaca*' (ibid., p. 357; our emphasis). Urbanization is positively valorized:

> Even if we grant the *rise* of the Oaxaca peoples from band-level hunters and gatherers to state-level stratified societies, this *rise* is insufficient to explain the differences between Mixtec and Zapotec culture . . . If we are genuinely interested in understanding individual Mesoamerican cultures, we cannot ignore drift, adaptive divergence, convergence, and parallel evolution while concentrating single mindedly on *advance through stages of sociopolitical organization*.
>
> (Ibid., p. 360; our emphasis)

Later 'stages' of social evolution are positively evaluated. Bands may eventually 'rise' to the status of a state or a civilization; the latter can only 'decline' or 'fall'.

The direction in which evolution is invariably depicted as leading is from the simple to the complex. The terms simple and complex in evolutionary discourses also imply the absent presence of two other strongly normative related concepts: respectively, the superior and the inferior. Both complexity and simplicity are multidimensional concepts and they cannot be defined except with reference to some entity or social form. They are relative, not fixed, terms. In evolutionary theories 'complex' is invariably associated with the state or those social forms which are gratuitously labelled civilizations. Any use of terms such as 'complex', 'civilization' or 'state' – they are virtually interchangeable in the literature on evolution – is inevitably predicated on the basis of its difference from its absent other, the uncivilized (savage), the simple, the non-state. Such a notion of complexity is ideologically loaded. Despite the fact that differentiation can be argued to exist in all societies from the palaeolithic to the present, this differentiation only counts in the case of a limited number of societies which become labelled complex. Furthermore complex does not imply better organized, better adapted, having better societal self-maintenance etc. (witness Chernobyl). Nevertheless the complex always becomes valorized vis à vis the simple, its polar opposite. As Rowlands points out,

> the significance of these categories of social life owe their origin to European deliberation on the important innovations marking the beginnings of modernity. Projected backwards such categories can be explored historically in order to address the degree of similarity and difference that provides us with an understanding on their contemporary unique forms . . . A universal monologue on the nature of social complexity has . . . been successfully disseminated from its original European power base.
>
> (Rowlands 1986 pp. 1–2)

Such a perspective permits a situation in which the 'simple' or the 'savage' is not only temporally distant in evolutionary frameworks from the West but is also transposed spatially in contemporary anthropological discourse which has a persistent tendency to place the societies that anthropologists study in a time other than the present of the anthropological researcher (figure 6.3; see Fabian, 1983, pp. 31ff). Temporal and spatial distanciation reinforce each other.

The schemes of 'explanation' in evolutionary theories easily slip into ideologies of self-justification or assert the priorities of the West in relation to other cultures whose primary importance is precisely to act as offsets for our contemporary 'civilization'. Genuine difference and radical incompatibility of social forms become relegated in terms of schemes which permit the evaluation of social life and the celebration of one social form *vis à vis* others. This 'knowledge' is a political act, a form of power. Societies become classified in an evaluative hierarchy judged implicitly or explicitly by their degree of deviation from ours. Hence complexity is elevated in relation to simplicity, differentiation in relation to homogeneity, the urban form in relation to the rural and so on. Lévi-Strauss has cogently noted that

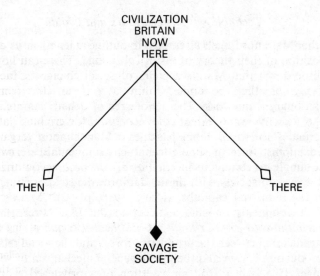

FIGURE 6.3 Contemporary time/space distanciation and the constitution
of the primitive, after Fabian
Source: From J. Fabian (1983), pp. 31ff.

'if the criterion chosen had been the degree of ability to overcome
even the most inhospitable geographical conditions, there can be
scarcely any doubt that the Eskimos, on the one hand and the
Bedouins, on the other would carry off the palm' (Lévi-Strauss,
1975, p. 113).

MARXISM, STRUCTURAL MARXISM AND
EVOLUTIONARY CHANGE

Marx's materialist conception of the historical process has been
subject to a very large number of specific interpretations both by
writers favourable to his work and by those deeply critical of it.
Here we shall not be concerned to attempt to review in any detail
Marx's vast corpus of writings and subsequent developments but
wish, rather, to draw out a few key features of Marx's conception
of social change and that employed more recently in structural
Marxist literature while analysing, in particular, the manner in
which this work has influenced archaeological theorizations of
change.

Technology: between Marx and Childe

Neither Marx nor Engels attempted to outline at length a systematic exposition of their theory of historical change. There can however be little doubt that Marx's account of social change asserted the primacy of the economic within a general developmental evolutionary framework. The major area of debate has been, and is, to exactly what extent the economy 'determines' and/or 'dominates' the social. Some passages in Marx support very clearly a reductionist form of simple techno-environmental determinism, for example his comments in *The Poverty of Philosophy*: 'the hand mill gives you society with the feudal lord; the steam mill, society with the industrial capitalist (Marx, 1936, p. 92).' Marx's most explicit comments on change occur in the 1859 'Preface to *A Contribution to the Critique of Political Economy*' in which contradiction between the productive forces and the social relations of production is viewed as being the general mechanism of societal change. This is based on an assertion of a privileged economic causality determining the entire structure of society:

> In the social production of their existence, men inevitably enter into definite relations, which are independent of their will, namely relations of production appropriate to a given stage in the development of their material forces of production. The totality of these relations of production constitutes the economic structure of society, the real foundation, on which arises a legal and political superstructure and to which correspond definite forms of social consciousness . . . At a certain stage of development, the material productive forces of society come into conflict with the existing relations of production . . . From forms of development of the productive forces these relations turn into their fetters. Then begins an era of social revolution. The changes in the economic foundation lead sooner or later to the transformation of the whole immense superstructure.
>
> (1968, pp. 20–1)

In Marx's conception, the economic base of society provides 'the real foundation on which arises a legal and political superstructure'. If this economic base changes, then the superstructure will also. In other words the base is assigned a privileged causality in relation to the superstructure, and the base and superstructure correspond to each other. The actual dynamics promoting change are located in a contradictory relation between the forces of production (labour power, land, tools, raw materials, technical knowledge and organization of production) and the social relations of production (relations between people in the production process which result from working on and with materials using specific technologies). Beyond a certain conjuncture the social relations of production act so as to restrict the further development of the forces of production and this will ultimately result in conflict between classes composing the relations of production becoming social revolution. This specific conception of historical change (at least partially contradicted elsewhere in Marx's writings) was coupled by Marx and Engels to an evolutionary conception of the historical process in which various stages or 'epochs' in the development of human society are outlined as specific modes of production: tribal, ancient or slave, feudal, capitalist and socialist (Marx and Engels, 1970, pp. 43–56), with an asiatic form being added later to the list.

Childe's interpretation of Marxism was in terms of the provision of a technological model for the understanding of social evolution, a model which he reiterated over and over again:

> The way people get their living should be expected in the long run to 'determine' their beliefs and institutions. But the way people get their living is determined on the one hand by environment . . . on the other by science and technology.
>
> (Childe, 1979, p. 93)

Although Childe indicates by his use of the term 'determine' that social change may not be rigidly determined by technology and the environment in any immediate and automatic fashion, technological development did amount to firmly conditioning possible courses of social trajectories.

> The environments to which societies are adjusted are worlds of ideas, collective representations . . . these worlds of knowledge must each have been, and be, conditioned by the whole of society's culture and particularly its technologies.
>
> (Childe, 1949, pp. 22–3)

Here Childe is clearly willing to allow some room for the social construction of reality, but in the last analysis, archaeology reveals:

> the progressive extension of humanity's control over external nature by the invention and discovery of more efficient tools and processes. Marx and Engels were the first to remark that this technological development is the foundation for the whole of history, conditioning and limiting all other human activities . . . If science and technology

are to progress, the relations of production must be adjusted accordingly.

(Childe, 1947, pp. 69, 73)

Technological determinism and the requirement for environmental adaptation become the essential motors of the historical process.

Structural Marxism and the economic/non-economic relation

It can be argued that when Marx, in the 1859 'Preface' (cited above), writes about the economic as a *foundation* on which arises a juridico-political superstructure, to which definite forms of social consciousness *correspond*, no unmediated and direct economic causation is, in fact, implied (Hindness and Hirst, 1975, p. 16). The manner in which the economic/non-economic relation may be theorized in relation to processes of social change constitutes a major part of what has been termed a 'structural Marxist' problematic. Comparatively recent work within Marxism and anthropology has attempted to build open and extend basic Marxian concepts and elucidate Marx's conception of social structure with reference to contemporary structuralist thought (Althusser, 1977; Althusser and Balibar, 1970; Godelier, 1972, 1977, 1978; Poulantzas, 1973; among others). Poulantzas outlines a threefold classification of Marxist concepts:

1 Marxism provides a theory of history and historical change insofar as its concepts can be considered to be transhistorical, i.e. applicable to all historically documented social forms such as mode of production, social relations of production, forces of production, labour or praxis, social formation and different structural levels within any particular social formation (economic, political, ideological).
2 Marxism utilizes specific sets of concepts in order to analyse each particular mode of production (tribal, ancient, asiatic, feudal, capitalist, socialist) as theoretically constituted in general theory; for example commodity relations, exchange and use value in the capitalist mode of production.
3 Marxism analyses particular structures or structural levels or regions within each mode of production; for example the ideological and political structures constituting the feudal or ancient mode. (Poulantzas, 1973, pp. 11–23)

For Althusser, the social totality or social formation is conceived as:

1   A complex unity of specific levels or 'instances', minimally the economic, ideological and political, constituting a 'structure in dominance'. It is not to be conceived in terms of a radical distinction between an economic base, conceived as an 'essence', and an ethereal superstructure that simply reflects the base and is ultimately reducible to it.

2   The levels or instances are relatively autonomous of each other. The economic instance is made up of a mode or modes of production constituted by an articulation between the social relations and forces of production. The former are always dominant hence a simple techno-economic determinism is avoided.

3   The totality is asymmetric. It may be dominated by one of its elements but the economy is always 'determinant in the last instance'.

4   Change is not a simple matter of a contradiction between the social relations and forces of production but is metonymic and overdetermined. All instances condition each other, and the structure of the whole totality affects the internal and external relations of the instances.

Godelier's conception of the social totality is similar in many respects, but rather than to consider specific points of similarity or difference in the overall conception, we wish to concentrate on the notion of change and the specific theorization of the economic/non-economic relation with reference to pre-capitalist social formations. In small-scale 'tribal' societies institutions and social practices are thoroughly embedded in each other. There simply is no apparent economic 'level' to be distinguished from 'superstructural levels'. In other words, it is difficult to characterize the economy as being either dominant or determinant. However, Godelier argues that kin relations are both infrastructure and superstructure:

> the determining role of the economy, apparently contradicted by the dominant role of kinship, is rediscovered in this dominant role, since kinship functions as, *inter alia*, production-relations. Here the relationship between economy and kinship appears as an internal relationship *without* the economic relationships of the kinsfolk *merging* for all that, with their political, sexual, etc., relationships.
>
> (Godelier, 1972, p. 95)

For Godelier, as for Althusser, the economic 'level' is an independent domain and yet forms an aspect of other areas of social life at the same time. Both Althusser and Godelier assert the ultimately determining role of the economic which raises the question as to how the 'relative autonomy' of other levels, areas or aspects of the social can be maintained if the economic ultimately holds sway. Both distinguish between primary contradictions providing the motility for structural change and secondary contradictions developing around the primary contradictions. The specific theorizations are different (for a detailed analysis see Goodfriend, 1978) and need not concern us here. The important point is that the primary motor of change is still situated in the economic domain between the productive forces and social relations. For Godelier this is a contradiction *between* structures composing the forces and relations; for Althusser it resides in a single structure composed of the productive forces and relations.

Epigenesis and change

The work of Godelier and, to a lesser extent, of Althusser has had some considerable impact upon archaeological analyses of change, especially through the influence of Friedman (1974, 1975) and Friedman and Rowlands (1978), and we will now examine this specific framework. Situating their work within an evolutionary frame of reference, Friedman and Rowlands adopt a dynamic model of change. Evolution is conceived as a set of 'homoeorhetic' processes in which there is a structurally determined order. The model is epigenetic in that the scheme that they present has no static stages and at any one moment the seeds of future change are contained within the social order. They present an abstract outline of certain 'evolutionary' processes with examples of varied concrete appearances in the archaeological and ethnographic record. As for Godelier, this abstract outline is based on a logic of social relations of production – a designation of the *essential*. The model is an attempt to reveal basic transformational processes forming both necessary and sufficient determinants of social evolution.

The specific model adopted owes much to Althusser and Godelier and is, of course, a variant of Marx's base/superstructure conception with the social formation being divided into a number of structurally autonomous functional levels. The properties of one level cannot be derived from those of the others. The levels are integrated in a single structure of material reproduction by two types of relations. From the ecosystem upwards there is a hierarchy of constraints determining the limits of functional compatibility between the levels. Such constraints are characterized as being negative, i.e. they determine what cannot occur rather than everything that does occur. Friedman and Rowlands note that 'positive determination would only exist where we could find necessary and sufficient conditions for the occurrence of a given structure, i.e. where only one set of productive relations could dominate the process of reproduction' (1978, p. 203). Relations of production are the dominant aspects of the social formation. They determine the use to be made of the environment within the limits of the available technology, the division of productive labour and the form of the appropriation and distribution of the social product of labour. In short, they define the rationality of the economic system. The forces of production form the basic techno-ecological conditions of production. These are the objective energy costs of reproduction and the rate of potential surplus. The manner in which the social relations of production relate to the objective conditions of the forces of production determines the long-term behaviour of the system and limits the conditions of its existence. Friedman and Rowlands stress that social formations cannot be conceived as isolated units because social reproduction is a spatial as well as temporal process. Social formations are always linked and 'production for exchange seems to be a constant factor in social evolution' (1978, p. 204). Social evolution becomes a multifaceted and multilineal set of interlinked spatial and temporal transformations between individual social formations. Change comes about because 'dominant relations of production determine a given developmental pathway and functional incompatibilities in the larger totality generate divergent transformations over time' (1978, p. 204). In such a framework traditional archaeological stadial typologies become no more than arbitrary cross-sections through a continuously operating complex of processes.

This framework remains one of the most attractive and sophisticated conceptualizations of societal change to have been used in archaeology, generating many specific studies (e.g. Frankenstein and Rowlands, 1978; Haselgrove, 1982). However, it has a number of shortcomings shared with both functionalist and other evolutionary theories of change which detract from its usefulness. Firstly, the notion of contradiction is simply reduced to *functional incompatibility* between the levels of the social formation; but as we argued in chapter 2, the idea of function and functionality provides, at best, a low-level description of aspects of the social and in no way provides an adequate explanation. Secondly, the characterization of the social formation artificially separates the organizational function of kinship systems in small-scale societies in organizing production (as the social relations of production) from their ideational and juridico-political components which take place in the sphere of the superstructure. This results in a damaging theoretical barrier being imposed to understanding the relationship between the economic and the non-economic.

Thirdly, the totalizing framework of the model *requires* a reductionist essentialism. It is proposed that history, the social, the relations of production have essences or essential features which operate as their principle of unity irrespective of any particular society. But the timeless universality of this logos (economic process) is dependent on that which it systematically excludes: the contingent, social difference, particularity. The primary essence of history is the dominance accredited to the social relations of production in relation to both the superstructure and the forces of production. While the latter may constrain the social relations, the superstructure appears to have no primary role whatsoever in social transformation. It becomes a pure effect of the dominance of the social relations of production. What does this superstructure consist of? The levels of the social formation in the model (see figure 6.4) clearly boil down to the economic – productive forces and relations – and the rest. What is the remainder, this apparently inessential and contingent left-over? The superstructure, of course, includes law, politics, religion, philosophy, ideology, art, etc., and it is this 'etc.' that is of importance because the 'etc.' implies that we can simply substitute the terms 'society' and 'culture', the social totality as a lived totality apart from abstract economic process. Now this 'etc.' would seem to be of fundamental importance for explaining and understanding the nature of social transformations but in the model provided the entire superstructure becomes an unreal set of data, of appearances projected from an underlying economic reality. It is secondary, derivative and ultimately an accidental effect of the economic.

The opposition economy/superstructure requires that the economic be conceived as something natural and prior to the superstructure, to power, ideology and political force. Such a model would seem to systematically evade or efface the role of subjective labour in constituting the social world and it tends to have the effect of neutralizing the coercive nature of political or superstructural relations. There can be no clear boundary between the economic and the superstructure. The economic cannot occur independently of political force and such force is never likely to be exercised purely for its own sake but for economic reasons. The economic can not be free of the superstructure as an independently

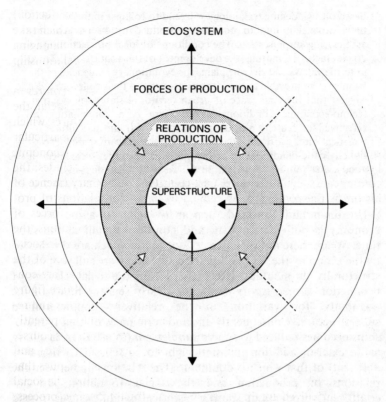

FIGURE 6.4 The 'Local population model' of Friedman and Rowlands
Notes: The solid line represents dominance; the broken line represents constraints.
Source: J. Friedman and M. Rowlands (1978). Reprinted by permission of
Duckworth & Co.

structuring dominant entity. The nature of labour, the work form itself is inextricably bound up with coercive power and politics. To isolate the economic and present it as dominant is to ignore the composition of the economic itself with politics.

Although the constraints of the productive forces and the ecosystem in the model are proposed as purely negative, in practice this 'negativity' seems to have considerable selective power:

> The developmental situation of the chiefdom depends very much on techno-ecological conditions . . . In montane areas, for example, where soils are shallow and runoff a major problem, chiefdoms

based on swiddening technology will tend to collapse in the course of their expansion due to decreasing productivity in an economy accelerating surpluses . . . The conditions of local production are a crucial factor permitting [the development of the asiatic state]. Thus, in fertile valleys and riverine plains the evolutionary tendencies of the tribal system are able to work themselves out to their fullest . . . We suggest that the emergence of urban territorial states will occur in techno-economic conditions where there is a combination of effective land scarcity plus the possibility of extreme agricultural intensification . . . Both Cuicuilco and Teotihuacan shared exceptionally good conditions for urban growth, since they were sited on good water sources for irrigation and near obsidian deposits.

(Friedman and Rowlands, 1978, pp. 213, 216, 234, 260)

Friedman and Rowlands appear to want to argue that the economy is both determinant and non-determinant at the same time. While there are vast areas of social life which are dominated by the economy (i.e. in the superstructure) they are still supposedly structurally autonomous. However, positing the social relations of production as *necessarily dominant* clearly sets the limits of the possibility for variation in the relatively non-determined superstructure. Consequently the indeterminacy of this relationships becomes reduced to a mere *supplement* (to use Derrida's term as an exterior addition to what ought to be self-sufficient but is deficient) of that which is dominant. The relationship between the relations of production and the social formation are not contingent, products of specific historical conditions but instead become an a priori necessity in which the conditions for social transformation are known in advance. If the social relations of production are dominant or determinant in *every* type of social formation then their conditions of existence must be deduced independently from any concrete manifestation of social relations. However, in this case, the only reality they would have would be to assure in tautological fashion the existence of the economy as a separate entity with a determining or dominant role.

While the notion of contradiction between levels or instances of the social formation is not explicitly introduced in Friedman and Rowlands's paper, Gledhill and Rowlands (1982) do usefully elevate the concept to an important causative role in social transformation while stating that 'economic and socio-political conditions cannot . . . be separated, and both are equally "material": we cannot understand economic processes in the narrowest sense in isolation, but neither can we argue that real developmental trajectories are determined by purely "cultural" or "political" processes' (Gledhill and Rowlands, 1982, p. 145). We entirely agree with such a position and the implicit criticism of the earlier model that it makes. What is required is a truly dialectical theorization in which the economic, the political and the cultural are viewed as being linked together in a relation of mutual mediation without any a priori hierarchy of dominance or determination.

BEYOND EVOLUTION: THE SOCIAL TEXTURE OF CHANGE

When considering social change in archaeology over either the long or the short term, evolutionary frameworks appear to be inadequate. The prospect before us is not to invent a new or a better evolutionary framework or model but to abandon the notion of evolution altogether. There is no difficulty in sustaining the reality of a conception, such as White's, that there is a fundamental difference between microlith technology and microchip technology or that energy capture has increased through time, so long as this is devoid of ethnocentric valorization. However, such observations do not take us very far in explaining the social and they certainly do not merit being placed within a totalizing evolutionary framework. It is far better to employ a simpler and far less loaded and contentious concept – 'change'. What we should be thinking in terms of are: social strategies, social transformation, power, ideology, altereity, plurality, relationality, displacement, substitution, difference – all terms that cannot be properly compressed or integrated into an evolutionary framework. Ultimately we may say that history is another term for undecidability. What this means is that we must regard social change as being an open, polysemous text, a text to be written and interpreted, not something that decides in any degree of finality what we write. Archaeology as a historical science is fundamentally open-ended. Evolutionary theories suggest that history is essentially closed in on itself, residing in a basic set of processes; but there are no such basic processes to be found. Processes exist but they are always different, singular, non-identical with each other. It is this non-identity, this singularity that we should be stressing. Rather than attempting to formulate positions which would once and for all explain the past in an absolute sense, we should be emphasizing that there are no absolutes, no fundamentals to dig down to in order to ground our analyses. The attempt to isolate series of events or essential elements and processes results in a turning away from history which becomes overlooked. It results in the production of a reductionist and ideological History.

In discussing an alternative theoretical position all we can hope to do is to outline a conceptual strategy for understanding social change in *general*. The level of generality involved will mean that such a perspective will only serve any useful purpose insofar as it is worked through, mediated, modified, and transformed in practice, in the act of trying to understand a particular case of social change.

Contingency and conjuncture

We start from two basic premises: (1) all social life is contingent; (2) all episodes of social change are conjunctural. By stressing the contingent and conjunctural nature of change we hope to avoid the pitfalls of essentialism and reductionism discussed earlier in this chapter. To say that social change is contingent is to adopt the position that history is indelibly a social creation: it has no predetermined teleological essence and there is no deterministic necessity to the working through of the historical process – history could have happened otherwise. Social change is conjunctural in that any particular episode of change depends on the convergence of overlapping sets of circumstances, actions and events which differ in form and nature from case to case according to differences in social context. By social change we specifically refer to the structural transformation rather than the reproduction of the social order. Such episodes of transformation are always *endogenously mediated* processes resulting in ruptures or structural disjunctions. This means that we conceive history as a series of ruptures and discontinuities separated by periods of social reproduction of variable duration. However, both stability and change are part and parcel of structural transformation and reproduction.

We are not dealing with a simplistic either/or distinction in which structural reproduction is conceived in some sense as absolute stability and structural transformation as a totalized set of changes. The difference between one situation and another is a matter of degree. Discontinuities depend on underlying continuities and vice versa. So history is a dialectic of continuity–discontinuity mediated by structural contingency and conjunctural events and circumstances. There is nothing in the archaeological or historical record which suggests that we should privilege or give methodological priority to change, or its conceptual polar opposite, stability. Indeed a radical opposition between the two terms would seem to be unhelpful because in an obvious manner societies are changing all the time in terms of the actual physical and bodily composition of the population, interactions between individuals, losses and gains in the transmission of knowledge and information, use of specific artefacts, etc. On the other hand, basic structural features of society, values and principles for conduct, may remain unaltered. No society can be absolutely stable, nor will social changes of even the most drastic sort alter every aspect of action, thought and feeling. Stability and change are both relative terms, neither can be conceptualized except in terms of the other, and both reside in all social forms.

It is important to stress that societies do not just exist in motion or action, in human praxis, but also in thought, either at a level of discursive or practical consciousness. In other words social actors always draw on stocks of knowledge and may know to a greater or lesser extent *why* they are acting in any particular manner and be able to justify or rationalize their actions; or, alternatively, they may know *how* to act without being able to verbalize the principles on which they are acting. Hence actions may have intended or unintended consequences and in any particular situation one or the other, or both, may provide an important motor for change. Thought and action are thoroughly interwoven and to avoid essentialism we must posit a dialectic between thought and action such that neither stands in relation to the other in a situation of dominance or determination. Social being does not determine consciousness nor can we reverse this Marxian formula. At any particular conjuncture and with reference to a particular set of contingent circumstances one may dominate the other but the nature of this domination, always remaining partial in scope, is a matter of practical demonstration rather than a priori theoretical determination.

The social world while being a practical world of situated action is also a conceptualized world consisting of codes, signs and symbols which are in a constant process of production and reproduction, structuration and destruction. It is always ordered in different societies according to a meaningful scheme and sets of values. Agents act in terms of socially constituted categories involving other persons, institutions and material culture.

Societies do not, of course, exist in isolation – social life involves interaction with and mediation of an environmental field and a social field of other individuals and groups. This 'external' natural and social field exerts influence. It may promote social transformation but such radical change is not automatic; it always involves an internalization of external factors. The 'risk' of carrying out various possible subsistence strategies and the effects of natural disasters are conceived and transformed within the structures of the social. That usually termed 'economic' has a style – it is itself part of a symbolic referential field. Similarly, contact between qualitatively different kinds of societies, such as hunter-gatherer band groups and socially stratified agrarian groups, or Captain Cook's arrival in Polynesia (Sahlins, 1981, 1985), is mediated by internal structure and signification. Acculturation is never a passive, but always an active and transformative process.

Social change: space and time

Space and time do not merely form containers within which social life is played out but constitute a medium through which social relations are produced and reproduced. Both are social productions and in turn are actively involved in social reproduction and transformation. As we argued in chapter 5 traditional archaeological practices resulting in the formulation of chronologies and periodizations of materials depend upon and presuppose a linear and abstract time. We argue instead that social practice and event have their own rhythms and their own time. Such a perspective questions the validity of traditional archaeological conceptions of time and the implicit identification of time with change which results in the 'problem' of the reality of archaeological periodizations (e.g. Halstatt and La Tène of the European Iron Age) and how transitions might develop between them.

Regarding time as a medium in which social action and change is played out means that societal transformation cannot be conceived as chaotic, as structureless – a point to which we will return below. Social change is not a single movement pervading the entire social totality but is articulated in time and space forming a medium for the restructuring of social relations. Spatiality and temporality form a component of social life in a situational social context in which purposeful human agency is structurally positioned and this positioning serves to shape day-to-day activities and alterations in their form and nature. Space and time are socially produced as concrete material spatialities and temporalities (e.g. the time-space of architectural forms) and as a set of relations between individuals and groups. Such space-time is not abstract and apart from human social existence but dense – filled up with the contents of social existence related dialectically to physical space and physiological ageing and society's cognitive image of itself as a continuing form. The spaces and times of the natural world (physical geography, passage of the seasons, lunar cycles etc.) and those related to the way the social field is conceptualized are incorporated into the social production of temporality and spatiality and transformed in the process. Social spatio-temporal production incorporates nature and the physical world into a 'second nature' and this socially constituted second nature may be redefined, reinforced, reinterpreted, reproduced or transformed into something qualitatively new. So, the historical sequence is one of contingent and conjunctural spatiality and temporality. Space and time form a medium serving to structure social life and are in turn structured by social relations in a recursive manner (Giddens, 1981; Soja, 1985; Pred, 1985).

But this spatio-temporal medium for social reproduction and transformation is not an indifferent one. The social constitution of time-space is not just a routinized process but one pregnant with contradictions, conflicts and struggles. Space and time form a medium for the networking of power and ideology in relation to competing interests and social strategies of individuals and groups. Power, ideology, contradiction, conflict, space and time can only be understood relationally. Each is infused with and partially encompassed by the others. Furthermore, all these concepts are not neutral but critical categories which can be turned in on themselves and in relation to an analysis of the social production of archaeological knowledge.

Signification, interests and structure

In discussing the nature of change we must make reference to the social world

1 As constituted a conceptual scheme of signs and codes for the ordering and reordering of human existence.
2 As a determinate patterning of actions and event sequences.
3 As mediated by structures dialectically related to strategies of individual and/or group *interest*.

In other words we are concerned with the linkage between signs, actions and constellations of actions or events, structures and power. People are always inseparable from meaning and from the world. The relationship between subject and object or thought and action is not one of radical opposition, nor of identity, but rather one of dialectical mediation. Subjects and objects form part of each other, help to constitute each other, but do not collapse into a single unitary entity.

The cultural schemes by means of which the social order is constituted are always arbitrary, never the only possibility for the realization of action. As we argued in chapter 3 the individual agent is always positioned in accordance with structure or relational sets of signs providing principles for conduct. Although positioned in the social field individuals do *act* and the consequences of these actions are just as likely to be unintended as intended. Such action is historically situated. It draws upon existing structured sign systems or conceptual schemes for the ordering of experience, but every manifestation of structure in an action event is a concretization of structure through its effects on social practice. This concretization of structure through action contains within itself the possibility of the reordering or structuration of structures because meanings and principles for conduct become re-evaluated in practice, in the contingent and conjunctural social circumstances of human practical activities. The practical projects of people take place within a context of received structured meanings and signification. However, this meaning and signification becoming concretized in and through action is at one and the same time re-evaluated through the course of this action and may be reproduced or transformed. Action, in other words, is in dialectical relation to structure and situational social context. It begins in structure, is mediated by structure, and ends in structure but its realization in the world may result in the rearticulation or transformation of structure.

Power, ideology and change

Power and ideology are integrally linked to the reproduction and transformation of the social order and to structure. While power is intimately involved in both social reproduction and transformation, ideology as a limited material practice and form of power is to be fundamentally linked with societal reproduction (see chapter 3). Power may take on a directly coercive form bolstering social domination in terms of direct physical control of subjects (e.g. military regimes). In social situations in which social control and exploitation are regularized features of life, the maintenance of this control by sheer force alone is likely to be both unstable and inefficient in the long run. In such cases repressive power may rest far more efficiently on some basis of perceived and maintained legitimacy, however achieved.

This form of power not directly involving physical coercion is ideological power which may (1) naturalize the social order through the manipulation of the past making what is mutable appear to be immutable; (2) represent as coherent aspects of the social order which are contradictory; (3) represent that which is partial as universal; (4) represent the social as being a pre-ordained natural order; (5) represent the ideas and modes of organization operating in terms of the specific interests of individuals or groups as being in the interests of everyone. So, in various ways, ideology relates the contingency of the present (social inequality) to a natural and timeless order or to a mythical past. Ideology is the presentation of antithesis, a strategy of social containment. Its structural effect in society is to disperse, conceal, dilute, displace or deny contradictions. Such a structural effect serves the interests of those in positions of social dominance and justifies or provides apologies for the social order. Hence ideology is a specific and limited material form of social practice with structural effects. It is not simply generalizable to 'world view' or to be conceived as 'false consciousness' or as a 'pre-scientific' form of knowledge. Instead it may be regarded as a solution at the level of social consciousness to structural contradictions that cannot be dissipated or resolved in practice.

Ideology is neither true nor false. It is a misrepresentation or denial of contradiction. To claim that ideology is a 'solution in consciousness' is not to suggest it merely operates in the realm of consciousness or ideas. Ideology, insofar as it is conceived as a set of ideas embodied in social action, is a real material force in the social contributing to the maintenance or reproduction of society. Although ideological relations may misrepresent contradictions and the concrete social practices operating in terms of these contradictions, at the same time they designate a real relation, both material and necessary, rather than purely illusory. As a material form ideology is bound up with, works through, and has definite effects on social practices. It does not appear as some kind of purely gratuitous invention of consciousness intentionally manipulating reality, nor is it the result of a conspiracy on the part of those whose interests it serves. However, the effects of the operation of ideology as a form of power are the concealment of contradictions obviously playing a powerful role in the reproduction of structure mediating social practices. So ideology operates in such a manner as to block the translation of structural contradiction into conjunctural struggle between social actors.

Contradiction

Structure, conceived as a set of signs and categories, principles and resources, resulting from and making possible human social experience and action, should not be conceived simplistically as a dovetailing of a harmoniously ordered entity. To the contrary, the principles embodied in structure exist in a relation of contradiction; one may deny or oppose another. *Difference* and contrast required in any sign system invites contradiction but this contradictory relationship between signs and meanings only realizes itself in the social through the practical effects of structure in action and situated event. Signs have, of course, conceptual value by virtue of their contrast to other signs, but in action signs become articulated with respect to the referential meaning of what may be, in any particular instance, the opposing interests of different social strategies. Contradiction may be conceived as a component of the · social world giving rise to a potentiality for change in at least two major senses. First, contradiction is an existential part of social being. It is always and will always be present because it is part of what it is to be human. Individual persons may consider themselves to have a continuing identity, irrespective of any particular action or action sequence, and yet can only be to others what they are at a particular time and place. The activities of individuals and groups result in the production of social conditions which, in some respects, constrain and set limits to the possibilities of future actions. These conditions are produced by individuals but become independent of their wills and hence social reality is a contradictory reality. Material production in most cases requires a division of labour, and this must be seen as a result of productive activity and by no means a consciously intended outcome.

A second source of existential contradiction is in the contrast between the 'natural' and the 'cultural' orders:

> the human being as *Dasein*, originates and disappears into the world of Being, the world of nature, yet as a conscious, reflective agent is the negation of the inorganic. The mediator of the contradictory character of human existence is society itself, for only in and through membership of a society does the human being acquire 'second nature'.
>
> (Giddens, 1981, p. 236; cf. Goldmann, 1977, p. 101)

This notion of contradiction as residing in the very nature of social being has to be complemented by a second sense of the term, if we are to claim that contradiction provides the root of motility in the social order.

Earlier in this chapter we rejected the position that the social order can adequately be conceived as a definite series of structural levels or instances. Such a view is intimately linked with the extensive debate over the concept of contradiction: whether it refers to real or logical opposition; whether logical contradictions can be real (see e.g. Colletti, 1975; Meikle, 1979; Elster, 1978; Larrain, 1983, ch. 4). In accordance with our arguments in other chapters contradiction is not a logical concept nor does it refer to real opposition or conflict. Furthermore, the notion of contradiction does not suggest functional incompatibility between structures, levels or instances of a social formation but refers to opposing principles, drawn on in social action, but which are nevertheless dependent on each other for their existence in any particular type of society (cf. Giddens, 1979, ch. 4).

Contradiction is an opposition between elements of structures residing in practices which presuppose one another and constitute conditions of existence for each other. It is to be conceived not as an opposition between fixed identities but as an internal relation where the identities of each contradictory element depend on each other. These contradictions will differ in nature and form from one society to another. In other words we avoid any essentialist notion of contradiction such as the classic Marxist formula in the 1859 'Preface' where contradiction arises between the forces and relations of production with primacy being given to the former in the determination and working-out of the historical process. We argue, instead, that contradiction is constitutive of the social field as a whole and is never likely to be a simple matter of an opposition between different areas of the economic or between economic and social processes. Contradiction is to be conceived as a reality lying within the very structuring of the social order itself. Adopting such a position it is possible to argue that all societies are contradictory totalities with the contradictions differing temporally between different forms of society. Such contradictions can never by dispelled except in terms of the transformation of the principles structuring the social field as a whole. Following from such an argument it is possible to argue that we can distinguish between primary and secondary contradictions, the former giving rise to and promoting the development of the latter. A primary contradiction is one that presages a new social system. Giddens, for example, argues that the primary contradiction of capitalism is that between private appropriation of wealth by the few, and a structural principle it presumes which negates it, socialized production (1979, p. 142). However, the ranking of contradictions in an evaluative hierarchy of importance appears to us as a rather dubious and contentious exercise and in itself may provide little insight into an understanding of why structural transformations occur. Following Althusser (1977, pp. 106–16) we will suggest that contradictions are always *overdetermined*. For example, the contradiction between private appropriation of wealth and socialized production in capitalist society is always dependent on the historically contingent and concrete forms and circumstances in which it takes place. In other words, the contradiction is inseparable from the overall structuration of the social order, and from its concrete realization in human practices.

Structural transformation is likely to occur when there is a multiplicity of contradictions between structuring principles, each affecting the other, which may give rise to further contradictions. However, structural contradiction can only be realized in human social practices, in situated action. So contradictions in structure, between structural principles drawn upon by actors in their day-to-day conduct, result in competing beliefs, evaluations and rationalizations for socially situated actions. These ultimately alter the conditions of existence for the form and nature of social relations, and concomitantly the nature of these relations themselves change. In other words, contradiction at the level of structure becomes translated into a conflict of interests between social actors which ultimately may become transcribed into the entire social body at any particular historical conjuncture producing a radical 'break' or rupture in the social process. The outcome of such a conflictual rupture will be a transformation of the structures underlying social action. Contradictions, then, are the precondition for social change, but they do not bring it about. Change, as discussed above, depends on episodes, conjunctures of events and conditions which build on each other around contradiction producing conflicts which may be resolved by social change.

The accumulation of time in such conjunctures may or may not involve a standard conception of chronology (see chapter 5). It may not be chronology which is important but the intersection of contradiction and event. In other words, meaningful connections may transcend chronology. Chronology may be crucial to social change, at points of sudden discontinuity, but for the most part we may expect it to be irrelevant in pre-capitalist social forms because of the absence of events which build on each other. Conjunctures, clusterings of events, must be understood in terms of their determinate temporality. The time of the events may overlap, but the time in common between the events may not extend beyond the clustering, the episode.

CONCLUSION: SPECIFICITY AND CHANGE

In considering the nature of social change it is vital to avoid theoretical frameworks which produce a totalizing history, a history of the whole of humanity which does not recognize rupture, difference, non-correspondence between social forms. Any adequate analysis of change must take into account the subjective constitution of the social as an active and differentiated set of strategies involving power, group and individual interest and signification. These cannot be simply reduced to a set of unitary processes.

We must take into consideration that the tempos, times, spaces, nature and form of change in contemporary Western society are fundamentally different from the prehistoric past. Furthermore, societies constitute their own spaces and their own times. Change has to be analysed in all the detail of its specificity. The concepts we have outlined in the final part of this chapter are of necessity general, but their purpose is to allow us to *think historical and contextual specificity* in attempting to understand social reproduction and transformation.

In attempting to understand change we are always faced with issues as to what type and degree of alteration in what is being considered, and why this is thought to be of interest or importance anyway. Ultimately these are practical questions that always presuppose a politics. This issue of the politics of theory is one we address in the next chapter.

7

Archaeology and the Politics of Theory

It is not my fault if reality is Marxist
Sartre quoting Che Guevara
Humanity is by nature political being.
Aristotle, *Politics* 1253ª3

Throughout this book we have been concerned to stress that archaeology is an active production of the past, an intellectual and cultural labour. Archaeology is to be situated in the present as discourse in a political field, and as a practice located in relation to structures of power. This has involved reference to the mediation of present and past, theory and data, abstract and concrete, epistemological subject and object in the practice of archaeology. By the term mediation we mean that there can be no radical separation and conclusive definition of these categories in themselves, nor can they be conceived as separate but interacting in some way; the categories are instead held together in a tension in determinate practices. In this chapter we wish to draw out the implications for archaeology of the proceeding discussions, and explore the major issues further. These concern the development of a critical archaeology.

THE EMERGENCE OF A CRITICALLY
SELF–CONSCIOUS ARCHAEOLOGY

It has been argued that particular archaeologies reflect contemporary cultural concerns or categories. For example, Trigger has related theoretical changes in Anglo-American archaeology to the changing fortunes (according to him, 1960s optimism and 1970s pessimism) of the middle classes:

a sense of helplessness is . . . emphasized by framing much of the discussion of evolutionary change in terms of general systems theory . . . disillusionment about present day affairs has led many archaeologists to reject the view that cultural progress is inevitable or even desirable . . . What emerges is an eschatological materialism in which human consciousness plays no significant role.

(Trigger, 1981, p. 151)

In another paper Trigger (1984) has described archaeologies as being nationalist, colonialist or imperialist. Archaeology has been, and is still, important in the establishment of national identities. Colonial archaeologies denigrate non-Western societies to the status of static yet living museums from which the nature of the past might be inferred. Imperialist archaeologies (largely those developed in Britain and America) exert theoretical hegemony over research in the rest of the world through extensively engaging in research abroad, playing a major role in training either foreign students or those who subsequently obtain employment abroad, and in the dissemination of texts. The American expression of the new archaeology, advocating high-level generalization and a cross-cultural comparative perspective, 'asserts the unimportance of national traditions . . . and of anything that stands in the way of American economic activity and political influence' (Trigger, 1984, p. 366). At an even more general level, Friedman (1986) has inserted archaeology into what he claims to be world cycles of 'traditionalist-culturalist', 'modernist' and 'post-modernist' cultural identities or cosmologies.

There has been criticism of particular archaeologies as vulgar ideology: that they are distorted fabrications lending support to a system of 'false consciousness'. Kohl (1981, p. 92) has remarked on the connection between ideas of hyperdiffusionism (spread of the Aryan race) and fascism in the 1920s, while other work has focused on ideological distortion in museum presentations of the past (see below). More sophisticated ideology critique has focused on the philosophical and methodological assumptions that lie behind many archaeologies and that work ideologically. This may involve representing particular social or political interests as universal, misrepresenting crucial contradictions in society or theory, or reifying particular categories (assuming that they are natural, objective and concrete, rather than relating them to their social conditions of production). As we mentioned in chapter 1, Rowlands has questioned the validity of the idea of a prehistory of Europe (1984, p. 154) and criticized a prehistoric metanarrative of development of societies from 'simple' to 'complex' forms:

the meta-narrative of simple to complex is a dominant ideology that organises the writing of contemporary world pre-history in favour of a modernising ethos and the primacy of the West. That the political context of colonialism is its natural progenitor. That for these reasons, such constructions of history have formed the dominant ideologies of the metropolitan centres, although changing their content from British imperialism to American neo-evolutionary, multi-lineal trajectories of the Modernisation kind . . . claims to autonomy and independence have taken the form of cognitive apartheid. If the West isn't the only area that has states, cities, writing, rationality etc. you show that you have something similar that is either equivalent or better. A universal dialogue about the nature of universal humanity is sustained but now with a radical emphasis on difference and comparison.

(Rowlands, 1986, pp. 3–4)

Elsewhere (Shanks and Tilley, 1987, ch. 3; Tilley, 1985) we have extensively criticized theoretical perspectives advanced in the new archaeology as lending explicit or implicit support to the value systems of a capitalist society. For example, the projection of present-day economic values such as maximizing returns and minimizing costs to 'explain' resource utilization among prehistoric hunter-gatherers naturalizes what are historically and culturally specific values as universal features of humanity.

The notion that archaeology can be separated from current political events has been challenged: strongly held conceptions of academic freedom have recently come into question. This questioning of a virtually dominant ideology – that archaeology constitutes a neutral academic discipline and its practitioners should have scholarly freedom and disciplinary autonomy – has been precipitated by events surrounding the World Archaeological Congress of 1986. As a result of a ban on South African and Namibian participants by the British organizers, the UISPP (International Union of Prehistoric and Protohistoric Sciences) withdrew its official recognition of the Congress, and set up an alternative congress. Many archaeologists from the West withdrew as a result of the ban. This withdrawal, both of official recognition and of discontented individuals, was justified in the cause of academic freedom, the claimed infringement of the freedom of South African archaeologists to attend the Congress, and in the cause of keeping the pollution of politics out of archaeology. Shaw (1986) and Hodder (1986a) have drawn attention to the complexity of the issues and have effectively criticized a position which would uphold an abstracted, detached and reified value of 'academic freedom', however strong and evocative its connotations.

The domination of the UISPP, a supposedly internationally representative body, by unelected authority figures of European archaeology, brings up the issue of the relationships between an academic West and non-Western 'developing' countries in a post-colonial world capitalist economy. Rowlands (1986a), Sinclair (1986) and Ray (1986) have considered the issues of a decolonialized archaeology in non-Western countries. This was also a feature of many papers at the World Archaeology Congress. Sinclair notes that:

> Differences between development strategies which attempt to reproduce capitalist relations of production in the Third World and those which attempt to support economic and cultural disassociation from the capitalist system directly influence the context in which archaeological research is carried out. On the one hand, forms of archaeological practice based on neo-colonial dualistic conceptions of 'traditional' and 'modern' society can often result in a preservationist and academically exclusionist attitude to the remnants of 'traditional' society. On the other hand, the focus on the 'traditional' can also lead to biases emerging against the 'modern'. This differs markedly from a programme of research which seeks to recover and present archaeological data in a form relevant to the widespread extension of an historical consciousness as part of a non-capitalist development strategy.
>
> (1986, p. 81)

Another focus for discussion has been the relationship between archaeological research and minority interests. The distortions and political implications of archaeologies of the Native Americans (Trigger, 1980), Australian Aborigines (Langford, 1983; Ucko, 1983), Norwegian Saami (Olsen, 1986) and the black community in Britain (Belgrave, 1986), have been discussed. This, and other work, (e.g. Hall, 1984; Fawcett, 1986) has involved a consideration of the politics of ethnicity and the issue of nationalist archaeologies. Academic archaeology, as often as not, operates as part of a wider cultural discourse serving to reproduce the relationship between the dominant and the dominated.

The controversy surrounding the World Archaeology Congress highlighted the conventional relationship between archaeology and politics as entirely exterior, concerning government and educational policy, administration and funding, public archaeology and the 'rescue' and 'preservation' of the past, and what has come to be termed cultural resource management. Here again the dominant ideology emphasizes neutrality, consensus with regard to conservation goals, and the disinterested pursuit of knowledge in the hands of professional administrators and academics: archaeology as a public service (cf. Cleere (ed.), 1984; Green (ed.), 1984). There has been a notable lack of critical reflection resulting in calls for archaeology to be explicitly marketed to an uneducated public (Macleod, 1977), and the specification of administrative and management strategies for maximizing archaeological productivity (Stephenson, 1977). Such a perspective turns the past into the cultural capital of a supposedly enlightened elite, who then may disseminate it at will to a passive, and ultimately alienated, public (see Shanks and Tilley, 1987, Chs 1 and 3).

The relationship of archaeology to the present necessarily involves that between archaeology as an academic discipline and its wider societal context. Hodder has reported preliminary results of an attitude survey of what people think about archaeology. The results are not surprising: 'certain groups of people in contemporary Britain know more about the past than others . . . these people have often had more education . . . often have higher valued jobs with more control over people and resources . . . are more likely to be male' (1986, p. 162). Popular representations of archaeology in books and magazines have also come under scrutiny. Gero and Root (1986), in an analysis of the *National Geographic Magazine*, illustrate the manner in which the past of 'exotic' countries becomes systematically incorporated into the American imperialist present, a conception involving an utterly materialistic and commodified conception of the past. The past is frequently enlivened by reference to contemporary categories and social relations, ultimately becoming homogenized and connected to the 'rise' of Western 'civilization'. Photographs of modern natives humanize the archaeological landscapes depicted, connecting past with present and offsetting the present-past of exotic countries with contemporary America. In the pages of the *National Geographic*, 'archaeology contributes to the rationalisation of imperialism, legitimating these activities with a congruent view of the past' (Gero and Root, 1986, p. 9).

Investigations have also been made of the major institutional relationship between the public and the discipline, the museum. Many criticisms have been made of distorted representations of the past (e.g. Leone, 1981, 1981a; Horne, 1984). Leone shows how the representation of Shaker society at the outdoor 'living-history' museum at Pleasant Hill, Lexington, Kentucky imposes the values of contemporary American capitalism. Efficiency, calculating rationality, industry, export, profit, innovation and inventive ingenuity comprise the major organizing themes in the displays. That Shaker society was based on an utterly different set of values in which they laboured to avoid sin, rather than for profit and 'the only efficiency they knew was the kind created between self-mortification and a hair shirt' (Leone, 1981a, p. 312) is almost entirely 'forgotten'. We have produced an extended ideology critique of the museum's aesthetic (see chapter 1; and Shanks and Tilley, 1987), concentrating on the way it produces its message in a number of individual museum exhibitions in Britain.

Finally, an important but surprisingly undeveloped focus in the emergence of a critically self-conscious archaeology is feminist archaeology, work that has raised the consciousness of the absence of women in archaeology, both conceptually in archaeological discourses and substantively in terms of a male-dominated profession (Conkey and Spector, 1984; Gero, 1985).

Despite growing awareness of the relationship between archaeology and present-day national and global structures of power and social domination, a great deal of critical work in archaeology remains political but without any politics. For so many the relation between present context and archaeology as disciplinary practice is neutral. The purpose of critique is thus regarded as one of consciousness raising and the correction of bias. Ideology, a concept central to so much of this work, is often regarded as false consciousness to be expelled by enlightened reason. A view of ideology as false consciousness depends on the classical empiricist conception of knowledge. In such a view knowledge is to be derived from the subject's experience of an external object. The *telos* is a better version of the past, the inculcation of critical judgements. Another view underlying some of the studies is a notion of ideology as related to class or social position. This raises the question of why critique should be accepted. Might not the critique also be socially determined? If the epistemological issues are not considered the prospect is of infinite regress and relativism, each group having its own legitimate past.

Critique and contextual archaeology

Hodder has presented a critique of the concept ideology in proposing a 'contextual' archaeology. He objects to the cross-cultural connotations of the concept, that it may be taken to be a historical universal and consequently fail to account for historical particularity. He regards the concept as being incompatible with a view of social actors as knowledgeable, who are not necessarily fooled by ideologies into a relation of false consciousness with regard to their social conditions of existence. He backs up this argument with the findings of public opinion surveys showing that people do not believe everything they are told about the past. Instead, Hodder argues all ideologies both mask and reveal: 'ideology can be socially active, revealing rather than masking, enabling rather than repressing' (1986a, p. 117). Here the concept of ideology is neutralized and depoliticized. It is simply regarded by Hodder as a 'world view' or conceptual structure, linked to knowledgeability on the part of social actors and power. This knowledgeability, according to him, allows the possibility of critical debate, and social change through social debate (ibid., p. 113). For Hodder, the solution to the problem of the verification of a critical theory which would criticize on the basis of the social and historical determination of truth and meaning is to abandon both the project and a conception of ideology as tied to the reproduction rather than the transformation of the social order.

As an alternative Hodder stresses a particular and determinant historical context within a structured cultural field produced by knowledgeable social actors. There remains the problem of relativism: if archaeological knowledges are contextual, with a subjective dimension, and tied to the negotiation of power, how are different archaeologies to be evaluated? Hodder's answer seems to be to refer to a project of self-knowledge and debate. Debate operates on a real, but not objective past. This allows critical evaluation, but no right answers, no certainty:

> There is no finishing position since there can never be any way of evaluating whether the 'right' interpretation has been arrived at . . .
> But better and better accommodations and new insights can be achieved in a continuing process of interpretation.
>
> (Hodder, 1986, p. 155)

Hodder has faced issues vital to the emergence of a post-processual archaeology of the 1980s and 1990s, but there are problems. He states that 'since the past cannot be known with certainty, we do not have the right to impose our own universals on the data and to present them as truth' (1986, p. 102). But this argument appears to come close to a disabling relativism. Hodder argues in the same context that universals deny people freedom, but such a statement has no *epistemological* relevance. Hodder's only resistance to relativism is the material reality of the past and a faith in the effectivity of liberal and critical debate.

All archaeology is contextual and archaeologies in opposition to mainstream academic archaeology are possible: non-Western indigenous archaeologies, feminist archaeologies, 'fringe' archaeologies. Hodder's answer to the compatibility or incompatibility of these different archaeologies is rightly to resist methodology – the specification of a universal method. Instead he relies on epistemology, the manner in which we can hope to *know* the past. He takes some points from a reading of Collingwood (1946): data are not objective but they are nevertheless real and are constituted in theory; they are activated by questions involving a historical imagination giving insight into particular historical circumstances. This is a process of thinking ourselves into the past, reliving the past (Hodder, 1986, p. 94). Such insights can be evaluated according to the internal coherence of an argument and the manner in which they correspond to evidence.

The result of such a position is a vision of an ideal of a discipline of archaeology characterized by open debate and operating in a pluralistic society; archaeologists creating better and better accommodations to the past in a continuous process of interpretation, aiming at self-knowledge of the present. Hodder's references (almost nostalgic) to the value of traditional archaeologies and his affirmation of the personal roots of his approach to archaeology (1986a, p. 171) become simply symptoms of his desire for civilized academic debate, the right to choose one's own past (within reason), an affirmation of the particularity of the lived past. But such a position seems all too readily to embrace a regressive liberalism and a fragmentary relativism – consequences of a shaky epistemology. Here we must ask whether a contextual archaeology will really change anything; can it act as social critique as Hodder seems to believe (1984, 1986a, p. 113)? He has admitted that critical debate seems, in the context of the events surrounding the World Archaeological Congress, to have had little effect on established ideologies and views even among supposedly enlightened intellectuals (1986a, pp. 118–19).

The vital question to be faced is the real implications of power to the discipline of archaeology. Here we need to consider the power relations between the academic community and the power interests of educational and governmental state apparatuses, and their linkage with a capitalist economy. These decide which educated and creative individuals are *allowed* to exercise and publicize their historical 'imaginations' in pursuit of *their* 'self-knowledge'. The corollary is that no matter how many subordinated individuals, minorities, classes or groups may realize, for example, the nonsense of a museum's representation of the past, it makes no difference. A contextual archaeology, as Hodder conceives it, runs the very real danger of disguising the reality of contemporary relations of repressive power and social domination behind a spurious plurality of archaeologies, neutralizing social objection, transforming it into a point of liberal and critical debate. Such a position also overlooks the contradictory relation of critical debate to contemporary society. Critique may be highly valued and yet matters little in reality as a feature of capitalism's hypocritical acknowledgement of 'civilized' values.

Marxist archaeology and political critique

Most Marxist approaches in archaeology have remained just that –alternative approaches to the past. They have a strong tendency to scientism. They may introduce different perspectives on the data which are claimed to be truer or better representations of society or the past than those produced by conventional archaeologies. This also applies to those predominantly Marxist inspired critical archaeologies which depend on a distinction between science and ideology: Marxist science dispelling the false consciousness of ideology, correcting the bias of those archaeologies remaining rooted in present ideologies.

There has been little serious consideration of what may be termed Marxism's critical tradition which does not emphasize a science/ideology distinction. Kristiansen explicitly discounts the critical theory of the Frankfurt school as being irrelevant to archaeology (1984, p. 96); Hodder's discussion of it, condensed into a few pages (1986, pp. 164–6), is inevitably somewhat lacking. We consider this critical tradition of Marxism as one of the most important and essential sources for reconstructing archaeological theory and practice (Shanks and Tilley, 1987). It would be a serious matter if archaeology remained content to simply borrow from alternative definitions of the social, as found for example in Marxist anthropology, while making the odd rhetorical gesture to critical radicalism. Spriggs astonishingly claims the French 'situationists' Vaneigem and Debord and the black leader Marcus Garvey as precursors of the contributors to *Marxist Perspectives in Archaeology* (1984, p. v: dedication)!

CRITICISM AND ARCHAEOLOGICAL PRACTICE

Gouldner (1980) has discussed at length the dual aspects of Marxism we mentioned above which stand in a relation of considerable tension: Marxism as science and Marxism as cultural critique. For scientific Marxism in traditional or structural Marxist form, the emergence of socialism depends on a prior set of objective economic conditions produced through an accumulation of antagonistic contradictions in the capitalist mode of production. In aspects of Marx's own formulations impersonal and necessary laws supposedly guarantee the organic evolution of socialism. Such a position is subject to the criticisms made of evolutionary theories discussed in chapter 6. However, the critical side of Marxism has never been content to sit back and permit blind historical forces to come to fruition but has been concerned to actively incite people to change the course of their history. If capitalism really is doomed to suffer a cultural demise there would seem to be little point in preparing its graveyard.

In situating archaeology as a social production taking place in the present we wish to draw on the Marxist critical tradition and stress the practice of critique. The past is a reconstruction, a cultural product, an artefact. And as Benjamin remarked, every document of civilization is at the same time a document of barbarism (1979, p. 359). Critique is essential but it is not to be conceived as the criticism of a theory we don't like. It is not simply open debate. Critique does not arise from method but from *objection* (Faris, 1986, p. 4), political and social objection. Critique breaks with established epistemologies, abstractions and totalities in the service of present social change.

Marx's eleventh thesis on Feuerbach states that 'the philosophers have only *interpreted* the world, in various ways; the point is to *change it*' (Marx and Engels, 1970, p. 123). We will elaborate several aspects we may take from this. The point of archaeology is not merely to interpret the past but to change the manner in which the past is interpreted in the service of social reconstruction in the present. There is no way of choosing between alternative pasts except on essentially political grounds, in terms of a definite value system, a morality. So, criteria for truth and falsity are not to be understood purely in terms of the logic and rationality, or other-wise, of discourses but require judgements in terms of the practical consequences of archaeological theory and practice for contemporary social change.

Critique: past, present, future

Hodder has talked of the aim of archaeology being self-knowledge, knowledge of the present. Such a view is not very different from the traditional justification of archaeology as forming part of the human pursuit of knowledge. We will clarify some important points.

The study of the past as an end in itself seems to amount to an antiquarian desire to escape from the burden of living in the present, perhaps for personal self-gratification; it may also amount to a nostalgic yearning for values, social structures and social relations that are, and can be, no more. The historian, or the archaeologist, becomes a kind of 'cultural necrophile', as White puts it (1978, p. 41). We challenge this traditional view of the discipline which would represent it as a disinterested study of the past for the sake of 'knowledge'. Such a position has the effect of concealing the work of archaeology as a contemporary cultural practice. Hodder's notion of archaeology as self-knowledge includes an awareness of archaeology's location in the present (see above); but we go further in arguing for a mediation of past and present, held in tension in the practice of archaeology, involving a temporality of 'presencing' (see chapters 1 and 5).

A critical archaeology involves us in a reading of the past which at the same time invites us to shape a different future. The study of the past is a means of providing a medium for a critical challenge to the present. It becomes an operation to change the world as we know and experience it. The study of archaeology is not something done to 'remind' men and women of the past but is a form of cultural action that attempts to forge a transition from our present to a different future. This involves an awareness of history as the outcome of human agency. Humanity creates its own history and so can change, or alter, the consequences of this historical development through specific forms of social action and intervention. This does not imply that the course of history is solely to be regarded as an intentional production, a function of the desires of individual agents, but such a perspective does stress the sociality of that history and that no future is assured or inevitable. The future is always open to construction and reconstruction in the present. There is no iron cage of historical inevitability. The only inevitability is that people make history with an awareness of history, and may extend or rupture it through their day-to-day praxis in the world. A critical archaeology is an invitation to live this awareness of our historicity, this potentiality.

Knowledge, hegemony, truth

The knowledge derived from archaeology can be regarded as a means and an instrument for carrying out work in and on the world. Such a position regards knowledge as being a form of power, being constituted in definite material circumstances, and having specific material effects. Archaeological knowledge has material effects by virtue of the fact that it arises from the situated practices of individuals living and working in society. In this sense we can say that all archaeologists live a dialectic between their life and work and the social order in which they find themselves. Knowledge, characterized by a particular material mode of production is always a production of positioned agents situated within classes, institutions and disciplines.

This relation of power and knowledge can be refined by considering the concept of hegemony. From a classical Marxist perspective consciousness was always determined by social being and this was conceived in terms of determinance by the economic base. In other words, consciousness of social reality was deemed to be a more or less automatic reflection of deeper socio-economic processes. In elevating the role of consciousness in the constitution of the social Gramsci stressed the key role of hegemony or ideological ascendancy, arguing that class-bound social control is not simply dependent on brute force but that another vital and equally material element for the dominant class to exercise power was the establishment of its own political, moral and social values as supposedly self-evident and conventional norms for living. For Gramsci, a hegemonic order is one in which a common coded value system is expressed in which one conception of social reality is dominant, affecting other modes of thought and action. Hegemony is quintessentially ideological power, or power over others achieved through consent rather than brute force. The coercive power of the capitalist state is derived in part from intellectual and moral leadership enforced through 'civil society' or the entire ensemble of educational, religious and cultural institutions. Gramsci cogently notes that

> One of the commonest totems is the belief about everything that exists, that it is 'natural' that it should exist, that it could not do otherwise than exist, and that however badly one's attempts at reform may go they will not stop life going on, since the traditional forces will continue to operate and precisely will keep life going on.
> (Gramsci, 1971, p. 157)

We stress the working of hegemony as a nexus (not necessarily coherent or singular) of encoded value systems, working through institutions and the day-to-day practices of individuals and groups, involving the acceptance (not necessarily in its entirety) of the social and political order as being right, just, or at the very least legitimate. So, yes, people are knowledgeable and may not be fooled by ideology – no one may be fooled by that museum exhibit – but the important feature is that people 'know' it doesn't matter: it is only a museum, or a television programme, a book. The 'working classes' do not generally go to museums, and anyway museums are places you visit on rainy days, just one *leisure* activity among others. But, precisely, this *is* the working of hegemony. The point is that the past does matter; that story of the past or that museum exhibit does matter. This is not because it educates the public, teaches them critical awareness or whatever, but because it forms part of our present, part of our conception of the present which always involves the past. We are not born free of this connection between past and present.

There are no essential and obligatory foundations for making truth claims which are not themselves the product of a *politics of truth*. We must be concerned to investigate what kinds of power and determinate social conditions make the truth of a text or a museum's representation of the past appear plausible. Truth in archaeology is always to be related to the kinds of vision of material culture that are relevant to us, that respond to our social need. So a critical archaeology is an invitation to engage in a transformative practice. We must aim to detach the power of truth from all repressive forms of class-bound social hegemony.

Archaeologists, for example, have established a hegemony over the distant past, a hegemony currently being reinforced by a populist discourse of heritage, of communal tradition: a past that 'belongs' equally to everyone and yet at the same time is to be ordered and preserved by the trained professional, applying his or her knowledge. We must investigate the meaning and significance of such discourses, their power effects, whom they serve and to what end. In terms of society as a whole archaeology obviously has very little economic or political significance, but it does constitute a cultural practice, integrated in the general hegemonic regime of power in society. As such, archaeology is nothing if it is not cultural critique.

Any notion that academic archaeology has its own sectional apolitical concerns and interests by and large irrelevant to, and untainted by, contemporary social processes is impossible and dangerous to attempt to sustain. Such a position amounts to containing whatever might be deemed 'archaeological' within its own limited academic space. But any attempt to artificially separate archaeology from politics only serves to benefit existing power structures. A 'neutral' archaeology serves to sustain the existing social order by its failure to engage actively with it and criticize it. Thus any advocacy of an apolitical archaeology remains itself a form of political action.

The position we are taking involves the inscription of a fresh politics of truth, itself a form of power. This is a struggle waged in terms of the production of alternative regimes of truth. Truth is to be conceived as a series of coded rules which permit divisions to be drawn between various types of discourses in terms of a polar truth/falsity opposition. We should not do battle 'in favour of truth' but, rather, situate truths in relation to the social, economic and political roles they play in society. Our aim is not so much to change people's consciousness as to change the manner in which truth is produced and becomes accepted. Power can never be detached from truth; but we can work to subvert the power of truth being attached to the existing social order and instead link truth to a political future.

Critique and pluralism

This emphasis on the relation of truth and power, on the location of the truth of the past in the contemporary cultural practice of archaeology, an emphasis on the politics of theory, does not open the way for an anarchic play with meaning, a profusion of archaeologies each rooted in their own politics. Hodder is right to stress the material resistance of the past: not just anything can be said about it. But a simple reference to the materiality of the past does not explain its facticity, that it is fact in the present. Such an ontology requires a mediation of subject and object, a subjectivity and objectivity constituted in social practice. Fabian, in another context, notes:

> The object's present is founded in the writer's past. In that sense, facticity itself, that cornerstone of scientific thought, is autobiographic. This, incidentally, is why in anthropology objectivity can never be defined in opposition to subjectivity.
>
> (Fabian, 1983, p. 89)

And social practice always implies a politics (where the political refers to debate as to how social relations should be arranged). This begins in the present and ends in a future. It must form the arena of any critical debate concerning the archaeological past. It goes far beyond the narrow forum of archaeology as academic discipline. A critique of traditional, 'new' or standard 'Marxist' archaeologies in terms of their deficient understanding of the past may be necessary, but is by no means sufficient. Such archaeologies require not just intellectual challenge but active displacement. This displacement, we suggest, is a matter of condemning or supporting particular archaeologies according to social and political values. Here it is important to note that value is not something inherently residing in archaeology as a whole or in some forms of archaeology as opposed to others. It is, rather, something *produced* for archaeology and in the *practice* of doing archaeology.

We have already discussed the notion of a radical pluralism in archaeology and counterposed this to a repressive pluralism (see chapter 1). A realization of the social conditions underlying archaeological practice must shatter the illusion, fostered in the new archaeology with its emphasis on cross-cultural generalization, that the results of archaeological research are applicable to the whole of humanity. Archaeology, as the product of social conditions and forms of social existence, is always produced in terms of specific interests and values. There is not, and cannot be, one correct archaeological view of the past, one indivisible archaeology. There are instead many archaeologies, and frameworks for understanding them must become sites of struggle. Hence archaeology is always dependent on the political and social position of the investigator and his or her awareness of the social conditions in which archaeological production takes place. But we must reassert that this is an issue itself with no necessary or final solution. Rowlands has warned against the vitalism that might be involved in supporting local knowledges, 'authentic' knowledges deriving from a life-world organic and specific to those it encompasses. He also remarks that a fragmented past may discourage collective identity and reinforce hierarchization in that while 'the subordinated and the powerless may have identity, the powerful will have science' (1986a, p. 4). Rowlands is arguing in the context of relations between the developed West and the third world: 'a stress on radical heterogeneity and cultural difference would . . . be more compatible with the aims of dominant elites in an industrialising third world seeking autonomy and identity in order to obscure and mystify the sources of their own power' (ibid., p. 4). This serves again to emphasize the importance of the politics of theory and the manner in which such a politics need to be situated in relation to a determinate social context.

INTELLECTUAL LABOUR AND THE SOCIO-POLITICAL ROLE OF THE ARCHAEOLOGIST

Il faut être absolument moderne.

Baudelaire

Intellectuals and power

What is to be done? What is the role of the individual archaeologist? We have defined archaeology as a cultural practice and referred to the mediation of the individual and the social in practice. The question that follows from this is the nature of what actually is involved in the production of cultural or intellectual work.

Traditionally, in Marxist thought, the intellectual has been regarded as being a bearer of universal truths, acting in the role of the political consciousness of the masses. The intellectual spoke in the name of freedom, equality and social justice. For Sartre, the role of the thinker was, in the last analysis, a class situation with the mode of production providing a horizon for thought undermining the pretence that reason alone could somehow be in itself the final arbiter of knowledge: reason is historical and class-bound. Sartre's definition of the intellectual is provocative:

> *someone who attends to what concerns him* (in exteriority – the principles which guide the conduct of his life; and in interiority – his lived experience in society) and to whom others refer to a man *who interferes in what does not concern him.*
>
> (Sartre, 1983, p. 244)

The relationship of the intellectual to the powers that be in society is an *oppositional* one. The role of the intellectual is to call into question the established socio-political order. The intellectual must ceaselessly combat his or her own class (usually petty bourgeois), itself moulded by hegemonic culture, thought and sentiment. Reason must be related to the life and situation of the researcher, and it is only in this manner that the limits that ideology pose on knowledge may be questioned. It is at the level of concrete situations in which the intellectual finds himself or herself that Sartre's dialectic of exteriority and interiority operates. So the radical intellectual combines life and work, seeking

> to produce, both in himself and in others, a true unity of the personality, a recuperation by each agent of the ends imposed on his

activity, a suppression of alienations, a real freedom for thought – by defeating *external* social prohibitions dictated by the class structure, and *internal* inhibitions and self-censorship.

(Sartre, 1983, pp. 250–1)

The intellectual must be entirely modern, of his or her own time, constantly aware of and concerned about events in the society in which he or she lives.

Radical and intellectual commitment are vital components of critique. Here we can say that those archaeologists who seek simply to preserve and transmit information about the past are forced to adopt a conservative position. If other archaeologists step out of line and relinquish this role by criticizing the relationship of the discipline to society they will probably be accused of mistaking their proper role and purpose. Conceiving of archaeology as, in part, an act of socio-political intellectual struggle will, no doubt, be denounced as scandalous or denigrated as misrepresenting the true goals of the discipline. Another means of coping with such a perspective may be to attempt to neutralize it by integrating it with mainstream archaeology as yet another facet. A third strategy may be a conspiracy of silence; time will tell.

For Foucault, intellectual knowledge is itself inserted within a system of power and may serve either explicitly or inadvertently to block or invalidate lay discourse and knowledge. Consequently, the intellectual's role is

> no longer to place himself 'somewhat ahead and to the side' in order to express the stifled truth of the collectivity; rather, it is to struggle against the forms of power that transform him into its object and instrument in the sphere of 'knowledge,' 'truth,' 'consciousness,' and 'discourse.'
>
> (Foucault, 1977a, p. 208)

The *universalizing* intellectual has, in such a perspective, to be replaced by the *specific* intellectual. The specific intellectual fights against repression and carries this work on in the determinate social situations in which he or she is located in society and on the terms of his or her expertise in a certain field. The specific intellectual, then, is one who works at a particular node within society inevitably involved in what can only be a localized and regionalized struggle. The work of the specific intellectual is intimately related to class position, the conditions of his or her personal life and work and particular area of research and expertise. The intellectual fights and struggles in all areas of society against prevailing power–

knowledge–truth strategies, and engages in concrete and real everyday struggles. This is a process of undermining or burrowing away in the midst of a multitude of different sectors, points and intersections within the social system (Foucault, 1977b, 1980).

This conception of the specific intellectual corresponds with Foucault's view of theory:

> theory does not express, translate, or serve to apply practice: it is practice. But it is local and regional . . . and not totalizing. This is a struggle against power, a struggle aimed at revealing and undermining power where it is most invisible and insidious. It is not to 'awaken consciousness' that we struggle . . . but to sap power, to take power; it is an activity conducted alongside those who struggle for power, and not for their illumination from a safe distance. A 'theory' is the regional system of this struggle.
>
> (Foucault, 1977a, p. 208)

Power is not simply coercion and social order is not just a creation of force. Hegemony is vital to maintaining order. Hence any attempt to transform society cannot just concentrate on altering that which appears to be most obviously economic and political: the economic and the political are not at all to be considered as strictly delimited 'subsystems', 'spheres', 'levels' or 'instances' but pervade and permeate every aspect of living from the micro-context of familial relations to the macro-institutional context and affect everything from poetry and plays to sport and patterns of food consumption, and not least the work of the archaeologist.

Gramsci distinguishes two fundamental dimensions of social change, the organic and the conjunctural (1971, pp. 210–76). The organic component is a 'war of position', the establishment of a counter-hegemony. The conjunctural component involves the physical contestation for state power. A war of position on the cultural front necessitates the penetration and subversion of the complex and multifarious channels of ideological diffusion through which hegemony becomes sustained and is bolstered, but hegemony is never total but riddled with inconsistencies and fissures. This means that we need to question educational objectives, archaeological courses and archaeological practices so as to challenge the relation of the archaeologist to society.

A 'radical' archaeologist might become involved in a trade union, a party political organization, in demonstrations in the streets or organize extra-curricula discussions about, say, radical discrimination, or the violation of human rights. These may be, of course, genuine and important political acts. The problem is that they have no *necessary* relationship to the archaeologist's day-to-day work. The most powerful political work the archaeologist is able to produce will be likely to be in that field he or she knows best – archaeological theory and practice. It is vital not to forget that archaeology forms part of contemporary culture. It works and acts upon, influences and informs opinion in the present. Hegemony has to be constantly reproduced, and one of the main sites of this reproduction is located in educational institutions. As Lentricchia puts it:

> struggles for hegemony are sometimes fought out in (certainly relayed through) colleges and universities; fought undramatically, yard for yard, and sometimes over minor texts of Balzac: no epic heroes, no epic acts.
>
> (Lentricchia, 1985, p. 10)

It might be suggested that a critical archaeology must, firstly, take up an oppositional role to contemporary society; secondly, embrace a conception of the archaeologist as specific, or at times universal, intellectual fighting at his or her institutional site against the prevailing regime of the production of truth; this involves, thirdly, taking up a notion of archaeological discourse as being part of a war of position. This will be a value-committed archaeology.

Value-committed archaeology

Contemporary academic archaeology determines effectively both what archaeology *is* and *how* it should be taught and learnt; i.e. what archaeological questions, problems, means, methods and modes of analysis are. This certainly has a profound effect on the entire gamut of secondary and tertiary education and the teaching of archaeology in these sectors of the educational system; on fictional writing about the past (e.g. Auel, 1981); and on presentations in museums and the media – areas of hegemonic culture. Unless its challenges extend this far, a critical archaeology is likely to amount to little more than a self-congratulatory stance that we are aware of biases and distortions in our work and that this heightened consciousness will lead to better work being done in the future.

Discussions about the form and nature of archaeology in academia inevitably filter back in one form or another to affect the manner in which millions of people make sense of, or have sense made for them, of *their* past, and its connection with the present. It is quite evident that the past may be used for expressing a wide variety of supportive ideas and values for a capitalist society, naturalized and legitimized through an emphasis on tradition and long-term time scales: myths of genius; individuality; patriarchy; humanity's essential economic nature; the universality and inevitability of technological development as progressive; the naturalness of social stability as opposed to contradiction; the inferiority or superiority of certain forms of social organization, etc. Such views may be strongly supported by archaeological texts (they usually are), or they may be challenged.

There is no possibility of a neutral and autonomous 'middle way'. The effect of archaeology in socio-political terms depends on the place that it chooses to occupy within a wider socio-cultural field. A value-committed archaeology is one rejecting any position which would suggest that research merely mirrors the past. Instead it insists that research forms part of a process in which the archaeologist *actively decides* upon one past rather than another. Interpretation in archaeology constructs a *socio-political position* in the process of engagement with the artefactual traces of the past. Anything 'discovered' about the past is not a passive reflection of what the 'facts' may or may not tell us. Archaeological texts which re-present the past have an expressive, rhetorical and persuasive purpose. They are not, and cannot be, neutral expositions of the facticity of the past (see chapter 1). What is their influence on those who read them?

> Any specialized activity participates in a larger unit of action. 'Identification' is a word for the . . . activity's place in this wider context, a place with which the agent may be unconcerned. The shepherd *qua* shepherd, acts for the good of the sheep to protect them from discomfiture and harm. But he may be 'identified' with a project that is raising the sheep for market.
>
> (Burke, 1969, p. 27, cited in Lentricchia, 1985, p. 88)

The shepherd's concern for the sheep, although it may appear genuine enough, when set in its wider context is hardly disinterested. Placing academic archaeology firmly within its social context as a cultural practice in late capitalist society in the West brings into focus the inadequacy of a 'disinterested' concern with the past. Such an educational role for archaeology may go quite some way towards fulfilling the goal of socializing individuals both to accept and wish to participate in the reproduction of the capitalist market. By contrast a value-committed archaeology is one that situates disciplinary practice critically within its present social context. There is no disinterested interpretation of the past because it always makes a *difference* in what manner it is represented.

A value-committed archaeology inevitably demands personal commitment on the part of the archaeologist who must be wary of being incorporated into upholding the established institutional framework. Such an archaeology would require a reorientation of power structures within archaeological institutions. At present the academic world all too faithfully mirrors wider social processes in capitalist society with its emphasis on competition between individuals for academic prestige and power in the framework of a hierarchical professorial structure; the 'ownership' of ideas as if they were equivalent to television sets; pressures to publish; the maintenance of strict disciplinary boundaries hindering understanding; and the often ritualized paying of homage to authority figures in acknowledgements, prefaces, citations and references. Here we can do no better than to refer to Gouldner's passionate denouncement of the petty personal aspirations held by many self-styled radicals:

> The man who can voice support for Black Power or who can denounce American imperialism in Latin America or Vietnam, but who plays the sycophant to the most petty authorities in his university, is no radical; the man who mouths phrases about the need for revolution abroad, but who is a coiled spring ready to punish the rebels among his own graduate students, is no radical; the academician who with mighty oaths denounces the President of the United States, but subserviently fawns upon his Department Chairman, is no radical; the man who denounces opportunistic power politics, but practices it daily among his university colleagues, is no radical. Such men are playing one of the oldest games in personal politics; they are seeking to maintain a creditable image of themselves, while accommodating to the most vulgar careerism. Such men are seeking neither to change nor to know the world; their aim is to grap a piece of it for themselves.
>
> (Gouldner, 1970, p. 503)

A radical value-committed archaeology involves a way of living that requires that intellectual struggle be carried into the heart of the discipline, on a daily basis as a willed personal act, and irrespective of the possible personal consequences of the reactions of those in authority.

Writing the past

How is the past to be written? It may be dominated by a style of textuality that either claims it has arrived at some truth in the past or is groping towards this ultimate aim. This is almost exclusively the position taken in archaeology at present, irrespective of differences in the specific frameworks advanced. The object of archaeology, then, is the production of knowledge about some aspect of the past. However, this knowledge is generally conceived in purely informational terms. 'Knowing' the past is to collect together more and more bits of information about it by inductive or deductive research strategies, or whatever. The information so derived is pieced together into what basically amounts to a pictorial statement. Such a knowledge of the past is at the same time a form of domination and control. It is ill-suited to an increase in self-awareness on the part of the investigator, the discipline, or society at large. No doubt it satisfies those for whom the primary rationale for archaeology is to provide either privatized or disciplinary intellectual pleasure.

Another way in which the past may be written is to provide a position on it which does not establish closure in a picture but dispels finality in a creative juxtaposition of past and present. Sartre states:

> this is the measure we propose to the writer: as long as his books arouse anger, discomfort, shame, hatred, love, even if he is no more than a shade, he will live.
>
> (Sartre, 1950, p. 238)

We might argue that what is needed is not the production of archaeological texts that provide and permit a passive understanding of the past, texts to be simply 'absorbed' (see the discussion of archaeological texts in chapter 1), but texts that challenge the reader: *writerly* texts (Barthes, 1974, p. 4) that have the effect of dissonance creating and actively inviting discussion, debate, 'completion'. Polemic and rhetoric should be an essential part of archaeological textual production to stimulate the reader to be a producer of the text's meaning and its relation to the meaning of the past, not a passive consumer of a bland and smooth narrative, or unapproachable information report inviting acquiescence rather than critical reflection. A critical archaeology will produce texts which interrogate the past in the form of a social document forged in the present, stimulating a reply, a reaction, another text. This raises a whole host of questions such as how should a site be represented? what is the significance of a measured pot drawing? is a list of artefacts objective? what is the origin, the meaning of a list? Whatever the answers, a politics of archaeology is also an aesthetics and a poetics, a production of texts which interrogate the past but do not pin it down to a set of mechanical and reified essences, texts which subvert those archaeologies that would deny the study of material culture as being fundamentally a study of power, the mediation, representation and articulation of power strategies through material forms.

CONCLUSION

An oppositional role for archaeology; the archaeologist as specific or universal intellectual; war of position; establishment of a counter-hegemony; value-commitment; the question of how reality is to be represented, written according to a radical aesthetic and poetic: we might also make reference to the idea of an avant-garde, or the debate over socialist realism, or the emergence of a so-called post-modernist culture. All are issues in a cultural practice, in a politics of archaeology. These issues need to be faced – archaeology must embrace a commitment to the present through a consideration of the present's past. Archaeology should be conceived as acting as a catalyst in the transformation of the present, for without commitment to one's own historicity, the discipline becomes little more than an escape from our own time and place.

Appendix

Notes Towards a New Problematic

1. ARCHAEOLOGY AND THEORY

1.1. Archaeology is immediately theoretical. There can be no meaningful separation of theory, method and practice in archaeology.

1.1.1. The idea of applying theories or models or concepts to archaeological data and the idea of theories as abstract heuristics (different ways of looking at the same data) both involve a disabling split between the theory and practice of archaeology.

1.2. It is not possible to provide a set of abstract rules of archaeological method. Method is in part style, or rhetoric, aspect of the relation between theorizing and the practice of archaeology.

1.2.1. A stress on methodology associated most recently with the advocacy of 'middle-range theory', or the attempt to produce a science of the archaeological record, represent a retreat into a practical empiricism of the most antitheoretical kind. Methodology is to be criticized as determining the past in advance of its confrontation in archaeological practice.

1.3. What is needed are not new answers to the old archaeological questions such as the origin of the state or 'civilization' but the redefinition of these questions in terms of a fresh problematic for social archaeology. This problematic focuses on archaeology's specific object and context: the place and meaning of material culture within the changing social worlds of past and present, and the meaning and form of gaining knowledge of this complex.

2. THE SOCIAL AND THE INDIVIDUAL

2.1. There is no such thing as 'society'; there can be no abstract and universal definition of society.

2.1.1. Social typologies or hierarchies of determination (such as ritual practices determined by material economic logic) are both essentialist and reductionist.

2.2. The concepts of function, adaptation and evolution have no explanatory role in a consideration of the social and need to be either completely abandoned or reduced to a simple descriptive vocabulary.

2.3. The social is an open field fixed in the politics of social relations and strategies and in the interpretative practices of discourses.

2.4 The individual cannot be screened out of archaeological analysis. The individual is to be conceived as knowledgeable and active and yet at the same time positioned in relation to social structures and strategies, a trace within a structured social field. This means that social relations cannot be reduced to interacting creative individuals.

2.5. The social practices of agents are always to be regarded as situated in relation to power, group or individual interests, ideology and symbolic and signifying practices.

2.6. Power is central to social analysis; power (both productive and repressive) is coextensive with the social field.

2.6.1 Power does not simply involve social stratification, nor does it simply arise from the logic of economic base or control over resources.

2.7. Ideology as a technology of power is a strategy for social containment and is fundamentally implicated in the reproduction as opposed to the transformation of the social. It is never a unitary phenomenon and is related both to forms of domination and the way in which agents must necessarily relate to and live through forms of social signification within a field of asymmetrical power relations.

3. MATERIAL CULTURE

3.1. Material culture does not provide a window through which we can see through and read-off past social reality.

3.2. Actions refer and relate to sign systems. Material culture is to be conceived as a sign system, a non-verbal discourse.

3.2.1. As a sign system there are multiple transformations involved in the elements of material culture: parallelism, opposition, inversion, linearity, equivalence.

3.3. Material culture is a social, not an individual creation.

3.4.   Material culture is active. Meaning is always actively created; the meaning attributed to any item always has to be argued for and against; meanings are mediated in relation to interests and social strategies.

3.4.1.   Material culture constitutes an open system, a chain of signifiers. It is irreducibly polysemous.

3.5.   Material culture forms a reified channel of communication and can be drawn on as a significative resource, activiated in the contextualized matrices of particular social strategies.

3.6.   Understanding material culture is an act of translation. Meaning depends on context and the position of the interpreter in relation to this context, whether prehistoric social actor or contemporary archaeologist. There is no original meaning to be discovered.

4.   TIME AND ARCHAEOLOGY

4.1.   There is no singular time, but temporalities. Time is related to social practice. It is part of the social construction of reality. As with space, it does not simply form a container for action but is a medium giving form to action and establishing action as meaningful. Different structures of temporality are implicated in different practices.

4.1.1.   Time as chronometry, measured as date, is not a universal temporality and only emerged as a dominant frame within capitalism.

4.2.   Archaeology is in part a history of times, times to be related substantially rather than abstractly to social structures and practices. Different temporal orientations shape history itself.

4.3.   History is a contingent and not a necessary progress, contingent upon determinate and historically variable sets of social relations. There can be no universal histories.

4.4.   Archaeology is a mediation of past, present and future. It is a social practice involving a temporal mode of *presencing*, uniting and yet holding apart past, present and future, constituting each other in their difference.

4.4.1.   The past exists not as the past studied in itself but represents a project in the present.

4.4.2.   The past requires completion by the interpreting archaeologist.

4.4.3.   Archaeology as contemporary practice reinscribes the past within our own society. The interpretation of the past does not transport a truth or property of the past into the present; it transforms or translates.

4.4.4. Choosing a past, constituting a past, is choosing a future. The meaning of the past is political and belongs to the present.

4.5. Capitalism is unique in relation to the past. This requires the rejection of uniformitarian assumptions as regards a connection between past and present. The uniqueness of capitalism – in terms of (1) rapidity and tempo of change; (2) dominance of the economy; (3) stress on the individual as discrete centre of consciousness; (4) mass production and mass consumption; (5) abstract or spatialized notion of time – has to be offset against the otherness, the difference of the past. Conceptual tools are required to theorize the otherness, this difference.

5.   SOCIAL CHANGE

5.1. It is stability rather than social change that needs explaining.

5.1.1. Both stability and change are intimately connected, specific, located in determinate historical and social conditions and not amenable to redescription in terms of an atemporal aspatial 'culture process'.

5.2. Social change is a process of the mediation of strategic practice and structure.

5.2.1. The social is immediately temporal. Social action, structured and situated in relation to schemes of signification, involves the constant reproduction of these structures and schemes within political, strategic interests.

5.2.2. Social change involves structural contradiction and particular, contingent historical conjunctures of actions and events.

5.3. The separation of statics and dynamics, synchrony and diachrony depends on the abstract temporality characteristic of the alienating calculus of the capitalist labour process. Analysis of social change which involves such a duality and temporality may thus be ideological.

5.4. Any notion of social causality in the form of cause–effect type relationships, however complex, needs to be abandoned.

6.   THE FORM AND POLITICS OF THEORY

6.1. Archaeology, as cultural practice, is always a politics, a morality.

6.2. Theory is thoroughly subjective. It is not a technical product of a specialist but a delimited and localized production, arising from a specific contextualized interaction between individuals, the experiences of these individuals, the manner in which their life and work interacts, and the way in which the archaeologist manages to arrive at a specific picture of the past based on the scraps of contingent materials (texts, knowledges, artefacts) and life experiences at his or her disposal.

6.3. No discourse on the past is neutral. The validity of a theory hinges on intention and interest: it is to be assessed in terms of the ends and goals of its archaeology, its politics and morality.

6.3.1. There can be no neutral algorithm (such as simplicity, comprehensiveness) for evaluating particular archaeologies.

6.4. Archaeology is a signifying practice, expressive and transformative. The past is written. Past and present are mediated in the archaeological text.

6.4.1. Self-reflection: it is necessary to consider archaeological discourse in terms of systems of concepts, rules and conventions for the production of knowledges.

6.4.2. What is needed is an archaeological topology, a rhetoric; an archaeological tropology, a stylistics: an archaeological poetics concerned with how the archaeological past may be written.

6.4.3. Established archaeologies need to be engaged in terms of a dialogue with their always present, absent other – that which is systematically suppressed or marginalized in the text.

6.5. Archaeology is nothing if it is not critique.

6.5.1. We do not argue for truths about the past but argue through the medium of the past to detach the power of truth from the present social order.

6.5.2. A critical archaeology is value-committed, a willed personal act with the aim of transforming the present in terms of its conceived connection with the past.

6.5.3. The past is not to be dispossessed of its difference by erecting it as a mirror reflecting the present. The difference, the tension between past and present subverts the legitimacy of the present.

Suggestions for
Further Reading

We recommend a number of general works here for the reader who is interested in following up in more detail some of the arguments that we have put forward in this book. Articles and works of a more specific nature are cited in full in the list of references.

In archaeology it might be most useful to follow through Hodder's work from the early strident advocacy of positivism in *Spatial Analysis in Archaeology* (Hodder and Orton, 1976), to the neo-structuralist orientation of *Symbols in Action* (1982) and *The Present Past* (1982c), to the more hermeneutic historical and contextualist positions reached in *Reading the Past* (1986). *Symbolic and Structural Archaeology* (Hodder (ed.), 1982), *Ideology, Power and Prehistory* (Miller and Tilley (eds), 1984) and *Re-constructing Archaeology* (Shanks and Tilley 1987) elaborate on some of the ideas we have discussed.

The works which follow are best read as sources of ideas on the key issues of a critical archaeology involving the conceptualization of the place of material culture in society, archaeology as a contemporary cultural practice, and ways in which we may begin to understand the form and nature of social reproduction and transformation.

The critical tradition in Marxist theory

Held's *Introduction to Critical Theory* (1980) is an excellent starting point and should be considered in conjunction with Jay's book, *The Dialectical Imagination* (1973), which places the ideas in a more historical perspective. Buck-Morss in *The Origin of Negative Dialectics* (1977) provides a detailed account of the work of Adorno and Benjamin. Eagleton in *Walter Benjamin or Towards a Revolutionary Criticism* (1981) provides a very stimulating exposition of the possibility and form of a revolutionary critical practice. Gouldner's *The Coming Crisis of Western Sociology* (1970) gives an excellent account of one of the forms a self-reflexive critical approach to disciplinary practice might take.

Structuralism, post-structuralism and Marxism

Two introductory books provide useful accounts of structuralism and post-structuralism: Culler *Structuralist Poetics* (1975) and Sturrock (ed.) *Structuralism and Since* (1979). Leitch's *Deconstructive Criticism* (1983) gives an advanced and extensive general introduction to many of the major issues in a post-structuralist critical practice. Some of the most illuminating of Barthes' work is collected together in two readers: *Image, Music, Text* (1977) and *Barthes: Selected Writings* (1982). An edited selection of Foucault's writings are reproduced in *The Foucault Reader* (1986). The most comprehensive discussion of Foucault's work to have been published so far is by Dreyfus and Rabinow (1982). Coward and Ellis's book *Language and Materialism* (1977) links structuralist and post-structuralist thought to a Marxist dialectical materialist position in an illuminating manner, while Ryan in *Marxism and Deconstruction* (1982) attempts an interesting synthesis of Marxism and aspects of Derrida's writings. It is important to point out that one of the most valuable aspects of post-structuralism is its attempt to critically undermine widely held notions of neutral academic theory but much of this is lost in American 'deconstruction'.

The social constitution of time and space

Works by Bourdieu, *An Outline of a Theory of Practice* (1977), and Giddens, *A Contemporary Critique of Historical Materialism* (1981), are essential starting points. Gregory and Urry (1985) in their edited volume *Social Relations and Spatial Structures* collect together a series of very useful papers on space, while Fabian's *Time and the Other* (1983) and Berger's book *And our Faces, my Heart, brief as Photos* (1984) discuss elegantly the social nature of time.

Power, ideology and subjectivity

Some of Foucault's writings collected together by Gordon in *Power/Knowledge* (1980) are stimulating. Wrong in *Power* (1979) provides a very broad overview of various uses of the concept but does not discuss Foucault. There are excellent discussions of theories of ideology in the volume *On Ideology* (1978) produced by the Centre for Contemporary Cultural Studies, and Larrain's *The Concept of Ideology* (1979) gives an insightful historical perspective. Althusser's work is discussed extensively in a collection of Hirst's writings *On Law and Ideology* (1979). A recent book, *The Category of the Person* (1986), edited by Carrithers, Collins and Lukes contains anthropological, philosophical and historical perspectives on the constitution of subjectivity.

On the notion of social form, reproduction and transformation

The following general works on social theory provide a number of contrasting and informative accounts: Keat and Urry, *Social Theory as Science* (1982); Bernstein, *The Restructuring of Social and Political Theory* (1976); and Jay, *Marxism and Totality* (1984). Giddens has produced two major and important syntheses, *Central Problems in Social Theory* (1979) and *The Constitution of Society* (1984). Bourdieu's *Outline of a Theory of Practice* (1977) works through in an extremely valuable fashion a parallel account to that provided by Giddens in relation to non-industrial societies.

References

Adorno, T. W. (1973) *Negative Dialectics*, Routledge and Kegan Paul, London.

Allen, W. and Richardson, J. (1971) 'The reconstruction of kinship from archaeological data: the concepts, the methods and the feasibility', *American Antiquity* 36: 41–53.

Althusser, L. (1971) 'Ideology and ideological state apparatuses', *Lenin and Philosophy and other Essays*, New Left Books, London.

Althusser, L. (1977) *For Marx*, Verso, London.

Althusser, L. and Balibar, E. (1970) *Reading Capital*, New Left Books, London.

Anderson, P. (1974) *Passages from Antiquity to Feudalism*, Verso, London.

Arnold, D. (1971) 'Ethnomineralogy of Ticul, Yucatan potters: ethics and emics', *American Antiquity* 36: 20–40.

Arnold, D. (1985) *Ceramic Theory and Cultural Process*, Cambridge University Press, Cambridge.

Auel, J. (1981) *The Clan of the Cave Bear*, Coronet Books, London.

Bailey, G. (1981) 'Concepts, time-scales and explanations in economic prehistory', in A. Sheridan and G. Bailey (eds), *Economic Archaeology*, British Archaeological Reports (International Series) 96, Oxford.

Bailey, G. (1983) 'Concepts of time in Quaternary prehistory', *Annual Review of Anthropology* 12: 165–92.

Barker, P. (1977) *Techniques of Archaeological Excavation*, Batsford, London.

Barthes, R. (1967) *Elements of Semiology*, Jonathan Cape, London.

Barthes, R. (1973) *Mythologies*, Paladin, London.

Barthes, R. (1974) *S/Z*, Hill and Wang, New York.

Barthes, R. (1977) *Image, Music, Text*, Hill and Wang, New York.

Barthes, R. (1982) *Selected Writings*, ed. S. Sontag, Fontana, London.

Barthes, R. (1982a) 'The plates of the encyclopaedia', in Barthes, 1982.

Baudrillard, J. (1981) *For a Critique of the Political Economy of the Sign*, Telos Press, St. Louis, Mo.

Belgrave, R. (1986) 'Southampton's Caribbean heritage: an analysis of the Oral History Project carried out by Southampton Museums,

218   REFERENCES

1983–1984',. Paper presented at the World Archaeological Congress 1986.

Bender, B. (1978) 'Gatherer-hunter to farmer', *World Archaeology* 10: 203–22.

Benjamin, W. (1970) 'The task of the translator', *Illuminations*, Fontana, London.

Benjamin W. (1979) 'Edward Fuchs, collector and historian', *One Way Street*, New Left Books, London.

Berger, J. (1984) *And our Faces, my Heart, brief as Photos*, Writers and Readers, London.

Bernstein, R. (1976) *The Restructuring of Social and Political Theory*, Methuen, London.

Binford, L. (1962) 'Archaeology as anthropology', *American Antiquity* 28: 217–25.

Binford, L. (1964) 'A consideration of archaeological research design', *American Antiquity* 30: 425–51.

Binford, L. (1965) 'Archaeological systematics and the study of culture process', *American Antiquity* 31: 203–10.

Binford, L. (1972) *An Archaeological Perspective*, Seminar Press, London.

Binford, L. (1972a) 'Mortuary practices: their study and their potential', in Binford, 1972.

Binford, L. (1973) 'Interassemblage variability: the Mousterian and the "functional" argument', in C. Renfrew (ed.), *The Explanation of Culture Change: Models in Prehistory*, Duckworth, London.

Binford, L. (1977) 'General introduction', in L. Binford (ed.), *For Theory Building in Archaeology*, Academic Press, London.

Binford, L. (1978) *Nunamiut Ethnoarchaeology*, Academic Press, London.

Binford, L. (1979) 'Organization and formation processes: looking at curated technologies', *Journal of Anthropological Research* 35: 255–73.

Binford, L. (1981) *Bones: Ancient Men and Modern Myths*, Academic Press, London.

Binford, L. (1983) *Working at Archaeology*, Academic Press, London.

Binford, L. and Sabloff, J. (1982) 'Paradigms, systematics and archaeology', *Journal of Anthropological Research* 38: 137–53.

Bintliff, J. (ed.) (1984) *European Social Evolution*, Bradford University Press, Bradford.

Bintliff, J. (1984) 'Introduction', in J. Bintliff (ed.)

Bintliff, J. (1984a) 'Iron Age Europe in the context of social evolution from the Bronze Age through to historic times', in J. Bintliff (ed.)

Bordes, F. (1973) 'On the chronology and contemporaneity of different palaeolithic cultures in France', in C. Renfrew (ed.), *The Explanation of Culture Change: Models in Prehistory*, Duckworth, London.

Borges, J. L. (1981) 'Tlön, Uqbar, Orbis Tertius', *Labyrinths*, Penguin.

Bourdieu, P. (1963) 'The attitude of the Algerian peasant toward time', in J. Pitt-Rivers (ed.), *Mediterranean Countrymen*, Mouton, The Hague.

Bourdieu, P. (1977) *Outline of a Theory of Practice*, Cambridge University Press, Cambridge.

Bradley, R. (1981) '"Various styles of urn": cemeteries and settlement in southern England c.1400–1000 BC', in R. Chapman, I. Kinnes and K. Randsborg (eds), *The Archaeology of Death*, Cambridge University Press, Cambridge.

Bradley, R. (1984) *The Social Foundations of Prehistoric Britain*, Longman, London.

Braithwaite, M. (1982) 'Decoration as ritual symbol: a theoretical proposal and an ethnographic study in southern Sudan', in I. Hodder (ed.)

Braun, D. (1983) 'Pots as tools', in J. Moore and A. Keene (eds), *Archaeological Hammers and Theories*, Academic Press, London.

Braun, D. and Plog, S. (1982) 'Evolution of tribal "social" networks: theory and prehistoric North American evidence', *American Antiquity* 47: 504–25.

Buck-Morss, S. (1977) *The Origin of Negative Dialectics: Theodor W. Adorno, Walter Benjamin, and the Frankfurt Institute*, Harvester Press, Hassocks.

Buikstra, J. (1981) 'Mortuary practices, palaeodemography and palaeopathology: a case study from the Koster site (Illinois)', in R. Chapman, I. Kinnes and K. Randsborg (eds), *The Archaeology of Death*, Cambridge University Press, Cambridge.

Burgess, C. (1980) *The Age of Stonehenge*, Dent, London.

Burke, K. (1969) *A Rhetoric of Motives*, University of California Press, Berkeley.

Burrow, J. (1966) *Evolution and Society*, Cambridge University Press, Cambridge.

Carrithers, M., Collins, S. and Lukes, S. (1986) *The Category of the Person*, Cambridge University Press, Cambridge.

Centre for Contemporary Cultural Studies (1978) *On Ideology*, Hutchinson, London.

Champion, T., Gamble, C., Shennan, S. and Whittle, A. (1984) *Prehistoric Europe*, Academic Press, London.

Chapman, R. and Randsborg, K. (1981) 'Approaches to the archaeology of death', in R. Chapman, I. Kinnes and K. Randsborg (eds).

Chapman, R., Kinnes, I. and Randsborg, K. (eds) (1981) *The Archaeology of Death*, Cambridge University Press, Cambridge.

Chang, K. (1967) *Rethinking Archaeology*, Random House, New York.

Cherry, J., Gamble, C. and Shennan, S. (eds) (1978) *Sampling in Contemporary British Archaeology*, British Archaeological Reports, Oxford.

Childe, V. G. (1929) *The Danube in Prehistory*, Oxford University Press, Oxford.

Childe, V. G. (1936) *Man Makes Himself*, Watts, London.

Childe, V. G. (1944) *Progress and Archaeology*, Watts, London.

Childe, V. G. (1947) *History*, Cobbett, London.

Childe, V. G. (1949) 'Social worlds of knowledge', L. T. Hobhouse Memorial Trust Lecture No. 19, Oxford University Press, London.

Childe, V. G. (1951) *Social Evolution*, Watts, London.

Childe, V. G. (1979) 'Prehistory and Marxism', *Antiquity* LIII: 93–5.

Clark, J. G. D. (1969) 'Foreword', in D. Brothwell and E. Higgs (eds), *Science in Archaeology*, Thames and Hudson, London.

Clark, J. G. D. (1972) *Archaeology and Society*, Methuen, London.

Clarke, D. (1968) *Analytical Archaeology*, Methuen, London.

Clarke, D. (1972) 'Models and paradigms in contemporary archaeology', in D. Clarke (ed.), *Models in Archaeology*, Methuen, London.

Clarke, D. (1973) 'Archaeology: the loss of innocence', *Antiquity* XLVII: 6–18.

Cleere, H. (ed.) (1984) *Archaeological Approaches to our Heritage*, Cambridge University Press, Cambridge.

Cohen, G. (1978) *Karl Marx's Theory of History: a Defence*, Oxford University Press, Oxford.

Cohen, M. (1977) *The Food Crisis in Prehistory*, Yale University Press, New Haven.

Cohen, Y. (1983) 'A theory and model of social change and evolution', *Journal of Anthropological Archaeology* 2: 164–207.

Colletti, L. (1975) 'Marxism and the dialectic', *New Left Review* 93.

Collingwood, R. (1946) *The Idea of History*, Oxford University Press, Oxford.

Collis, J. (1984) *The European Iron Age*, Batsford, London.

Cooke, K. and Renfrew, C. (1979) 'An experiment on the simulation of culture changes', in C. Renfrew and K. Cooke (eds), *Transformations: Mathematical Approaches to Culture Change*, Academic Press, London.

Conkey, M. (1978) 'Style and information in cultural evolution: towards a predictive model for the palaeolithic', in C. Redman et al. (eds), *Social Archaeology: Beyond Subsistence and Dating*, Academic Press, London.

Conkey, M. and Spector, J. (1984) 'Archaeology and the study of gender', in M. Schiffer (ed.), *Advances in Archaeological Method and Theory*, vol. 7., Academic Press, London.

Coward, R. and Ellis, J. (1977) *Language and Materialism*, Routledge and Kegan Paul, London.

Culler, J. (1975) *Structuralist Poetics*, Routledge and Kegan Paul, London.

Dahrendorf, R. (1968) *Essays in the Theory of Society*, Routledge and Kegan Paul, London.

David, N. (1972) 'On the life span of pottery, type frequencies and archaeological inference', *American Antiquity* 37: 141–2.

Daniel, G. (1981) *A Short History of Archaeology*, Thames and Hudson, London.

Deetz, J. (1965) 'The dynamics of stylistic change in Arikara ceramics', *Illinois Studies in Anthropology* 4.

DeBoer, W. and Lathrap, D. (1979) 'The making and breaking of Shipibo-Conibo ceramics', in C. Kramer (ed.), *Ethnoarchaeology: implications of ethnography for archaeology*, Columbia University Press, New York.

de Paor, L. (1967) *Archaeology: an Illustrated Introduction*, Penguin, Harmondsworth.

Derrida, J. (1976) *Of Grammatology*, Johns Hopkins University Press, Baltimore.

Derrida, J. (1978) 'Structure, sign, and play in the discourse of the human sciences', *Writing and Difference*, Routledge and Kegan Paul, London.

Derrida, J. (1981) 'Plato's pharmacy', *Dissemination*, Athlone Press, London.

de Ste. Croix, G. E. M. (1981) *The Class Struggle in the Ancient Greek World*, Duckworth, London.

Doran, J. and Hodson, R. (1975) *Mathematics and Computers in Archaeology*, Edinburgh University Press, Edinburgh.

Douglas, M. (1970) *Natural Symbols*, Penguin, Harmondsworth.

Dolukhanov, P. (1986) 'The late mesolithic and the transition to food production in Eastern Europe', in M. Zvelebil (ed.), *Hunters in Transition*, Cambridge University Press, Cambridge.

Dreyfus, H. and Rabinow, P. (1982) *Michel Foucault: Beyond Structuralism and Hermeneutics*, Harvester Press, Hassocks.

Dufrenne, M. (1967) 'La philosophie du néo-positivisme', *Esprit* 360.

Dunnell, R. (1971) *Systematics in Prehistory*, Free Press, New York.

Dunnell, R. (1978) 'Style and function: a fundamental dichotomy', *American Antiquity* 43: 192–202.

Dunnell, R. (1980) 'Evolutionary theory and archaeology', in M. Schiffer (ed.), *Advances in Archaeological Method and Theory*, Vol. 3., Academic Press, London.

Eagleton, T. (1981) *Walter Benjamin or Towards a Revolutionary Criticism*, Verso, London.

Earle, T. and Ericson, J. (1977) *Exchange Systems in Prehistory*, Academic Press, London.

Eggert, M. (1977) 'Prehistory, archaeology and the problem of ethno-cognition', *Anthropos*: 242–55.

Elster, J. (1978) *Logic and Society*, Wiley, Chichester.

Engelbrecht, W. (1978) 'Ceramic patterning between New York Iroquois sites', in I. Hodder (ed.), *The Spatial Organization of Culture*, Duckworth, London.

Ericson, J. and Earle, T. (eds) (1982) *Contexts for Prehistoric Exchange*, Academic Press, London.

Fabian, J. (1983) *Time and the Other: how Anthropology makes its Object*, Columbia University Press, New York.

Faris, J. (1986) 'Comments on the symposium "The past is the present"', Paper presented at the meetings of the Society for American Archaeology, New Orleans.

Fawcett, C. (1986) 'The politics of assimilation in Japanese archaeology', *Archaeological Review from Cambridge* 5: 43–57.

Firth, R. (1971) *Elements of Social Organization*, Tavistock, London.

Flannery, K. (1968) 'Archaeological systems theory and early Mesoamerica', in B. Meggers (ed.), *Anthropological Archaeology in the Americas*, Washington.

Flannery, K. (1972) 'The cultural evolution of civilisations', *Annual Review of Ecology and Systematics* 3: 399–426.

Flannery, K. (1982) 'The golden marshalltown: a parable for the archaeology of the 1980s', *American Anthropologist* 84: 256–78.

Flannery, K. (1983) 'Divergent evolution', in K. Flannery and J. Marcus (eds).

Flannery, K. and Marcus, J. (eds) (1983) *The Cloud People: Divergent Evolution of the Zapotec and Mixtec Civilisations*, Academic Press, London.

Fletcher, R. (1977) 'Settlement studies (micro and semi-micro)', in D. Clarke (ed.), *Spatial Archaeology*, Academic Press, London.

Foley, R. (ed.) (1984) *Hominid Evolution and Community Ecology*, Academic Press, London.

Ford, J. (1954a) 'The type concept revisited', *American Anthropologist* 56: 42–54.

Ford, J. (1954b) 'Comment on A. C. Spaulding, "statistical techniques for the discovery of artefact types"', *American Antiquity* 19: 390–1.

Foucault, M. (1974) *The Order of Things*, Tavistock, London.

Foucault, M. (1977) *Discipline and Punish*, Vantage, New York.

Foucault, M. (1977a) 'Intellectuals and power', *Language, Counter-Memory, Practice*, ed. D. Bouchard, Cornell University Press, New York.

Foucault, M. (1977b) 'The political function of the intellectual', *Radical Philosophy*, Summer 1977: 12–14.

Foucault, M. (1980) 'Truth and power', *Power/Knowledge*, ed. C. Gordon, Harvester, Hassocks.

Foucault, M. (1981) 'The order of discourse', in R. Young (ed.), *Untying the Text*, Routledge and Kegan Paul, London.

Foucault, M. (1986) *The Foucault Reader,* ed. P. Rabinow, Penguin, Harmondsworth.

Fowler, P. (1977) *Approaches to Archaeology*, Adam and Charles Black, London.

Frankenstein, S. and Rowlands, M. (1978) 'The internal structure and regional context of early Iron Age society in south-western Germany', *Bulletin of the Institute of Archaeology, London* 15: 73–112.

Fried, M. (1967) *The Evolution of Political Society*, Random House, New York.

Friedman, J. (1974) 'Marxism, structuralism and vulgar materialism', *Man* 9: 444–69.

Friedman, J. (1975) 'Tribes, states and transformations', in M. Bloch (ed.), *Marxist Analyses and Social Anthropology*, Malaby, London.

Friedman, J. (1986) 'Culture, identity and world process', Paper presented at the World Archaeological Congress, 1986.

Friedman, J. and Rowlands, M. (1978) 'Notes towards an epigenetic model of the evolution of "civilisation"', in J. Friedman and M. Rowlands (eds), *The Evolution of Social Systems*, Duckworth, London.

Friedrich, M. (1970) 'Design structure and social interaction:

archaeological implications of an ethnographic analysis', *American Antiquity* 35: 332–43.

Fritz, J. (1978) 'Palaeopsychology today: ideational systems and human adaptation in prehistory', in C. Redman et al. (eds), *Social Archaeology: Beyond Dating and Subsistence*, Academic Press, London.

Fritz, J. and Plog, F. (1970) 'The nature of archaeological explanation', *American Antiquity* 35: 405–12.

Gall, P. and Saxe, A. (1977) 'The ecological evolution of culture: the state as predator in succession theory', in T. Earle and J. Ericson (eds).

Geertz, C. (1979) 'From the native's point of view: on the nature of anthropological understanding', in P. Rabinow and W. Sullivan (eds), *Interpretative Social Science: a Reader*, University of California Press, Berkeley.

Gero, J. (1985) 'Socio-politics and the woman-at-home ideology', *American Antiquity* 50: 342–50.

Gero, J. and Root, D. (1986) 'Public presentations and private concerns: archaeology in the passages of *National Geographic*', Paper presented at the World Archaeological Congress, 1986.

Gibson, A. (1982) *Beaker Domestic Sites: a Study of the Domestic Pottery of the Late Third and Early Second Millenia B.C. in the British Isles*, British Archaeological Reports, Oxford.

Giddens, A. (1976) *New Rules of Sociological Method*, Hutchinson, London.

Giddens, A. (1979) *Central Problems in Social Theory*, Macmillan, London.

Giddens, A. (1981) *A Contemporary Critique of Historical Materialism*, Macmillan, London.

Giddens, A. (1984) *The Constitution of Society*, Polity Press, Cambridge.

Gifford, J. (1960) 'The type-variety method of ceramic classification as an indicator of cultural phenomena', *American Antiquity* 25: 341–7.

Gledhill, J. and Rowlands, M. (1982) 'Materialism and socio-economic process in multilinear evolution', in C. Renfrew and S. Shennan (eds).

Godelier, M. (1972) *Rationality and Irrationality in Economics*, New Left Books, London.

Godelier, M. (1977) *Perspectives in Marxist Anthropology*, Cambridge University Press, Cambridge.

Godelier, M. (1978) 'Politics as infrastructure: an anthropologist's thoughts on the example of classical Greece', in J. Friedman and M. Rowlands (eds), *The Evolution of Social Systems*, Duckworth, London.

Goldmann, L. (1977) *Lukács and Heidegger*, Routledge and Kegan Paul, London.

Goodfriend, D. (1978) 'Plus ça change, plus c'est la même chose: the dilemma of the French structural Marxists', in S. Diamond (ed.), *Toward a Marxist Anthropology*, Mouton, The Hague.

Goodenough, W. (1965) 'Rethinking "status" and "role": toward a general model of the cultural organization of social relationships', in M. Banton (ed.), *The Relevance of Models for Social Anthropology*, Malaby, London.

Goody, J. (1978) *The Domestication of the Savage Mind*, Cambridge University Press, Cambridge.

Gould, R. (ed.) (1978) *Explorations in Ethnoarchaeology*, University of New Mexico Press, Albuquerque.

Gould, R. (1980) *Living Archaeology*, Cambridge University Press, Cambridge.

Gould, R. and Schiffer, M. (eds) (1981) *Modern Material Culture: the Archaeology of Us*, Academic Press, London.

Gouldner, A. (1970) *The Coming Crisis of Western Sociology*, Heineman, London.

Gouldner, A. (1980) *The Two Marxisms*, Macmillan, London.

Gramsci, A. (1971) *Selections from Prison Notebooks*, Q. Hoare and G. Nowell Smith (eds and trans), Lawrence and Wishart, London.

Graves, M. (1982) 'Breaking down ceramic variation: testing models of White Mountain Redware design development', *Journal of Anthropological Archaeology* 1: 305–54.

Green, E. (ed.) (1984) *Ethics and Values in Archaeology*, The Free Press, New York.

Greene, K. (1983) *Archaeology: an Introduction. The History, Principles and Methods of Modern Archaeology*, Batsford, London.

Gregory, D. and Urry, J. (eds) (1985) *Social Relations and Spatial Structures*, Macmillan, London.

Grinsell, L., Rahtz, P. and Williams, D. (1974) *The Preparation of Archaeological Reports*, John Baker, London.

Gurvitch, G. (1964) *The Spectrum of Social Time*, D. Reidel, Dordrecht.

Habermas, J. (1979) 'Toward a reconstruction of historical materialism', *Communication and the Evolution of Society*, Heinemann, London.

Hall, M. (1984) 'The burden of tribalism: the social context of southern African Iron Age Studies', *American Antiquity* 49: 455–67.

Hally, D. (1986) 'The identification of vessel function: a case study from northwest Georgia', *American Antiquity* 51: 267–95.

Haselgrove, C. (1982) 'Wealth, prestige and power: the dynamics of late Iron Age political centralisation in south-east England', in C. Renfrew and S. Shennan (eds).

Hardin, M. (1979) 'The cognitive basis of productivity in a decorative art style: implications of an ethnographic study for archaeologists' taxonomies', in C. Kramer (ed.), *Ethnoarchaeology: Implications of Ethnography for Archaeology*, Columbia University Press, New York.

Hardin, M. (1983) 'The structure of Tarascan pottery painting', in D. Washburn (ed.), *Structure and Cognition in Art*, Cambridge University Press, Cambridge.

Hargrave, L. (1932) 'Guide to forty pottery types from the Hopi country and the San Francisco mountains', *Museum of Northern Arizona Bulletin*, No. 1., Arizona.

Hawkes, C. (1954) 'Archaeological theory and method: some suggestions from the old world', *American Anthropologist* LVI: 55–68.

Hayden, B. (ed.) (1979) *Lithic Use–Wear Analysis,* Academic Press, London.

Held, D. (1980) *Introduction to Critical Theory: Horkheimer to Habermas*, Hutchinson, London.

Hiedegger, M. (1972) 'Time and being', *On Time and Being*, Harper and Row, New York.

Hietala, H. (ed.) (1984) *Intrasite Spatial Analysis in Archaeology*, Cambridge University Press, Cambridge.

Higgs, E. (ed.) (1972) *Papers in Economic Prehistory*, Cambridge University Press, Cambridge.

Higgs, E. (ed.) (1975) *Palaeoeconomy*, Cambridge University Press, Cambridge.

Hill, J. (1970) *Broken K Pueblo: Prehistoric Social Organization in the American South-West*, Anthropological Papers of the University of Arizona 18, Tucson, Arizona.

Hill, J. (1972) 'The methodological debate in contemporary archaeology: a model', in D. Clarke (ed.), *Models in Archaeology*, Methuen, London.

Hill, J. (1977) 'Systems theory and the explanation of change', in J. Hill (ed.), *The Explanation of Prehistoric Change*, University of New Mexico Press, Albuquerque.

Hill, J. and Evans, R. (1972) 'A model for classification and typology', in D. Clarke (ed.), *Models in Archaeology*, Methuen, London.

Hill, J. and Gunn, J. (eds) (1977) *The Individual in Prehistory*, Academic Press, London.

Hindess, B. and Hirst, P. (1975) *Pre-Capitalist Modes of Production*, Routledge and Kegan Paul, London.

Hirst, P. (1979) *On Law and Ideology*, Macmillan, London.

Hirst, P. (1980) 'Law, socialism and rights', in P. Carlen and M. Collinson (eds), *Radical Issues in Criminology*, Martin Robertson, Oxford.

Hodder, I. (ed.) (1978) *The Spatial Organization of Culture*, Duckworth, London.

Hodder, I. (1982) *Symbols in Action*, Cambridge University Press, Cambridge.

Hodder, I. (ed.) (1982) *Symbolic and Structural Archaeology*, Cambridge University Press, Cambridge.

Hodder, I. (1982a) 'Theoretical archaeology: a reactionary view', in I. Hodder (ed.)

Hodder, I. (1982b) 'The identification and interpretation of ranking in prehistory: a contextual perspective', in C. Renfrew and S. Shennan (eds).

Hodder, I. (1982c) *The Present Past*, Batsford, London.

Hodder, I. (1982d) 'Sequences of structural change in the Dutch neolithic', in I. Hodder (ed.)

Hodder, I. (1984) 'Archaeology in 1984', *Antiquity* 58: 25–32.

Hodder, I. (1985) 'Post processual archaeology' in M. Schiffer (ed.) *Advances in Archaeological Method and Theory*, vol. 8, Academic Press, London.

Hodder, I. (1986) *Reading the Past*, Cambridge University Press, Cambridge.

Hodder, I. (1986a) 'Politics and ideology in the World Archaeological Congress 1986', *Archaeological Review from Cambridge* 5: 113–18.

Hodder, I. and Orton, C. (1976) *Spatial Analysis in Archaeology*, Cambridge University Press, Cambridge.

Horne, D. (1984) *The Great Museum: the Re-Presentation of History*, Pluto Press, London.

Howard, H. and Morris, E. (eds) (1981) *Production and Distribution: a Ceramic Viewpoint*, British Archaeological Reports 120, Oxford.

Jay, M. (1973) *The Dialectical Imagination: a History of the Frankfurt School and the Institute of Social Research, 1923–1950*, Little, Brown, Boston.

Jay, M. (1984) *Marxism and Totality: the Adventures of a Concept from Lukács to Habermas*, Polity Press, Cambridge.

Jochim, M. (1983) 'Palaeolithic cave art in ecological perspective', in G. Bailey (ed.), *Hunter-Gatherer Economy in Prehistory*, Cambridge University Press, Cambridge.

Johnson, G. (1978) 'Information sources and the development of decision-making organisations', in C. Redman et al. (eds), *Social Archaeology: Beyond Dating and Subsistence*, Academic Press, London.

Juteson, J. and Hampson, S. (1985) 'Closed models of open systems: boundary considerations', in S. Green and S. Perlman (eds), *The Archaeology of Frontiers and Boundaries*, Academic Press, London.

Keat, R. and Urry, J. (1982) *Social Theory as Science*, Routledge and Kegan Paul, London.

Kent, S. (1984) *Analyzing Activity Areas*, University of New Mexico Press, Albuquerque.

Kohl, P. (1981) 'Materialist approaches in prehistory', *Annual Review of Anthropology* 10: 89–118.

Kramer, C. (1985) 'Ceramic ethnoarchaeology', *Annual Review of Anthropology* 14: 77–102.

Kreiger, A. (1944) 'The typological concept', *American Antiquity* 9: 271–88.

Kristiansen, K. (1984) 'Ideology and material culture: an archaeological perspective', in M. Spriggs (ed.), *Perspectives in Marxist Archaeology*, Cambridge University Press, Cambridge.

Kroeber, A. (1948) *Anthropology*, Harcourt Brace, New York.

Lacan, J. (1973) *Le Séminaire, Livre XI*, Seuil, Paris.

Lacan, J. (1977) *Écrits. A Selection*, Tavistock, London.

Laclau, E. and Mouffe, C. (1985) *Hegemony and Socialist Strategy*, Verso, London.

Langford, R. (1983) 'Our heritage – your playground', *Australian Archaeology* 16: 1–6.

Larrain, J. (1979) *The Concept of Ideology*, Hutchinson, London.

Larrain, J. (1983) *Marxism and Ideology*, Macmillan, London.

Leach, E. (1954) *Political Systems of Highland Burma*, Athlone, London.

Leitch, V. (1983) *Deconstructive Criticism: an Advanced Introduction*, Hutchinson, London.

Leone, M. (1981) 'Archaeology's relationship to the present and the past', in R. Gould and M. Schiffer (eds), *Modern Material Culture: the Archaeology of Us*, Academic Press, London.

Leone, M. (1981a) 'The relationship between artifacts and the public in outdoor history museums', *Annals of the New York Academy of Sciences* 376: 301–14.

Leroi-Gourhan, A. (1965) *Préhistoire de l'art occidental*, Mazenod, Paris.

Lentricchia, F. (1985) *Criticism and Social Change*, University of Chicago Press, Chicago.

Lévi-Strauss, C. (1966) *The Savage Mind*, Weidenfeld and Nicolson, London.

Lévi-Strauss, C. (1968) *Structural Anthropology*, Allen Lane, London.

Lévi-Strauss, C. (1969) *Totemism*, Penguin, Harmondsworth.

Lévi-Strauss, C. (1975) 'Race and history', *Race, Science and Society*, George Allen and Unwin, London.

Longacre, W. (1970) *Archaeology as Anthropology: a Case Study*, Anthropological Papers of the University of Arizona 17, University of Arizona Press.

Longacre, W. (1981) 'Kalinga pottery: an ethnoarchaeological study', in I. Hodder, G. Isaac and N. Hammond (eds), *Pattern of the Past*, Cambridge University Press, Cambridge.

Lowe, D. (1982) *History of Bourgeois Perception*, University of Chicago Press, Chicago.

Lubbock, J. (1865) *Prehistoric Times*, Williams and Norgate, London.

Macleod, D. (1977) 'Peddle or perish: archaeological marketing from concept to product delivery', in M. Schiffer and G. Gummerman (eds), *Conservation Archaeology*, Academic Press, London.

Martin, P. (1971) 'The revolution in archaeology', *American Antiquity* 36: 1–8.

Marx, K. (1936) *The Poverty of Philosophy*, Martin Lawrence, London.

Marx, K. (1968) 'Preface to *A Contribution to the Critique of Political Economy*' (1859) in Marx, K. and Engels, F. *Selected Works*, Lawrence and Wishart, London.

Marx, K. and Engels, F. (1970) *The German Ideology*, ed. C. Arthur, Lawrence and Wishart, London (Appendix includes 'Theses on Feuerbach').

Mauss, M. (1979) 'A category of the human mind: the notion of person, the notion of self', *Sociology and Psychology*, Routledge and Kegan Paul, London.

McGuire, R. (1983) 'Breaking down cultural complexity: inequality and heterogeneity', in M. Schiffer (ed.), *Advances in Archaeological Method and Theory*, vol. 6, Academic Press, London.

Merleau-Ponty, M. (1982), trans C. Smith, *Phenomenology of Perception*, Routledge and Kegan Paul, London.

Meikle, S. (1979) 'Dialectical contradiction and necessity', in J. Mepham and D. Ruben (eds), *Issues in Marxist Philosophy*, vol. 1, *Dialectics and Method*, Harvester, Hassocks.

Meltzer, D. (1979) 'Paradigms and the nature of change in American archaeology', *American Antiquity* 44: 644–57.

Meltzer, D. (1981) 'Ideology and material culture', in R. Gould and M. Schiffer (eds), *Modern Material Culture: the Archaeology of Us* Academic Press, London.

Merton, R. (1957) *Social Theory and Social Structure*, Free Press, New York.

Miller, D. (1985) *Artefacts as Categories*, Cambridge University Press, Cambridge.

Miller, D. (1985a) 'Ideology and the Harappan civilisation', *Journal of Anthropological Archaeology* 4: 34–71.

Miller, D. and Tilley, C. (eds) (1984) *Ideology, Power and Prehistory*, Cambridge University Press, Cambridge.

Miller, D. and Tilley, C. 'Ideology, power and prehistory: an introduction', in D. Miller and C. Tilley (eds).

Miller, D. and Tilley, C. 'Ideology, power and long-term social change', in D. Miller and C. Tilley (eds).

Morgan, L. (1963) *Ancient Society*, Meridan Books, Cleveland.

Mueller, J. (ed.) (1975) *Sampling in Archaeology*, University of Arizona Press, Tucson.

Nadel, S. (1957) *The Theory of Social Structure*, Cohen and West, London.

Olsen, B. (1986) 'Norwegian archaeology and the people without (pre-)history: or how to create a myth of a uniform past', *Archaeological Review from Cambridge* 5: 25–42.

Ong, W. (1967) *The Presence of the Word*, Yale University Press, New Haven.

Orton, C. (1980) *Mathematics in Archaeology*, Collins, London.

O'Shea, J. (1981) 'Social configurations and the archaeological study of mortuary practices: a case study', in R. Chapman, I. Kinnes and K. Randsborg (eds).

O'Shea, J. (1984) *Mortuary Variability: an Archaeological Investigation*, Academic Press, London.

Parker Pearson, M. (1984a) 'Social change, ideology and the archaeological record', in M. Spriggs (ed.)

Parker Pearson, M. (1984b) 'Economic and ideological change: cyclical growth in the pre-state societies of Jutland', in D. Miller and C. Tilley (eds).

Parsons, T. (1952) *The Social System*, Routledge and Kegan Paul, London.

Parsons, T. (1964) 'Evolutionary universals in society', *American Sociological Review* 29: 329–57.

Peel, J. (1971) *Herbert Spencer: the Evolution of a Sociologist*, Heinemann, London.

Piggott, S. (1959) *Approach to Archaeology*, A. and C. Black, London.

Piggott, S. (1965) *Ancient Europe*, Edinburgh University Press, Edinburgh.

Plog, F. (1974) *The Study of Prehistoric Change*, Academic Press, London.

Plog, S. (1976) 'Measurement of prehistoric interaction between communities', in K. Flannery (ed.), *The Early Mesoamerican Village*, Academic Press, London.

Plog, S. (1978) 'Social interaction and stylistic similarity: a reanalysis', in M. Schiffer (ed.), *Advances in Archaeological Method and Theory*, Academic Press, London.

Plog, S. (1980) *Stylistic Variation in Prehistoric Ceramics*, Cambridge University Press, Cambridge.

Popper, K. (1959) *The Logic of Scientific Discovery*, Hutchinson, London.

Pollock, S. (1983) 'Style and information: an analysis of Susiana ceramics', *Journal of Anthropological Archaeology* 2: 354–90.

Poulantzas, N. (1973) *Political Power and Social Classes*, New Left Books, London.

Pred, A. (1985) 'The social becomes the spatial, the spatial becomes the social: enclosures, social change and the becoming of places in the Swedish province of Skåne', in D. Gregory and J. Urry (eds), *Social Relations and Spatial Structures*, Macmillan, London.

Preiswerk, R. and Perrot, D. (1978) *Ethnocentrism and History*, Nok, London.

Prigogine, L., Allen, P. and Herman, R. (1977) 'Long term trends and the evolution of complexity', in E. Laszlo and J. Bierman (eds), *Goals in a Community: a Report to the Club of Rome*, vol. 1, *Studies on the Conceptual Foundations*, Pergamon Press, New York.

Racevskis, K. (1983) *Michel Foucault and the Subversion of Intellect*, Cornell University Press, New York.

Radcliffe-Brown, A. (1952) *Structure and Function in Primitive Society*, Cohen and West, London.

Ray, K. (1986) 'Archaeological praxis in West African historic preservation: Senegambia 1981', *Archaeological Review from Cambridge* 5: 58–76.

Reason, D. (1979) 'Classification, time and the organization of production', in R. Ellen and D. Reason (eds), *Classifications in their Social Context*, Academic Press, London.

Renfrew, C. (1969) 'Trade and culture process in European prehistory', *Current Anthropology* 10: 151–69.

Renfrew, C. (1972) *The Emergence of Civilisation: the Cyclades and the Aegean in the Third Millenium B.C.*, Methuen, London.

Renfrew, C. (1973) 'Monuments, mobilization and social organization in neolithic Wessex', in C. Renfrew (ed.), *The Explanation of Culture Change: Models in Prehistory*, Duckworth, London.

Renfrew, C. (1978) 'Space, time and polity', in J. Friedman and M. Rowlands (eds), *The Evolution of Social Systems*, Duckworth, London.

Renfrew, C. (1978a) 'Trajectory, discontinuity and morphogenesis: the implications of catastrophe theory for archaeology', *American Antiquity* 43: 202–22.

Renfrew, C. (1979) 'Systems collapse as social transformation: catastrophe and anastrophe in early state societies', in C. Renfrew and K. Cooke (eds), *Transformations: Mathematical Approaches to Culture Change*, Academic Press, London.

Renfrew, C. (1982) 'Discussion: contrasting paradigms', in C. Renfrew and S. Shennan (eds).

Renfrew, C. (1983) 'Divided we stand: aspects of archaeology and information', *American Antiquity* 48: 3–16.

Renfrew, C. and Cherry, J. (eds) (1986) *Peer Polity Interaction and Sociopolitical Change*, Cambridge University Press, Cambridge.

Renfrew, C., Rowlands, M. and Segraves, B. (eds) (1982) *Theory and Explanation in Archaeology*, Academic Press, London.

Renfrew, C. and Shennan, S. (eds) (1982) *Ranking Resource and Exchange: Aspects of the Archaeology of Early European Society*, Cambridge University Press, Cambridge.

Richards, J. and Ryan, N. (1985) *Data Processing in Archaeology*, Cambridge University Press, Cambridge.

Rossi-Landi, F. *Linguistics and Economics*, Mouton, The Hague.

Rouse, I. (1939) *Prehistory in Haiti. A Study in Method*, Yale University Publications in Anthropology No. 21, New Haven.

Rouse, I. (1960) 'The classification of artifacts in archaeology', *American Antiquity* 25: 313–23.

Rowlands, M. (1982) 'Processual archaeology as historical social science', in C. Renfrew, M. Rowlands and B. Segraves (eds).

Rowlands, M. (1984) 'Conceptualising the European Bronze and early Iron Ages', in J. Bintliff (ed.), *European Social Evolution*, Bradford University Press, Bradford.

Rowlands, M. (1984a) 'Objectivity and subjectivity in archaeology', in M. Spriggs (ed.), *Marxist Perspectives in Archaeology*, Cambridge University Press, Cambridge.

Rowlands, M. (1986) 'From simple to complex: a modernist fantasy in prehistory', Paper presented at the World Archaeology Congress, 1986.

Rowlands, M. (1986a) 'Colonialism, archaeology and constituting the African peasantry', Paper presented at the World Archaeological Congress, 1986.

Rowley-Conwy, P. (1986) 'Between cave painters and crop planters: aspects of the temperate European mesolithic', in M. Zvelebil (ed.), *Hunters in Transition*, Cambridge University Press, Cambridge.

Ryan, M. (1982) *Marxism and Deconstruction: a Critical Articulation*, Johns Hopkins University Press, Baltimore.

Sabloff, J. and Lamberg-Karlovsky, C. (eds) (1975) *Ancient Civilisation and Trade*, University of New Mexico Press, Albuquerque.

Sackett, J. (1973) 'Style, function and artifact variability in palaeolithic assemblages', in C. Renfrew (ed.), *The Explanation of Culture Change: Models in Prehistory*, Duckworth, London.

Sackett, J. (1977) 'The meaning of style: a general model', *American Antiquity* 42: 369–80.

Sackett, J. (1982) 'Approaches to style in lithic archaeology', *Journal of Anthropological Archaeology* 1: 59–112.

Sackett, J. (1985) 'Style and ethnicity in the Kalahari: a reply to Weissner', *American Antiquity* 50: 154–9.

Sahlins, M. (1968) *Tribesmen*, Prentice-Hall, Englewood Cliffs.

Sahlins, M. (1981) *Historical Metaphors and Mythical Realities*, University of Michigan Press, Ann Arbor.

Sahlins, M. (1985) *Islands of History*, University of Chicago Press, Chicago.

Sahlins, M. and Service, E. (1960) *Evolution and Culture*, University of Michigan Press, Ann Arbor.

Sanders, W. and Webster, D. (1978) 'Unilinealism, multilinealism, and the evolution of complex societies', in C. Redman et al (eds)., *Social Archaeology: Beyond Dating and Subsistence*, Academic Press, London.

Sartre, J.-P. (1950) 'Writing for one's age', *What is Literature?*, Methuen, London.

Sartre, J.-P. (1983) 'A plea for intellectuals', *Between Existentialism and Marxism*, Verso, London.

Saussure, F. de (1978) *Course in General Linguistics*, Peter Owen, London.

Saxe, A. (1970) *Social Dimensions of Mortuary Practices*, doctoral dissertation, University Microfilms, Ann Arbor.

Schapiro, G. (1984) 'Ceramic vessels, site permanence and group size: a Mississippian example', *American Antiquity* 49: 696–712.

Schiffer, M. (1976) *Behavioural Archaeology*, Academic Press, London.

Schiffer, M. (1978) 'Taking the pulse of method and theory in American archaeology', *American Antiquity* 43: 153–8.

Schiffer, M. (1981) 'Some issues in the philosophy of archaeology', *American Antiquity* 46: 899–908.

Sears, W. (1960) 'Ceramic systems and eastern archaeology', *American Antiquity* 25: 324–9.

Segraves, B. (1982) 'Central elements in the construction of a general theory of the evolution of societal complexity', in C. Renfrew, M. Rowlands and B. Segraves (eds).

Semenov, S. (1964) *Prehistoric Technology*, Adams and Dart, Bath.

Service, E. (1962) *Primitive Social Organization*, Random House, New York.

Service, E. (1975) *Origins of the State and Civilisation*, Norton, New York.

Shanks, M. and Tilley, C. (1982) 'Ideology, symbolic power and ritual communication: a reinterpretation of neolithic mortuary practices', in I. Hodder (ed.)

Shanks, M. and Tilley, C. (1987) *Re-Constructing Archaeology: Theory and Practice*, Cambridge University Press, Cambridge.

Shaw, T. (1986) 'Archaeology and the politics of academic freedom', *Archaeological Review from Cambridge* 5: 5–24.

Shennan, S. E. (1975) 'The social organisation at Branč', *Antiquity* 49: 279–88.

Shennan, S. J. (1978) 'Archaeological "cultures": an empirical investigation', in I. Hodder (ed.)

Shennan, S. J. (1982) 'Ideology, change and the European early Bronze Age' in I. Hodder (ed.)

Shennan, S. J. (1986) 'Interaction and change in third millennium B.C. western and central Europe', in C. Renfrew and J. Cherry (eds).

Sherratt, A. (1981) 'Plough and pastoralism: aspects of the secondary products revolution', in I. Hodder, G. Isaac and N. Hammond (eds), *Pattern of the Past*, Cambridge University Press, Cambridge.

Sherratt, A. (1982) 'Mobile resources: settlement and exchange in early agricultural Europe', in C. Renfrew and S. Shennan (eds).

Sinclair, P. (1986) 'Archaeology, ideology and development: Mozambican perspectives', *Archaeological Review from Cambridge* 5: 77–87.

Sklair, L. (1970) *The Sociology of Progress*, Routledge and Kegan Paul, London.

Smith, A. (1973) *The Concept of Social Change*, Routledge and Kegan Paul, London.

Soja, E. (1985) 'The spatiality of social life: towards a transformative retheorisation', in D. Gregory and J. Urry (eds), *Social Relations and Spatial Structures*, Macmillan, London.

Spaulding, A. (1953) 'Statistical techniques for the discovery of artifact types', *American Antiquity* 18: 305–13.

Spaulding, A. (1954) 'Reply to Ford', *American Antiquity* 19: 391–3.

Spencer, H. (1852) 'A theory of population deduced from the general laws of animal fertility', *Westminster Review* 57: 468–501.

Spencer, H. (1967) *The Evolution of Society*, University of Chicago Press, Chicago.

Spencer, H. (1972) *On Social Evolution*, ed. J. Peel, University of Chicago Press, Chicago.

Spriggs, M. (ed.) (1984) *Perspectives in Marxist Archaeology*, Cambridge University Press, Cambridge.

Stanislawski, M. and Stanislawski, B. (1978) 'Hopi and Hopi-Tewa ceramic tradition networks', in I. Hodder (ed.)

Stephenson, R. (1977) 'A strategy for getting the job done', in S. South (ed.), *Research Strategies in Historical Archaeology,* Academic Press, London.

Steponaitis, V. (1983) *Ceramics, Chronology, and Community Patterns: an Archaeological Study at Moundville*, Academic Press, London.

Sterud, E. (1973) 'A paradigmatic view of prehistory', in C. Renfrew (ed.), *The Explanation of Culture Change: Models in Prehistory*, Duckworth, London.

Sterud, E. (1978) 'Changing aims of Americanist archaeology: a citations analysis of "American Antiquity" 1946–1975', *American Antiquity* 43: 294–302.

Steward, J. (1955) *Theory of Culture Change*, University of Illinois Press, London.

Sturrock, J. (ed.) (1979) *Structuralism and Since*, Oxford University Press, Oxford.

Tainter, J. (1975) 'Social inference and mortuary practices: an experiment in numerical classification', *World Archaeology* 7: 1–5.

Tainter, J. (1977) 'Modelling change in prehistoric social systems', in L. Binford (ed.), *For Theory Building in Archaeology*, Academic Press, London.

Tainter, J. (1978) 'Mortuary practices and the study of prehistoric social systems', in M. Schiffer (ed.), *Advances in Archaeological Method and Theory*, vol. 1., Academic Press, London.

Thompson, E. P. (1978) *The Poverty of Theory*, Merlin, London.

Thorpe, I. and Richards, C. 'The decline of ritual authority and the introduction of beakers into Britain', in R. Bradley and J. Gardiner (eds), *Neolithic Studies*, British Archaeological Reports 133, Oxford.

Tilley, C. (1981a) 'Conceptual frameworks for the explanation of socio-cultural change', in I. Hodder, G. Isaac and N. Hammond (eds), *Pattern of the Past*, Cambridge University Press, Cambridge.

Tilley, C. (1981b) 'Economy and society: what relationship?', in A. Sheridan and G. Bailey (eds), *Economic Archaeology*, British Archaeological Reports, Oxford.

Tilley, C. (1982) 'Social formation, social structures and social change', in I. Hodder (ed.)

Tilley, C. (1984) 'Ideology and the legitimation of power in the middle neolithic of southern Sweden', in D. Miller and C. Tilley (eds).

Tilley, C. (1985) 'Archaeology as sociopolitical action in the present', in V. Pinsky and A. Wylie (eds), *Critical Traditions in Contemporary Archaeology*, Cambridge University Press, Cambridge.

Trigger, B. (1978) *Time and Traditions: Essays in Archaeological Interpretation*, Edinburgh University Press, Edinburgh.

Trigger, B. (1980) 'Archaeology and the image of the American indian', *American Antiquity* 45: 662–76.

Trigger, B. (1981) 'Anglo-American archaeology', *World Archaeology* 13: 138–55.

Trigger, B. (1984) 'Alternative archaeologies: nationalist, colonialist, imperialist', *Man* 19: 355–70.

Tylor, E. (1958) *Primitive Culture* (1871), 2 vols, Harper Torchbooks, New York.

Tylor, E. (1881) *Anthropology: an Introduction to the Study of Man*, D. Appleton, New York.

Ucko, P. (1983) 'Australian academic archaeology: aboriginal transformation of its aims and practices', *Australian Archaeology* 16: 11–26.

Van de Leeuw, S. (1976) *Studies in the Technology of Ancient Pottery*, doctoral dissertation, University of Amsterdam.

Van de Leeuw, S. (1981) 'Information flows, flow structures and the explanation of change in human institutions', in S. Van de Leeuw (ed.)

Van de Leeuw, S. (ed.) (1981) *Archaeological Approaches to the Study of Complexity*, University of Amsterdam Press, Amsterdam.

Wainwright, G. (1979) *Gussage All Saints: an Iron Age Settlement in Dorset*, Department of the Environment Archaeological Reports No. 10, Her Majesty's Stationery Office, London.

Washburn, D. (1978) 'A symmetry classification of pueblo ceramic design', in P. Grebinger (ed.), *Discovering Past Behaviour*, Gordon and Breach, New York.

Washburn, D. (1983) 'Symmetry analysis of ceramic design: two tests of the method on neolithic material from Greece and the Aegean', in D.

Washburn (ed.), *Structure and Cognition in Art*, Cambridge University Press, Cambridge.

Watson, P., LeBlanc, S. and Redman, C. (1971) *Explanation in Archaeology: an Explicitly Scientific Approach*, Columbia University Press, New York.

Weissner, P. (1983) 'Style and social information in Kalahari San projectile points', *American Antiquity* 48: 253–76.

Wenke, R. (1981) 'Explaining the evolution of cultural complexity: a review', in M. Schiffer (ed.), *Advances in Archaeological Method and Theory*, vol. 5, Academic Press, London.

Whallon, R. (1968) 'Investigations of late prehistoric social organisation in New York state', in L. and S. Binford (eds), *New Perspectives in Archaeology*, Aldine, Chicago.

Whallon, R. (1982) 'Comments on "explanation", in C. Renfrew and S. Shennan (eds).

Wheeler, M. (1954) *Archaeology from the Earth*, Penguin, Harmondsworth.

White, H. (1978) *Tropics of Discourse*, Johns Hopkins University Press, Baltimore.

White, L. (1959) *The Evolution of Culture*, McGraw-Hill, New York.

Wilmsen, E. (1968) 'Functional analysis of flaked stone artifacts', *American Antiquity* 33: 156–61.

Wobst, M. (1977) 'Stylistic behaviour and information exchange', *University of Michigan, Museum of Anthropology Anthropological Papers* 61: 317–42.

Wrong, D. (1979) *Power: its Forms, Bases and Uses*, Basil Blackwell, Oxford.

Yoffee, N. (1979) 'The decline and rise of Mesopotamian civilisation: an ethnoarchaeological perspective on the evolution of societal complexity', *American Antiquity* 44: 5–34.

Zubrow, E. (1972) 'Environment, subsistence and society: the changing archaeological perspective', *Annual Review of Anthropology* 1: 179–206.

Index

8 JAN 12 1988

Lecture Notes in Mathematics

Edited by A. Dold and B. Eckmann

804

Michihiko Matsuda

First Order Algebraic Differential Equations

A Differential Algebraic Approach

Springer-Verlag

Berlin Heidelberg New York 1980

W9-ABN-291

Author

Michihiko Matsuda
Department of Mathematics, Kyoto Sangyo University
Kamigamo, Kyoto 603/Japan

AMS Subject Classifications (1980): 12 H 05

ISBN 3-540-09997-2 Springer-Verlag Berlin Heidelberg New York
ISBN 0-387-09997-2 Springer-Verlag New York Heidelberg Berlin

This work is subject to copyright. All rights are reserved, whether the whole or
part of the material is concerned, specifically those of translation, reprinting,
re-use of illustrations, broadcasting, reproduction by photocopying machine or
similar means, and storage in data banks. Under § 54 of the German Copyright
Law where copies are made for other than private use, a fee is payable to the
publisher, the amount of the fee to be determined by agreement with the publisher.
© by Springer-Verlag Berlin Heidelberg 1980
Printed in Germany

Printing and binding: Beltz Offsetdruck, Hemsbach/Bergstr.
2141/3140-543210

Introduction

The study of first order algebraic differential equations
produced fruitful results around the end of the last century. The
classification of equations free of movable singularities was
carried out successfully. The investigations were carried out in
the complex plane and the main tool of investigation was "analytic
continuation". Fuchs tried to clarify the algebraic aspect making
use of "Puiseux series", but his work was not developed fully at
that time.

The modern theory of differential algebra and algebraic
function fields of one variable has enabled us to give an abstract
treatment, leaving the complex plane. Recently the author presented a differential-algebraic criterion for a first order algebraic differential equation to have no movable singularity suggested by Fuchs' criterion for this property. From this standpoint we reconstructed some classical theorems due to Briot,
Bouquet, Fuchs and Poincaré. In this treatment the coefficient
field is an arbitrary algebraically-closed differential field of
characteristic 0.

E. R. Kolchin , using Galois theory of differential fields,
obtained in 1953 a theorem containing a criterion for a first order algebraic differential equation to define elliptic functions
(cf. §12). The author would like to note that his work was motiv-
ated by this excellent theorem. M. Rosenlicht applied valuation
theory to the problem of explicit solvability of certain algebraic

differential equations successfully.

In this note we shall consider the general case in which the coefficient field is an arbitrary differential field: It is not necessarily of characteristic 0 nor algebraically closed. We assume the reader to be familiar with the contents of the first six chapters of the book "Introduction to the theory of algebraic functions of one variable" by Chevalley (Amer. Math. Soc. 4th printing, 1971), which will be referenced as [C]. Any theorem not contained in this book and used here will be proved, even if the proof is well known. A familiarity with differential algebra is not assumed except in §18.

In §§16-17 recent results of Keiji Nishioka will be introduced: They are valid only in the case of characteristic 0.

The author would like to express his sincere gratitude to Professor I. Laine and Professor M. Rosenlicht for their invitation to the Colloquium on Complex Analysis, Joensuu, Finland, August 24-27, 1978 and the Special Lecture at the University of California, Berkeley, July 18, 1978 respectively.

August 1979

Michihiko Matsuda

Preliminaries

Let M be a commutative ring and N be a subring of M. A derivation of N into M is a mapping δ which satisfies the following conditions:

$$\delta(y + z) = \delta y + \delta z, \quad \delta(yz) = y\delta z + z\delta y.$$

A derivation of M into itself is called simply a derivation of M: If M has no proper zero divisors, then it can be extended to a derivation of the quotient field of M in one and only one way.

Suppose that M is a field and N is a subfield of M. The derivation δ of N into M satisfies

$$\delta(y/z) = (z\,\delta y - y\delta z)/z^2, \quad z \neq 0.$$

If two derivations of N into M coincide on some subset E of N, then they coincide on the subfield of N generated by the elements of E.

Let x be an element of the field M. If x is transcendental over the subfield N, the derivation δ can be extended to a derivation D of N(x) into M such that Dx is an arbitrarily chosen element of M(cf. §1, p.3). Suppose that x is algebraic over N. If x is separable over N, δ can be extended to a derivation of N(x) into M in one and only one way. If an element u of N is the p-th power of x, δ can be extended to a derivation D of N(x) into M if and only if $\delta u = 0$, where p is the characteristic of N. In this case an arbitrary element of M may be taken for Dx if x $\notin$ N(cf. for instance pp.12-13 of the book "Foundations of algebraic geometry" by Weil(Amer. Math. Soc., 2nd Edition, 1962)).

Table of Contents

§1. Differential algebraic function field of one variable

A differential field is a field to which a derivation of it is attached. The affixed derivation is called the differentiation and signed with the prime "'".

An element of a differential field whose derivative vanishes is a constant. The totality of constants forms a field, the field of constants. If the characteristic p of a differential field is positive, the p-th power of any element is a constant. Hence, a perfect differential field consists of constants if p is positive.

A subfield of a differential field is called a differential subfield if it is closed under the differentiation. The overfield is called a differential extension of it.

An algebraic function field of one variable over a field K is a field R containing K as a subfield which satisfies the following condition: There is an element x of R which is transcendental over K, and R is algebraic of finite degree over K(x). The coefficient field of R is the totality of those elements of R which are algebraic over K: It is the one called the field of constants of R in [C]: This term is used here for the meaning stated ahead.

In case R is of the form K(x, y), the coefficient field of R coincides with K if the characteristic polynomial f(Y) of y with respect to K(x) is irreducible in $\bar{K}(x)[Y]$, where $\bar{K}$ is the algebraic closure of K: For, if u is an element of R which is algebraic over K, we have

$$[R : K(x)] = [R : K(x, u)],$$

whence u $\in$ K(x): Since K is relatively algebraically closed in K(x), u belongs to K. In case R is separably generated over K, the converse is true; the coefficient field K* of R contains K properly if f(Y) is reducible in $\bar{K}$(x)[Y]: For there are an element u of $\bar{K}$ and an intermediary field L between K and $\bar{K}$ such that f(Y) is irreducible in L(x)[Y] but reducible in L(u, x)[Y]: Let g(U) be the characteristic polynomial of u in L(u) with respect to L: It is irreducible in L(x)[Y] because L is relatively algebraically closed in L(x), whence

$$[L(u, x) : L(x)] = [L(u) : L]:$$

We set T = R(L) and consider it an algebraic function field of one variable over L: The coefficient field of T is L if L contains K*, since R is assumed to be separably generated over K([C, p.91]): If K* were K, L would contain K*, whence L would be relatively algebraically closed in T and g(U) would be irreducible in T[U]: We would have

$$[T(u) : T] = [L(u) : L],$$

but it is impossible because

$$[T(u) : L(u, x)] < [T : L(x)]$$

by our assumption that f(Y) is reducible in L(u, x)[Y]. In the general case our converse is not true; we can find a counter example in [C, p.91] .

An algebraic function field R of one variable over K will be called a <u>differential</u> <u>algebraic</u> <u>function</u> <u>field</u> <u>of</u> <u>one</u> <u>variable</u>

over K if R is a differential field in which K is closed under the differentiation.

In case R is separably generated over K, the coefficient field of R is closed under the differentiation, because it is algebraic and separable over K. In the general case it is not true: Assume for instance that R = K(a, x), where K is a field of positive characteristic p and x is transcendental over K, while $a^p \in K$, a $\notin$ K. If we define

x' = 0, a' = x, c' = 0, c $\in$ K,

R is a differential algebraic function field of one variable over K, but the coefficient field K(a) of R is not closed under the differentiation.

Let R be an algebraic function field of one variable over a given field K. We shall suppose that K is a differential field and see how R becomes a differential extension of K under the assumption that R is separably generated over K. For this purpose take a separating variable x in R: We shall show that for any element y of R there is a derivation D of K(x) into R such that Dx = y and it coincides with the given derivation on K. If ϕ is an element of K[x] of the form $\Sigma a_i x^i$, we define

$$D\phi = \Sigma a_i' x^i + y\Sigma i a_i x^{i-1}.$$

Clearly it is a derivation of K[x] into R, which satisfies

Dx = y, Da = a', a $\in$ K.

We may extend it to a derivation D of K(x) into R by

$$D(w) = (\psi D\phi - \phi D\psi)\psi^{-2}, \quad w = \phi/\psi, \quad \phi, \psi \in K[x];$$

it is well-defined on K(x). The derivation D thus defined can be extended to a derivation of R in one and only way, since R is algebraic and separable over K(x).

This being said, let f(X, Y) be an irreducible polynomial with the coefficients in a given field K such that $f_Y(X, Y) \neq 0$. If K is a differential field, there is a differential algebraic function field R of one variable over K such that R = K(x, x') with f(x, x') = 0. In case f(X, Y) is irreducible in $\bar{K}[X, Y]$, the coefficient field of R is K.

Let R be a differential algebraic function field of one variable over K. We shall show that if $\wp$ is a place in R, the differentiation is continuous on R in the topology induced by $\wp$. In case the coefficient field K* of R is closed under the differentiation, the proof is found in [C, p.114]. In the general case the proof goes through if the number s_0 presented there is replaced by $s_0 + s_1$, where s_1 is the number defined below. Let $\{\omega_1, \ldots, \omega_r\}$ be a base of K* with respect to K. We set

$$s_1 = \max \{0, -\nu_{\wp}(\omega_i'); 1 \leq i \leq r\};$$

here $\nu_{\wp}$ is the order function at $\wp$. If a is an element of K*;

$$a = \Sigma c_i \omega_i \ (1 \leq i \leq r), \quad c_i \in K,$$

then we have

$$a' = \Sigma c_i' \omega_i + \Sigma c_i \omega_i',$$

whence

$$\nu_{\wp}(a') \geq \min \{\nu_{\wp}(\omega_i'); 1 \leq i \leq r\} \geq -s_1$$

because $c_i' \in K$.

This being said, if $\wp$ is a place in a differential algebraic function field R of one variable over K, the differentiation can be extended to a derivation of the $\wp$-adic completion $\bar{R}$ of R which is continuous on $\bar{R}$ in one and only way. The extended derivation will be called the differentiation of $\bar{R}$ and denoted by the same sign "'".

Throughout this note we shall use the notation $\nu_\wp$ to represent the order function at a place $\wp$ in an algebraic function field of one variable.

We shall give an example of a differential algebraic function field of one variable over K which is not separably generated over K: Assume for instance that $R = K(x, y_1, y_2)$ with

$$y_i^p + a_i x^p + b_i = 0, \quad i = 1, 2$$

and $K = P(a_1, b_1, a_2, b_2)$, where P is any differential field of positive characteristic p and the a_i, b_i are algebraically independent over P. If we define $a_i' = b_i' = 0 (i = 1, 2)$ and take arbitrary elements of R for the derivatives of x, y_1, y_2, then R is a differential algebraic function field of one variable over K. The coefficient field K^* of R is K: For, if K^* were not K, then the p-th roots of the a_i, $b_i (i = 1, 2)$ would be contained in R, but it is impossible because the degree of R over K(x) is p^2. If L is the field generated by the p-th roots of a_1, a_2 over K, the coefficient field L^* of R(L) is not L because L^* contains the p-th roots of b_1, b_2, where R(L) is the field deduced from R by adjoining the elements of L to K. Therefore, R is not separably generated over K([C, p.91]). We note that R can not take the form

$K(u, v)$: For if it were $K(u, v)$ then the degree of R over $K(x^p)$ would be p^2, but it is impossible because it is equal to p^3.

Remark. A field to which several derivations $\delta_1, \ldots, \delta_m$ ($m > 1$) are attached is called a partial differential field if $\delta_i \delta_j = \delta_j \delta_i$ ($1 \le i < j \le m$): If $m = 1$, which is our case, it is called an ordinary differential field in case it is necessary to distinguish it from a partial one.

§2.   Movable singularities

We shall give the following:

Definition.   Let R be a differential algebraic function field of one variable over K.   It is said to have no movable singularity if the ring $\mathcal{O}$ of any place $\mathfrak{p}$ in R is closed under the differentiation.

Let R be a differential algebraic function field of one variable over K, and x be an element of R which is transcendental over K.   We shall examine when the ring $\mathfrak{O}$ of a given place $\mathfrak{P}$ in R is closed under the differentiation if the derivative x' of x is known.   We may assume that $\mathfrak{P}$ is not a pole of x; if it is a pole of x, we replace x by x^{-1}.   The ring $\mathcal{O}$ of the place $\mathfrak{p}$ in K(x) which lies below $\mathfrak{P}$ is mapped by the differentiation into $\mathfrak{O}$ if and only if x' is integral at $\mathfrak{P}$: For an element z of $\mathcal{O}$ may be written in the form y_1/y_2, y_1, $y_2 \in K[x]$ with $v_{\mathfrak{p}}(y_2) = 0$, and

$$z' = (y_1'y_2 - y_1y_2')y_2^{-2},$$

whence $z' \in \mathfrak{O}$ if $x' \in \mathfrak{O}$ because K is closed under the differentiation.   Now assume that the differentiation maps $\mathcal{O}$ into $\mathfrak{O}$.   Let u be a uniformizing variable at $\mathfrak{P}$ and v_1, ... , v_f be integral elements of the $\mathfrak{P}$-adic completion $\bar{R}$ of R whose residue classes modulo $\mathfrak{P}$ form a base of the residue field of $\mathfrak{P}$ with respect to the residue field of $\mathfrak{p}$.   Every integral element w of $\bar{R}$ may be written in the form

$$\Sigma z_{ij}u^iv_j, \quad 0 \le i \le e, \quad 1 \le j \le f$$

with z_{ij} in the ring of integral elements of the $\wp$-adic completion of $K(x)$ ([C, p.61]). Their derivatives are integral at $\mathfrak{P}$ because the differentiation is continuous on $\bar{R}$, whence w' is integral at $\mathfrak{P}$ if the derivatives of u, v_1, ... , v_f are integral at $\mathfrak{P}$.

Let R be a differential algebraic function field of one variable over K, and $\wp$ be a place in R. We shall assume that the residue field $\Sigma(\wp)$ of $\wp$ is separable over K, and see that the ring $\mathcal{O}$ of $\wp$ is closed under the differentiation if there is in $\bar{R}$ a uniformizing variable t at $\wp$ whose derivative is integral at $\wp$. The $\wp$-adic completion $\bar{R}$ of R has a subfield Σ which contains K and which is a system of representatives for the elements of $\Sigma(\wp)$ ([C, p.44]). An integral element w of $\bar{R}$ can be represented in the form

$$\Sigma a_k t^k, \quad 0 \leq k < \infty, \quad a_k \in \Sigma$$

with a uniformizing variable t at $\wp$ ([C, p.46]). Since the differentiation is continuous on $\bar{R}$,

$$w' = \Sigma a_k' t^k + t' \Sigma k a_k t^{k-1}.$$

By hypothesis Σ is algebraic and separable over K, and it is closed under the differentiation, whence $a_k' \in \Sigma$: Thus w' is integral at $\wp$ if t' is integral at $\wp$. In particular the derivative of every uniformizing variable in $\bar{R}$ is integral at $\wp$ if t' is integral at $\wp$.

In case $\Sigma(\wp)$ is unseparable over K, there is an example of R such that $\mathcal{O}$ is not closed under the differentiation although there exists a uniformizing variable at $\wp$ whose derivative is integral at $\wp$. Assume for instance that R = K(x) and K is a field of positive characteristic p containing some element a whose p-th root is not in K. If we define $c' = 0$, $c \in K$ and $x' = y^{-1}$ with $y = x^p - a$, then R is a differential algebraic function field of one variable over K. Let a place $\wp$ in R be a zero of y. The residue field of $\wp$ is $K(a^{1/p})$, which is unseparable over K. In R, y is a uniformizing variable at $\wp$, and $y' = 0$. We have $x \in \mathcal{O}$, but $x' \notin \mathcal{O}$ although $y' \in \mathcal{O}$.

Now return to the case where $\Sigma(\wp)$ is separable over K. The notation being as above, any uniformizing variable t_1 at $\wp$ satisfies

$$v_{\wp}(t_1') = v_{\wp}(t')$$

if $v_{\wp}(t') \leq 0$: For t_1 can be represented in the form

$$\Sigma a_k t^k, \quad 1 \leq k < \infty, \quad a_k \in \Sigma, \quad a_1 \neq 0,$$

whence

$$t_1' = a_1 t' + \Sigma(k + 1)a_{k+1} t^k t' + \Sigma a_k' t^k, \quad 1 \leq k < \infty.$$

In case $v_{\wp}(t') > 0$, we have $v_{\wp}(t_1') > 0$, but the equality $v_{\wp}(t_1') = v_{\wp}(t')$ does not hold in general. Assume for instance that $R = K(x)$ with $K = P(a)$, where P is a field and a is transcendental over P. If we define

$$x' = x, \quad a' = a, \quad c' = 0, \quad c \in P,$$

R is a differential algebraic function field of one variable over K. Let a place $\wp$ in R be a zero of x. Then $\Sigma(\wp)$ is K and x is a uniformizing variable at $\wp$, which satisfies $v_{\wp}(x') = 1$. The element x/a is also a uniformizing variable at $\wp$, but it is a constant, whence $v_{\wp}((x/a)') = \infty$.

We note that if R has no movable singularity then the coefficient field K* of R is closed under the differentiation: For

the derivative a' of an element a of K* has no pole in R, whence
a' belongs to K*([C, p.9]).

Let R and S be algebraic function fields of one variable
over K and L respectively such that S contains R as a subfield.
We assume that any element of R which is algebraic over K is algebraic over L and that any element of R which is transcendental
over K is transcendental over L.

Theorem 1. The notation being as above, suppose that R
and S are differential algebraic function fields of one variable
over K and L respectively, and that S is a differential extension
of R. Then R has no movable singularity if S has no movable singularity.

If $\mathfrak{p}$ is a place of R, there exists at least one place $\mathfrak{P}$
of S which lies above $\mathfrak{p}$ ([C, p.52]). Since the ring $\mathfrak{D}$ of $\mathfrak{P}$ is
closed under the differentiation, the ring $\mathfrak{O}$ of $\mathfrak{p}$ is closed under the differentiation because $\mathfrak{O} = \mathfrak{D} \cap R$.

§3. Fuchs' theorem

We shall prove the following theorem which is essentially
due to Fuchs:

Theorem 2. Let R be a differential algebraic function field
of one variable over K, and x be an element of R which is transcendental over K. We denote by f(Y) the minimal polynomial of x' over
K(x);

$$f(Y) = \Sigma a_i(x) Y^{n-i}, \quad 0 \leq i \leq n, \ a_0 = 1, \ a_i \in K(x).$$

If R has no movable singularity, then $a_i(x)$ is a polynomial of x
with coefficients in K whose degree is at most equal to 2i unless
$a_i = 0$.

Let $\wp$ be a place in K(x). If it is not a pole of x, the
derivative x' of x is integral at any place in R which lies above
$\wp$, whence f(Y) has the coefficients in the ring of $\wp$ ([C, p.56]),
and they are polynomials of x with coefficients in K([C, p.23]).
If $\wp$ is a pole of x, we set $z = x^{-1}$. The characteristic polynomial of z' with respect to K(z) is

$$\Sigma (-1)^i z^{2i} a_i(z^{-1}) Y^{n-i}, \quad 0 \leq i \leq n.$$

The coefficient is a polynomial of z with coefficients in K, whence
the degree of $a_i(x)$ with respect to x is at most 2i unless $a_i = 0$.

Let R be a differential algebraic function field of one
variable over K. We assume that R takes the form K(x, y) and that
R is algebraic and separable over K(x). By f(Y) we denote the

characteristic polynomial of y with respect to K(x) and see that
the ring $\mathcal{O}$ of $\mathfrak{P}$ is closed under the differentiation if $\mathfrak{P}$ is
neither a pole of x' and any coefficient of f(Y) nor a zero of the
discriminant Δ of f(Y). The differentiation maps the ring $\mathcal{O}$ of
the place $\mathfrak{p}$ in K(x) which lies below $\mathfrak{P}$ into $\mathcal{O}$ because x' is integral at $\mathfrak{P}$ (§2, p.7). Since y is integral over $\mathcal{O}$, it is integral at $\mathfrak{P}$. The $\mathfrak{P}$-adic completion $\bar{R}$ of R takes the form T(y) with
the $\mathfrak{p}$-adic completion T of K(x) ([C, p.63]). If g(Y) is the characteristic polynomial of y with respect to T, it has the coefficients in the ring of integral elements of T at $\mathfrak{p}$ because y is
integral at $\mathfrak{p}$ ([C, p.62]). Let g*(Y) be the polynomial obtained
from g(Y) by replacing the coefficients by their residue classes
modulo $\mathfrak{p}$; then it divides f*(Y) similarly obtained from f(Y)
in Σ[Y], where Σ is the residue field of $\mathfrak{p}$; g*(Y) is irreducible
in Σ[Y]: For, if it were reducible in Σ[Y], it would take the form
h*(Y)$^\lambda$ with $\lambda > 1$ by Hensel's lemma, since g(Y) is irreducible in
T[Y] ([C, p.43]), but it is impossible because f*(Y) has only simple
roots by our assumption that $\mathfrak{P}$ is not a zero of Δ. Thus, the residue field of $\mathfrak{P}$ is generated by the residue class $\bar{y}$ of y modulo $\mathfrak{P}$
over Σ and $\mathfrak{P}$ is unramified with respect to K(x) ([C, p.61]). The
derivative y' of y is integral at $\mathfrak{P}$: For if g(Y) takes the form
$$\Sigma a_i y^{f-i}, \quad 0 \le i \le f, \quad a_0 = 1,$$
we have
$$\Sigma a_i' y^{f-i} + g_Y(y) y' = 0;$$
the derivatives of a_i are integral at $\mathfrak{P}$ and $g_Y^*(\bar{y}) \ne 0$. Hence, $\mathcal{O}$
is closed under the differentiation (§2, pp.7-8).

A differential algebraic function field R of one variable over K is called a <u>Riccati</u> <u>field</u> over K if R = K(x) with

$$x' = a + bx + cx^2, \quad a, b, c \in K.$$

A Riccati field R over K has no movable singularity: For if a place $\mathcal{P}$ in R is not a pole of x, the ring of $\mathcal{P}$ is closed under the differentiation by the above arguments: If $\mathcal{P}$ is a pole of x, we have

$$- (x^{-1})' = c + bx^{-1} + cx^{-2},$$

whence the ring of $\mathcal{P}$ is closed under the differentiation.

<u>Theorem</u> 3.   Let R be a differential algebraic function field of one variable over K of genus 0 such that R has a place of degree 1.   If R has no movable singularity, it is a Riccati field over the coefficient field K*.

By hypothesis R is a rational function field K*(x) over K*. Since R has no movable singularity, K* is closed under the differentiation(§2, p.9).   The derivative of x is a rational function of x over K* and it is a polynomial of x over K* whose degree is at most equal to 2 unless it vanishes by Theorem 2.

There is an example of R of genus 0 such that R has no movable singularity while it has no place of degree 1.   Assume for instance that R takes the form K(x, y) with $y^2 + x^2 + 4a = 0$ and that K is of the form P(a), where a is transcendental over P, while P is a field which does not contain a quadratic root of -1. The characteristic p of K satisfies $p \equiv -1 \pmod 4$ unless p = 0. Every place in R is proved to be of degree greater than 1.   If we define x' = y and c' = 0, c $\in$ K, then R is a differential algebraic function field of one variable over K. Let L be the

overfield of K obtained from K by the adjunction of a quadratic

root i of -1. Then L is separable over K and $R(L) = L(t)$ with

$$t = - i(1 + a - iy)/(1 - a + x);$$

$$x = - \{(1 - a)t^2 + 2i(1 + a)t - (1 - a)\}/(1 + t^2).$$

The genus of $R(L)$ is 0, whence the genus of R is 0 because L is

separable over K([C, p.99]). We have

$$t' = - (x + ty)/(1 - a + x) = (1 - t^2)/2,$$

whence $R(L)$ has no movable singularity. By Theorem 1(§2), R has

no movable singularity.

Remark (Fuchs' criterion). Let R be a differential algebra-

ic function field of one variable over K of the form $K(x, x')$.

We assume that K is algebraically closed and of characteristic 0.

Let $f(Y)$ be the characteristic polynomial of x' with respect to

$K(x)$;

$$f(Y) = \Sigma a_i(x) Y^{n-i}, \quad a_i(x) \in K(x), \quad a_0 = 1.$$

Then R has no movable singularity if and only if the following

three conditions are satisfied:

(i) Each coefficient $a_i(x)$ of $f(Y)$ is a polynomial of x

over K whose degree is at most equal to 2i unless $a_i(x) = 0$:

(ii) If a place $\mathfrak{p}$ in R which is not a pole of x is rami-

fied with respect to $K(x)$, the residue classes ξ, η of x, x' modulo

$\mathfrak{p}$ satisfy $\xi' = \eta$ and

$$v_{\mathfrak{p}}(x' - \eta) \geq e_{\mathfrak{p}} - 1,$$

where $e_{\mathfrak{p}}$ is the ramification index of $\mathfrak{p}$ with respect to $K(x)$:

(iii) If a place $\mathfrak{p}$ in R which is a pole of x is ramified with respect to $K(x)$, then

$$\nu_{\wp}(x') \geq \nu_{\wp}(x) - 1.$$

We shall prove that our statement is true. If R has no movable singularity, the condition (i) is satisfied by Theorem 2. We assume that the condition (i) is satisfied: x' is integral at any place in R which is not a pole of x and $(x^{-1})'$ is integral at any place which is a pole of x. If a place $\wp$ in R is not a pole of x, x may be written in the form $\xi + t^e$ with a uniformizing variable t at $\wp$ in the $\wp$-adic completion of R, where e is the ramification index of $\wp$ with respect to $K(x)$ ([C, p.64]). We have

$$x' = \xi' + et^{e-1}t',$$

whence t' is integral at $\wp$ if $e = 1$. In case $e > 1$, t' is integral at $\wp$ if and only if the condition (ii) is satisfied. If a place $\wp$ in R is a pole of x, x^{-1} may be written in the form $x^{-1} = t^e$ with a uniformizing variable t at $\wp$ in the $\wp$-adic completion of R, where e is the ramification index of $\wp$ with respect to $K(x)$. We have

$$(x^{-1})' = - x't^{2e} = et^{e-1}t',$$

whence t' is integral at $\wp$ if $e = 1$. In case $e > 1$, t' is integral at $\wp$ if and only if the condition (iii) is satisfied.

Fuchs failed to notice that the condition (iii) is necessary for R to have no movable singularity. There is an example of R which has movable singularities although the conditions (i) and (ii) are satisfied. Assume for instance that $R = K(x, x')$ with

$$(x')^{\ell} - x^m = 0,$$

where ℓ and m are positive integers having no common divisor which satisfy

$$2\ell \geq m \geq \ell + 1,$$

while K is any algebraically closed differential field of characteristic 0. The condition (i) is satisfied. If a place $\wp$ in R is neither a zero of x nor a pole of x, it is unramified with respect to K(x). In case $\wp$ is a zero of x, we have

$$\xi = \eta = 0, \quad e_{\wp} = \ell, \quad \nu_{\wp}(x') = m,$$

whence the condition (ii) is satisfied. Suppose that $\wp$ is a pole of x. Then x^{-1} may be written in the form $x^{-1} = t^{\ell}$ with a uniformizing variable t at $\wp$. We have

$$\nu_{\wp}(x') = -m$$

and

$$\ell t^{\ell-1} t' = (x^{-1})' = -x' x^{-2} = -x' t^{2\ell},$$

whence

$$\nu_{\wp}(t') = -m + \ell + 1 < 0.$$

For Fuchs' work (Ueber Differentialgleichungen, deren Integrale feste Verzweigungspunkte besitzen, S.-B. der Königl. preussischen Akad. Wiss. Berlin, 32(1884), 699-710), confer with §§116-121 of the book "Theory of differential equations (Vol. 2, Ordinary equations, not linear)" by Forsyth (Cambridge Univ. Press, London, 1906).

§4. Extensions of the coefficient field

Let R be an algebraic function field of one variable, and
K be the coefficient field. If L is an overfield of K, we have
the field $R(L)$ deduced from R by adjoining the elements of L to
$K([C, p.88])$; $R(L)$ is an algebraic function field of one variable
over L, and L is the coefficient field of $R(L)$ if either R or L
is separable over $K([C, p.91])$. The genus g' of $R(L)$ is not
greater than the genus g of R, and g' is equal to g if L is separable over $K([C, p.99])$.

We shall suppose that R is a differential algebraic func-
tion field of one variable over the coefficient field K and that
L is a differential extension of K. If y is an element of the
Kronecker product $R \otimes L$ over K of the form

$$\Sigma x_i a_i, \quad x_i \in R, \ a_i \in L,$$

we may define the derivative Dy by

$$Dy = \Sigma x_i' a_i + \Sigma x_i a_i';$$

it is well defined: For, if $(\xi_\lambda)_{\lambda \in \Lambda}$ is a base of L with respect
to K with the set Λ of indices which may be finite or infinite,
then each a_i may be written in the form

$$a_i = \Sigma c_{i\lambda} \xi_\lambda, \quad c_{i\lambda} \in K$$

and

$$y = \Sigma z_\lambda \xi_\lambda, \quad z_\lambda = \Sigma x_i c_{i\lambda}:$$

We have

$$\Sigma z_\lambda' \xi_\lambda + \Sigma z_\lambda \xi_\lambda' = \Sigma (\Sigma x_i' c_{i\lambda} + \Sigma x_i c_{i\lambda}') \xi_\lambda + \Sigma\Sigma x_i c_{i\lambda} \xi_\lambda'$$

$$= \Sigma x_i' \Sigma c_{i\lambda} \xi_\lambda + \Sigma x_i \Sigma (c_{i\lambda}' \xi_\lambda + c_{i\lambda} \xi_\lambda') = \Sigma x_i a_i' + \Sigma x_i' a_i.$$

In case the radical $\mathfrak{n}$ of $R \otimes L$ is closed under the operation D, $R(L)$ becomes a differential field of which R and L are differential subfields by the definition of $R(L)$ ([C, p.88]).

This being said, $R(L)$ is called the _differential field deduced from R by adjoining the elements of L to K_ if $\mathfrak{n}$ is closed under D. It is a differential algebraic function field of one variable over L.

If either R or L is separable over K, the radical $\mathfrak{n}$ of $R \otimes L$ consists of only 0 ([C, p.90]). In general $\mathfrak{n}$ is not necessarily closed under D. Assume for instance that $R = K(x, y)$ with

$$y^p + ax^p + b = 0,$$

where $K = P(a, b)$ with a, b which are algebraically independent over P, while P is any differential field of positive characteristic p. If we define $a' = b' = 0$ and take arbitrary elements of R for x' and y', R is a differential algebraic function field of one variable over K. Let L be $P(\alpha, \beta)$, where $\alpha^p = a$, $\beta^p = b$. If we take arbitrary elements of L for α' and β', L is a differential extension of K. The radical of $R \otimes L$ is generated by

$$y + \alpha x + \beta,$$

whence $\mathfrak{n}$ is closed under D if and only if

$$y' + \alpha'x + \alpha x' + \beta' \in \mathfrak{n}.$$

It does not hold in general.

Let R be an algebraic function field of one variable and L be an overfield of the coefficient field K of R. If there is a derivation δ_1 of the field $R(L)$ deduced from R by adjoining the elements of L to K which coincides with the given differentiation on R and L which are assumed to be differential extensions of K, then the radical $\mathfrak{n}$ of $R \otimes L$ is closed under the derivation D and $\phi D = D_1 \phi$ on $R \otimes L$, where ϕ is the natural homomorphism of $R \otimes L$ onto $R \otimes L / \mathfrak{n}$, while D_1 is the restriction of δ_1 to $R \otimes L / \mathfrak{n}$ whose quotient field is $R(L)$ by the definition: For, the transformation $D_1 \phi - \phi D$ of $R \otimes L$ into $R \otimes L / \mathfrak{n}$ coincides with 0 on R and L, whence $D_1 \phi = \phi D$ on $R \otimes L$ and the radical $\mathfrak{n}$ of $R \otimes L$ is closed under the derivation D.

We shall prove the following:

Theorem 4. Let R be a differential algebraic function field of one variable over the coefficient field K and L be a separable differential extension of K. The differential field $R(L)$ deduced from R by adjoining the elements of L to K has no movable singularity if and only if R has no movable singularity.

"Only if" part has been already proved by Theorem 1(§2). We shall prove the "if" part. Let $\mathfrak{P}$ be a place in $R(L)$. If $\mathfrak{P}$ is fixed with respect to R, it is unramified with respect to R([C, p.92]). Let z be an element of the ring $\mathfrak{O}$ of $\mathfrak{P}$. We define a repartition $\mathfrak{X}$ in $R(L)$ by

$$\mathfrak{X}(\mathfrak{P}) = z, \quad \mathfrak{X}(\mathfrak{Q}) = 0, \quad \mathfrak{Q} \neq \mathfrak{P}.$$

Take a place $\mathfrak{q}$ in R which is different from the place $\mathfrak{p}$ in R lying below $\mathfrak{P}$: Then there is an element y of $R(L)$ such that

$$y \equiv \mathfrak{X} \pmod{\mathfrak{P} \ \mathrm{Con}_{R/R(L)} \ \mathfrak{q}^{-\lambda}}$$

if λ is sufficiently large by the theorem of Riemann-Roch ([C; p. 30, p.32]). It satisfies

$$\nu_{\mathfrak{P}} (y - z) > 0$$

and

$$y \equiv 0 \,(\mathrm{mod}\ \mathrm{Con}_{R/R(L)}\,\mathfrak{l}^{-\lambda}).$$

We can represent y as a linear combination with coefficients in L of elements of R which are

$$\equiv 0 \,(\mathrm{mod}\ \mathrm{Con}_{R/R(L)}\,\mathfrak{l}^{-\lambda})$$

([C, p.96)]. These elements of R are integral at $\mathfrak{p}$ and their derivatives are integral at $\mathfrak{p}$, whence y' is integral at $\mathfrak{P}$ because L is closed under the differentiation. Take an element x of R which is transcendental over K such that $\mathfrak{p}$ is not a pole of x. Then x' is integral at $\mathfrak{p}$, and the derivative of every integral element of L(x) at $\mathfrak{P}$ is integral at $\mathfrak{P}$. If $\mathfrak{P}_0$ is the place in L(x) which lies below $\mathfrak{P}$, we can take integral elements $y_1, \ldots , y_f$ of R(L) at $\mathfrak{P}$ whose residue classes modulo $\mathfrak{P}$ form a base of the residue field of $\mathfrak{P}$ with respect to the residue field of $\mathfrak{P}_0$ such that the derivatives of $y_1, \ldots , y_f$ are integral at $\mathfrak{P}$. A uniformizing variable t at $\mathfrak{p}$ is a uniformizing variable at $\mathfrak{P}$ because $\mathfrak{P}$ is unramified with respect to R; the derivative of t is integral at $\mathfrak{P}$. The ring of $\mathfrak{P}$ is therefore closed under the differentiation (§2, pp.7-8).

Next suppose that $\mathfrak{P}$ is variable with respect to R. If z is an integral element of R(L) at $\mathfrak{P}$, we define a repartition $\mathfrak{E}$ in R(L) by

$$\mathfrak{E} (\mathfrak{P}) = z, \quad \mathfrak{E} (\mathfrak{Q}) = 0, \quad \mathfrak{Q} \neq \mathfrak{P}.$$

Take a place $\mathfrak{q}$ in R. There is an element y of R(L) such that

$$y \equiv \mathfrak{z} \pmod{\mathfrak{P}^2 \mathrm{Con}_{R/R(L)} \mathfrak{z}^{-\lambda}}$$

if λ is sufficiently large by the theorem of Riemann-Roch ([C, p. 30, p.32]). It satisfies

$$\nu_{\mathfrak{P}}(y - z) > 1,$$

and y does not have any variable pole with respect to R. We can represent y as a linear combination of elements of R with coefficients in L([C, p.98]). Hence the derivative of y is integral at $\mathfrak{P}$ because R and L are closed under the differentiation. If z is a uniformizing variable at $\mathfrak{P}$, y is also a uniformizing variable at $\mathfrak{P}$. Take an element x of R which is transcendental over K. Then x' is integral at $\mathfrak{P}$, and the derivative of every integral element of L(x) at $\mathfrak{P}$ is integral at $\mathfrak{P}$. We can take a uniformizing variable at $\mathfrak{P}$ whose derivative is integral at $\mathfrak{P}$. Therefore the ring of $\mathfrak{P}$ is proved to be closed under the differentiation in a similar way as above.

In case L is not separable over K, there is an example of R(L) such that R(L) has movable singularities although R has no movable singularity. Such an example will be given at the end of the next section.

§5. Briot-Bouquet's theorem

We shall prove the following theorem which is essentially
due to Briot and Bouquet:

Theorem 5. Let R be a differential algebraic function field
of one variable over its coefficient field K. Assume that K is a
perfect field and that it consists of constants in case the characteristic of K is 0. Then the genus g of R is either 0 or 1 if
R has no movable singularity, unless R consists of constants.

Since K is perfect, there is a separating variable x in R
([C, p.81]). Let $\wp$ be a place in R. If t is a uniformizing variable at $\wp$, it is a separating variable in R: For if t were not
a separating variable in R, the characteristic polynomial f(X) of
x in K(t, x) with respect to K(t) would be a polynomial of x^p with
coefficients in K(t);

$$f(X) = \Sigma a_i x^{ip}.$$

The coefficient a_i is the p-th power of b_i in $K(t^{1/p})$. If we define

$$g(X) = \Sigma b_i x^i,$$

then

$$g(x)^p = f(x) = 0$$

in $K(t^{1/p}, x)$, whence $g(x) = 0$ and it would follow that

$$[K(t^{1/p}, x) : K(t)] = p[K(t^{1/p}, x) : K(t^{1/p})]$$

$$\leq [K(t, x) : K(t)],$$

whence $t^{1/p}$ would belong to K(t, x), but it is impossible because

$v_{\wp}(t) = 1$. It may be assumed that $x' \neq 0$ if R has a non constant element, because it is not a p-th power in R: We have

$$dx = (D_t x)dt$$

with the derivation D_t of R with respect to t which maps every element of K upon 0 and t upon 1([C, p.116]). In the divisor $\delta(dt)$ of dt, $\wp$ enters with the exponent 0: For we have

$$\delta(dt) = \delta_t \mathfrak{N}_t^{-2},$$

where δ_t is the different of R with respect to K(t), while $\mathfrak{N}_t$ is the divisor of poles of t([C, p.110]): The place $\wp$ is unramified with respect to K(t), whence $\wp$ does not divide δ_t because the residue field $\Sigma(\wp)$ of $\wp$ is separable over K which is perfect ([C, p.69]). Thus $\wp$ enters in the divisors $\delta(dx)$ and $\delta(D_t x)$ with the same exponent, where $\delta(D_t x)$ is the divisor of $D_t x$. The $\wp$-adic completion $\bar{R}$ of R has a subfield Σ which contains K and which is a system of representatives for the elements of $\Sigma(\wp)$ ([C, p.44]). We can represent x in the form

$$x = \Sigma a_i t^i, \quad r \leq i < \infty, \quad a_i \in \Sigma, \quad a_r \neq 0, \quad r = v_{\wp}(x)$$

([C, p.46]). The field Σ is algebraic and separable over K, whence it consists of constants. Hence we have

$$x' = t' D_t x \neq 0,$$

since the differentiation and D_t are continuous on $\bar{R}$. If $\wp$ enters in the divisor $\delta(x')$ of x' and the divisor $\delta(dx)$ of dx with the exponents $e_{\wp}(x')$ and $e_{\wp}(dx)$ respectively, the inequality

$$e_{\wp}(x') \geq e_{\wp}(dx)$$

holds because t' is integral at $\wp$. Thus we have

$$0 = \delta(\delta(x')) = \Sigma d_{\wp} e_{\wp}(x') \geq$$

$$\geq \Sigma d_{\wp} e_{\wp} (dx) = \delta (\delta (dx)) = 2g - 2$$

with $\wp$ which runs through all places in R, where δ denotes the degree of the divisors, while $d_{\wp}$ is the degree of $\wp$.

In case K is not a perfect field, there is an example of R such that the genus of R is greater than 1 although R has no movable singularity. Assume for instance that $R = K(x, y)$ with

$$y^2 = x^p - u, \quad u \in K, \quad u' = 0,$$

where K is a differential field of positive characteristic $p(\neq 2)$, while $u^{1/p} \notin K$. Then R is separable over $K(x)$. If we define

$$x' = a + bx, \quad a, b \in K,$$

R is a differential algebraic function field over K, which is the coefficient field of R. The genus g of R is $(p - 1)/2$: For, if $m(\wp)$ is the differential exponent of $\wp$ with respect to $K(x)$, we have $m(\wp) = 0$ in case $\wp$ is neither a zero nor a pole of y: If $\wp$ is either a zero or a pole of y, the ramification index and the relative degree of $\wp$ with respect to $K(x)$ is 2 and 1 respectively. The divisor of y is of the form $\wp_0 \wp_\infty^{-1}$: We have

$$m(\wp_0) = m(\wp_\infty) = 1.$$

The degree of $\wp_0$ is p and that of $\wp_\infty$ is 1, whence

$$g - 1 = - 2 + (p + 1)/2$$

([C, p.106]). Let us see that R has no movable singularity. We take a place $\wp$ in R. If $\wp$ is neither $\wp_0$ nor $\wp_\infty$, the ring $\mathcal{O}$ of $\wp$ is closed under the differentiation, because x' is integral at $\wp$ (§3, pp.11-12). In case $\wp = \wp_\infty$, an uniformizing variable at $\wp_\infty$ is given by

$$t = x^s y^{-1}, \quad s = (p - 1)/2 = g:$$

We have

$$t' = sx^{s-1} x' y^{-1} = sx^{s-1}(a + bx)y^{-1},$$

since $y' = 0$. It is integral at $\wp_\infty$, whence $\diamondsuit$ is closed under the differentiation because the residue field of $\wp_\infty$ is K. In case $\wp = \wp_0$, y is a uniformizing variable at $\wp_0$ and $y' = 0$. The residue field of $\wp_0$ is generated by the residue class of x over K, whence $\diamondsuit$ is closed under the differentiation because x' is integral at $\wp_0$ (§2, pp.7-8). Thus our R has the required property in case $p > 3$.

Let us set $L = K(w)$ with $w = u^{1/p}$ and take an arbitrary element of L for w'. Then L is a differential extension of K, because $u' = 0$. If $R(w)$ is the field obtained from R by the adjunction of w, then there is a derivation of $R(w)$ which coincides with the given differentiation on R and L, whence $R(L)$ is the differential field deduced from R by adjoining the elements of L to K. If we set

$$z = (x - w)^{-s} y, \quad s = (p - 1)/2,$$

then

$$x = z^2 + w, \quad y = z^p,$$

whence $R = L(z)$. Since $y' = 0$, we have

$$- z' = s(x' - w')(x - w)^{-s-1} y$$
$$= s(a + bx - w')z^{-2s-2+p}$$
$$= s\{a + bw - w' + b(x - w)\}z^{-1}$$
$$= s(a + bw - w' + bz^2)z^{-1},$$

whence $R(L)$ has movable singularities if and only if $w' \neq a + bw$ (§3).

In the above example, if we replace $y^2 = x^p - u$ by $y^{2p+1} = x^p - u$, then similar arguments may be done with

$$t = x^{-1}y^2, \quad z = (x - w)y^{-2}.$$

In this case the genus of R is $p(p - 1)$ which is greater than 1, whence we obtain a required example in the remained case where $p = 2, 3$.

For Briot-Bouquet's theorem in the complex plane, confer with pp.62-64 of the book "Traité d'analyse", Tome III, by Picard (2e Edition, Gauthier-Villars, Paris, 1908) and Fuchs' paper quoted at the end of §3.

§6. Clairaut fields

We shall state some well known results on constants of a differential field. Let Ω be a differential field and k be a differential subfield of Ω. We denote by Ω_0 and k_0 the fields of constants of Ω and k respectively. If $u_1, \ldots, u_n$ are elements of k, we define

$$W(u_1, \ldots, u_n) = \det(u_j^{(i)}), \quad 0 \leq i < n, \ 1 \leq j \leq n,$$

where $u_j^{(i)}$ is the i-th derivative of u_j. It is an element of k, which vanishes if $u_1, \ldots, u_n$ are linearly dependent over Ω_0:

For, if

$$\Sigma c_i u_i = 0, \quad c_i \in \Omega_0, \ (c_1, \ldots, c_n) \neq (0, \ldots, 0),$$

then we have

$$\Sigma c_i u_i^{(j)} = 0 \ (1 \leq i \leq n), \quad 0 \leq j < n.$$

We show that they are linearly dependent over k_0 if $W(u_1, \ldots, u_n)$ vanishes. It is obviously true in case n = 1. Suppose that it is true for n - 1 elements of k. We may assume that

(1) $W(u_1, \ldots, u_{n-1}) \neq 0$:

For if it vanishes $u_1, \ldots, u_{n-1}$ are linearly dependent over k_0 by our assumption. Since

$$W(u_1, \ldots, u_n) = 0,$$

there are n elements $a_1, \ldots, a_n$ of k which satisfy

$$\Sigma a_i u_i^{(j)} = 0 \ (1 \leq i \leq n), \quad 0 < j \leq n.$$

By our assumption (1), $a_n \neq 0$, whence a_n may be assumed to be 1. If j is less than n, then

$$\Sigma a_i' u_i^{(j)} = 0 \ (1 \leq i \leq n),$$

but $a_n' = 0$, whence every a_i is a constant.

It follows that k and Ω_0 are linearly disjoint over k_0: If a constant of Ω is algebraic over k, it is algebraic over k_0.

We see that the field of constants of $k(\Sigma_0)$ is $k_0(\Sigma_0)$ if Σ_0 is a subfield of Ω_0. An element $x(\neq 0)$ of $k(\Sigma_0)$ may be written in the form

$$x = \Sigma a_i \alpha_i / \Sigma b_j \beta_j \quad (1 \leq i \leq r, \ 1 \leq j \leq s),$$
$$a_i, \ b_j \in k, \quad \alpha_i, \ \beta_j \in k_0(\Sigma_0),$$

where $\alpha_1, \ \ldots, \ \alpha_r$ and $\beta_1, \ \ldots, \ \beta_s$ are respectively linearly independent over k_0. We may assume that our expression has the minimal s in those possible expressions of x and that $b_s = 1$. If x is a constant, then

$$x \Sigma b_j' \beta_j = \Sigma a_i' \alpha_i.$$

Since $b_s' = 0$, we have

$$\Sigma b_j' \beta_j = \Sigma a_i' \alpha_i = 0$$

by our assumption on s, whence $a_i, \ b_j$ are constants. Thus x belongs to $k_0(\Sigma_0)$.

Let R be a differential algebraic function field of one variable over K. In case the characteristic of K is 0, we assume that there is a constant of R which is transcendental over K. If K_0 represents the field of constants of K, the field of constants R_0 of R is an algebraic function field of one variable over K_0: For, if γ is a constant of R which is transcendental over K, the field of constants of $K(\gamma)$ is $K_0(\gamma)$. We have

$$[K(\gamma_1, \ \ldots, \ \gamma_n, \ \gamma) : K(\gamma)] =$$

$$= [K_0(\gamma_1, \ldots, \gamma_n, \gamma) : K_0(\gamma)]$$

if $\gamma_1, \ldots, \gamma_n$ are constants of R, because $K(\gamma)$ and R_0 are linearly disjoint over $K_0(\gamma)$. Therefore, R_0 is of finite degree over $K_0(\gamma)$ and the degree is $[K(R_0) : K(\gamma)]$. If K^* is the coefficient field of R, the coefficient field of R_0 is the field of constants of K^*.

Remark 1. The notation being as above, assume that the characteristic of K is 0. Then the genus g_0 of R_0 is equal to the genus of $K(R_0)$, since K is separable over K_0 ([C, p.99]): It is at most equal to the genus g of R([C, p.106]), whence $g_0 \leq g$. This inequality is due to M. Rosenlicht [10].

A differential algebraic function field R of one variable over K is called a Clairaut field over K if R is generated by its constants over K. We shall prove the following:

Theorem 6. A Clairaut field over K has no movable singularity if the characteristic of K is 0.

If K^* and K_0^* represent the coefficient fields of R and R_0 respectively, we may consider R as the differential field $R_0(K^*)$ deduced from R_0 by adjoining the elements of K^* to K_0^* because K^* and R_0 are linearly disjoint over K_0^* ([C, p.89]). Clearly R_0 has no movable singularity, whence R has no movable singularity by Theorem 3(§4) because K^* is separable over K_0^*.

In case the characteristic p of K is positive, there is an example of a Clairaut field R over K which has movable singularities. Assume for instance that $R = K(x, y)$ with

$$y^p = x^p + a,$$

where $K = P(a, b)$ and P is any differential field of positive characteristic p, while a, b are algebraically independent over K. If we define

$$a' = 0, \quad x' = 0, \quad b' = b^p, \quad y' = y^p,$$

then R is a Clairaut field over K: For, if we set

$$\gamma = y^{-p+1} - b^{-p+1},$$

then it is a constant and

$$y = y^p(\gamma + b^{-p+1}) = (x^p + a)(\gamma + b^{-p+1}),$$

whence $R = K(x, y) = K(\gamma, x)$ with $\gamma' = x' = 0$. If a place $\wp$ in R is a pole of x, y/x is integral at $\wp$, since

$$(y/x)^p = 1 + ax^{-p}.$$

We have

$$(y/x)' = y^p/x = x^{p-1} + ax^{-1}$$

which is not integral at $\wp$, whence R has movable singularities.

This example shows that, if two differential subfields R_1 and R_2 of R containing K have no movable singularity, the subfield R_1R_2 generated by R_1 and R_2 does not necessarily have no movable singularity: For in the above example $K(x)$ and $K(\gamma)$ have no movable singularity. However, in case of characteristic 0, we shall see that R_1R_2 has no movable singularity if R_1 and R_2 have no movable singularity by a theorem of K. Nishioka in §17.

Theorem 7. If R is a Riccati field over the coefficient field K, there is a differential extension field L of K which is separable over K such that the differential field $R(L)$ deduced from R by adjoining the elements of L to K is a Clairaut field over L.

By hypothesis R takes the form $K(x)$ with

$$x' = a + bx + cx^2, \quad a, b, c \in K.$$

Let us set $L = K(x_1, x_2, x_3)$, where x_1, x_2, x_3 are algebraically independent over K, while

$$x_i' = a + bx_i + cx_i^2, \quad 1 \leq i \leq 3.$$

Then L is a differential extension of K which is separable over K. The cross ratio

$$\gamma = (x - x_1)/(x - x_2) : (x_3 - x_1)/(x_3 - x_2)$$

is a constant;

$$\gamma'/\gamma = (x' - x_1')/(x - x_1) - (x' - x_2')/(x - x_2)$$
$$- (x_3' - x_1')/(x_3 - x_1) + (x_3' - x_2')/(x_3 - x_2)$$
$$= b + c(x + x_1) - \{b + c(x + x_2)\}$$
$$- \{b + c(x_3 + x_1)\} + b + c(x_3 + x_2) = 0,$$

whence $R(L) = L(x) = L(\gamma)$ with $\gamma' = 0$.

We shall see that the term "Clairaut field" is a reasonable one. Let R be a Clairaut field over K. Assume that K has an element ξ whose derivative is 1 and that R_0 is separable over K_0. Then R_0 takes the form $K_0(a, b)$ and a, b satisfy an irreducible algebraic equation $G(a, b) = 0$ over K_0 and $G_b \neq 0$. If

$$x = a\xi + b,$$

then $R = K(x, x')$ with $G(x', x - \xi x') = 0$ because $x' = a$. Conversely suppose that R takes the form $K(x, x')$ with

$$F(x, x') = G(x', x - \xi x') = 0,$$

where ξ is an element of K satisfying $\xi' = 1$, while $G(A, B)$ is an irreducible polynomial over K_0 satisfying $G_B \neq 0$. Then differentiating $G = 0$ we have

$$x''G_A - \xi x''G_B = x''(G_A - \xi G_B) = 0.$$

The polynomial $G_A - \xi G_B$ of A, B does not vanish identically because $\xi' \neq 0$, whence $x'' = 0$, since

$$\partial F/\partial x' = (G_A - \xi G_B)(x', x - \xi x') \neq 0.$$

If we set

$$a = x', \quad b = x - \xi x',$$

they are constants and $R = K(a, b)$. The field of constants R_0 is $K_0(a, b)$, which is separable over K_0 with $G(a, b) = 0$.

Remark 2. If the characteristic of K is 0, we may take L in Theorem 7 which satisfies an additional condition that any constant of L is algebraic over K(cf. Remark 2, §18).

§7. Poincaré fields

An elliptic field is an algebraic function field of one variable whose genus is 1. Suppose that an elliptic field R has a place $\mathfrak{p}$ of degree 1. We denote by $\mathcal{L}(\mathfrak{a})$ the space of elements of R which are $\equiv 0 \pmod{\mathfrak{a}}$, where $\mathfrak{a}$ is a divisor in R: It is a linear space over the coefficient field K of R and its dimension is denoted by $\ell(\mathfrak{a})$ which is finite. If n is a positive integer,

$$\ell(\mathfrak{p}^{-n}) = n$$

by the theorem of Riemann-Roch ([C, p.33]). There is an element x of $\mathcal{L}(\mathfrak{p}^{-2})$ which is not in K. The divisor of poles of x is $\mathfrak{p}^2$: For if it were $\mathfrak{p}$ then R would be K(x). Therefore R is of degree 2 over K(x). An element z of R which is linearly independent of 1 and x over K is contained in $\mathcal{L}(\mathfrak{p}^{-3})$. The divisor of poles of z is $\mathfrak{p}^3$ and R = K(x, z): For if z were contained in K(x) then the order of z at $\mathfrak{p}$ would be even. The space $\mathcal{L}(\mathfrak{p}^{-6})$ contains $1, x, z, x^2, xz, x^3, z^2$, whence they satisfy a linear relation over K, where the coefficient of z^2 does not vanish. If the characteristic of K is not 2, we have R = K(x, y) with $y^2 = A(x)$, where A(x) is a polynomial of x over K of degree 3: It has no common factor with $A_x(x)$ unless $A_x = 0$.

Conversely suppose that R = K(x, y) with $y^2 = A(x)$, where A(x) is a polynomial of x over K of degree 3 which has no common factor with $A_x(x)$ unless $A_x = 0$, while the characteristic p of K is not 2. Then we see that the genus of R is 1. Since $p \neq 2$, R is separable over K(x). Let $\mathfrak{P}$ be a place in R, and $\mathfrak{p}$ be the place in K(x) which lies below $\mathfrak{P}$. In case $\mathfrak{P}$ is neither a pole nor a zero of y, the residue field $\Sigma(\mathfrak{P})$ of $\mathfrak{P}$ coincides with the residue field $\Sigma(\mathfrak{p})$ of $\mathfrak{p}$ if and only if $\Sigma(\mathfrak{p})$ contains a quadratic root of $A(\bar{x})$, where $\bar{x}$ is the residue class of x modulo $\mathfrak{p}$; in this case $\text{Con}_{K(x)/R}\,\mathfrak{p} = \mathfrak{P}\mathfrak{P}_1$ with $\mathfrak{P} \neq \mathfrak{P}_1$ and $\mathfrak{P}$ is unramified with respect to K(x): In the other case the relative degree of $\mathfrak{P}$ with respect to K(x) is 2 and $\mathfrak{P}$ is unramified with respect to K(x). If $\mathfrak{P}$ is a pole of y, the ramification index of $\mathfrak{P}$ with respect to K(x) is 2 and the degree of $\mathfrak{P}$ is 1. If $\mathfrak{P}$ is a zero of y, the ramification index of $\mathfrak{P}$ with respect to K(x) is 2 and the relative degree of $\mathfrak{P}$ with respect to K(x) is 1. Thus the genus of R is 1 ([C; p.69, p.106]). We note that the genus of the field R(L) deduced from R by adjoining the elements of L to K is 1 for any overfield L of K if $A_x \neq 0$.

Let R be an algebraic function field of one variable. An automorphism of R over the coefficient field K is an automorphism of R which coincides with the identity on K. If ϕ is an automorphism of R over K, the image of a V-ring in R by ϕ is also a V-ring in R([C, p.1]). Thus ϕ transforms a place in R to another place in R.

Now return to an elliptic field R having a place $\mathfrak{p}$ of degree 1. We shall see that if $\mathfrak{p}_1$ is a place in R of degree 1 different from $\mathfrak{p}$ then there is an automorphism of R over the coefficient field K which transforms $\mathfrak{p}$ to $\mathfrak{p}_1$. By the theorem of Riemann-Roch

$$\ell(\mathfrak{p}_1^{-n}\mathfrak{p}^{-n}) = 2n,$$

whence there is an element w of $\mathcal{L}(\wp^{-1}\wp_1^{-1})$ which is not contained in K. The divisor of poles of w is $\wp\wp_1$. Let x and x_1 be elements of $\mathcal{L}(\wp^{-2})$ and $\mathcal{L}(\wp_1^{-2})$ respectively which are not in K. They are not contained in K(w): For if x for instance were in K(w), $\wp_1$ would be a pole of x. The space $\mathcal{L}(\wp^{-2}\wp_1^{-2})$ contains 1, x, x_1, w, w^2, xx_1, whence we have the following two linear relations between them over K:

$$a + bx + cx_1 + dw + ew^2 = 0, \quad bc \neq 0$$

$$a_1 + b_1x + c_1xx_1 + d_1w + e_1w^2 = 0, \quad c_1 \neq 0.$$

If we set

$$v = b(x - c), \quad v_1 = c(x_1 - b + b_1/c_1),$$

then

$$v + v_1 = - (a + dw + ew^2) - c(b - b_1/c_1),$$

$$vv_1 = - c_1^{-1}b(a_1 + d_1w + e_1w^2) + bc(a + dw + ew^2)$$

$$+ bc^2(b - b_1/c_1),$$

whence v and v_1 are distinct roots of a quadratic equation over K(w), and we have an automorphism of R which coincides with the identity on K(w) and which maps v upon v_1: Clearly it transforms $\wp$ to $\wp_1$.

Assume that R is a differential algebraic function field of one variable over the coefficient field K which is an elliptic field possessing a place $\wp$ of degree 1. Let the notation be as above: $\mathcal{L}(\wp^{-2})$ and $\mathcal{L}(\wp^{-3})$ are spanned by 1, x and 1, x, z over K respectively. The ring $\mathcal{O}$ of $\wp$ is closed under the differentiation if the following conditions are satisfied: z' is a linear combination of 1, x, z, x^2 over K and x' is a linear combination of 1, x, z over K: For, if we set t = x/z, it is a uniformizing variable at $\wp$ and

$$t' = x'/z - xz'/z^2$$

which is integral at $\wp$, whence $\diamondsuit$ is closed under the differentiation because $\wp$ is of degree 1. We shall see that our conditions are satisfied if R has no movable singularity. The derivative u' of

$$u = x^{-1}t^{-2} = z^{-1}t^{-3} = x^{-3}z^2$$

is integral at $\wp$, since u is integral at $\wp$. We have

$$x' = - x^2(2tt'u + t^2u'),$$

$$z' = - z^2(3tt'u + t^3u'),$$

whence

$$x' \in \mathcal{L}(\wp^{-3}), \quad z' \in \mathcal{L}(\wp^{-5})$$

because x' and z' are integral at any place in R different from $\wp$ by our assumption. These spaces are spanned by 1, x, z and 1, x, x^2, z respectively over K.

A differential algebraic function field of one variable over the coefficient field K is called a <u>Poincaré field</u> if it takes the form K(x, y) with x' = y and

$$y^2 = A(x) = \lambda\Pi(x - a_i), \quad 1 \leq i \leq 3, \quad \lambda, a_i \in K, \lambda \neq 0,$$

where $a_i \neq a_j (i \neq j)$, while the a_i are constants.

If R is a Poincaré field, its characteristic is not 2: For, if it were 2, we would have

$$0 = \lambda'A(x) + \lambda A_x(x)y$$

which is impossible because $A_x \neq 0$. Therefore the Poincaré field

R is separable over K(x).

We shall show that a Poincaré field has no movable singularity. The notation being as above we have

$$2y' = \lambda'\lambda^{-1}y + \lambda A_x(x).$$

Let $\wp$ be a place in R. If $\wp$ is neither a pole nor a zero of y, the ring $\mathcal{O}$ of $\wp$ is closed under the differentiation(§3, pp.11-12). If $\wp$ is a pole of y, $\mathcal{O}$ is closed under the differentiation by the above discussions. Suppose that $\wp$ is a zero of y. Then its degree is 1 and y is a uniformizing variable at $\wp$ whose derivative is integral at $\wp$, whence $\mathcal{O}$ is closed under the differentiation. We shall prove the following theorem which is essentially due to Poincaré:

Theorem 8. Let R be a differential algebraic function field of one variable over the coefficient field K. Assume that R is an elliptic field possessing a place of degree 1 and that the characteristic p of K is neither 2 nor 3. Then, if R has no movable singularity, there is an overfield L of K which is algebraic and separable over K such that the differential field R(L) deduced from R by adjoining the elements of L to K is either a Poincaré field or a Clairaut field over L.

By hypothesis R takes the form K(x, y) with $y^2 = A(x)$, where A is a polynomial of x over K of degree 3. For L we take the splitting field of A over K, which is separable over K because $p \neq 3$. The polynomial A has three distinct roots x_1, x_2, x_3, since the genus of R(L) is 1([C, p.99]). By Theorem 4(§4), R(L) has no movable singularity. If we set

$$w = (x - x_1)/(x_2 - x_1),$$

then

$$y^2 = \mu w (w - 1) (w - \delta),$$

where

$$\mu = \lambda (x_2 - x_1)^3, \quad \delta = (x_3 - x_1)/(x_2 - x_1),$$

while λ is the leading coefficient of A. By the above arguments
w' is a linear combination of 1, w, y over the coefficient field L:

$$w' = a + bw + cy, \quad a, b, c \in L.$$

Let $\mathfrak{P}$ be a place in R(L) which is a zero of y. Then it is of
degree 1 and y is a uniformizing variable at $\mathfrak{P}$. If $\bar{w}$ represents
the residue class of w modulo $\mathfrak{P}$, we have

$$w - \bar{w} = y^2 u, \quad \nu_{\mathfrak{P}} (u) = 0$$

and

$$w' - \bar{w}' = 2yy'u + y^2 u',$$

whence $\bar{w}'$ is the residue class of w' modulo $\mathfrak{P}$ because u' is integral at $\mathfrak{P}$. We may set $\bar{w} = 0$, which gives us a = 0. Setting
$\bar{w} = 1$ we have b = 0. Therefore $w' = cy$ and $\delta' = 0$ because we may
set $\bar{w} = \delta$. If $c \neq 0$, R(L) is a Poincaré field. In case c = 0,
we set $L_1 = L(\omega)$ with a quadratic root ω of μ which is separable
over L because $p \neq 2$. Since $\delta' = 0$, y/ω is a constant, whence
$R(L_1)$ is a Clairaut field over L_1.

Our assumption that $p \neq 3$ can not be taken out of Theorem 8.
Assume for instance that R = K(x, y) with

$$y^2 = x^3 - u, \quad u \in K, \quad x' = 1,$$

where K is a differential field of characteristic 3 which consists of constants, while $u^{1/3} \notin K$. The genus of R is 1, and it has no movable singularity because y' = 0. If L is any overfield of K which is algebraic and separable over K, R(L) is not a Poincaré field: For, if we set $L_1 = L(u^{1/3})$, the genus of R(L) is 0 (cf. p.34). It is not a Clairaut field over L, since L consists of constants while R contains a nonconstant element x.

The assumption that $p \neq 2$ also can not be taken out of Theorem 8: Assume for instance that R = K(x, y) with

$$y^2 + y + x^3 = 0, \quad x' = 1,$$

where K is any algebraically closed field of characteristic 2: K consists of constants. Then R is separable over K(x) and

$$y' = -3x^2:$$

It has no movable singularity and it is neither a Poincaré field nor a Clairut field over K. We shall see that the genus of R is 1. Let $\wp$ be a place in R, and $m(\wp)$ be the differential exponent of $\wp$ with respect to K(x). If $\wp$ is not a pole of x then $m(\wp)$ = 0 because $\wp$ is unramified with respect to K(x) and the relative degree is 1([C, p.69]). Suppose that $\wp$ is a pole of x. Then the ramification index of $\wp$ with respect to K(x) is 2 and the degree of $\wp$ is 1. If t = x/y, it is a uniformizing variable at $\wp$ and 1, t form an integral base with respect to K(x) ([C, p.61]). We have

$$t^2 + x^{-2}t + x^{-1} = 0$$

and its discriminant is x^{-4}, whence $m(\wp)$ = 4 because x^{-1} is a uniformizing variable at the place in K(x) which lies below $\wp$ ([C, p.70]). Thus the genus of R is 1([C, p.106]).

There is an example of R in Theorem 8 such that K itself can not be taken for L. Assume for instance that $K = P(a)$ and $R = K(x, y)$ with

$$y^2 = x(x^2 - a), \quad x' = x, \quad a' = 2a,$$

where P is any differential field of characteristic 0 consisting of constants, while a is transcendental over P. Then the genus of R is 1 and R has no movable singularity since $2y' = 3y$. If R takes the form $K(u, v)$ with $v^2 = A(u)$, where A is a polynomial of u over K of degree 1, then we may assume that y and v have the same pole because there is an automorphism of R over K which transforms the pole of y to that of $v(p.34)$. Therefore u may be assumed to be a linear combination of 1 and x over K, and $K(u) = K(x)$. The polynomial A can not be decomposed to the product of linear factors because we have only three places in R which are ramified with respect to $K(x)$. Thus R is not a Poincaré field. It is not a Clairaut field over K. To prove it, for a moment suppose that $R = K(R_0)$ with the field of constants R_0. Then, $R = R_0(a)$ and a is transcendental over R_0. The element x is a rational function of a over R_0: $x = \Pi f(a)$, where f is an irreducible polynomial of a over R_0. We would have

$$a^{-1} = a^{-1}x'/x = 2\Sigma f_a(a)/f(a),$$

which is impossible because the characteristic of R_0 is 0.

Another example is given by

$$R = K(x, y), \quad y^2 = A(x), \quad x' = y,$$

where K is any differential field consisting of constants whose characteristic is not 2, while A is an irreducible polynomial of

x over K of degree 3.   It is neither a Poincaré field nor a
Clairaut field over K while it has no movable singularity.

For Poincaré's work (Sur un théorème de M. Fuchs, Acta Math.,
7(1885), 1-32), confer with §124 of the book by Forsyth quoted at
the end of §3.

§8. Analogs of addition formulae for elliptic functions

We shall prove the following:

Lemma 1. Let k be a differential field whose characteristic is not 2, and α, β be constants of k which satisfy

$$\beta^2 = S(\alpha) = (1 - \alpha^2)(1 - \kappa^2\alpha^2),$$

where κ^2 is a constant of k different from 0 and 1. If y is a non constant solution of $(y')^2 = S(y)$ then an element z of k defined by

$$z = (\alpha y' + \beta y)/(1 - \kappa^2\alpha^2 y^2)$$

is a solution of $(z')^2 = S(z)$.

We have

$$y'' = - y(1 + \kappa^2 - 2\kappa^2 y^2)$$

because $y' \neq 0$, and

$$z' = (\alpha y Q + \beta y' P)/A,$$
$$P(\alpha, y; \kappa^2) = 1 + \kappa^2\alpha^2 y^2,$$
$$Q(\alpha, y; \kappa^2) = 1 + \kappa^2 - 2\kappa^2(\alpha^2 + y^2) + \kappa^2(1 + \kappa^2)\alpha^2 y^2,$$
$$A(\alpha, y; \kappa^2) = (1 - \kappa^2\alpha^2 y^2)^2.$$

On the other hand

$$\begin{aligned}
S(z) &= (1 - z^2)(1 - \kappa^2 z^2) \\
&= A^{-2}[(A - B)(A - \kappa^2 B) + 4\kappa^2\alpha^2\beta^2 y^2 S(y) \\
&\quad + 2\alpha\beta y y'\{(1 + \kappa^2)A - 2\kappa^2 B\}],
\end{aligned}$$

where

$$B(\alpha, y; \kappa^2) = \alpha^2 S(y) + \beta^2 y^2.$$

The following identities in α, y, κ^2 hold:

$$P^2 - 4\kappa^2\alpha^2 y^2 = A,$$

$$(1 + \kappa^2)A - 2\kappa^2 B = PQ,$$

$$Q^2 = 4\kappa^2\beta^2 S(y) + (1 - \kappa^2)^2 A,$$

whence

$$A^2(S(z) - z'^2) = (A - B)(A - \kappa^2 B) + 4\kappa^2\alpha^2\beta^2 y^2 S(y)$$

$$+ 2\alpha\beta yy'\{(1 + \kappa^2)A - 2\kappa^2 B\} - \{\alpha^2 y^2 Q^2 + \beta^2 S(y)P^2 + 2\alpha\beta yy'PQ\}$$

$$= (A - B)(A - \kappa^2 B) - \{\alpha^2 y^2 Q^2 + \beta^2 S(y)A\},$$

which vanishes because

$$4\kappa^2\{\alpha^2 y^2 Q^2 + \beta^2 S(y)A\}$$

$$= (P^2 - A)Q^2 + 4\kappa^2\beta^2 S(y)A$$

$$= \{(1 + \kappa^2)A - 2\kappa^2 B\}^2 - A\{4\kappa^2\beta^2 S(y) + (1 - \kappa^2)^2 A\}$$

$$+ 4\kappa^2\beta^2 S(y)A$$

$$= 4\kappa^2\{A^2 - (1 + \kappa^2)AB + \kappa^2 B^2\}$$

$$= 4\kappa^2(A - B)(A - \kappa^2 B).$$

We shall prove the following:

Lemma 2. Let k be a differential field whose characteristic is not 2, and y_1, y_2 be non constant solutions in k of

$$(y')^2 = S(y) = (1 - y^2)(1 - \kappa^2 y^2)$$

satisfying $1 - \kappa^2 y_1^2 y_2^2 \neq 0$, where κ^2 is a constant different from 0 and 1. If we define

$$\alpha = (y_1 y_2' - y_1' y_2)/(1 - \kappa^2 y_1^2 y_2^2),$$

$$\beta = [y_1 y_2\{(1 + \kappa^2)(1 + \kappa^2 y_1^2 y_2^2) - 2\kappa^2(y_1^2 + y_2^2)$$

$$+ (1 + \kappa^2 y_1^2 y_2^2)y_1' y_2']/(1 - \kappa^2 y_1^2 y_2^2)^2,$$

then they are constants and $\beta^2 = S(\alpha)$.

We have

$$y_i'' = - y_i(1 + \kappa^2 - 2\kappa^2 y_i^2), \quad i = 1, 2$$

and

$$(1 - \kappa^2 y_1^2 y_2^2)^2 \alpha'$$

$$= (y_1 y_2'' - y_1'' y_2)(1 - \kappa^2 y_1^2 y_2^2)$$

$$+ 2\kappa^2 y_1 y_2 (y_1 y_2' - y_1' y_2)(y_1' y_2 + y_1 y_2')$$

$$= 2\kappa^2 y_1 y_2 (y_2^2 - y_1^2)(1 - \kappa^2 y_1^2 y_2^2)$$

$$+ 2\kappa^2 y_1 y_2 (y_1^2 y_2'^2 - y_1'^2 y_2^2)$$

$$= 2\kappa^2 y_1 y_2 \{(y_2^2 - y_1^2)(1 - \kappa^2 y_1^2 y_2^2) + y_1^2(1 - y_2^2)(1 - \kappa^2 y_2^2)$$

$$- y_2^2(1 - y_1^2)(1 - \kappa^2 y_1^2)\} = 0,$$

whence α is a constant. The equality

(1) $$\alpha y_2' + \beta y_2 = y_1(1 - \kappa^2 \alpha^2 y_2^2)$$

holds because

$$(1 - \kappa^2 y_1^2 y_2^2)^2 (\alpha y_2' + \beta y_2)$$

$$= (1 - \kappa^2 y_1^2 y_2^2)(y_1 S(y_2) - y_2 y_1' y_2')$$

$$+ y_2 [y_1 y_2 \{(1 + \kappa^2)(1 + \kappa^2 y_1^2 y_2^2) - 2\kappa^2 (y_1^2 + y_2^2)\}$$

$$+ (1 + \kappa^2 y_1^2 y_2^2) y_1' y_2']$$

$$= y_1 [(1 - \kappa^2 y_1^2 y_2^2) S(y_2) + y_2^2 \{(1 + \kappa^2)(1 + \kappa^2 y_1^2 y_2^2)$$

$$- 2\kappa^2 (y_1^2 + y_2^2)\} + 2\kappa^2 y_2^3 y_1 y_1' y_2']$$

$$= y_1 [-\kappa^2 y_1^2 y_2^2 S(y_2) + 1 + \kappa^2 y_2^4$$

$$+ \kappa^2 y_2^2 \{(1 + \kappa^2) y_1^2 y_2^2 - 2(y_1^2 + y_2^2)\} + 2\kappa^2 y_2^3 y_1 y_1' y_2']$$

$$= y_1 \{- \kappa^2 y_1^2 y_2^2 S(y_2) + (1 - \kappa^2 y_1^2 y_2^2)^2 - \kappa^2 y_2^4 S(y_1) + 2\kappa^2 y_2^3 y_1 y_1' y_2'\}$$

$$= y_1(1 - \kappa^2 y_1^2 y_2^2)^2 (1 - \kappa^2 \alpha^2 y_2^2).$$

We have

$$S(y_1)y_2^2 = (y_1'y_2)^2$$

$$= \{(1 - \kappa^2 y_1^2 y_2^2)\alpha - y_1 y_2'\}^2$$

$$= y_1^2 S(y_2) - 2(1 - \kappa^2 y_1^2 y_2^2)\alpha y_1 y_2',$$

whence

$$(1 - \kappa^2 y_1^2 y_2^2)\{(1 - \kappa^2 y_1^2 y_2^2)\alpha^2 - 2\alpha y_1 y_2' + y_1^2 - y_2^2\} = 0$$

because

$$y_1^2 S(y_2) - y_2^2 S(y_1) = (y_1^2 - y_2^2)(1 - \kappa^2 y_1^2 y_2^2).$$

Therefore

(2) $\qquad (1 - \kappa^2 \alpha^2 y_2^2)y_1^2 - 2\alpha y_1 y_2' + \alpha^2 - y_2^2 = 0.$

From the equality (1)

$$(\beta y_2)^2 = \{(1 - \kappa^2 \alpha^2 y_2^2)y_1 - \alpha y_2'\}^2$$

$$= (1 - \kappa^2 \alpha^2 y_2^2)\{(1 - \kappa^2 \alpha^2 y_2^2)y_1^2 - 2\alpha y_1 y_2'\} + \alpha^2 S(y_2).$$

By (2) it is equal to

$$(1 - \kappa^2 \alpha^2 y_2^2)(y_2^2 - \alpha^2) + \alpha^2 S(y_2) = y_2^2 S(\alpha),$$

whence $\beta^2 = S(\alpha)$. Since the characteristic of k is not 2, β is a constant.

Remark. If k is the field of elliptic functions with modulus κ, then we may set by Jacobi's elliptic functions in Lemma 1

$$y = \text{sn } x, \quad \alpha = \text{sn } c, \quad \beta = \text{cn } c \cdot \text{dn } c$$

and in Lemma 2

$$y_1 = \text{sn}(x + c), \quad y_2 = \text{sn } x,$$

where x is variable and c is constant. By addition formulae

$$z = \text{sn}(x + c)$$

in Lemma 1 because $d(\text{sn } x)/dx = \text{cn } x \cdot \text{dn } x$, and

$$\alpha = \text{sn } c, \quad \beta = \text{cn } c \cdot \text{dn } c$$

in Lemma 2. Confer for instance with §§42-44 of the book by
Weber "Lehrbuch der Algebra", Band III, 2. Aufl., Druck und
Verlag von Friedr. Vieweg & Sohn Akt.- Ges., Braunschweig, 1908.

§9. Poincaré fields generated by the constants

We shall prove the following:

__Theorem__ 9. Let R be a differential algebraic function field of one variable over the coefficient field K whose characteristic is neither 2 nor 3. Assume that R is an elliptic field possessing a place of degree 1 and that R contains a non constant element. If R has no movable singularity, there is an overfield L of K which is algebraic and separable over K such that the differential field R(L) deduced from R by adjoining the elements of L to K is a Poincaré field.

The notation being as in the proof of Theorem 8 (§7), we may assume that $w' = 0$ and $R(L) = L(w, y)$ with
$$y^2 = w(w - 1)(w - \delta),$$
where δ is a constant of L different from 0 and 1. Let us set
$$L_1 = L(\kappa^{1/2}),$$
where κ is a root of the quadratic equation
$$0 = \kappa^2 - 2(2\delta - 1)\kappa + 1 = (1 + \kappa)^2 - 4\delta\kappa.$$
Then $\kappa \neq 0, \pm 1$, and L_1 is separable over L. We define
$$u = -(1 + \kappa - 2w)/(1 + \kappa - 2w),$$
$$v = 4\kappa^{1/2}(\kappa u + 1)^2 y/(1 - \kappa^2),$$
which satisfy
$$2(\kappa u + 1)w = (1 + \kappa)(u + 1),$$
$$2(\kappa u + 1)(w - 1) = (1 - \kappa)(u - 1),$$
$$4\kappa(\kappa u + 1)(w - \delta) = (1 - \kappa^2)(\kappa u - 1)$$

and

$$v^2 = S(u) = (1 - u^2)(1 - \kappa^2 u^2).$$

By assumption R contains a non constant element ξ. We set

$$L_2 = L_1(\lambda^{1/2}), \quad \lambda = (\xi')^2/S(\xi),$$

which is separable over L_1, and define a new differentiation of $R(L_2)$ signed with the dot by $\dot{X} = \lambda^{-1/2}X'$. In this new differentiation

$$\dot{\xi}^2 = S(\xi).$$

We may apply Lemma 1 (§8) to $R(L_2)$ setting

$$\alpha = u, \quad \beta = v, \quad y = \xi.$$

The element z of $R(L_2)$ defined there is a solution of $\dot{z}^2 = S(z)$: By the definition

$$R(L_2) = L_2(u, v) = L_2(u, z),$$

whose genus is 1, and z is transcendental over L_2. We have

$$(1 - \kappa^2\xi^2 z^2)u^2 - 2\dot{\xi}zu + z^2 - \xi^2 = 0$$

(cf. equality (2), §8, p.45), whence

$$[R(L_2) : L_2(z)] = 2.$$

Since $\dot{z}^2 = S(z)$, $\dot{z}$ is not a rational function of z over L_2, whence

$$R(L_2) = L_2(z, \dot{z}) = L_2(z, z')$$

with $(z')^2 = \lambda S(z)$.

We shall prove the following:

Theorem 10. If R is a Poincaré field, there is a differential extension field L of the coefficient field K which is separable over K such that the differential field R(L) deduced from R by adjoining the elements of L to K is a Clairaut field over L.

By hypothesis R takes the form $K(x, x')$ with

$$(x')^2 = \lambda \Pi (x - a_i), \quad 1 \leq i \leq 3, \quad \lambda, a_i \in K, \quad \lambda \neq 0,$$

where $a_i \neq a_j (i \neq j)$ and they are constants. We set

$$L_1 = K(\kappa),$$

where κ is a root of the quadratic equation

$$(a_2 - a_1)\kappa^2 + 2(a_1 + a_2 - 2a_3)\kappa + a_2 - a_1 = 0,$$

and define

$$u = N(x)/M(x),$$

$$M(x) = -2x + (1 - \kappa)a_1 + (1 + \kappa)a_2,$$

$$N(x) = 2\kappa x + (1 - \kappa)a_1 - (1 + \kappa)a_2,$$

which satisfies

$$1 - u = 2(1 + \kappa)(x - a_1)/M(x),$$

$$1 + u = -2(1 - \kappa)(x - a_2)/M(x),$$

$$1 - \kappa u = 4(x - a_3)/M(x),$$

$$1 + \kappa u = (1 - \kappa^2)(a_1 - a_2)/M(x)$$

and

$$S(u) = (1 - u^2)(1 - \kappa^2 u^2)$$
$$= 16(1 - \kappa^2)^2 \kappa (a_2 - a_1)\lambda^{-1}(x')^2/M(x)^4.$$

Differentiating $u = N(x)/M(x)$ we have

$$M(x)^2 u' = 2\kappa x' M(x) + 2x' N(x) = 2x'(1 - \kappa^2)(a_1 - a_2),$$

whence

$$(u')^2 = \mu S(u), \quad \mu = \lambda(a_2 - a_1)/(4\kappa).$$

We set

$$L_2 = L_1(\mu^{1/2}),$$

which is separable over K, and define a new differentiation of $R(L_2)$ signed with the dot by $\dot{X} = \mu^{-1/2} x'$. In this new differentiation

$$\dot{u}^2 = S(u).$$

We define a differential extension field L of K by

$$L = L_2(\eta), \quad \dot{\eta}^2 = S(\eta),$$

where η is assumed to be transcendental over L_2: L is separable over K. Lemma 2 (§8) may be applied to R(L) if we set

$$y_1 = u, \quad y_2 = \eta.$$

The elements α, β of R(L) defined there are constants which satisfy $\beta^2 = S(\alpha)$: By the definition of α

$$R(L) = L(u, \dot{u}) = L(u, \alpha),$$

whose genus is 1, and α is transcendental over L. We have

$$(1 - \kappa^2\eta^2 u^2)\alpha^2 - 2\dot{\eta}u\alpha + u^2 - \eta^2 = 0$$

by the equality (2), §8, p.45, whence R(L) is of degree 2 over $L(\alpha)$ and $R(L) = L(\alpha, \beta)$ because $\beta^2 = S(\alpha)$.

Remark. Suppose that R is a Poincaré field of the form $K(x, x')$ with

$$(x')^2 = \lambda S(x) = \lambda(1 - x^2)(1 - \kappa^2 x^2), \quad \lambda, \kappa \in K,$$

$$\lambda \neq 0, \kappa \neq 0, \pm 1, \quad \kappa' = 0.$$

Then there is a differential extension field L of K which is separable over K such that R(L) takes the form $L(z, z')$ with $(z')^2 = S(z)$, where the multiplier λ is replaced by 1. This result is due to K. Nishioka [6].

We shall sketch the proof. Let us define

$$L_1 = K(\eta, \eta'), \quad (\eta')^2 = \lambda S(\eta),$$

where η is assumed to be transcendental over K. Then by Lemma 2

(§8), there are constants α, β of $R(L_1)$ such that $\beta^2 = S(\alpha)$ and $R(L_1) = L_1(\alpha, \beta)$. For L we take

$$L = L_1(\zeta, \zeta'), \quad (\zeta')^2 = S(\zeta),$$

where ζ is assumed to be transcendental over L_1. By Lemma 1(§8) there is a solution z of $(z')^2 = S(z)$ in $R(L)$ such that $R(L) = L(z, z')$.

An example of R of characteristic 0 such that the algebraic closure of K can not be taken for L in our Remark will be given in the next section.

If the characteristic of K is 0, we may take L in Theorem 10 and Remark which satisfies an additional condition that any constant of L is algebraic over K(cf. Remark 2, §18).

§10. Poincaré fields of characteristic 0

Let R be a differential algebraic function field of one
variable over the coefficient field K of characteristic 0, which
takes the form K(x, y) with x' = y and F(x, y) = 0, where F is
an irreducible polynomial over K. The residue field of a place
$\mathscr{p}$ in R is a differential extension of K, since it is separable
over K. If the ideal $\mathscr{p}$ in its ring is closed under the differentiation, the derivative z' of an integral element z of R at $\mathscr{p}$
is integral at $\mathscr{p}$ and the residue class of z' modulo $\mathscr{p}$ is the
derivative of the residue class of z modulo $\mathscr{p}$. In case x is
integral at $\mathscr{p}$, the residue class ξ of x satisfies F(ξ, ξ') = 0.
If g(X) is the characteristic polynomial of ξ with respect to
K, $\mathscr{p}$ is a zero of g(x).

We shall see that the ideal $\mathscr{p}$ in its ring is closed under
the differentiation if $\mathscr{p}$ is a zero of a constant γ of R which is
transcendental over K. The $\mathscr{p}$-adic completion $\bar{R}$ has a subfield
Σ which contains K and which is a system of representatives for
the elements of the residue field of $\mathscr{p}$ ([C, p.44]). The constant
γ is represented in the form
$$\gamma = \Sigma a_i t^i, \quad 1 \leq i < \infty, \quad a_i \in \Sigma$$
in $\bar{R}$ with a uniformizing variable t at $\mathscr{p}$ ([C, p.46]). Since the
differentiation is continuous on $\bar{R}$, we have
$$0 = \gamma' = t'\Sigma i a_i t^{i-1} + \Sigma a_i' t^i \; (1 \leq i < \infty),$$
whence t' belongs to $\mathscr{p}$.

With a constant c of K, γ + c is a constant of R which is transcendental over K. Therefore, if R has a constant which is transcendental over K, there are infinitely many solutions of $F(\xi, \xi') = 0$ in the algebraic closure of K, which is a differential extension of K.

Let R be a Poincaré field over the coefficient field K of characteristic 0: $R = K(x, y)$ with $x' = y$ and

$$F(x, y) = y^2 - \lambda f(x) = 0, \qquad f(x) = \Pi(x - a_i), \quad 1 \leq i \leq 3,$$
$$\lambda, a_i \in K, \quad \lambda \neq 0, \quad a_i' = 0, \quad a_i \neq a_j (i \neq j).$$

We have

$$2y' = \lambda'\lambda^{-1}y + \lambda f_x(x).$$

If a place $\wp$ in R is a pole of y, then $x/y \in \wp$ and

$$2(x/y)' = 2 - 2xy'y^{-2} = 2 - xf_x(x)/f(x) - \lambda'\lambda^{-1}x/y$$
$$\equiv -1 \pmod{\wp},$$

whence the ideal $\wp$ in its ring is not closed under the differentiation. In case $\wp$ is a zero of y, it is not a zero of y'. Therefore, if there is a place $\wp$ in R such that the ideal $\wp$ in its ring is closed under the differentiation, we have a non constant solution of $F(\xi, \xi') = 0$ which is algebraic over K.

Assume that $K = P(\zeta)$ with $\zeta' = 1$, where P is a differential field of characteristic 0 consisting of constants: The field of constants of K is P. We shall prove that if λ is a constant then the solutions of $F(\xi, \xi') = 0$ which are algebraic over K are $a_i (1 \leq i \leq 3)$. For a moment suppose that there were a non constant solution ξ of $F(\xi, \xi') = 0$ which is algebraic over K. We may consider $P(\zeta, \xi, \xi')$ as a differential algebraic function field of one variable over P, since $\lambda \in P$. Take a place $\wp$ in

$P(\zeta, \xi, \xi')$ which is a pole of ζ. In its $\mathfrak{P}$-adic completion we have an overfield Σ of K which may be identified with the residue field of $\mathfrak{P}$ and ζ is represented in the form

$$\zeta = \Sigma b_i t^i \, (d \leq i < \infty), \quad b_i \in \Sigma, \quad b_d \neq 0, \quad d = \nu_{\mathfrak{P}}(\zeta) < 0$$

with a uniformizing variable t at $\mathfrak{P}$. Since Σ consists of constants, we have

$$1 = \zeta' = t' \Sigma i b_i t^{i-1} \, (d \leq i < \infty),$$

whence t' belongs to $\mathfrak{P}$ because $d < 0$. Thus $\mathfrak{P}$ would be closed under the differentiation. We may consider $P(\xi, \xi')$ as a differential algebraic function field of one variable over P, since ξ is transcendental over P. If $\mathfrak{p}$ is the place in $P(\xi, \xi')$ which lies below $\mathfrak{P}$, the ideal $\mathfrak{p}$ in its ring would be closed under the differentiation, but it impossible because the algebraic closure of P consists of constants.

Remark. The notation being as above, any non constant solution of $F(\xi, \xi') = 0$ is not contained in a liouvillian extension of K if λ is a constant. It is due to M. Rosenlicht(An analogue of L'Hospital's rule, Proc. Amer. Math. Soc., 37(1973), 369 -373).

Let us give an example of R which has the property required at the end of the previous section. Assume that $R = K(\alpha, \beta)$ with

$$\beta^2 = \alpha(\alpha^2 - 1), \quad \alpha' = 0,$$

where K is $P(\zeta)$ defined above and α is transcendental over K. By Theorem 6(§6) it has no movable singularity. If L is the algebraic closure of K, $R(L)$ has no movable singularity by Theorem 4(§4).

We have $R(L) = L(x, y)$ with $x' = y$ and $F = 0$ above defined replacing K by L by Theorem 8 (§8): $\lambda \in L$ and a_i belongs to the field L_0 of constants of L. The constant α is transcendental over L, whence there is a non constant solution of $F(\xi, \xi') = 0$ in L, which is algebraic over $L_0(\zeta)$. Therefore, λ can not be a constant.

§11. Automorphisms of an elliptic field

Let R be an elliptic field which is assumed to have a place $\mathfrak{p}_0$ of degree 1. We see that if $\mathfrak{a}$ is a divisor in R of degree 0 then there is a place $\mathfrak{p}$ in R of degree 1 such that $\mathfrak{a}\mathfrak{p}_0\mathfrak{p}^{-1}$ is the divisor (w) of an element w of R. By the theorem of Riemann-Roch,

$$\ell(\mathfrak{a}^{-1}\mathfrak{p}_0^{-1}) = 1,$$

whence there is an element $w(\neq 0)$ of R such that

$$w \equiv 0 \pmod{\mathfrak{a}^{-1}\mathfrak{p}_0^{-1}}$$

and (w)$\mathfrak{a}\mathfrak{p}_0$ is an integral divisor of degree 1, which is a place $\mathfrak{p}$ in R of degree 1. If $\mathfrak{p}_1$, $\mathfrak{p}_2$ are places in R of degree 1, the degree of $\mathfrak{p}_1\mathfrak{p}_2\mathfrak{p}_0^{-2}$ is 0, whence there is a place $\mathfrak{p}_3$ in R of degree 1 such that $\mathfrak{p}_1\mathfrak{p}_2\mathfrak{p}_3^{-1}\mathfrak{p}_0^{-1}$ is the divisor of an element of R. Such a place $\mathfrak{p}_3$ is determined uniquely: For if $\mathfrak{p}$ has the required property, $\mathfrak{p}_3\mathfrak{p}^{-1}$ is the divisor (x) of an element x of R, whence $\mathfrak{p} = \mathfrak{p}_3$ because R is not a rational function field K(x). We define

$$\mathfrak{p}_3 = \mathfrak{p}_1 + \mathfrak{p}_2 = \mathfrak{p}_2 + \mathfrak{p}_1.$$

The place $\mathfrak{p}_0$ satisfies

$$\mathfrak{p} + \mathfrak{p}_0 = \mathfrak{p}.$$

If $\mathfrak{p}_1$ is a place in R of degree 1, there is a place $\mathfrak{p}_2$ in R such that $\mathfrak{p}_1 + \mathfrak{p}_2 = \mathfrak{p}_0$: For the degree of $\mathfrak{p}_0\mathfrak{p}_1^{-1}$ is 0 and there is a place $\mathfrak{p}_2$ of degree 0 such that $\mathfrak{p}_0^2\mathfrak{p}_1^{-1}\mathfrak{p}_2^{-1}$ is the divisor of an element of R. If $\mathfrak{p}_1$, $\mathfrak{p}_2$, $\mathfrak{p}_3$ are places in R of degree 1, there is a place $\mathfrak{p}_4$ in R of degree 1 such that

$$\mathfrak{P}_1 \mathfrak{P}_2 \mathfrak{P}_3 \mathfrak{P}_4^{-1} \mathfrak{P}_0^{-2}$$

is the divisor of an element of R. It is determined uniquely, whence

$$(\mathfrak{P}_1 + \mathfrak{P}_2) + \mathfrak{P}_3 = \mathfrak{P}_1 + (\mathfrak{P}_2 + \mathfrak{P}_3).$$

Thus the set of places in R of degree 1 forms an Abelian group with the identity $\mathfrak{P}_0$. An automorphism Φ of R over the coefficient field K transforms $\mathfrak{P}_1 + \mathfrak{P}_2$ to $^\Phi\mathfrak{P}_1 + {}^\Phi\mathfrak{P}_2 - {}^\Phi\mathfrak{P}_0$: For, if $\mathfrak{P}_1\mathfrak{P}_2 = (w)\,\mathfrak{P}_3\mathfrak{P}_0$, then $^\Phi\mathfrak{P}_1{}^\Phi\mathfrak{P}_2 = (\Phi(w))\,{}^\Phi\mathfrak{P}_3{}^\Phi\mathfrak{P}_0$. We have

$$\ell(\mathfrak{P}_0^{-3}) = 3,$$

whence the linear space $\mathcal{L}(\mathfrak{P}_0^{-3})$ is spanned by 1, ξ, η over K. If $\mathfrak{P}_1 + \mathfrak{P}_2 + \mathfrak{Q} = \mathfrak{P}_0$, then $\mathfrak{P}_1\mathfrak{P}_2\mathfrak{Q} = (w)\,\mathfrak{P}_0^3$ with a linear combination w of 1, ξ, η over K, which is determined uniquely up to a factor of K because $\ell(\mathfrak{P}_1\mathfrak{P}_2\mathfrak{P}_0^{-3}) = 1$.

Assume that R takes the form K(x, y) with

$$y^2 = S(x) = (1 - x^2)(1 - \kappa^2 x^2), \quad \kappa \in K(\neq 0, \pm 1)$$

and that the characteristic of K is not 2. If a place $\mathfrak{P}$ in R is a pole of x, it is a pole of y and

$$(yx^{-2} + \kappa)(yx^{-2} - \kappa) = x^{-4} - (1 + \kappa^2)x^{-2},$$

whence yx^{-2} is integral at $\mathfrak{P}$. We define $\mathfrak{P}_\infty$ and $\bar{\mathfrak{P}}_\infty$ as follows: The divisor of poles of x is $\mathfrak{P}_\infty\bar{\mathfrak{P}}_\infty$ and the residue class of yx^{-2} modulo $\mathfrak{P}_\infty$, $\bar{\mathfrak{P}}_\infty$ is $-\kappa$, κ respectively. They are of degree 1. The divisor of poles of y is $\mathfrak{P}_\infty^2\bar{\mathfrak{P}}_\infty^2$ and

$$v_{\mathfrak{P}_\infty}(yx^{-2} + \kappa) \geq 2, \quad v_{\bar{\mathfrak{P}}_\infty}(yx^{-2} - \kappa) \geq 2,$$
$$v_{\bar{\mathfrak{P}}_\infty}(yx^{-2} + \kappa) = 0, \quad v_{\mathfrak{P}_\infty}(yx^{-2} - \kappa) = 0.$$

If a place $\mathfrak{P}$ in R of degree 1 is not a pole of x, the residue classes a, b of x, y modulo $\mathfrak{P}$ are elements of K which satisfy

$b^2 = S(a)$. Conversely if elements a, b of K satisfy $b^2 = S(a)$, there is a place $\mathfrak{p}$ in R of degree 1 which is not a pole of x such that a, b are the residue classes of x, y modulo $\mathfrak{p}$. We define $\mathfrak{p}_0$ and $\bar{\mathfrak{p}}_0$ as follows: The divisor of zeros of x is $\mathfrak{p}_0\bar{\mathfrak{p}}_0$ and the residue class of y modulo $\mathfrak{p}_0, \bar{\mathfrak{p}}_0$ is 1, $-$ 1 respectively. They are of degree 1.

If we set

$$\Phi_{\mathfrak{p}_\infty}(x) = \kappa^{-1}x^{-1}, \quad \Phi_{\mathfrak{p}_\infty}(y) = -\kappa^{-1}x^{-2}y$$

and

$$\Phi_{\bar{\mathfrak{p}}_\infty}(x) = -\kappa^{-1}x^{-1}, \quad \Phi_{\bar{\mathfrak{p}}_\infty}(y) = \kappa^{-1}x^{-2}y,$$

then they define automorphisms of R over K:

$$\Phi_{\mathfrak{p}}(y)^2 = S(\Phi_{\mathfrak{p}}(x)), \quad \mathfrak{p} = \mathfrak{p}_\infty, \bar{\mathfrak{p}}_\infty.$$

We have

$$\Phi_{\mathfrak{p}_\infty}\mathfrak{p}_\infty = \mathfrak{p}_0, \quad \Phi_{\bar{\mathfrak{p}}_\infty}\bar{\mathfrak{p}}_\infty = \mathfrak{p}_0:$$

For, if $\mathfrak{p} = \mathfrak{p}_\infty$ for instance, then

$$0 > \nu_{\mathfrak{p}_\infty}(x) = \nu_{\Phi\mathfrak{p}_\infty}(\kappa^{-1}x^{-1}) = -\nu_{\Phi\mathfrak{p}_\infty}(x),$$

whence $\Phi\mathfrak{p}_\infty$ is a zero of x: We have

$$0 > \nu_{\mathfrak{p}_\infty}(yx^{-2} + \kappa) = \nu_{\Phi\mathfrak{p}_\infty}(-\kappa y + \kappa) = \nu_{\Phi\mathfrak{p}_\infty}(y - 1),$$

whence $\Phi\mathfrak{p}_\infty = \mathfrak{p}_0$.

If $\mathfrak{p}$ is a place in R of degree 1 which is not a pole of x, we set

$$\Phi_{\mathfrak{p}}(x) = (bx + ay)/(1 - \kappa^2 a^2 x^2),$$

$$\Phi_{\mathfrak{p}}(y) = [ax\{2\kappa^2(a^2 + x^2) - (1 + \kappa^2)(1 + \kappa^2 a^2 x^2)\}$$
$$+ (1 + \kappa^2 a^2 x^2)by]/(1 - \kappa^2 a^2 x^2)^2,$$

where a, b are the residue classes of x, y modulo $\mathfrak{p}$. Replacing y_1, y_1', y_2, y_2' in Lemma 2 (§8) by x, y, $-$ a, b respectively, we have

$$b\Phi_{\mathfrak{p}}(x) - a\Phi_{\mathfrak{p}}(y) = x(1 - \kappa^2 a^2 \Phi_{\mathfrak{p}}(x)^2)$$

(§8, p.44) and

$$\Phi_{\mathfrak{p}}(y)^2 = S(\Phi_{\mathfrak{p}}(x))$$

(§8, p.45), whence $\Phi_{\mathfrak{p}}$ defines an automorphism of R over K. It satisfies

$$\Phi_{\mathfrak{p}}\mathfrak{p} = \mathfrak{p}_0:$$

For, if $\Phi = \Phi_{\mathfrak{p}}$, then

$$0 < \nu_{\mathfrak{p}_0}(\Phi(x) - a) = \nu_{\Phi^{-1}\mathfrak{p}_0}(x - a),$$
$$0 < \nu_{\mathfrak{p}_0}(\Phi(y) - b) = \nu_{\Phi^{-1}\mathfrak{p}_0}(y - b).$$

In case $\mathfrak{p} = \mathfrak{p}_0$, $\Phi_{\mathfrak{p}_0}$ is the identity.

We define elements u, v of R by

$$u = (1 + \kappa x^2 - y)/2,$$
$$v = x(1 + \kappa^2 - 2\kappa^2 x^2 + 2\kappa y)/\{2(1 + \kappa)\}$$

and an element λ^2 of K by

$$\lambda^2 = 4\kappa/(1 + \kappa)^2.$$

They satisfy

$$1 - u = (1 - \kappa x^2 + y)/2,$$
$$1 - \lambda^2 u = (1 + \kappa^2 - 2\kappa^2 x^2 + 2\kappa y)/(1 + \kappa)^2,$$
$$v^2 = T(u) = u(1 - u)(1 - \lambda^2 u)$$

because

(1) $\quad (1 + \kappa x^2 - y)(1 - \kappa x^2 + y) = x^2(1 + \kappa^2 - 2\kappa^2 x^2 + 2\kappa y),$

and $\lambda^2 \neq 0, 1$. We have

$$x = 2v/\{(1 + \kappa)(1 - \lambda^2 u)\},$$
$$y = (1 - 2u + \lambda^2 u^2)/(1 - \lambda^2 u)$$

because

$$(1 - u)/(1 - \lambda^2 u) = (1 + \kappa x^2 + y)/2 = u + y,$$

whence $R = K(u, v)$. The divisors of u, $1 - u$, $1 - \lambda^2 u$, v are given by

$$(u) = \mathfrak{p}_0^2 \mathfrak{p}_\infty^{-2}, \quad (1 - u) = \bar{\mathfrak{p}}_0^2 \mathfrak{p}_\infty^{-2},$$

$$(1 - \lambda^2 u) = \bar{\bar{\mathfrak{p}}}_\infty^2 \mathfrak{p}_\infty^{-2}, \quad (v) = \mathfrak{p}_0 \bar{\mathfrak{p}}_0 \bar{\bar{\mathfrak{p}}}_\infty \mathfrak{p}_\infty^{-3}.$$

Therfore,

$$2 \mathfrak{p}_\infty = 2 \bar{\mathfrak{p}}_0 = 2 \bar{\bar{\mathfrak{p}}}_\infty = \mathfrak{p}_0, \quad \bar{\mathfrak{p}}_0 + \bar{\bar{\mathfrak{p}}}_\infty = \mathfrak{p}_\infty.$$

The residue class of $v^2 u^{-3}$ modulo $\mathfrak{p}_\infty$ is λ^2, and the residue class of $v^2 u^{-1}$ modulo $\mathfrak{p}_0$ is 1. If a place $\mathfrak{p}$ in R of degree 1 is not a pole of u, the residue classes α, β of u, v modulo $\mathfrak{p}$ satisfy $\beta^2 = T(\alpha)$. Conversely if elements α, β of K satisfy $\beta^2 = T(\alpha)$, there is a place $\mathfrak{p}$ in R of degree 1 which is not a pole of u such that the residue classes of u, v modulo $\mathfrak{p}$ are α, β. It is uniquely determined, and we set $\mathfrak{p} = \mathfrak{p}(\alpha, \beta)$, which satisfies

$$\mathfrak{p}(\alpha, \beta) + \mathfrak{p}(\alpha, - \beta) = \mathfrak{p}_0,$$

because the divisor of $(u - \alpha)/u$ is $\mathfrak{p}(\alpha, \beta) \mathfrak{p}(\alpha, - \beta) \mathfrak{p}_0^{-2}$. The linear space $\mathcal{L}(\mathfrak{p}_0^{-3})$ is spanned by 1, u^{-1}, $u^{-2}v$ over K.

If $\mathfrak{p}$ is a place in R of degree 1, there is an automorphism of R over K which transforms $\mathfrak{p}$ to $\mathfrak{p}_\infty$ (§7, p.34). The linear space $\mathcal{L}(\mathfrak{p}_\infty^{-2})$, $\mathcal{L}(\mathfrak{p}_\infty^{-3})$ are spanned by 1, u and 1, u, v respectively over K. If an automorphism Φ of R over K leaves $\mathfrak{p}_\infty$ fixed, then

$$\Phi(u) = \omega u + \gamma, \quad \omega, \gamma \in K,$$

$$\Phi(v) = \rho v + \xi u + \eta, \quad \rho, \xi, \eta \in K.$$

They satisfy

$$\Phi(v)^2 = T(\Phi(u)),$$

whence

$$\xi = \eta = 0, \qquad \rho^2 = \omega^3, \qquad T(\gamma) = 0$$

$$(1 + \lambda^2)\omega = 1 + \lambda^2 - 3\lambda^2\gamma,$$

$$\omega^2 = 3\lambda^2\gamma^2 - 2(1 + \lambda^2)\gamma + 1.$$

The group of automorphisms of R over K leaving $\wp_\infty$ fixed is finite. If $1 + \lambda^2 = 0$, then $\gamma = 0$ in case the characteristic p of K is not 3. In this case $\omega = 1$. In case $p = 3$ we have $\omega = \pm 1$ and $\gamma = 0$, ± 1. Suppose that $1 + \lambda^2 \neq 0$: If $\gamma = 1$ then

$$(\lambda^2 - 2)(\lambda^4 - \lambda^2 + 1) = 0, \quad \omega = (1 - 2\lambda^2)/(1 + \lambda^2):$$

If $\gamma = \lambda^{-2}$ then

$$(2\lambda^2 - 1)(\lambda^4 - \lambda^2 + 1) = 0, \quad \omega = (\lambda^2 - 2)/(1 + \lambda^2):$$

In case $\lambda^4 - \lambda^2 + 1 = 0$ we have $\omega^3 = 1$: If $\gamma = 0$ then $\omega = 1$. At most three places in R of degree 1 are left fixed by Φ.

It follows that if an automorphism of R over K leaves four places in R of degree 1 fixed then it is the identity.

We have

$$\Phi_{\wp_\infty}(u) = \Phi_{\wp_\infty}(1 + \kappa x^2 - y)/2 = (1 + \kappa^{-1}x^{-2} + \kappa^{-1}x^{-2}y)/2$$

$$= \kappa^{-1}x^{-2}(1 + \kappa x^2 + y)/2 = \lambda^{-2}u^{-1}$$

because

(2) $\qquad (1 + \kappa x^2 + y)(1 + \kappa x^2 - y) = (1 + \kappa)^2 x^2,$

and

$$\Phi_{\wp_\infty}(v) = 2^{-1}(1 + \kappa)^{-1}\kappa^{-1}x^{-1}(1 + \kappa^2 - 2x^{-2} - 2x^{-2}y)$$

$$= -2^{-1}(1 + \kappa)^{-1}\kappa^{-1}x^{-3}\{2 - (1 + \kappa^2)x^2 + 2y\} = -\lambda^{-2}u^{-2}v$$

by (1) and (2), because

$$2 - (1 + \kappa^2)x^2 + 2y = (1 + \kappa x^2 + y)(1 - \kappa x^2 + y).$$

We shall see that

$$\Phi_{\mathfrak{p}_\infty}^{-1}\mathfrak{p} = \mathfrak{p} + \mathfrak{p}_\infty.$$

In case $\mathfrak{p} = \mathfrak{p}_0$, the left side is $\mathfrak{p}_\infty$ which is equal to the right side. If $\mathfrak{p} = \mathfrak{p}_\infty$, the left side is $\mathfrak{p}_0$ and the right side is $2\mathfrak{p}_\infty$ which is equal to $\mathfrak{p}_0$. If $\mathfrak{p} = \mathfrak{p}(\alpha, \beta)$ with $\alpha \neq 0$, then the left side is

$$\mathfrak{p}(\lambda^{-2}\alpha^{-1}, -\lambda^{-2}\alpha^{-2}\beta),$$

and the divisor of $(\alpha v - \beta u)/u^2$ is

$$\mathfrak{p}(\alpha, \beta)\, \mathfrak{p}(\lambda^{-2}\alpha^{-1}, \lambda^{-2}\alpha^{-2}\beta)\, \mathfrak{p}_\infty \mathfrak{p}_0^{-3},$$

whence

$$\mathfrak{p} + \mathfrak{p}_\infty - \Phi_{\mathfrak{p}_\infty}^{-1}\mathfrak{p} = 3\mathfrak{p}_0 = \mathfrak{p}_0.$$

If $\mathfrak{p} = \mathfrak{p}(\alpha, \beta)$ with $\alpha \neq 0$, we set

$$\Psi_{\mathfrak{p}}(u) = \{u(1 - \alpha)(1 - \lambda^2\alpha) + 2\beta v$$
$$+ \alpha(1 - u)(1 - \lambda^2 u)\}/(1 - \lambda^2\alpha u)^2$$
$$= \{(\beta u + \alpha v)/(1 - \lambda^2\alpha u)\}^2/(\alpha u)$$

and

$$\Psi_{\mathfrak{p}}(v) = (\beta u + \alpha v)\{(1 - \alpha)(1 - u) - \beta v\}\cdot$$
$$\cdot\{(1 - \lambda^2\alpha)(1 - \lambda^2 u) - \lambda^2\beta v\}/\{\beta v(1 - \lambda^2\alpha u)^3\}.$$

They satisfy

$$1 - \Psi_{\mathfrak{p}}(u) = \{(1 - \alpha)(1 - u) - \beta v\}^2\cdot$$
$$\cdot\{(1 - \alpha)(1 - u)(1 - \lambda^2\alpha u)^2\}^{-1},$$

$$1 - \lambda^2\Psi_{\mathfrak{p}}(u) = \{(1 - \lambda^2\alpha)(1 - \lambda^2 u) - \beta v\}^2\cdot$$
$$\cdot\{(1 - \lambda^2\alpha)(1 - \lambda^2 u)(1 - \lambda^2\alpha u)^2\}^{-1}$$

and

$$\Psi_{\mathfrak{p}}(v)^2 = \Psi_{\mathfrak{p}}(u)(1 - \Psi_{\mathfrak{p}}(u))(1 - \lambda^2\Psi_{\mathfrak{p}}(u)).$$

We have

$$(1 - \lambda^2\alpha u)^3(\beta\Psi_{\mathfrak{p}}(u) - \alpha\Psi_{\mathfrak{p}}(v)) = (\beta u + \alpha v)W,$$

where

$$W = 1 - \lambda^2\alpha\{\alpha + 3u - 2(1 + \lambda^2)\alpha u + \lambda^2\alpha^2 u + 2\beta v\},$$

which satisfies

$$(1 - \lambda^2\alpha u)^2(1 - \lambda^2\alpha\Psi_\wp(u)) = W,$$

whence

(3) $\quad (1 - \lambda^2\alpha u)(\beta\Psi_\wp(u) - \alpha\Psi_\wp(v)) = (\beta u + \alpha v)(1 - \lambda^2\alpha\Psi_\wp(u)).$

Therefore,

$$u = \{(\beta\Psi_\wp(u) - \alpha\Psi_\wp(v))/(1 - \lambda^2\alpha\Psi_\wp(u)\}^2/(\alpha\Psi_\wp(u)),$$

and $\Psi_\wp$ defines an automorphism of R over K. We shall see that

$$\Psi_\wp = \Phi_\wp.$$

By the definition $\Psi^{-1}\wp_0 = \wp$. We have

$$\Psi_\wp^{-1}\bar{\wp}_0 = \wp((1 - \alpha)(1 - \lambda^2\alpha)^{-1}, \ -(1 - \lambda^2)\beta(1 - \lambda^2\alpha)^{-2}),$$
$$\alpha \neq \lambda^{-2},$$
$$\Psi_\wp^{-1}\wp_\infty = \wp(\lambda^{-2}\alpha^{-1}, \ -\lambda^{-2}\alpha^{-2}\beta),$$
$$\Psi_\wp^{-1}\bar{\wp}_\infty = \wp(\lambda^{-2}(1 - \alpha)^{-1}(1 - \lambda^2\alpha),$$
$$\lambda^{-2}(1 - \lambda^2)(1 - \alpha)^{-3}\beta), \quad \alpha \neq 1$$

and

$$\Psi_{\bar{\wp}_\infty}^{-1}\wp_0 = \Psi_{\bar{\wp}_0}^{-1}\bar{\wp}_\infty = \wp_\infty.$$

In case $\wp = \bar{\wp}_\infty$ we have

$$\Phi_{\bar{\wp}_\infty}^{-1}\bar{\wp}_0 = \wp_\infty = \Psi_{\bar{\wp}_\infty}^{-1}\bar{\wp}_0, \quad \Phi_{\bar{\wp}_\infty}^{-1}\wp_\infty = \bar{\wp}_0 = \Psi_{\bar{\wp}_\infty}^{-1}\wp_\infty,$$
$$\Phi_{\bar{\wp}_\infty}^{-1}\wp_\infty = \wp_0 = \Psi_{\bar{\wp}_\infty}^{-1}\wp_\infty,$$

whence $\Phi_{\bar{\wp}_\infty} = \Psi_{\bar{\wp}_\infty}$. If $\wp = \bar{\wp}_0$, we have

$$\Phi_{\bar{\wp}_0}^{-1}\bar{\wp}_0 = \wp_0 = \Psi_{\bar{\wp}_0}^{-1}\wp_0, \quad \Phi_{\bar{\wp}_0}^{-1}\wp_\infty = \wp_\infty = \Psi_{\bar{\wp}_0}^{-1}\wp_\infty,$$
$$\Phi_{\bar{\wp}_0}^{-1}\bar{\wp}_\infty = \wp_\infty = \Psi_{\bar{\wp}_0}^{-1}\bar{\wp}_\infty,$$

whence $\Phi_{\bar{\wp}_0} = \Psi_{\bar{\wp}_0}$. We denote by $a(\wp)$, $b(\wp)$ the residue classes of x, y modulo $\mathfrak{p}$ which is not a pole of x. If a, b are the residue classes of x, y modulo $\mathfrak{p}$ which is neither a pole nor a zero of x, then

$$a(\Phi_{\mathfrak{p}}^{-1}\,\bar{\mathfrak{p}}_0) = -\,a, \quad b(\Phi_{\mathfrak{p}}^{-1}\,\bar{\mathfrak{p}}_0) = -\,b,$$
$$a(\Phi_{\mathfrak{p}}^{-1}\,\mathfrak{p}_\infty) = \kappa^{-1}a^{-1}, \quad b(\Phi_{\mathfrak{p}}^{-1}\,\mathfrak{p}_\infty) = -\,\kappa^{-1}a^{-2}b,$$
$$a(\Phi_{\mathfrak{p}}^{-1}\,\bar{\mathfrak{p}}_\infty) = -\,\kappa^{-1}a^{-1}, \quad b(\Phi_{\mathfrak{p}}^{-1}\,\bar{\mathfrak{p}}_\infty) = \kappa^{-1}a^{-2}b.$$

If a, b are the residue classes of x, y modulo $\mathfrak{p}(\alpha, \beta)$ which is not a pole of x, then

$$\alpha = A(a, b) = 2^{-1}(1 + \kappa a^2 - b),$$
$$\beta = B(a, b) = 2^{-1}(1 + \kappa)^{-1}a(1 + \kappa^2 - 2\kappa^2 a^2 + 2\kappa b).$$

These functions A, B of a, b satisfy

$$(1 - A)(1 - \lambda^2 A)^{-1} = A(-\,a, -\,b),$$
$$-\,(1 - \lambda^2)B(1 - \lambda^2 A)^{-2} = B(-\,a, -\,b);$$
$$\lambda^{-2}A^{-1} = A(\kappa^{-1}a^{-1}, -\,\kappa^{-1}a^{-2}b),$$
$$-\,\lambda^{-2}A^{-2}B = B(\kappa^{-1}a^{-1}, -\,\kappa^{-1}a^{-2}b);$$
$$\lambda^{-2}(1 - A)^{-1}(1 - \lambda^2 A) = A(-\,\kappa^{-1}a^{-1}, \kappa^{-1}a^{-2}b),$$
$$\lambda^{-2}(1 - \lambda^2)(1 - A)^{-3}B = B(-\,\kappa^{-1}a^{-1}, \kappa^{-1}a^{-2}b),$$

whence $\Phi_{\mathfrak{p}}^{-1}\,\mathfrak{z} = \Psi_{\mathfrak{p}}^{-1}\,\mathfrak{z}$, $\mathfrak{z} = \bar{\mathfrak{p}}_0$, $\mathfrak{p}_\infty$, $\bar{\mathfrak{p}}_\infty$, and $\Phi_{\mathfrak{p}} = \Psi_{\mathfrak{p}}$.

We shall prove that

$$\Phi_{\mathfrak{p}}^{-1}\,\mathfrak{p}^* = \mathfrak{p} + \mathfrak{p}^*.$$

It may be assumed that $\mathfrak{p} \neq \mathfrak{p}_0, \mathfrak{p}_\infty$ and $\mathfrak{p}^* \neq \mathfrak{p}_0$. If $\mathfrak{p}^* = \mathfrak{p}_\infty$, then

$$\Phi_{\mathfrak{p}}^{-1}\,\mathfrak{p}_\infty = \mathfrak{p}(\lambda^{-2}\alpha^{-1}, -\,\lambda^{-2}\alpha^{-2}\beta) = \Phi_{\mathfrak{p}_\infty}^{-1}\,\mathfrak{p} = \mathfrak{p} + \mathfrak{p}_\infty$$

with $\mathfrak{p} = \mathfrak{p}(\alpha, \beta)$, whence we may assume that $\mathfrak{p}^* \neq \mathfrak{p}_\infty$. Suppose that $\mathfrak{p}^* = \mathfrak{p}$. We define an element z of R by

$$z = u^{-2}[(1 - \lambda^2\alpha^2)u^2 - \alpha\{3 - 2(1 + \lambda^2)\alpha + \lambda^2\alpha^2\}u + 2\alpha\beta v].$$

The divisor of poles of z is $\wp_0^3$. We shall see that $\wp^2$ divides the divisor of zeros of z. If $t = u - \alpha$ then

$$u^2z = t[(1 - \lambda^2\alpha^2)(t + 2\alpha) - \alpha\{3 - 2(1 + \lambda^2)\alpha + \lambda^2\alpha^2\}$$

$$+ 2\alpha\beta(v + \beta)^{-1}\{\lambda^2t^2 + (3\lambda^2\alpha - 1 - \lambda^2)t$$

$$+ 3\lambda^2\alpha^2 - 2(1 + \lambda^2)\alpha + 1\}].$$

The residue class of $t^{-1}u^2z$ modulo $\wp$ is

$$2\alpha(1 - \lambda^2\alpha^2) - \alpha\{3 - 2(1 + \lambda^2)\alpha + \lambda^2\alpha^2\}$$

$$+ \alpha\{3\lambda^2\alpha^2 - 2(1 + \lambda^2)\alpha + 1\},$$

which vanishes. We have

$$\Phi_{\wp}^{-1}\wp = \wp(X, Y)$$

with

$$X = 4\beta^2(1 - \lambda^2\alpha^2)^{-2},$$

$$Y = 2\beta(1 - 2\alpha + \lambda^2\alpha^2)(1 - 2\lambda^2\alpha + \lambda^2\alpha^2)(1 - \lambda^2\alpha^2)^{-3}$$

in case $1 - \lambda^2\alpha^2 \neq 0$. If it vanishes, then $\Phi_{\wp}^{-1}\wp = \wp_\infty$ and $\wp_\infty$ is a zero of z. The place $\wp(X, -Y)$ is a zero of z:

$$(1 - \lambda^2\alpha^2)X^2 - \alpha\{3 - 2(1 + \lambda^2)\alpha + \lambda^2\alpha^2\}X - 2\alpha\beta Y$$

$$= 4(1 - \lambda^2\alpha^2)^{-3}\beta^2[4\beta^2 - \alpha(1 - \lambda^2\alpha^2)\{3 - 2(1 + \lambda^2)\alpha + \lambda^2\alpha^2\}$$

$$- \alpha(1 - 2\alpha + \lambda^2\alpha^2)(1 - 2\lambda^2\alpha + \lambda^2\alpha^2)]$$

$$= 4(1 - \lambda^2\alpha^2)^{-3}\beta^2\{4\beta^2 - 4\alpha(1 - \alpha)(1 - \lambda^2\alpha)\} = 0.$$

Thus $(z) = \wp^2\wp(X, -Y)\wp_0^{-3}$ and $\Phi_{\wp}^{-1}\wp = 2\wp$ because

$$\Phi_{\wp}^{-1}\wp = \wp(X, Y) = -\wp(X, -Y).$$

If $\wp* = -\wp$, then $\wp + \wp* = \wp_0$ and

$$\Phi_{\wp}^{-1}\wp + \Phi_{\wp}^{-1}\wp* - \Phi_{\wp}^{-1}\wp_0 = \Phi_{\wp}^{-1}\wp_0 = \wp,$$

whence $\Phi_{\wp}^{-1}\wp* = \wp_0 = \wp + \wp*$. Therefore we may assume that

$\wp* \neq \pm \wp$. Let us define an element w of R by

$$w = u^{-2}\{(\alpha\beta* - \alpha*\beta)u^2 - (\beta*\alpha^2 - \beta\alpha*^2)u + \alpha\alpha*(\alpha - \alpha*)v\},$$

where $\wp(\alpha*, \beta*) = \wp*$. The divisor of poles of w is $\wp_0^3$ and $\wp$, $\wp*$ are zeros of w. The place $\wp_\infty$ is a zero of w if and only if $\wp* = -\wp - \wp_\infty$, that is

$$\alpha* = \lambda^{-2}\alpha^{-1}, \qquad \beta* = \lambda^{-2}\alpha^{-2}\beta$$

because $\Phi_{\wp_\infty}^{-1}\wp = \wp + \wp_\infty$. In this case we have

$$\Phi_{\wp}^{-1}\wp* = \wp_\infty = \wp + \wp*.$$

If $\wp* = \wp + \wp_\infty$, then

$$\Phi_{\wp}^{-1}\wp* = \Phi_{\wp}^{-1}\wp + \Phi_{\wp}^{-1}\wp_\infty - \Phi_{\wp}^{-1}\wp_0 = 2\wp + \wp + \wp_\infty - \wp$$

$$= 2\wp + \wp_\infty = \wp + \wp*.$$

Therefore we may assume that $1 - \lambda^2\alpha\alpha* \neq 0$. The place $\Phi_{\wp}^{-1}\wp*$ is $\wp(U, V)$ with

$$U = \{(\beta\alpha* + \alpha\beta*)/(1 - \lambda^2\alpha\alpha*)\}^2/(\alpha\alpha*)$$

$$= \{(1 - \alpha)(1 - \lambda^2\alpha)\alpha* + 2\beta\beta* + (1 - \alpha*)(1 - \lambda^2\alpha*)\} \cdot$$

$$\cdot (1 - \lambda^2\alpha\alpha*)^{-2},$$

$$V = (\beta\alpha* + \alpha\beta*)\{(1 - \alpha)(1 - \alpha*) - \beta\beta*\} \cdot$$

$$\cdot \{(1 - \lambda^2\alpha)(1 - \lambda^2\alpha*) - \lambda^2\beta\beta*\}\{\beta\beta*(1 - \lambda^2\alpha\alpha*)^3\}^{-1}.$$

Here,

(4) $(\beta\alpha* + \alpha\beta*)(\beta\alpha* - \alpha\beta*) = \alpha\alpha*(\alpha* - \alpha)(1 - \lambda^2\alpha\alpha*) \neq 0$.

We shall show that $\wp(U, - V)$ is a zero of w. By (3),

$$\alpha V = \beta U - (\beta\alpha* + \alpha\beta*)(1 - \lambda^2\alpha U)/(1 - \lambda^2\alpha\alpha*).$$

Let Z be the value of $u^2 w$ by the replacement of $u = U$, $v = V$:

$$Z = (\alpha\beta* - \alpha*\beta)U^2 - (\beta*\alpha^2 - \beta\alpha*^2)U - \alpha\alpha*(\alpha - \alpha*)V$$

$$= U\{(\alpha\beta* - \alpha*\beta)U + 2\alpha*^2\beta - \beta*\alpha^2 - \alpha\alpha*\beta\} -$$

$$- \alpha^*(\alpha^* - \alpha)(\alpha^*\beta + \beta^*\alpha)(1 - \lambda^2\alpha U)/(1 - \lambda^2\alpha\alpha^*),$$

and

$$U^{-1}Z = (\alpha\beta^* - \alpha^*\beta)U + 2\alpha^{*2}\beta - \beta^*\alpha^2 - \alpha\alpha^*\beta$$

$$- \alpha\alpha^{*2}(\alpha^* - \alpha)(1 - \lambda^2\alpha\alpha^*)(1 - \lambda^2\alpha U)/(\alpha^*\beta + \beta^*\alpha);$$

here,

$$(\alpha\beta^* + \beta\alpha^*)(2\alpha^*\beta - \beta^*\alpha^2 - \alpha\alpha^*\beta)$$

$$= \alpha\alpha^* \cdot (\alpha^* - \alpha)\{\alpha^*(1 - \alpha)(1 - \lambda^2\alpha) + 2\beta\beta^*$$

$$+ \alpha(1 - \alpha^*)(1 - \lambda^2\alpha^*) + \alpha^*(1 - \lambda^2\alpha\alpha^*)\}.$$

By (4) we have

$$(\beta^*\alpha - \alpha^*\beta)^{-1}U^{-1}Z$$

$$= U - \{\alpha^*(1 - \alpha)(1 - \lambda^2\alpha) + 2\beta\beta^* + \alpha(1 - \alpha^*)(1 - \lambda^2\alpha^*)$$

$$+ \alpha^*(1 - \lambda^2\alpha\alpha^*)\}/(1 - \lambda^2\alpha\alpha^*) + \alpha^*(1 - \lambda^2\alpha U)$$

$$= (1 - \lambda^2\alpha\alpha^*)U$$

$$- \{\alpha^*(1 - \alpha)(1 - \lambda^2\alpha) + 2\beta\beta^* + \alpha(1 - \alpha^*)(1 - \lambda^2\alpha^*)\} \cdot$$

$$\cdot (1 - \lambda^2\alpha\alpha^*)^{-1} = 0$$

(p. 66). Thus, $(\hat{w}) = \wp\wp^*\wp(U, -V)\wp_0^{-3}$ and

(5) $\qquad \Phi_\wp^{-1}\wp^* = \wp + \wp^*.$

<u>Remark</u>. If R is the field of elliptic functions with modulus κ we may express x and y by Jacobi's elliptic functions:

$$x = \text{sn }\zeta, \qquad y = \text{cn }\zeta \cdot \text{dn }\zeta$$

with a complex variable ζ, and u, v in the forms

$$u = \text{sn}^2[(1 + \kappa)\zeta/2, \lambda],$$

$$v = \text{sn}[(1 + \kappa)\zeta/2, \lambda] \cdot \text{cn}[(1 + \kappa)\zeta/2, \lambda] \cdot \text{dn}[(1 + \kappa)\zeta/2, \lambda]$$

by Jacobi's elliptic functions with modulus λ: Here, $\text{sn}[(1 + \kappa)\zeta, \lambda]$ is obtained from $\text{sn}(\zeta, \kappa)$ by Gauss' transformation;

$$sn[(1 + \kappa)\zeta, \lambda] = (1 + \kappa)sn\ \zeta/(1 + \kappa sn^2\zeta).$$

Confer for instance with p.147 of the book by Weber quoted at the end of §8. The formula (5) was proved by Euler, who made use of the identity in a, b, c;

$$\Sigma du_i/\ T(u_i)^{1/2} = 0, \quad 1 \le i \le 3,$$

where u_1, u_2, u_3 are the roots of

$$u(a + bu)^2 - c^2(1 - u)(1 - \lambda^2 u) = 0$$

with variables a, b, c(cf. pp.46-48 of the book quoted above).

§12. Differential automorphisms

Let R be an algebraic function field of one variable and
K be the coefficient field. If L is an overfield of K, an automorphism of R over K can be extended in one and only way to an
automorphism of R(L) which coincides with the identity on L by
the definition of the field R(L) deduced from R by adjoining the
elements of L to K. It coincides with the identity on the coefficient field L* of R(L) because L* is purely unseparable over L
([C, p.91]).

Suppose that R is a differential algebraic function field
of one variable over the coefficient field K. An automorphism ϕ
of R over K is a differential automorphism of R over K if $\phi\delta = \delta\phi$
on R with the differentiation δ of R. Assume that R(L) becomes
the differential field deduced from R by adjoining the elements
of L to K with the differentiation D (§4). If ϕ is a differential
automorphism of R over K, the extended automorphism Φ of R(L) over
L* satisfies $\Phi D = D\Phi$ on R because $\Phi D - D\Phi$ is a derivation of R(L)
which coincides with 0 on R and L. The coefficient field L* is
not necessarily closed under D: Consider for instance the example
given in §4, p.18. We take K(α) for L with $\alpha^p = a$ and an arbitrary
element of L for α'. The radical of R$\otimes$L consists only of 0, whence
R(L) is the differential field deduced from R by adjoining the elements of L to K. The coefficient field L* is P(α, β) with

$$\beta = - y - \alpha x, \qquad \beta^p = b$$

([C, p.91]). The derivative β' is $- y' - \alpha'x - \alpha x'$, which is not necessarily in L*.

If $\mathcal{P}$ is a place in R, the ring of $\phi\mathcal{P}$ is closed under the differentiation if and only if the ring of $\mathcal{P}$ is closed under the differentiation. We shall prove the following:

Theorem 11. Let R be a differential algebraic function field of one variable over the coefficient field K. The number of those places in R such that their rings are not closed under the differentiation is finite.

Take an element x of R which is transcendental over K. If $y_1, \ldots, y_n$ form a base of R with respect to K(x) it is an integral base at almost all places in R([C, 56]). The derivatives of $x, y_1, \ldots, y_n$ are integral at almost all places in R. Suppose that $y_1, \ldots, y_n$ form an integral base at a place $\mathcal{P}$ in R and that the derivatives of $x, y_1, \ldots, y_n$ are integral at $\mathcal{P}$. An integral element z of R at $\mathcal{P}$ may be expressed in the form

$$z = \Sigma u_i y_i, \quad 1 \le i \le n$$

with the coefficients in the ring of the place in K(x) which lies below $\mathcal{P}$, whose derivatives are integral at $\mathcal{P}$, whence z' is integral at $\mathcal{P}$.

Theorem 12. Let R be a differential algebraic function field of one variable over the coefficient field K whose characteristic is neither 2 nor 3. Assume that R is an elliptic field possessing a place of degree 1 and that R has a non constant element. If the group of differential automorphisms of R over K is infinite, then there is an overfield L of K which is algebraic and separable over K such that the differential field R(L) deduced from R adjoining the elements of L to K is a Poincaré field.

There is an overfield L of K which is algebraic and separable over K such that R(L) = L(x, y) with

$$y^2 = x(x - 1)(x - \delta),$$

where δ is an element of L different from 0 and 1, since the characteristic of K is neither 2 nor 3 (§7). The group of differential automorphisms of R(L) over L is infinite. Let Γ be the set of those places in R(L) of degree 1 such that their rings are not closed under the differentiation: It is finite by Theorem 11. We see that it is empty. By a differential automorphism of R(L) over L, Γ is left invariant. If Γ were not empty, there would be an element of Γ such that infinitely many differential automorphisms of R(L) over L leave it fixed, but it is impossible (§11, p.61). The places in R(L) which are zeros of y are of degree 1, whence their rings are closed under the differentiation. Therefore we have x' = cy with an element c of L and δ is a constant (§7, p.38); thus R(L) is a Poincaré field (cf. the proof of Theorem 9, §9).

The assumption that the characteristic of K is not 3 can not be taken out of Theorem 12. Assume for instance that R = K(x, y) with

$$y^2 = x^3 - u, \quad u \in K, \quad x' = x, \quad u' = 0,$$

where K is a differential field of characteristic 3 which satisfies the following conditions; an element ξ of K satisfies $\xi' = \xi$ and any

element of its algebraic closure which is separable over K is
contained in K, while $u^{1/3} \notin K$. Then there are infinitely many
constants of K: R has no movable singularity and its genus is 1.
Let $\wp$ be a place in R which is not a pole of x such that the residue class of x modulo $\wp$ is $c\xi$ with a constant c of K. It is of
degree 1 and an uniformizing variable t at $\wp$ is given by t = x -
$c\xi$, whose derivative is t, whence the ideal $\wp$ in its ring is closed
under the differentiation. If c_1 is a constant of K different
from c, we have a place $\wp_1$ in R of degree 1 such that the residue
class of x modulo $\wp_1$ is $c_1\xi$. The space $\mathcal{L}(\wp^{-1}\wp_1^{-1})$ contains an
element w which is not in K and the derivative w' is contained in
this space, whence w' is a linear combination of 1 and w over K
and K(w) is a differential subfield of R. The automorphism of R
over K constructed in §7, p.35 is a differential one, which transforms $\wp$ to $\wp_1$. Therefore the group of differential automorphisms
of R over K is infinite, while R is not a Poincaré field(§7).

Remark 1. In Theorem 12 suppose that the characteristic
is 0 and any constant of R is contained in K which is assumed to
be algebraically closed: Then the result is included in a theorem
of E. R. Kolchin [1, p.809]: It is stated in the general case of
partial differential field where K is not necessarily algebraically
closed, while the field of constants is algebraically closed. His
theorem has another part(cf. Remark, §14).

Confer with the arguments at the end of §13.

Remark 2. Let R be an algebraic function field of one var-

iable over an algebraically closed field K: Then the group of
automorphisms of R over K is finite if the genus of R is greater
than 1(cf. for instance K. Iwasawa and T. Tamagawa, On the group
of automorphisms of a function field, J. Math. Soc. Japan, 3(1951),
137-147).

In case of characteristic 0 the above theorem will be proved
in §15.

§13. Differential automorphisms of a Poincaré field

Let R be an elliptic field over K whose characteristic is not
2, which takes the form $K(x, y)$ with

$$y^2 = S(x) = (1 - x^2)(1 - \kappa^2 x^2), \quad \kappa \in K(\neq 0, \pm 1).$$

If $\mathfrak{p}$ is a place in R of degree 1, we have an automorphism $\Phi_{\mathfrak{p}}$ of R
over K which satisfies

$$\Phi_{\mathfrak{p}} \mathfrak{p} = \mathfrak{p}_0, \quad \Phi_{\mathfrak{p}}^{-1} \mathfrak{p}^* = \mathfrak{p} + \mathfrak{p}^*.$$

It is defined by

$$\Phi_{\mathfrak{p}}(x) = (bx + ay)/(1 - \kappa^2 a^2 x^2),$$

$$\Phi_{\mathfrak{p}}(y) = [(1 + \kappa^2 a^2 x^2)by - ax\{(1 + \kappa^2)(1 + \kappa^2 a^2 x^2)$$

$$- 2\kappa^2(a^2 + x^2)\}]/(1 - \kappa^2 a^2 x^2)^2$$

if $\mathfrak{p}$ is not a pole of x, where a, b are the residue classes of
x, y modulo $\mathfrak{p}$, and

$$\Phi_{\mathfrak{p}_\infty}(x) = \kappa^{-1} x^{-1}, \quad \Phi_{\mathfrak{p}_\infty}(y) = -\kappa^{-1} x^{-2} y,$$

$$\Phi_{\bar{\mathfrak{p}}_\infty}(x) = -\kappa^{-1} x^{-1}, \quad \Phi_{\bar{\mathfrak{p}}_\infty}(y) = \kappa^{-1} x^{-2} y$$

(§11).

Suppose that R is a Poincaré field with the differentiation δ
which satisfies $\delta x = y$ and $\delta \kappa = 0$:

$$\delta y = -(1 + \kappa^2)x + 2\kappa^2 x^3.$$

Differentiating $b^2 = S(a)$ we have

$$b\delta b = \{-(1 + \kappa^2)a + 2\kappa^2 a^3\}\delta a.$$

There exist derivations D_0 and D_x^* of R which satisfy respectively

$$D_0 x = 0, \quad D_0 = \delta \text{ on } K,$$

$$D_x^* x = y, \quad D_x^* = 0 \text{ on } K:$$

Since R is separable over K(x), we have

$$\delta = D_0 + D_x^*$$

and $D_0 y = 0$, $D_x^* y = \delta y$ because $\delta \kappa = 0$. If $\wp$ is a pole of x, then

$$D_x^* \Phi_{\wp_\infty}(x) = -\kappa^{-1}x^{-2}y = \Phi_{\wp_\infty}(y), \qquad D_0 \Phi_{\wp_\infty}(x) = 0$$

and

$$D_x^* \Phi_{\bar{\wp}_\infty}(x) = \kappa^{-1}x^{-2}y = \Phi_{\bar{\wp}_\infty}(y), \qquad D_0 \Phi_{\bar{\wp}_\infty}(x) = 0.$$

If $\wp$ is not a pole of x, then

$$D_x^* \Phi_{\wp}(x) = (1 - \kappa^2 a^2 x^2)^{-2}\{(by + a\delta y)(1 - \kappa^2 a^2 x^2)$$

$$+ 2\kappa^2 a^2 (bx + ay)xy\}$$

$$= (1 - \kappa^2 a^2 x^2)^{-2}[by \cdot (1 + \kappa^2 a^2 x^2)$$

$$+ a(1 - \kappa^2 a^2 x^2)\{-(1 + \kappa^2)x + 2\kappa^2 x^3\}$$

$$+ 2\kappa^2 a^3 x(1 - x^2)(1 - \kappa^2 x^2)\}] = \Phi_{\wp}(y)$$

and

$$D_0 \Phi_{\wp}(x) = (1 - \kappa^2 a^2 x^2)^{-2}\{(x\delta b + y\delta a)(1 - \kappa^2 a^2 x^2)$$

$$+ 2\kappa^2 ax^2(bx + ay)\delta a\}:$$

If $b = 0$, $D_0 \Phi_{\wp}(x) = 0$ because $\delta a = 0$: In case $b \neq 0$ we have

$$D_0 \Phi_{\wp}(x) = (1 - \kappa^2 a^2 x^2)^{-2}b^{-1}\delta a \cdot$$

$$\cdot [\{-(1 + \kappa^2)a + 2\kappa^2 a^3\}x(1 - \kappa^2 a^2 x^2)$$

$$+ b\{y(1 - \kappa^2 a^2 x^2) + 2\kappa^2 ax^2(bx + ay)\}]$$

$$= (1 - \kappa^2 a^2 x^2)^{-2}b^{-1}\delta a \cdot$$

$$\cdot [by(1 + \kappa^2 a^2 x^2) - ax\{(1 + \kappa^2 - 2\kappa^2 a^2)(1 - \kappa^2 a^2 x^2)$$

$$- 2\kappa^2(1 - a^2)(1 - \kappa^2 a^2)x^2\}] = b^{-1}\delta a \Phi_{\wp}(y).$$

Thus, if $\wp$ is neither a zero nor a pole of y,

$$\delta\Phi_{\wp}(x) = (1 + b^{-1}\delta a)\Phi_{\wp}(y):$$

In case $\wp$ is either a zero or a pole of y, $\delta\Phi_{\wp}(x) = \Phi_{\wp}(y)$.

Since R is separable over K(x), we have

$$\delta\Phi_{\wp} = (1 + b^{-1}\delta a)\Phi_{\wp}\delta - b^{-1}\delta aD_0$$

on R if $\wp$ is neither a zero nor a pole of y. In case $\wp$ is either a zero or a pole of y, $\delta\Phi_{\wp} = \Phi_{\wp}\delta$ on R.

In §11 we defined

$$u = 2^{-1}(1 + \kappa x^2 - y),$$

$$v = 2^{-1}(1 + \kappa)^{-1}x(1 + \kappa^2 - 2\kappa^2 x^2 + 2\kappa y),$$

which satisfy $D_0 u = D_0 v = 0$ because $\delta\kappa = 0$, and

$$\delta u = (2\kappa xy - \delta y)/2$$

$$= [2\kappa xy - \{-(1 + \kappa^2)x + 2\kappa^2 x^2\}]/2$$

$$= x(1 + \kappa^2 - 2\kappa^2 x^2 + 2\kappa y)/2 = (1 + \kappa)v.$$

If an automorphism Φ of R over K transforms $\wp + \wp_\infty$ to $\wp_\infty$, it takes the form

$$\Phi(u) = \omega\Phi_{\wp}(u) + \gamma, \qquad \Phi(v) = \rho\Phi_{\wp}(v),$$

where ω, γ, ρ are the constants of K determined in §11, p.61. We have

$$\delta\Phi(u) = \omega\delta\Phi_{\wp}(u) = \omega(1 + b^{-1}\delta a)\Phi_{\wp}(\delta u)$$

$$= (1 + \kappa)\omega(1 + b^{-1}\delta a)\Phi_{\wp}(v)$$

$$= (1 + \kappa)\omega\rho^{-1}(1 + b^{-1}\delta a)\Phi(v) = \omega\rho^{-1}(1 + b^{-1}\delta a)\Phi(\delta u)$$

if $\wp$ is neither a zero nor a pole of y. Thus, in this case,

$$\delta\Phi = \Phi\delta$$

on R if and only if

$$\omega\rho^{-1}(1 + b^{-1}\delta a) = 1,$$

since R is separable over K(u). In case $\wp$ is either a zero or a pole of y,

$$\delta\Phi(u) = \omega\delta\Phi_{\wp}(u) = \omega\Phi_{\wp}(\delta u) = (1 + \kappa)\omega\Phi_{\wp}(v)$$
$$= (1 + \kappa)\omega\rho^{-1}\Phi(v) = \omega\rho^{-1}\Phi(\delta u),$$

whence $\delta\Phi = \Phi\delta$ if and only if $\omega\rho^{-1} = 1$. The automorphism $\Phi_{\wp}$ of R over K is a differential one if and only if either $\delta a = 0$ or $\wp$ is a pole of x.

We shall show that if R and K have the same field of constants then any differential automorphism Φ of R over K coincides with some $\Phi_{\wp}$ (cf. E. R. Kolchin [1]; Remark 1, §12). We apply Lemma 2(§8) to R setting $y_1 = x$, $y_2 = \Phi(x)$. The constants α, β defined there belong to K by our assumption. Since they satisfy $\beta^2 = S(\alpha)$, there is a place $\wp$ in R such that α, β are the residue classes of x, y modulo $\wp$, and we have $\Phi = \Phi_{\wp}(§8, \text{p.44})$. If the characteristic is positive, R contains a constant which is transcendental over K. In the case of characteristic 0, R has a constant which is not in K if and only if there is a non constant solution of $(\xi')^2 = S(\xi)$ in the algebraic closure of K(§10).

Suppose that R and K have the same field of constants. If T is a differential subfield of R which contains K properly such that R is a Galois extension of T, then R is an Abelian extension of T: For an element of the Galois group is a differential automorphism of R over K and the group of differential automorphisms of R over K is an Abelian group according to the previous paragraph.

§14. Riccati fields of characteristic 0

Let R be a differential algebraic function field of one variable over K of characteristic 0 of the form $K(x)$. The derivative x' is a rational function of x over K: $x' = T(x)/S(x)$, where S, T are polynomials of x over K possessing no common divisor, while the leading coefficient of $S(x)$ is 1. If Φ is a differential automorphism of R over K which leaves the pole $\wp$ of x fixed, it takes the form

$$\Phi(x) = \alpha x + \beta, \quad \alpha, \beta \in K$$

because the space $\mathcal{L}(\wp^{-1})$ is spanned by 1 and x over K. We have the identity in x:

(1) $\alpha' x + \alpha T(x)/S(x) + \beta' = T(\alpha x + \beta)/S(\alpha x + \beta),$

since

$$\{\Phi(x)\}' = \alpha' x + \alpha x' + \beta' = \Phi(x') = T(\Phi(x))/S(\Phi(x)).$$

The rational function $T(x)/S(x)$ may be represented in the partial fraction

$$\sum_{f}\sum_{\lambda} g_\lambda(x)/f(x)^\lambda + h(x), \quad f, g_\lambda, h \in K[x]$$

in one and only way, where $f(x)$ is an irreducible divisor of $S(x)$, while $\deg g_\lambda < \deg f$. We shall see that if infinitely many differential automorphisms of R over K leave $\wp$ fixed then the ideal $\wp$ in its ring is closed under the differentiation and there is a generator t of R which satisfies t' or $t'/t \in K$. The denominator $S(x)$ of x' is 1: For, if S were not 1, there would be an irreducible factor $f(x)$ of $S(x)$ which is left invariant up to a factor of K by infinitely many differential automorphisms Φ of R over K;

$$\alpha^n f(x) = f(\alpha x + \beta), \quad n = \deg f:$$

We would have $\alpha^n f(0) = f(\beta)$ and by (1)

$$\alpha = \alpha^m, \quad m = \deg g_\lambda - \lambda n < 0,$$

which is impossible. Therefore $S = 1$ and

(2) $\qquad \alpha'x + \alpha T(x) + \beta' = T(\alpha x + \beta).$

The degree r of T is 1: For, if it were greater than 1, we would

have $\alpha = \alpha^r$ and

$$\alpha' + \alpha T_x(0) = \alpha T_x(\beta)$$

by (2), which is impossible. Thus

$$x' = a + bx, \quad a, b \in K$$

and the ideal $\wp$ in its ring is closed under the differentiation:

$$(1/x)' = -a(1/x)^2 - b(1/x).$$

We have

$$\alpha'x + \alpha(a + bx) + \beta' = a + b(\alpha x + \beta),$$

whence

$$\alpha' = 0, \quad \alpha a + \beta' = a + b\beta.$$

If $\alpha \neq 1$ for some Φ, we set

$$t = x - \gamma, \quad \gamma = (1 - \alpha)^{-1}\beta,$$

which satisfies $t' = bt$ because $\gamma' = a + b\gamma$. If $\alpha = 1$ for any Φ,

then $\beta \neq 0$ for some Φ and we set $t = x/\beta$, which satisfies $t' = a/\beta$

because $\beta' = \beta$.

Suppose that R is a Riccati field over K of characteristic 0:
$R = K(x)$ with

(3) $\qquad x' = T(x) = a + bx + cx^2, \quad a, b, c \in K.$

If a differential automorphism Φ of R over K which is not the iden-

tity leaves the pole $\wp$ of x fixed, the ideal $\wp$ in its ring is closed under the differentiation: For, we have by (2)

$$\alpha' = 2c\alpha\beta, \qquad \alpha^r = \alpha, \quad r = \deg T,$$

whence $c = 0$ and $r = 1$. We shall prove the following:

Theorem 13. Let R be a differential algebraic function field of one variable of genus 0 over the coefficient field K of characteristic 0. If the group of differential automorphisms of R over K is infinite, then there is an overfield L of K of finite degree such that the differential field $R(L)$ deduced from R by adjoining the elements of L to K takes the form $L(t)$ with t' or $t'/t \in L$.

We denote by R_1 the differential field deduced from R by adjoining the elements of the algebraic closure K_1 of K to K. The group $\mathcal{J}$ of those differential automorphisms of R_1 over K_1 which are the extensions of differential automorphisms of R over K is infinite (§12). The set of those places in R_1 such that their rings are not closed under the differentiation is finite by Theorem 11 (§12). We see that it is empty: For if it were not empty, there would be a place in R_1 such that infinitely many elements of $\mathcal{J}$ leave it fixed, but it is impossible by the above arguments. Therefore R_1 has no movable singularity, and by Theorem 4 (§4) R has no movable singularity. We may assume that R has a place of degree 1. By Theorem 3 (§3) R is a Riccati field over K: $R = K(x)$ with (3). If an element Ψ of $\mathcal{J}$ does not leave the pole $\mathfrak{p}$ of x fixed, it takes the form

$$\Psi(x) = (\alpha x + \beta)/(\gamma x + \partial), \quad \alpha, \beta, \gamma, \partial \in K, \quad \gamma \neq 0:$$

A root σ of the quadratic equation

$$\gamma\sigma^2 + (\gamma - \alpha)\gamma - \beta = 0$$

is a solution of (3): For a place Ω in R_1 which is a zero of $x - \sigma$ is left fixed by Ψ and the ideal Ω in its ring is closed under the differentiation by the above arguments. The set Λ of those places $\mathcal{P}*$ in R_1 such that the ideal $\mathcal{P}*$ in its ring is closed under the differentiation is not empty: For if an element of $\mathcal{G}$ which is not the identity leaves $\mathcal{p}$ fixed then the ideal $\mathcal{p}$ in its ring is closed under the differentiation. If Λ is finite, there is a place $\mathcal{P}*$ in R_1 such that infinitely many elements of $\mathcal{G}$ leave $\mathcal{P}*$ fixed. We have a subfield L of K_1 which is of finite degree over K such that the place in R(L) which lies below $\mathcal{P}*$ is of degree 1. By the above arguments R(L) takes the required form. In case Λ is infinite, there are in K_1 infinitely many solutions of (3). If σ_1, σ_2, σ_3 are solutions of (3) in K_1 different from each other, the element of R_1 defined by

$$(x - \sigma_1)/(x - \sigma_2):(\sigma_3 - \sigma_1)/(\sigma_3 - \sigma_2)$$

is a constant(§6, p.31). We may take $K(\sigma_1, \sigma_2, \sigma_3)$ for L.

Remark. Let k be a differential field of characteristic 0 and k_1 be a differential extension field of k with the same field of constants: If an element t of k_1 which is algebraic over k satisfies t' or t'/t $\in$ k, then we have t $\in$ k or $t^n \in$ k accordingly, where n is the degree of k(t) over k. It is well known and can be proved without difficulty, whence if R and K have the same field of constants then we can take K itself for L. This result is due to E. R. Kolchin [1, p.809]. His theorem is stated in the general case of partial differential field.

In case of positive characteristic p, there is an example of R of genus 0 which has movable singularity although R admits infinitely many differential automorphisms over the coefficient field K. Assume for instance that P is a differential field of characteristic p which contains an element ξ whose derivative is 1 and that $R = K(x)$ with $x' = x^p$, where K is the subfield of the algebraic closure of P of those elements which are separable over P. A $(p - 1)$th root α of $\{(1 - p)(\xi + c)\}^{-1}$ with a constant c of K satisfies $\alpha' = \alpha^p$, whence an automorphism Ψ of R over K defined by $\Psi(x) = x + \alpha$ is a differential one:

$$\Psi(x)' = x' + \alpha' = x^p + \alpha^p = (x + \alpha)^p = \Psi(x').$$

If $p > 2$, R has movable singularities by Theorem 2 (§3). In case $p = 2$, we have a required example if $p(= 2)$ is replaced by $p^2(= 4)$.

§15. Weierstrass points

Let R be an algebraic function field of one variable over an <u>algebraically</u> <u>closed</u> field K of <u>characteristic</u> <u>zero</u>. If α is a divisor in R we denote by $\mathcal{L}(\alpha)$ the space of those elements x of R which are $\equiv 0 \pmod{\alpha}$: It is a linear space over K of finite dimension which is denoted by $\ell(\alpha)$ ([C, p.21]). If the genus of R is g we have the theorem of Riemann-Roch ([C, p.33]):

(1) $\qquad \ell(\alpha^{-1}) = d(\alpha) - g + 1 + \ell(\alpha\delta^{-1})$,

where $d(\alpha)$ is the degree of α, while δ is the divisor of a differential $\omega (\neq 0)$ of R. Since K is assumed to be algebraically closed, any place $\wp$ in R is of degree 1. By (1)

$\qquad \ell(\wp^{-m}) = m - g + 1 + \ell(\wp^m \delta^{-1})$

with a positive integer m. We have

$\qquad 0 \leq \ell(\wp^{-m}) - \ell(\wp^{-m+1}) = 1 + \ell(\wp^m \delta^{-1}) - \ell(\wp^{m-1}\delta^{-1})$,

which is either 0 or 1 because

(2) $\qquad \ell(\wp^{m-1}\delta^{-1}) \geq \ell(\wp^m\delta^{-1})$.

If m > 2g - 1, then the equality holds in (2) ([C, p.32]) and

$\qquad \ell(\wp^{-m}) - \ell(\wp^{-m+1}) = 1$.

Therefore, we obtain

$\qquad 1 = \ell(\wp^0) \leq \ell(\wp^{-1}) \leq \dots \leq \ell(\wp^{1-2g}) < \ell(\wp^{-2g}) < \dots$.

By (1)

$\qquad \ell(\wp^{1-2g}) = 2g - 1 - g + 1 + 0 = g$:

The number of those m such that the equality

(3) $\qquad \ell(\wp^{-m+1}) = \ell(\wp^{-m})$

holds is equal to g. This equality holds if and only if any el-

elemt u of R does not satisfy

$$u \equiv 0 \,(\text{mod } \wp^{-m}), \quad v_{\wp}(u) = -m.$$

We have

$$1 = \ell(\wp^{-1}) = \ldots = \ell(\wp^{-g})$$

if and only if $\ell(\wp^{-g}) = 1$.

A place $\wp$ in R is a __Weierstrass__ __point__ of R if $\ell(\wp^{-g}) > 1$.

By definition there is no Weierstrass point of R if the genus of R is 0.

Every differential of R takes the form $x\omega$ with an element x of R([C, p.31]), and

$$\delta(x\omega) = \delta(x)\,\delta(\omega),$$

where $\delta(x)$ is the divisor of x([C, p.32]): We have

$$v_{\wp}(x\omega) = v_{\wp}(x) + v_{\wp}(\omega).$$

Since K is algebraically closed, x is represented in the form

$$x = \Sigma a_i t^i, \quad d \leq i < \infty, \quad a_i \in K, \quad a_d \neq 0, \quad d = v_{\wp}(x)$$

with a uniformizing variable t at $\wp$ in the $\wp$-adic completion $\bar{R}$ of R. The space of differentials of the first kind of R is a linear space over K of dimension g([C, p.30]). We may take a base $(\omega_1, \ldots, \omega_g)$ of this space with respect to K such that

$$v_{\wp}(\omega_1) < \ldots < v_{\wp}(\omega_g).$$

If we set

$$v_{\wp}(\omega_i) = \rho_i - 1, \quad 1 \leq i \leq g,$$

then the equality (3) holds if and only if m is equal to one of $\rho_1, \ldots, \rho_g$: For the equality (3) holds if and only if

$$\ell(\wp^{m-1}\delta^{-1}) > \ell(\wp^m \delta^{-1}):$$

It holds if and only if there is an element u of R such that

$$u \equiv 0 \pmod{\mathfrak{p}^{m-1}\delta^{-1}}, \qquad \not\equiv 0 \pmod{\mathfrak{p}^m \delta^{-1}};$$

it is possible if and only if $u\omega$ is a differential of the first kind such that $v_{\mathfrak{p}}(u\omega) = m - 1$. Thus, $\mathfrak{p}$ is a Weierstrass point of R if and only if $\rho_g > g$.

If u is an element of R which is not in K, the exact differential du is not 0 ([C, p.108]). Every differential ω^* of R takes the form ydu with an element y of R which is uniquely determined. We represent y by ω^*/du. Inductively let us define elements $y_{ij} (1 \leq i, j \leq g)$ of R by

$$y_{i1} = \omega_i/du, \qquad y_{ij} = dy_{i,j-1}/du$$

and denote

$$\det (y_{ij}), \quad 1 \leq i, j \leq g$$

by $\Delta(u)$, which is an element of R. If v is another element of R which is not in K, then

(4) $\qquad \Delta(u) = (dv/du)^{g(g+1)/2} \Delta(v):$

For, we have

$$y_{ij} = D_u^{j-1} y_{i1}, \quad 1 \leq i, j \leq g$$

with the derivation D_u of R with respect to u([C, p.116]): If

$$z_{ij} = D_v^{j-1} z_{i1}, \quad z_{i1} = \omega_i/dv$$

with the derivation of R with respect to v, then

$$y_{ij} = \Sigma w_{jh} z_{ih}, \quad 1 \leq h \leq j,$$

where $w_{jh} (1 \leq j \leq g, 1 \leq h \leq j)$ is determined inductively by

$$w_{11} = dv/du,$$

$$w_{j+1,h} = dw_{jh}/du + w_{j,h-1}(dv/du), \quad 1 < h \leq j,$$

$$w_{j+1,1} = dw_{j1}/du,$$

whence $w_{jj} = (dv/du)^j$, $1 \le j \le g$ (cf. [C, p.118]). A uniformizing variable t at $\wp$ satisfies $v_{\wp}(dt) = 0$ (§5, p.23). If ω_i takes the form $x_i dt$ with an element x_i of R, then

$$\Delta(t) = \det(D_t^j x_i), \quad 1 \le i \le g, \; 0 \le j < g$$

with the derivation D_t of R with respect to t. In $\bar{R}$ we have

$$x_i = \Sigma c_{ih} t^h, \quad \rho_i - 1 \le h < \infty, \quad c_{ih} \in K, \quad c_{i,\rho_i-1} \ne 0$$

and

$$D_t^j x_i = \Sigma c_{ih} D_t^j t^h,$$

whence

(5) $\qquad v_{\wp}(\Delta(t)) = - g(g+1)/2 + \Sigma \rho_i, \quad 1 \le i \le g:$

For, the following identity in t holds:

$$\det(D_t^j t^{\lambda_i}), \quad 1 \le i \le g, \; 0 \le j < g$$
$$= \Pi(\lambda_i - \lambda_j) t^{m(\lambda)}, \quad 1 \le i < j \le g,$$
$$m(\lambda) = \lambda_1 + \lambda_2 - 1 + \ldots + \lambda_g - g + 1 = - g(g-1)/2 + \Sigma \lambda_i,$$

where $\lambda_1, \ldots, \lambda_g$ are integers. The number (5) is a non negative integer which does not depend on the choice of a uniformizing variable t at $\wp$: It vanishes if and only if $\rho_i = i$, $1 \le i \le g$. Replacing v by t in (4) we have

$$v_{\wp}(\Delta(u)) = - \{g(g+1)/2\} v_{\wp}(du) + h(\wp),$$

where $h(\wp)$ is the number (5):

$$h(\wp) = - g(g+1)/2 + \Sigma \rho_i, \quad 1 \le i \le g.$$

The following equalities hold:

$$\delta(\Delta(u)) = \Sigma v_{\wp}(\Delta(u)) = 0$$

([C, p.18]) and

$$\delta(du) = \Sigma v_{\wp}(du) = 2g - 2$$

([C, p.32]), where $\wp$ runs over all places in R. Thus,

$$\Sigma h(\wp) = (g - 1)g(g + 1)$$

which is finite, and $h(\wp)$ is positive if and only if $\wp$ is a Weierstrass point of R: We have obtained the following theorem:

The number of Weierstrass points of R is finite and it is positive if the genus of R is greater than 1. In case R is an elliptic field there is no Weierstrass point of R.

Suppose that R is a hyperelliptic field: The subfield S generated by the ratios of differentials of R of the first kind is a proper subfield of R. The genus of S is 0 and R is of degree 2 over S([C, p.74]). There are exactly 2g + 2 places $\wp_1$, ... , $\wp_{2g+2}$ in R which are ramified with respect to S: We may express R in the form K(x, y) with

$$y^2 = \Pi(x - a_i), \quad 1 \le i \le 2g + 2, \quad a_i \in K, \quad a_i \neq a_j (i \neq j);$$

changing the indices if necessary we may assume that $\wp_i$ is a zero of $x - a_i$, $1 \le i \le 2g + 2$. The divisor of zeros of $x - a_i$ is $\wp_i^2$, whence $\mathcal{L}(\wp_i^{-2})$ contains $(x - a_i)^{-1}$ and $\wp_i$ is a Weierstrass point of R. We have $\rho_j = 2j - 1(1 \le j \le g)$ at $\wp_i$, since $\ell(\wp_i^{1-2g}) = g$. Threfore,

$$h(\wp_i) = -g(g + 1)/2 + \Sigma\rho_j, \quad 1 \le j \le g$$
$$= (g - 1)g/2$$

and the sum $\Sigma h(\wp_i)(1 \le i \le 2g + 2)$ attains $(g - 1)g(g + 1)$, whence the Weierstrass points of R are $\wp_i(1 \le i \le 2g + 2)$.

Assume that R is not a hyperelliptic field while the genus g of R is greater than 1. The divisor of poles of an element of R which is not in K is greater than 2([C, p.74]). Let $\wp$ be a

Weierstrass point of R: We denote by r the minimum of those m such that $\ell(\wp^{-m}) > 1$: There is an element u of $\mathcal{L}(\wp^{-r})$ such that $\wp$ is a pole of u of order r. If an element v of $\mathcal{L}(\wp^{-m})$ satisfies $v_{\wp}(v) = -m$, then $uv \in \mathcal{L}(\wp^{-r-m})$ and $v_{\wp}(uv) = -r - m$. Therefore the set of $\rho_1, \ldots, \rho_g$ is

$$1, \qquad 1 + r, \ldots, 1 + s_1 r,$$

$$2, \qquad 2 + r, \ldots, 2 + s_2 r,$$

$$\ldots\ldots$$

$$r - 1, \quad 2r - 1, \ldots, r - 1 + s_{r-1}r,$$

where $s_1, \ldots, s_{r-1}$ are non negative integers. If we set

$$t_i = i + s_i r, \quad 1 \le i < r,$$

then $t_i \le 2g - 1$ and

$$r(2g - r + 1)/2 = \Sigma t_i, \quad 1 \le i < r,$$

because

$$g = r - 1 + \Sigma s_i, \quad 1 \le i < r.$$

We have

$$h(\wp) = -g(g + 1)/2 + \Sigma\Sigma(i + jr), \quad 1 \le i < r, \quad 0 \le j \le s_i;$$

here

$$\Sigma(i + jr), \quad 0 \le j \le s_i$$

$$= (s_i + 1)(i + s_i r/2) = (t_i + i)(t_i + r - i)/(2r)$$

$$= (t_i^2 - i^2)/(2r) + t_i + i,$$

whence

$$\Sigma\Sigma(i + jr) = \Sigma t_i^2/(2r) - (r - 1)(2r - 1)/12$$

$$+ r(2g - r + 1)/4 + r(r - 1)/4.$$

Thus

$$h(\wp) = g(g - 1)/2 - (r - 1)(r - 2)/6 -$$

$$- \Sigma t_i (2g - 1 - t_i)/(2r), \quad 1 \leq i < r,$$

and

$$h(\wp) < g(g - 1)/2$$

because $r > 2$. If W is the number of Wieerstrass points of R, then

$$(g - 1)g(g + 1) = \Sigma h(\wp) < Wg(g - 1)/2,$$

whence $W > 2g + 2$. We have obtained the following theorem:

If the genus g of R is greater than 1, the number of Weierstrass points of R is greater than $2g + 2$ unless R is a hyperelliptic field. In the last case it is equal to $2g + 2$.

Let Φ be an automorphism of R over K. If Φ leaves every place in R fixed then it is the identity: For, if $\wp$ is a place in R, any element $z(\neq 0)$ of R satisfies

$$\nu_\wp(z) = \nu_{\Phi\wp}(z) = \nu_\wp(\Phi^{-1}z),$$

whence $z^{-1}\Phi^{-1}z$ is an element of K which we denote by $\phi(z)$: In case $z \in K$, $\phi(z) = z^{-1}z = 1$: If $z \notin K$, then

$$\Phi(z + 1) = \phi(z + 1)(z + 1) = \Phi(z) + 1 = \phi(z)z + 1,$$

whence $\phi(z) = \phi(z + 1) = 1$. If Φ leaves a place $\wp$ in R fixed, $\wp$ is a zero of $z - \Phi z$ for an integral element z at $\wp$: For, if c is the residue class of z modulo $\wp$, then

$$\nu_\wp(\Phi(z - c)) = \nu_{\Phi\wp}(z - c) = \nu_\wp(z - c) > 0,$$

whence

$$\nu_\wp(z - \Phi z) = \nu_\wp(z - c - \Phi(z - c)) > 0.$$

We shall prove that if Φ leaves r distinct places in R fixed with $r > 2g + 2$ then Φ is the identity. For a moment assume that there were a place $\mathfrak{p}$ in R such that $\Phi\mathfrak{p} \neq \mathfrak{p}$. We have an element z of R which is transcendental over K such that

$$z \equiv 0 \pmod{\mathfrak{p}^{-g-1}}$$

by the theorem of Riemann-Roch. If $w = z - \Phi z$, then $w \neq 0$ and its divisor of poles is $(\mathfrak{p}\Phi\mathfrak{p})^m$ with $m \leq g + 1$. The degree of zeros of w is 2m, but it is impossible because r distinct places in R are zeros of w according to the previous discussions.

The set of Weierstrass points of R is left invariant by Φ. If R is a hyperelliptic field then the subfield S of R is left invariant by Φ. The identity on S can be extended to an automorphism of R over K which differs from the identity in one and only way. There are exactly 2g + 2 places in S which lie below Weierstrass points, whence the group of automorphisms of R over K is finite because 2g + 2 > 3. In case R is not a hyperelliptic field, the number of Weierstrass points of R is greater than 2g + 2 if g > 1. We have obtained the following theorem:

The group of automorphisms of R over K is finite if the genus of R is greater than 1.

The arguments of this section are based on Hurwitz' work "Ueber algebraische Gebilde mit eindeutigen Transformationen in sich", Math. Ann. 41(1893), 403-442.

§16.   Clairaut fields of characteristic 0

Let R be an algebraic function field of one variable of characteristic 0.   We assume that the coefficient field K is algebraically closed and the genus g of R is positive.

Lemma 3.   The notation being as above, suppose that there are r distinct places $\wp_1, \ldots, \wp_r$ in R and r elements $u_1, \ldots, u_r$ of R such that $\wp_i$ is the only pole of $u_i (1 \le i \le r)$.   If r is at least equal to 2g + 2 then either R is of degree 2 over the subfield M generated by the u_i over K whose genus is 0 or R = M.

If $\mathcal{Z}_i$ is the place in M which lies below $\wp_i$, then

$$\mathrm{Con}_{M/R} \mathcal{Z}_i = \wp_i^e, \quad e = [R : M]$$

because $\mathcal{Z}_i$ is a pole of u_i in M and $\wp_i$ is its only pole in R. The differential exponent of $\wp_i$ with respect to M is e - 1, whence

$$g - 1 \ge e(g_0 - 1) + r(e - 1)/2,$$

where g_0 is the genus of M([C, p.106]).   By our assumption that $r \ge 2g + 2$ we have $g \ge (e - 1)g + eg_0$, whence either e = 2 and $g_0 = 0$ or e = 1 because $g > 0$.

We shall prove the following theorem which is due to K. Nishioka [7]:

Theorem 14.   Let R be a differential algebraic function field of one variable over K of characteristic 0.   Assume that the genus g of R is greater than 1.   Then R is a Clairaut field over K if R has no movable singularity.

Since $g > 1$, there are r Weierstrass points $\wp_1, \ldots, \wp_r$ of R with $r \geq 2g + 2 (\S15)$. If $\wp = \wp_1$, we have a positive integer n which is at most equal to g such that

(1) $\qquad 1 = \ell(\wp^{1-n}) < \ell(\wp^{-n}) = \ell(\wp^{-n-1}) = 2$

($\S15$): Take an element u of $\mathcal{L}(\wp^{-n})$ which is not in K. By our assumption that R has no movable singularity, $\wp$ is the only pole of the derivative u'. In the $\wp$-adic completion $\bar{R}$ of R, u may be represented in the form $u = t^{-n}$ with a uniformizing variable t at $\wp$. We have $\nu_\wp(t') \geq 0$ and $u' \in \mathcal{L}(\wp^{-n-1})$ because $u' = - nt^{-n-1}t'$. By (1) u' belongs to $\mathcal{L}(\wp^{-n})$, whence $\nu_\wp(t') > 0$ and the ideal $\wp$ in its ring is closed under the differentiation. The linear space $\mathcal{L}(\wp^{-n})$ is spanned by 1 and u over K, and

$$u' = a + bu, \qquad a, b \in K.$$

If $\mathcal{E}_i$ is the residue class of u modulo $\wp_i (i \neq 1)$, then

$$\mathcal{E}'_i = a + b\mathcal{E}_i$$

because the ideal $\wp_i$ in its ring is closed under the differentiation. The degree of the divisor of zeros of $u - \mathcal{E}_2$ is n, which satisfies

$$n \leq g < 2g + 1 \leq r - 1,$$

whence there is an index $j (\neq 2)$ such that $\wp_j$ is not a zero of $u - \mathcal{E}_2$. We set

$$w = (u - \mathcal{E}_2)/(\mathcal{E}_j - \mathcal{E}_2),$$

which is a constant ($\S6$, p.31). Thus there are constants $w_1, \ldots, w_r$ of R such that $\wp_i$ is the only pole of $w_i (1 \leq i \leq r)$. By Lemma 3, if $M = K(w_1, \ldots, w_r)$, either R is of degree 2 over M whose genus is 0 or R = M. In the latter case R is a Clairaut field over K.

In the former case M takes the form K(x) and R = K(x, y) with

$$y^2 = \prod(x - \beta_i), \quad 1 \leqq i \leqq 2g + 2, \quad \beta_i \in K, \quad \beta_i \neq \beta_j (i \neq j).$$

The Weierstrass point $\wp_1$ of R is a zero of $x - \beta_i$ for some i (§15).
We have n = 2 and $(x - \beta_i)^{-1} \in \mathcal{L}(\wp^{-2})$, whence it is a linear
combination of 1 and w over K. Therefore, R = K(w, z) with

$$z^2 = \prod(w - \alpha_j), \quad 2 \leqq j \leqq 2g + 2.$$

Places in R which are zeros of the $w - \alpha_j$ are Weierstrass points
of R (§15), and the α_j are constants because w' = 0, whence z is
a constant.

If K is not algebraically closed, there is an example of R
whose genus is greater than 1 such that R is not a Clairaut field
over K while R has no movable singularity. Assume for instance
that R = K(x, y) with

$$y^2 = x^s - u, \quad s = \text{odd} > 3,$$

where K = P(u) with a differential field P of characteristic 0
which consists of constants, while u is transcendental over P.
If we define u' = 2su, x' = 2x, then R is a differential algebraic
function field of one variable over K. The genus g of R is (s-1)/2
(§5, p.24) which is greater than 1. We have y' = sy, and if $\wp$ is
a place in R which is neither a zero nor a pole of y the ring $\mathcal{O}$
of $\wp$ is closed under the differentiation. In case $\wp$ is a pole
of y, an uniformizing variable t at $\wp$ is given by $t = x^g y^{-1}$,
which satisfies

$$t' = gx^{g-1}x'y^{-1} - x^g y^{-2}y' = (2g - s)t,$$

whence $\mathcal{O}$ is closed under the differentiation. If $\wp$ is a zero

of y, y is a uniformizing variable at $\wp$ and $\diamondsuit$ is closed under
the differentiation. Thus R has no movable singularity. We have
$K(R_0) = R_0(u)$, where R_0 is the field of constants of R. The
element y is not in $K(R_0)$: For, if y were in $K(R_0)$, it would be
a rational function $\phi(u)$ over R_0, whence it would follow that

$$1 = y'/(sy) = u' \cdot \phi_u(u)/(s \phi(u)) = 2u \cdot \phi_u(u)/ \phi(u),$$

but it is impossible. Therefore, R is not a Clairaut field over K.

In case of positive characteristic, if the coefficient field
K is perfect then the genus of R which has no movable singularity
is either 0 or 1 by Theorem 5 (§5) unless R consists of constants:
If K is not perfect, there is an example of R whose genus is greater
than 1 such that R is not a Clairaut field while it has no movable
singularity (§5).

§17. Movable singularities in case of characteristic 0

Let R be a differential algebraic function field of one variable over the coefficient field K of characteristic 0. If $\mathfrak{p}$ is a place in R, an element $u(\neq 0)$ of the $\mathfrak{p}$-adic completion $\bar{R}$ of R may be represented in the form

$$u = \Sigma a_i \tau^i, \quad d \leq i < \infty, \quad a_i \in \Sigma, \quad d = \nu_{\mathfrak{p}}(u), \quad a_d \neq 0$$

with a uniformizing variable τ at $\mathfrak{p}$, where Σ is the subfield of $\bar{R}$ containing K which is a system of representatives for the elements of the residue field of $\mathfrak{p}$ ([C, p.46]): The subfield Σ is closed under the differentiation.

Suppose that the ring $\mathcal{O}$ of $\mathfrak{p}$ is not closed under the differentiation. The negative integer $\nu_{\mathfrak{p}}(\tau')$ does not depend on the choice of an uniformizing variable τ at $\mathfrak{p}$ (§2, p.9). We set

$$r = -\nu_{\mathfrak{p}}(\tau') + 1,$$

which is a positive integer greater than 1. A __R-variable__ at $\mathfrak{p}$ is a uniformizing variable t at $\mathfrak{p}$ which satisfies

(1) $\quad t' = \gamma t^{1-r}, \quad \gamma \in \Sigma.$

We prove the existence of a R-variable at $\mathfrak{p}$, which is due to M. Rosenlicht [9]. In $\bar{R}$ we have

$$\tau' = \Sigma \gamma_i \tau^i, \quad 1 - r \leq i < \infty, \quad \gamma_i \in \Sigma, \quad \gamma_{1-r} \neq 0.$$

Take a uniformizing variable t at $\mathfrak{p}$:

$$t = \Sigma a_i \tau^i, \quad 1 \leq i < \infty, \quad a_i \in \Sigma, \quad a_1 \neq 0.$$

Its derivative t' is

$$\Sigma a_i' \tau^i + \tau' \Sigma i a_i \tau^{i-1} = \Sigma \alpha_i \tau^i, \quad 1 - r \leq i < \infty,$$

$$\alpha_i = a_i' + \Sigma h a_h \gamma_{i+1} - h$$

with $a_{1-r} = \ldots = a_0 = 0$. We have

$$t^{r-1} = \Sigma \beta_i \tau^i, \quad r - 1 \leq i < \infty,$$

$$\beta_i = \Sigma a_{j_1} \cdot \ldots \cdot a_{j_{r-1}}, \quad j_1 + \ldots + j_{r-1} = i$$

and

(2) $\qquad t^{r-1}t' = \Sigma (\Sigma \alpha_j \beta_{i-j}) \tau^i, \quad 0 \leq i < \infty$:

Here,

$$\alpha_{1-r} = a_1 \gamma_{1-r}, \quad \beta_{r-1} = a_1^{r-1}:$$

If $j < i - r$, then α_j does not contain a_i nor a_i', and

$$\alpha_{i-r} = i a_i \gamma_{1-r} + A_i,$$

where A_i does not contain a_i nor a_i': If $h < i + r - 2$, then β_h does not contain a_i, and

$$\beta_{i+r-2} = r a_1^{r-2} a_i + B_i$$

where B_i does not contain a_i. Therefore, if $j < i - 1$, the coefficient of τ^j in (2) does not contain a_i nor a_i': The coefficient of τ^{i-1} in (2) is

$$(r + i) a_1^{r-1} a_i + C_i,$$

where C_i does not contain a_i nor a_i'. If t is a R-variable at $\mathcal{P}$, then

(3) $\qquad (r + i) a_1^{r-1} a_i + C_i = 0, \quad i > 1.$

Conversely the element t of $\bar{R}$ defined by (3) with $a_1 \neq 0$ is a R-variable at $\mathcal{P}$.

Suppose that τ and t are R-variables at $\mathcal{P}$: $\gamma_i = 0$, $i > 1 - r$. Then, $A_i = a_{i-r}'$ and $C_2 = 0$, whence $a_2 = 0$. Inductively we have

$$a_i = 0, \quad 2 < i \leq r,$$

$$\alpha_i = 0, \quad 1 - r < i \leq 0, \quad \beta_i = 0, \quad r - 1 < i \leq 2r - 2$$

and

$$\alpha_1 = a' + (r + 1)\gamma_{1-r}a_{r+1}, \qquad \beta_{2r-1} = a_1^{r-2}a_{r+1}.$$

By successive induction we obtain

$$a_i = 0, \quad i \not\equiv 1 \pmod{r}.$$

Therefore,

$$t = \tau\Sigma a_{ir+1}\tau^{ir}, \quad 0 \le i < \infty;$$

here

$$a'_{ir+1} + \{1 + (i + 1)r\}\gamma_{1-r}a_{(i+1)r+1} = 0.$$

We denote by $S(\wp)$ the set of those elements x of R such that

$$x = \Sigma b_i t^{ir}, \quad b_i \in \Sigma$$

in $\bar{R}$ with a R-variable t at $\wp$: It does not depend on the choice of a R-variable t at $\wp$ and it is a subfield of R which contains K. If t satisfies (1) then

$$x' = \Sigma b'_i t^{ir} + t'\cdot\Sigma irb_i t^{ir-1} = \Sigma b'_i t^{ir} + \gamma\Sigma irb_i t^{(i-1)r},$$

whence $S(\wp)$ is closed under the differentiation. A constant w of R is contained in $S(\wp)$: For, if

$$w = \Sigma b_i t^i, \quad d \le i < \infty, \quad b_i \in \Sigma, \quad b_d \ne 0,$$

then

$$0 = w' = \Sigma b'_i t^i + t'\Sigma ib_i t^{i-1},$$

whence $d = 0$, $b_1 = \ldots = b_{r-1} = 0$ and

$$b'_i + (r + i)b_{r+i} = 0.$$

Inductively we have

$$b_i = 0, \quad i \not\equiv 0 \pmod{r}$$

and

$$b'_{(e-1)r} + erb_{er} = 0, \quad e \ge 1.$$

We define

$$P(R) = \bigcap S(\wp),$$

where $\wp$ runs over all places in R whose rings are not closed under the differentiation. It is a differential subfield of R which contains $K(R_0)$, where R_0 is the field of constants of R. If R has no movable singularity, $P(R) = R$. In case $P(R)$ contains K properly we may consider it as a differential algebraic function field of one variable over K, and it has no movable singularity: For, if $\wp$ is the place in $P(R)$ which lies below a place $\wp$ in R whose ring is not closed under the differentiation, a uniformizing variable u at $\wp$ is expressed in the form

$$u = \Sigma b_i t^{ir}, \quad 1 \leq i < \infty, \quad b_i \in \Sigma$$

in $\bar{R}$ with a R-variable t at $\wp$. If t satisfies (1) then

$$u' = \Sigma b_i' t^{ir} + \gamma \Sigma irb_i t^{(i-1)r},$$

whence u' is integral at $\wp$. We shall prove the following:

Theorem 15. Let R be a differential algebraic function field of one variable over the coefficient field K of characteristic 0, and L be a differential extension field of K. If $P(R) = K$ then $P(R(L)) = L$, where $R(L)$ is the differential field deduced from R by adjoining the elements of L to K. In case $P(R) \neq K$ we have

$$P(R(L)) = (P(R))(L),$$

where the right side is the differential field deduced from $P(R)$ by adjoining the elements of L to K.

The two fields R and L are linearly disjoint over K in $R(L)$ ([C, p.90]), whence $(P(R))(L)$ is generated by $P(R)$ and L if $P(R) \neq K$ ([C, p.81]). Let $\wp$ be a place in $R(L)$. If $\wp$ is variable with respect to R, the ring of $\wp$ is closed under the differentiation (§4, pp.20-21). If $\wp$ is fixed with respect to R, it is unramified with respect to R([C, p.92]). Suppose that the ring of $\mathscr{P}$ is not closed under the differentiation. Then the ring of the place $\wp$ in R which lies below $\mathscr{P}$ is not closed under the differentiation(§4, pp.19-20). If t is a R-variable at $\wp$, it is a R-variable at $\mathscr{P}$. Therefore P(R(L)) contains P(R). Suppose that $\wp$ is a place in R whose ring is not closed under the differentiation and take a R-variable t at $\wp$. If w is an element of $\bar{R}$ of the form $\Sigma a_i t^i$, $a_i \in \Sigma$ then we define $\bar{w} = \Sigma a_{ir} t^{ir} \in \bar{R}$. By definition $w \in S(\wp)$ if and only if $\bar{w} = w$. If $x(\neq 0)$ is an element of R(L), it may be expressed in the form

$$x = \Sigma a_i u_i / \Sigma b_j v_j \quad (1 \leq i \leq q, \ 1 \leq j \leq s),$$

$$a_i, \ b_j \in L, \quad u_i, \ v_j \in R, \quad v_s = 1,$$

where the a_i are linearly independent over R. We may assume that our expression of x has the minimal s in those expressions of x. By T we denote the subfield of R(L) generated by R and the a_i, b_j, which is not necessarily closed under the differentiation. In the Kronecker product $T \otimes \bar{R}$ over R we have

$$\Sigma a_i u_i - x \Sigma b_j v_j = 0.$$

Let us consider T as an algebraic function field of one variable over K. If $\bar{\mathscr{P}}_1, \ldots, \bar{\mathscr{P}}_h$ are the distinct places in T which lie above $\wp$, we may identify $T \otimes \bar{R}$ with the product of the $\bar{\mathscr{P}}_\lambda$-adic completions $\bar{T}_\lambda$ of $T(1 \leq \lambda \leq h)$([C, p.60]). Suppose that x belongs to P(R(L)). Then for each $\bar{\mathscr{P}}_\lambda$ x belongs to $S(\bar{\mathscr{P}}_\lambda)$, where $\mathscr{P}_\lambda$ is a place in R(L) which lies above $\bar{\mathscr{P}}_\lambda$, and we have $\Sigma a_i \bar{u}_i - x \Sigma b_j \bar{v}_j = 0$ in $\bar{T}_\lambda$. It holds in $T \otimes \bar{R}$ because each of its λ-component vanishes. Thus,

$$\Sigma a_i(u_i - \bar{u}_i) - x\Sigma b_j(v_j - \bar{v}_j) = 0$$

in $T \otimes \bar{R}$; here we have $v_s - \bar{v}_s = 0$ because $v_s = 1$. By our assumption on s,

(4) $\qquad a_1, \ldots, a_q, xb_1, \ldots, xb_{s-1}$

are linearly independent over R, since the a_i are linearly independent over R. By the definition of Kronecker product the members of (4) are linearly independent over $\bar{R}$, whence

$$u_i = \bar{u}_i, \quad v_j = \bar{v}_j, \quad 1 \le i \le q, \ 1 \le j < s.$$

Therefore, $P(R(L))$ is contained in the subfield of $R(L)$ generated by $P(R)$ and L.

Let R be an algebraic function field of one variable of characteristic 0 and T be a subfield of R which contains the coefficient field K of R. Let us indicate that if L is an overfield of K then $R \cap T(L) = T$, where $T(L)$ is a subfield of $R(L)$ generated by T and L, while $R(L)$ is the field deduced from R by adjoining the elements of L to K. If $x(\ne 0)$ is an element of $T(L)$, it is expressed in the form

$$x = \Sigma a_i u_i / \Sigma b_j v_j \ (1 \le i \le q, \ 1 \le j \le s),$$
$$a_i, b_j \in L, \quad u_i, v_j \in T,$$

where the u_i are linearly independent over K. In the Kronecker product $R \otimes L$ over K we have

$$\Sigma a_i u_i - x\Sigma b_j v_j = 0.$$

If x belongs to R then $u_1, \ldots, u_q, xv_1, \ldots, xv_s$ are linearly dependent over K in $R \otimes L$, whence x belongs to T.

We shall prove the following:

Theorem 16. Let R be a differential algebraic function field of one variable over the coefficient field K of characteristic 0, and T be a differential subfield of R which contains K properly. If T has no movable singularity then it is contained in P(R).

By Theorems 7(§6), 10(§9), 14(§16) there is a differential extension field L of K such that the differential field T(L) deduced from T by adjoining the elements of L to K is a Clairaut field over L. We may consider it as a subfield of R(L) generated by T and L, where R(L) is the differential field deduced from R by adjoining the elements of L to K. If T_0 and R_0 represent the fields of constants of T and R respectively, then P(R(L)) contains $L(R_0)$, whence

$$P(R(L)) \supset L(T_0) = T(L).$$
By Theorem 15 we have
$$P(R(L)) = (P(R))(L):$$
Therefore,
$$P(R) = R \cap P(R)(L) \supset R \cap T(L) = T$$
according to the previous arguments.

This theorem was proved by K. Nishioka [8] in case K is algebraically closed.

By Theorem 1(§2) any differential subfield of P(R) which contains K properly has no movable singularity. Thus we have the following:

Cororally. Let R be a differential algebraic function field

of one variable of characteristic 0, and R_1, R_2 be differential subfields of R which contain properly the coefficient field K of R. If R_1, R_2 have no movable singularity then the subfield of R generated by R_1 and R_2 have no movable singularity.

This is valid only in case of the characteristic 0 (§6, p. 30).

In case of positive characteristic p, there is an example of R which has a place $\wp$ such that a R-variable at $\wp$ does not exist. Assume for instance that $R = K(x)$ with

$$x' = x^{-p} + x^{p-1}$$

and K is algebraically closed. If a place $\wp$ in R is a zero of x, the ring of $\wp$ is not closed under the differentiation. A uniformizing variable t at $\wp$ is expressed in the form

$$t = \Sigma a_i x^i, \quad 1 \leq i < \infty, \quad a_i \in K, \quad a_1 \neq 0.$$

In this case $r = p + 1$ and

$$t^p t' = (\Sigma a_i x^i)^p (\Sigma i a_i x^{i-1})(x^{-p} + x^{p-1})$$

$$= (\Sigma a_i^p x^{ip-p})(\Sigma i a_i x^{i-1})(1 + x^{2p-1}).$$

The coefficient of x^{2p-1} in the right side is a_1^{p+1} because the coefficient of x^{p-1} in $\Sigma i a_i x^{i-1}$ vanishes, whence t is not a R-variable at $\wp$.

§18. Differential Lefschetz principle

In differential algebra we have an analog of Lefschetz principle for algebraic geometry("Algebraic geometry"(Appendix, p.224) by Lefschetz(Princeton Univ. Press, Princeton, 1953)) due to A. Seidenberg, Abstract differential algebra and the analytic case, Proc. Amer. Math. Soc., 9(1958), 159-164; II, ibidem, 23 (1969), 689-691:

Let k be a differential field of characteristic 0. If $(z_1, \ldots, z_m)$ is an indexed set of elements of k, there is an indexed set $(\zeta_1(x), \ldots, \zeta_m(x))$ of holomorphic functions of a single variable x at the origin O of the complex plane which is a generic differential specialization of $(z_1, \ldots, z_m)$ over the field of rational numbers Q.

In the following proof we presuppose the reader a familiarity with the contents of the first two chapters of the book "Differential algebra" by Ritt(Amer. Math. Soc. Colloq. Publ. Vol.33, New York, 1950). We shall state the notion of resolvent: Let Σ be a non trivial prime differential ideal in

$$Q\{u_1, \ldots, u_q, y_1, \ldots, y_p\},$$

where $(u_1, \ldots, u_q)$ is a parametric set for Σ with $q > 0$. There is a prime differential ideal Λ in

$$Q\{u_1, \ldots, u_q, w, y_1, \ldots, y_p\}$$

with a new indeterminate w which satisfies the following conditions:

(i) $\Lambda \cap Q\{u_1, \ldots, u_q, y_1, \ldots, y_p\} = \Sigma;$

(ii) Λ has a characteristic set A, A_1, ... , A_p in the order u_1, ... , u_q, w, y_1, ... , y_p such that A is algebraically irreducible element of $Q\{u_1,$ ... , $u_q,$ w$\}$ and A_i is expressed in the form $P_iy_i + Q_i$, where P_i, $Q_i \in Q\{u_1,$ ... , $u_q,$ w$\}$ and $P_i \neq 0$.

Because of (i), $(u_1,$ ... , $u_q)$ is a parametric set of Λ and A contains w. By (ii) P_i, Q_i are reduced with respect to A and their orders with respect to w are not greater than that of A. If $(u_1^*,$ ... , $u_q^*,$ w^*, y_1^*, ... , $y_p^*)$ is a generic zero of Λ over Q then $(u_1^*,,...,$ $u_q^*,$ y_1^*, ... , $y_p^*)$ is a generic zero of Σ over Q by (i). The equation A = 0 is called a resolvent of Σ.

Suppose that Σ is the prime differential ideal in $Q\{v_1,$ ... , $v_m\}$ consisting of all differential polynomials over Q which vanish at $(z_1,$ ... , $z_m)$. First we assume that Σ is the zero ideal. The set of all nonzero elements of $Q\{v_1,$ ... , $v_m\}$ is countable, whence there are complex numbers a_{ij} $(1 \leq i \leq m,$ $0 \leq j < \infty)$ such that $|a_{ij}| < 1$ and the replacement

$$v_i^{(j)} = a_{ij} \ (1 \leq i \leq m, \ 0 \leq j < \infty)$$

does not annihilate any nonzero element of $Q\{v_1,$ ... , $v_m\}$. We set

$$\zeta_i(x) = \Sigma a_{ij}x^j/j! \ (0 \leq j < \infty), \quad 1 \leq i \leq m,$$

which is an integral function of x. They satisfy

$$d^j\zeta_i/dx^j (0) = a_{ij}$$

and

$$F(\zeta_1(x), \ ... \ , \ \zeta_m(x)) \neq 0$$

if F is a nonzero differential polynomials of the v_i over Q, because $F(\zeta_1(0),$ ... , $\zeta_m(0)) \neq 0$.

Next we assume that Σ is not the zero ideal. Let us divide the v_i into the two sets $u_1, \ldots, u_q; y_1, \ldots, y_p$ such that the former is a parametric set for Σ. It may be assumed that $q > 0$: For, if $q = 0$ we adjoin an indeterminate z_0 to $z_1, \ldots, z_m$ and extend $(v_1, \ldots, v_m)$ to $(v_0, \ldots, v_m)$. Let Λ be a prime differential ideal in $Q\{u_1, \ldots, u_q, w, y_1, \ldots, y_p\}$ which satisfies the conditions (i), (ii). We denote by I the initial of A, by D the discriminant of A with respect to $w^{(r)}$, and by T_i the resultant of A and P_i in $w^{(r)}$, $1 \le i \le p$, where r is the order of A with respect to w. They are nonzero polynomials of $w^{(0)}, \ldots, w^{(r-1)}$ over $Q\{u_1, \ldots, u_q\}$. We take integral functions $\zeta_1(x), \ldots, \zeta_q(x)$ of x which satisfy

$$F(\zeta_1(0), \ldots, \zeta_q(0)) \neq 0$$

for any nonzero differential polynomial F of the u over Q. There are complex numbers $a_0, \ldots, a_{r-1}$ which satisfy

(1) $\quad (IDT_1 \cdot \ldots \cdot T_p)(\zeta_1(0), \ldots, \zeta_q(0); a_0, \ldots, a_{r-1}) \neq 0.$

If a_r is a root of an algebraic equation in $w^{(r)}$

$$A(\zeta_1(0), \ldots, \zeta_q(0); a_0, \ldots, a_{r-1}, w^{(r)}) = 0,$$

it is a simple root by (1), whence by the implicit function theorem we have

$$A(\zeta_1(x), \ldots, \zeta_q(x); w^{(0)}, \ldots, w^{(r)})$$

$$= (w^{(r)} - f(x; w^{(0)}, \ldots, w^{(r-1)}))\Phi(x; w^{(0)}, \ldots, w^{(r)})$$

with

$$\Phi = J_0(w^{(r)})^s + \ldots + J_{s-1}w^{(r)} + J_s,$$

where $f, J_0, \ldots, J_s$ are convergent power series in

$$x, w^{(0)} - a_0, \ldots, w^{(r-1)} - a_{r-1}$$

with complex coefficients which satisfy

$$f(0; a_0, \dots, a_{r-1}) = a_r,$$

$$\Phi(0; a_0, \dots, a_r) \neq 0,$$

while $s + 1$ is the degree of A with respect to $w^{(r)}$: We may suppose that they converge in the domain defined by

$$|x|, |w^{(0)} - a_0|, \dots, |w^{(r-1)} - a_{r-1}| < \rho$$

with a positive number ρ. Applying the existence theorem of solution for the initial value problem to the differential equation

$$d^r y/dx^r = f(x, y, y^{(1)}, \dots, y^{(r-1)}),$$

we obtain a power siries solution $\xi(x; \beta_0, \dots, \beta_{r-1})$ in

(2) $\qquad x, \beta_0 - a_0, \dots, \beta_{r-1} - a_{r-1}$

with complex coefficients which satisfies

$$\partial^i \xi/\partial x^i(0; \beta_0, \dots, \beta_{r-1}) = \beta_i, \quad 0 \leq i < r$$

and

$$|\partial^i \xi/\partial x^i - a_i| < \rho, \quad 0 \leq i < r$$

in the domain defined by

(3) $\quad |x|, |\beta_0 - a_0|, \dots, |\beta_{r-1} - a_{r-1}| < \delta < \rho,$

where ξ converges. By (1)

$$P_j(\zeta_1(0), \dots, \zeta_q(0); \xi(0; a_0, \dots, a_{r-1})) \neq 0, \quad 1 \leq j \leq p.$$

Let us set

$$u_i^* = \zeta_i(x), \quad 1 \leq i \leq q, \quad w^* = \xi(x; \beta_0, \dots, \beta_{r-1}),$$

$$y_j^* = -(Q_j/P_j)(u_1^*, \dots, u_q^*, w^*), \quad 1 \leq j \leq p,$$

which are convergent power series in (2) with complex coefficients. We shall see that $(u_1^*, \dots, u_q^*, w^*, y_1^*, \dots, y_p^*)$ is a generic zero of Λ over Q. It is sufficient to show that if $G(u_1, \dots, u_q, w)$ is a nonzero differential polynomial over Q reduced with respect to A then the convergent power series $G(u_1^*, \ldots, u_q^*, w^*)$ does not vanish identically in (2). The order of G with respect to w is not greater than r. The resultant E of A and G in $w^{(r)}$ is a nonzero element of $Q\{u_1, \ldots, u_q\}[w^{(0)}, \ldots, w^{(r-1)}]$. There are complex numbers $b_1, \ldots, b_{r-1}$ which satisfy

$$|b_h - a_h| < \delta, \quad 0 \leq h < r$$

and

$$(\text{IE}) \quad (\zeta_1(0), \ldots, \zeta_q(0); b_0, \ldots, b_{r-1}) \neq 0.$$

We have

$$G(\zeta_1(0), \ldots, \zeta_q(0), \xi(0; b_0, \ldots, b_{r-1})) \neq 0$$

because $\partial^r \xi / \partial x^r (0; b_0, \ldots, b_{r-1})$ is a root of

$$A(\zeta_1(0), \ldots, \zeta_q(0); b_0, \ldots, b_{r-1}, w^{(r)}) = 0,$$

whence $G(u_1^*, \ldots, u_q^*, w^*) \neq 0$. The set Γ of all nonzero differential polynomials $G(u_1, \ldots, u_q, w)$ over Q reduced with respect to A is countable, whence there are complex numbers $b_1^*, \ldots, b_{r-1}^*$ which satisfy $|b_h^* - a_h| < \delta$, $0 \leq h < r$ and

$$G(\zeta_1(0), \ldots, \zeta_q(0), \xi(0; b_0^*, \ldots, b_{r-1}^*)) \neq 0$$

if G is an element of Γ. If we replace the β_h by b_h^* then $u_1^*, \ldots, u_q^*, w^*, y_1^*, \ldots, y_p^*$ are holomorphic functions of x at the origin O which form a generic zero of Λ over Q, whence

$$(u_1^*, \ldots, u_q^*, y_1^*, \ldots, y_p^*)$$

is a generic zero of Σ over Q.

Remark 1. E. R. Kolchin [1, pp.768-771] proved that if k is a partial differential field of characteristic 0 there exists a differential extension field Ω of k which satisfies the following condition: If k_1 is a finitely generated differential extension field of k contained in Ω, any finitely generated differential extension field of k_1 has its differential isomorphic image over k_1 in Ω. In the case of positive characteristic confer with pp. 133-134 of the book [2] by Kolchin. For "differentially closed" field confer with A. Robinson, On the concept of differentially closed field, Bull. Res. Counc. Isr. Sect. F8(1959), 113-128 and M. Rosenlicht [10].

Remark 2. The following theorem is due to E. R. Kolchin, Existence theorems connected with the Picard-Vessiot theory of homogeneous linear ordinary differential equations, Bull. Amer. Math. Soc. 54(1948), 927-932:

Let k be a differential field of characteristic 0 and Σ be a perfect differential ideal in $k\{y_1, \ldots, y_n\}$. Given an element D of $k\{y_1, \ldots, y_n\}$ which is not in Σ, there is a point $(\xi_1, \ldots, \xi_n)$ in the manifold of Σ satisfying $D(\xi_1, \ldots, \xi_n) \neq 0$ such that any constant of $k<\xi_1, \ldots, \xi_n>$ is algebraic over the field of constants k_0 of k.

He proved it by the following theorem due to Ritt(cf. [2, pp.138-142]):

The notation being as above, let $\eta_1, \ldots, \eta_p, \zeta_1, \ldots, \zeta_q$ be elements of Ω. Given an element T of
$$k\{y_1, \ldots, y_p, z_1, \ldots, z_q\}$$
satisfying $T(\eta_1, \ldots, \eta_p, \zeta_1, \ldots, \zeta_q) \neq 0$, there is an element J of $k\{y_1, \ldots, y_p\}$ such that $J(\eta) \neq 0$ and a differential specialization $(\alpha_1, \ldots, \alpha_p)$ of $(\eta_1, \ldots, \eta_p)$ over k with $J(\alpha) \neq 0$ can be extended to a differential specialization $(\alpha_1, \ldots, \alpha_p, \beta_1, \ldots, \beta_q)$ of

$(\eta_1,\ldots,\eta_p,\ \zeta_1,\ \ldots,\ \zeta_q)$ over k with $T(\alpha,\ \beta) \neq 0$.

The former is induced from the latter as follows: The set Φ of all prime divisors of Σ in $k\{y_1,\ \ldots,\ y_n\}$ which do not contain D is not empty, since one of the essential prime divisors of Σ does not contain D. Let Δ be a maximal element of Φ in the relation of inclusion. If $(\xi_1,\ \ldots,\ \xi_n)$ is a generic zero of Δ over k, then $D(\xi) \neq 0$ and any differential specialization α of ξ over k is a generic one over k if $D(\alpha) \neq 0$, since Δ is maximal in Φ. We see that any constant of $k<\xi>$ is algebraic over k_0. For a moment suppose that there were a constant γ of $k<\xi>$ which is transcendental over k_0. It would be transcendental over k (§6, p.28), and

(4) $\gamma = Q(\xi)/P(\xi),\quad P,\ Q \in k\{y_1,\ \ldots,\ y_n\}.$

We apply the latter theorem to $(\gamma,\ \xi_1,\ \ldots,\ \xi_n)$ setting $T(y,\ z) = D(z)$: There is an element $J(u)$ of $k\{u\}$ satisfying $J(\gamma) \neq 0$ such that any differential specialization c of γ over k with $J(c)\neq0$ can be extended to a differential specialization $(c,\ \beta)$ of $(\gamma,\ \xi)$ over k with $D(\beta) \neq 0$. There is a constant c of k which satisfies $J(c) \neq 0$: It is a differential specialization of γ because γ is transcendental over k, whence we have a differential specialization $(c,\ \beta)$ of $(\gamma,\ \xi)$ over k with $D(\beta) \neq 0$ which satisfies $P(\beta)c = Q(\beta)$ by (4). Since β is a generic differential specialization of ξ over k, we have $P(\xi)c = Q(\xi)$ and $\gamma = c$, which contradicts our assumption that γ is transcendental over k_0.

Bibliography

1. E. R. Kolchin, Galois theory of differential fields, Amer. J. Math., 75(1953), 753-824.

2. ————— , Differential algebra and algebraic groups, Academic Press, New York, 1973.

3. M. Matsuda, An application of Ritt's low power theorem, Nagoya Math. J., 68(1977), 17-19.

4. ————— , Algebraic differential equations of the first order free from parametric singularities from the differential-algebraic standpoint, J. Math. Soc. Japan, 30(1978), 447-455.

5. ————— , The group of automorphisms of a differential algebraic function field, Nagoya Math. J., 74(1979), 87-94.

6. K. Nishioka, Transcendental constants over the coefficient fields in differential elliptic function fields, Pacific J. Math., 74(1978), 191-197.

7. ————— , Algebraic differential equations of Clairaut type from the differential-algebraic standpoint, J. Math. Soc. Japan, 31(1979), 553-560.

8. ————— , A theorem of Painlevé on parametric singularities of algebraic differential equations of the first order, to appear.

9. M. Rosenlicht, Canonical forms for local derivations, Pacific J. Math., 42(1972), 721-732.

10. ————— , The nonminimality of the differential closure, Pacific J. Math., 52(1974), 529-537.

Index

Vol. 700: Module Theory, Proceedings, 1977. Edited by C. Faith and S. Wiegand. X, 239 pages. 1979.

Vol. 701: Functional Analysis Methods in Numerical Analysis, Proceedings, 1977. Edited by M. Zuhair Nashed. VII, 333 pages. 1979.

Vol. 702: Yuri N. Bibikov, Local Theory of Nonlinear Analytic Ordinary Differential Equations. IX, 147 pages. 1979.

Vol. 703: Equadiff IV, Proceedings, 1977. Edited by J. Fábera. XIX, 441 pages. 1979.

Vol. 704: Computing Methods in Applied Sciences and Engineering, 1977, I. Proceedings, 1977. Edited by R. Glowinski and J. L. Lions. VI, 391 pages. 1979.

Vol. 705: O. Forster und K. Knorr, Konstruktion verseller Familien kompakter komplexer Räume. VII, 141 Seiten. 1979.

Vol. 706: Probability Measures on Groups, Proceedings, 1978. Edited by H. Heyer. XIII, 348 pages. 1979.

Vol. 707: R. Zielke, Discontinuous Čebyšev Systems. VI, 111 pages. 1979.

Vol. 708: J. P. Jouanolou, Equations de Pfaff algébriques. V, 255 pages. 1979.

Vol. 709: Probability in Banach Spaces II. Proceedings, 1978. Edited by A. Beck. V, 205 pages. 1979.

Vol. 710: Séminaire Bourbaki vol. 1977/78, Exposés 507–524. IV, 328 pages. 1979.

Vol. 711: Asymptotic Analysis. Edited by F. Verhulst. V, 240 pages. 1979.

Vol. 712: Equations Différentielles et Systèmes de Pfaff dans le Champ Complexe. Edité par R. Gérard et J.-P. Ramis. V, 364 pages. 1979.

Vol. 713: Séminaire de Théorie du Potentiel, Paris No. 4. Edité par F. Hirsch et G. Mokobodzki. VII, 281 pages. 1979.

Vol. 714: J. Jacod, Calcul Stochastique et Problèmes de Martingales. X, 539 pages. 1979.

Vol. 715: Inder Bir S. Passi, Group Rings and Their Augmentation Ideals. VI, 137 pages. 1979.

Vol. 716: M. A. Scheunert, The Theory of Lie Superalgebras. X, 271 pages. 1979.

Vol. 717: Grosser, Bidualräume und Vervollständigungen von Banachmoduln. III, 209 pages. 1979.

Vol. 718: J. Ferrante and C. W. Rackoff, The Computational Complexity of Logical Theories. X, 243 pages. 1979.

Vol. 719: Categorial Topology, Proceedings, 1978. Edited by H. Herrlich and G. Preuß. XII, 420 pages. 1979.

Vol. 720: E. Dubinsky, The Structure of Nuclear Fréchet Spaces. V, 187 pages. 1979.

Vol. 721: Séminaire de Probabilités XIII. Proceedings, Strasbourg, 1977/78. Edité par C. Dellacherie, P. A. Meyer et M. Weil. VII, 647 pages. 1979.

Vol. 722: Topology of Low-Dimensional Manifolds. Proceedings, 1977. Edited by R. Fenn. VI, 154 pages. 1979.

Vol. 723: W. Brandal, Commutative Rings whose Finitely Generated Modules Decompose. II, 116 pages. 1979.

Vol. 724: D. Griffeath, Additive and Cancellative Interacting Particle Systems. V, 108 pages. 1979.

Vol. 725: Algèbres d'Opérateurs. Proceedings, 1978. Edité par P. de la Harpe. VII, 309 pages. 1979.

Vol. 726: Y.-C. Wong, Schwartz Spaces, Nuclear Spaces and Tensor Products. VI, 418 pages. 1979.

Vol. 727: Y. Saito, Spectral Representations for Schrödinger Operators With Long-Range Potentials. V, 149 pages. 1979.

Vol. 728: Non-Commutative Harmonic Analysis. Proceedings, 1978. Edited by J. Carmona and M. Vergne. V, 244 pages. 1979.

Vol. 729: Ergodic Theory. Proceedings, 1978. Edited by M. Denker and K. Jacobs. XII, 209 pages. 1979.

Vol. 730: Functional Differential Equations and Approximation of Fixed Points. Proceedings, 1978. Edited by H.-O. Peitgen and H.-O. Walther. XV, 503 pages. 1979.

Vol. 731: Y. Nakagami and M. Takesaki, Duality for Crossed Products of von Neumann Algebras. IX, 139 pages. 1979.

Vol. 732: Algebraic Geometry. Proceedings, 1978. Edited by K. Lønsted. IV, 658 pages. 1979.

Vol. 733: F. Bloom, Modern Differential Geometric Techniques in the Theory of Continuous Distributions of Dislocations. XII, 206 pages. 1979.

Vol. 734: Ring Theory, Waterloo, 1978. Proceedings, 1978. Edited by D. Handelman and J. Lawrence. XI, 352 pages. 1979.

Vol. 735: B. Aupetit, Propriétés Spectrales des Algèbres de Banach. XII, 192 pages. 1979.

Vol. 736: E. Behrends, M-Structure and the Banach-Stone Theorem. X, 217 pages. 1979.

Vol. 737: Volterra Equations. Proceedings 1978. Edited by S.-O. Londen and O. J. Staffans. VIII, 314 pages. 1979.

Vol. 738: P. E. Conner, Differentiable Periodic Maps. 2nd edition, IV, 181 pages. 1979.

Vol. 739: Analyse Harmonique sur les Groupes de Lie II. Proceedings, 1976–78. Edited by P. Eymard et al. VI, 646 pages. 1979.

Vol. 740: Séminaire d'Algèbre Paul Dubreil. Proceedings, 1977–78. Edited by M.-P. Malliavin. V, 456 pages. 1979.

Vol. 741: Algebraic Topology, Waterloo 1978. Proceedings. Edited by P. Hoffman and V. Snaith. XI, 655 pages. 1979.

Vol. 742: K. Clancey, Seminormal Operators. VII, 125 pages. 1979.

Vol. 743: Romanian-Finnish Seminar on Complex Analysis. Proceedings, 1976. Edited by C. Andreian Cazacu et al. XVI, 713 pages. 1979.

Vol. 744: I. Reiner and K. W. Roggenkamp, Integral Representations. VIII, 275 pages. 1979.

Vol. 745: D. K. Haley, Equational Compactness in Rings. III, 167 pages. 1979.

Vol. 746: P. Hoffman, τ-Rings and Wreath Product Representations. V, 148 pages. 1979.

Vol. 747: Complex Analysis, Joensuu 1978. Proceedings, 1978. Edited by I. Laine, O. Lehto and T. Sorvali. XV, 450 pages. 1979.

Vol. 748: Combinatorial Mathematics VI. Proceedings, 1978. Edited by A. F. Horadam and W. D. Wallis. IX, 206 pages. 1979.

Vol. 749: V. Girault and P.-A. Raviart, Finite Element Approximation of the Navier-Stokes Equations. VII, 200 pages. 1979.

Vol. 750: J. C. Jantzen, Moduln mit einem höchsten Gewicht. III, 195 Seiten. 1979.

Vol. 751: Number Theory, Carbondale 1979. Proceedings. Edited by M. B. Nathanson. V, 342 pages. 1979.

Vol. 752: M. Barr, *-Autonomous Categories. VI, 140 pages. 1979.

Vol. 753: Applications of Sheaves. Proceedings, 1977. Edited by M. Fourman, C. Mulvey and D. Scott. XIV, 779 pages. 1979.

Vol. 754: O. A. Laudal, Formal Moduli of Algebraic Structures. III, 161 pages. 1979.

Vol. 755: Global Analysis. Proceedings, 1978. Edited by M. Grmela and J. E. Marsden. VII, 377 pages. 1979.

Vol. 756: H. O. Cordes, Elliptic Pseudo-Differential Operators – An Abstract Theory. IX, 331 pages. 1979.

Vol. 757: Smoothing Techniques for Curve Estimation. Proceedings, 1979. Edited by Th. Gasser and M. Rosenblatt. V, 245 pages. 1979.

Vol. 758: C. Năstăsescu and F. Van Oystaeyen; Graded and Filtered Rings and Modules. X, 148 pages. 1979.

This series reports new developments in mathematical research and teaching – quickly, informally and at a high level. The type of material considered for publication includes:

1. Preliminary drafts of original papers and monographs
2. Lectures on a new field or presentations of a new angle in a classical field
3. Seminar work-outs
4. Reports of meetings, provided they are
   a) of exceptional interest and
   b) devoted to a single topic.

Texts which are out of print but still in demand may also be considered if they fall within these categories.

The timeliness of a manuscript is more important than its form, which may be unfinished or tentative. Thus, in some instances, proofs may be merely outlined and results presented which have been or will later be published elsewhere. If possible, a subject index should be included. Publication of Lecture Notes is intended as a service to the international mathematical community, in that a commercial publisher, Springer-Verlag, can offer a wide distribution of documents which would otherwise have a restricted readership. Once published and copyrighted, they can be documented in the scientific literature.

Manuscripts

Manuscripts should be no less than 100 and preferably no more than 500 pages in length.
They are reproduced by a photographic process and therefore must be typed with extreme care. Symbols not on the typewriter should be inserted by hand in indelible black ink. Corrections to the typescript should be made by pasting in the new text or painting out errors with white correction fluid. Authors receive 75 free copies and are free to use the material in other publications. The typescript is reduced slightly in size during reproduction; best results will not be obtained unless the text on any one page is kept within the overall limit of 18 x 26.5 cm (7 x 10½ inches). On request, the publisher will supply special paper with the typing area outlined.

Manuscripts should be sent to Prof. A. Dold, Mathematisches Institut der Universität Heidelberg, Im Neuenheimer Feld 288, 6900 Heidelberg/Germany, Prof. B. Eckmann, Eidgenössische Technische Hochschule, CH-8092 Zürich/Switzerland, or directly to Springer-Verlag Heidelberg.

Springer-Verlag, Heidelberger Platz 3, D-1000 Berlin 33
Springer-Verlag, Neuenheimer Landstraße 28–30, D-6900 Heidelberg 1
Springer-Verlag, 175 Fifth Avenue, New York, NY 10010/USA

ISBN 3-540-09997-2
ISBN 0-387-09997-2

Lecture Notes in Mathematics

continuation on page 115

Lecture Notes in Mathematics

Edited by A. Dold and B. Eckmann

804

Michihiko Matsuda

First Order Algebraic Differential Equations

A Differential Algebraic Approach

Springer-Verlag
Berlin Heidelberg New York